CHATTO
The Life and Times of an
Indian Anti-Imperialist in Europe

CHATTO
The Life and Times of an Indian
Anti-Imperialist in Europe

Nirode K. Barooah

UNIVERSITY PRESS

OXFORD

UNIVERSITY PRESS

YMCA Library Building, Jai Singh Road, New Delhi 110 001

Oxford University Press is a department of the University of Oxford. It furthers the
University's objective of excellence in research, scholarship, and education
by publishing worldwide in

Oxford   New York

Auckland   Bangkok   Buenos Aires   Cape Town   Chennai
Dar es Salaam   Delhi   Hong Kong   Istanbul   Karachi   Kolkata
Kuala Lumpur   Madrid   Melbourne   Mexico City   Mumbai   Nairobi
São Paulo   Shanghai   Taipei   Tokyo   Toronto

Oxford is a registered trade mark of Oxford University Press
in the UK and in certain other countries

Published in India
By Oxford University Press, New Delhi

© Oxford University Press, 2004

The moral rights of the author have been asserted
Database right Oxford University Press (maker)

First published 2004

All rights reserved. No part of this publication may be reproduced,
stored in a retrieval system, or transmitted, in any form or by any means,
without the prior permission in writing of Oxford University Press,
or as expressly permitted by law, or under terms agreed with the appropriate
reprographics rights organization. Enquiries concerning reproduction
outside the scope of the above should be sent to the Rights Department,
Oxford University Press, at the address above

You must not circulate this book in any other binding or cover
and you must impose this same condition on any acquiror

ISBN 019 566547 3

Typeset in Goudy 10.5/12.5
By Laser Print Craft, New Delhi
Printed in India at Rashtriya Printers, Delhi 110 032
Published by Manzar Khan, Oxford University Press
YMCA Library Building, Jai Singh Road, New Delhi 110 001

To
Echen and Shah Shuja

Contents

Acknowledgements	x
Abbreviations	xii
INTRODUCTION	1

1. THE RADICAL NATIONALIST IN THE MAKING 1902–14   7
   Home background. Law, linguistics, and the 'India House' radicalism. Chatto, Krishnavarma, and the revolutionary ideology. The Paris years: 1910–14.

2. THE ENEMY OF OUR ENEMY IS OUR FRIEND 1914   34
   The war and Germany's 'threat to India' policy. Chatto and the formation of the Berlin India Committee. 'India Committee' in Indian hands.

3. ATTEMPTS AT REVOLUTIONIZING INDIA 1915–17   62
   Mission to Afghanistan. Activities in the Ottoman Empire. Problems of arms and failed revolution: Activities in New York, Chicago, San Francisco, Shanghai, Batavia, and Bangkok. Berlin Committee in the USA after the arms debacle. Chatto's leadership until the failure of the revolutionizing attempts.

4. INTERNATIONALIZING THE INDIAN QUESTION FROM STOCKHOLM 1917–21   100
   Experience with the Second International 1917. The first Indian contact with the Bolsheviks. Chatto's anti-British propaganda from Stockholm. British reaction to Indian propaganda in Sweden.

5. MISSING THE COMINTERN LINK   157
   Seeking a Comintern link. The Berlin Indians in Moscow. Chatto and the 'Thesis on India and the World Revolution'. The failure of the Moscow mission. Roy and Chatto.

6. HAZARDS IN PROMOTING INDO-GERMAN
   RELATIONS 1921–6 178
   Baron Ruedt and German commercial interests in India.
   Anglo-German plots against the Berlin Indians. Attacking
   the German racial trade policy 1925. 'Indians in Berlin
   Zoo'. The collapse of the INSIB.

7. CHATTO AND SMEDLEY: LOVE, DOMESTIC TYRANNY,
   NERVOUS BREAKDOWNS 1920–6 225
   Smedley: Her life and Indian work before 1920. Chatto-
   Smedley Union: Love and innate incompatibility. The final
   parting of ways.

8. THE LEAGUE AGAINST IMPERIALISM PHASE AND THE FATEFUL
   TURN OF EVENTS 1926–31 246
   Willi Muenzenberg and the idea of an international
   Congress on colonial oppression and imperialism. India and
   China at the Brussels Congress and the foundation of the
   League Against Imperialism. The LAI and the Chatto-
   Nehru relationship. Chatto's fateful ideological conversion.

9. THE BIRTH OF THE SOVIET-INDIAN SOCIAL SCIENTIST
   VIRENDRANAT AGORNATOVICH CHATOPADAYA 1933–7 . . . 283
   Escape to the Soviet Union. Academic appointment at
   Leningrad. Essays Extolling Engels and his *The Origin of the
   Family, Private Property and the State*. In defence of Marx
   and Engels against the influence of bourgeois scholarship.
   Other scientific researches, academic rewards, and
   dedication in teaching.

10. BRIEF INTERLUDE OF HAPPINESS AND SUDDEN DEATH . . . 314
    Chatto and Lidiya: Conjugal Happiness Nipped in the Bud.
    Chatto's arrest and execution; Kirov's *protégé*.

    Bibliography 328

    Index 349

PLATES* *(between pages 228 and 229)*
Official photograph of Chatto as Joint-Secretary of the League Against Imperialism
Chatto and Lidiya in their Moscow apartment
O.G. von Wesendonk
Agnes Smedley
Willi Muenzenberg

---

*Reproduced from photocopied material.

Acknowledgements

Much of the research for this book was carried out in Germany, with the help of a scholarship from the Alexander Humboldt Foundation during 1972–4, and it is with an abiding sense of gratitude that I acknowledge this assistance, without which it would not have been possible for me to collect material from so many different archives of Europe. I am only sorry that, although parts of this research appeared in some academic papers, this work has taken an inordinately long time to see the light of day.

I recall with a deep sense of gratitude the inspiration and encouragement that I received from the late Professor Theodor Schieder of the University of Cologne in the early phase of my research in the field of Indo-German relations. I am equally grateful to Professor Dietmar Rothermund of the University of Heidelberg for many kindnesses shown to me during the same period.

My grateful thanks are also due to the archives, libraries, and institutions that allowed me access to the material in their possession. Particular mention must be made of the Political Archive of the German Foreign Office in Bonn; the German Federal Archive in Koblenz; the German Central Archive in Potsdam (then GDR); Stadtgeschichtliches Museum, Leipzig (Dr Klaus Sohl); the Public Records Office, London; the India Office Library and Records, London; Riksarkivet, Stockholm; Det Koeniglige Bibliotek (Mr Palle Ringsted), Copenhagen; the Library of the University of Colorado at Boulder (Ms Kris McCusker); the Nehru Memorial Museum and Library, New Delhi; the archive of the St Petersburg Branch of the Institute of Oriental Studies of the Russian Academy of Sciences (Professor E.I. Kichanov); the International Institute of Social History, Amsterdam (Ms M. Ijzermans).

Among the many people I contacted at the earliest stages of my research, who had known Chattopadhyaya in action in Germany and who helped me enormously, were A.C.N. Nambiar, Lucie Hecht, O.W.

Hentig, and Fritz Grobba. I gratefully remember their cooperation and kindnesses. I am also grateful to Sven Stroemgren (Stockholm), Professor Tomas Hammar (Stockholm), Folke Ludwigs (Stockholm), and W. Pochhammer (then in Bremen) for giving me much valuable information. I am sad that some of them are no longer with us.

The publication of this book has been delayed primarily due to the inaccessibility of some of the most relevant material, preserved in the former Soviet Union. It was only towards the end of 1999 that I could see some of this long-awaited material through the kind mediation of Ambassador Ronen Sen, who contacted Professor Kichanov and Dr L.V. Mitrokhin on the subject. I also cannot forget the interest shown and help rendered in the matter by Sanjoy Hazarika, the well-known Indian journalist and author. I owe all of them my grateful thanks.

I received ungrudging help from several long-standing friends. At the earliest stages, José Leal-Ferreira sent me from New Delhi handwritten notes from some rare books I then needed; Dr Peter J.V. Willis of London checked for me some old issues of British newspapers from the period 1907–9; Dr A. Vasudevan of Bombay sent from the USA some books which were not available in Germany; Ms Rosi Schuermann translated for me some Swedish material; and Shah Shujatullah, now of Seattle, did me an immense service by going through the manuscript and giving invaluable suggestions for improvement. I am deeply grateful to each of them.

The help rendered by my wife is beyond description. Without her knowledge of various European languages, I would have been driven from pillar to post without making any substantial progress. She has translated for me innumerable documents, and has carefully gone through and neatly typed out the manuscript. In the process, she pointed out the passages that needed correction or further elucidation. Her help, particularly in translating the Russian material, has been invaluable beyond words. Although she has thus been inseparable from the work, I alone am responsible for any shortcomings.

The initial period of research for this book in Germany, almost three decades ago, was also the period when our two children were born. Looking back today in May 2002, I cannot but gratefully remember how the late Frau Johanna Ulrich kindly volunteered to take care of our children for a part of the day when both my wife and I used to be working at our offices.

NIRODE K. BAROOAH

Abbreviations

AA	Auswaertiges Amt (German Foreign Office)
AABI	Britische Besitzungen in Asien: Britisch Indien
ADGS	Akten der Deutschen Gesandtschaft Stockholm
DD	Deutsche Dokumente zum Kriegsausbruch
DML	Erstwhile Dimitroff Museum, Leipzig
FFI	Friends of Freedom for India
FLP	Florence Lennon Papers, University of Colorado at Boulder
FO	British Foreign Office
IAE	Institute of Anthropology and Ethnography, Leningrad
IC	India Committee, Berlin
IHR	*The Indian Historical Review*
IHZ	*Industrie- und Handelszeitung*
IIB	Indian Information Bureau
INC	Indian National Congress
Inprecor	*International Press Correspondence*, Moscow
Inprekorr	German edition of *Inprecor*
INSIB	Indian News Service and Information Bureau
IO	Indian Office, London
IOR	India Office Records
IQR	*Indian Quarterly Register*
ITRFI	*Industrial and Trade Review for India*
JNP	Jawaharlal Nehru Papers, NMML, New Delhi
KMP	Karin Michaelis Papers, Det Kongelige Bibliotek, Copenhagen
LAI	League Against Imperialism
MOPR	Mezhdunarodnaya Organizatsiya Pomoshchi Bortsam Revolyutsii (International Association for Aid to Revolutionary Fighters)
NMML	Nehru Memorial Museum and Library, New Delhi
PRO	Public Records Office, London
Wk	Weltkrieg (World War)

Introduction

The struggle for India's freedom was not confined to India alone, but extended beyond its borders, roughly from the first decade of the last century. Perhaps no other freedom fighter was as persistently and steadfastly anti-imperialist as Virendranath Chattopadhyaya (1880–1937), whose field of operations was Europe. Mahatma Gandhi, who led the mainstream Indian movement from 1920 until Independence in 1947 intermittently made compromises with British imperialism all through the movement. So did his lieutenant, Jawaharlal Nehru, often against his own instinct, in the interest of unity and loyalty to the supreme commander. The 'Lal-Bal-Pal' trio* of the so-called Indian 'extremists' of the earlier period had also eventually patched up with British imperialism. At the end of World War I, even Har Dayal, the fierce advocate of violent revolution, turned into an admirer of British rule in India. But Chatto, as Virendranath Chattopadhyaya was popularly known, never made any compromises with imperialism, apart from using the German imperial power against British imperialism in India during WWI, declaring at the same time his own anti-imperialism.

Chatto's tireless energy enabled him to involve the Indian freedom struggle with different anti-British and anti-imperialist forces in Europe such as the German Foreign Office, the 1917 Stockholm peace initiatives of the Socialist International, the Bolsheviks, the League Against Imperialism, and the Communist International. The effectiveness of his propaganda against the British in India in the foreign press, and his political activities in Europe before, during, and after WWI, remained a constant thorn in the side of the British government, and the British Secret Service made strenuous efforts until 1931, in Switzerland, Sweden, and Germany either to capture or kill him. In the

*Lala Lajpat Rai, Gangadhar Tilak, and Bipin Chandra Pal.

late–1920s, as secretary of the League Against Imperialism, he played a key role in radicalizing Jawaharlal Nehru, and in the 1930s, in the Soviet Union, he earned a name for himself as a social scientist and university teacher. And yet there is no full-scale biography of this distinguished patriot and fascinating figure. The government of independent India is lamentably indifferent to commemorating in a fitting manner the life-long sacrifices Chatto made for his countrymen's freedom. It is truly astonishing that in spite of Nehru's close relationship with Chatto during a very significant phase of the Indian freedom movement and his daughter Indira Gandhi's intimate knowledge of his work for India from Berlin when she was 18[1], the Nehru dynasty did next to nothing to honour the legacy of Chatto during its long tenure of power in India. The centenary of his birth in 1980 was allowed to pass unnoticed without even a token of remembrance and respect.

What is the reason for this neglect and indifference? We are not concerned here with the reason for the official neglect. But the obvious reason for the lack of a proper biography seems to be that not enough is known in India about Chatto's life in exile before and after WWI to awaken much curiosity. Even what little is known about his activities during WWI as an ally of Germany, is shrouded in myths, distortions, and half-truths. Another reason, probably, is the language problem. During his active life abroad Chatto spent most of his time in continental Europe, and with a knowledge of English alone, it is not possible to handle the basic materials preserved in the various European archives. Disregard of the original German sources is largely responsible for the perpetuation of the half-truths just mentioned. Yet another reason seems to be the remarks by M.N. Roy in his *Memoirs*, minimizing the importance of Chatto's work in Berlin.[2] Roy's supporters in India are still spreading baseless stories founded on his observations.[3] Last but not least, for many Indian Communists, the study and research of Chatto's life and work has remained taboo. Although the Soviet Union, throughout its existence, kept on feeding the Indian government concocted stories about the circumstances of Chatto's death, it has always been an open secret that he was liquidated in Stalin's mass purges. And Stalin, of course, is still held in great respect and admiration by many Indian Marxist academics and communist activists.

This book is based primarily on the original archival sources. The major portion is derived from various German official archives. They are supplemented by those from the British, Swedish, American, Russian, Danish, and Dutch archives. Although the book covers all aspects of Chatto's life, as far as possible, it is not a compact biography in the conventional sense. The nature of some of Chatto's activities was such, particularly during the War, that events developed without his actual presence. Yet, these events, being part and parcel of the full story, have to be detailed.

Chatto's political life began at the time of the emergence of revolutionary nationalism in Indian politics after the assassination of Curzon Wyllie by Madanlal Dhingra in London in 1909. This event instantly made both the moderates and the so-called 'extremists' almost disappear from the scene as far as the substance of nationalism is concerned. Surendranath Banerjea, the premier moderate leader, then in London, started praising British rule in India in every meeting and, on the opposite side, in the face of the current British hostility to Indian nationalism, Bipin Chandra Pal, the eminent 'extremist', also in London, declared that he had ceased to be an 'extremist'. Shyamaji Krishnavarma and Chatto debated, in the pages of the *Times*, the uses and abuses of Krishnavarma's revolutionary ideas. Although for tactical reasons Chatto at first discarded Krishnavarma's notions, he soon left London and Pal's camp to give a practical shape to those ideas from Germany as an ally of the German Foreign Office.

Although some welcome revision has lately taken place in projecting and judging the war-time 'German conspiracies' in India, in the wake of successive releases of erstwhile classified material by the British and American archives highlighting the equally underhand British tactics and conspiracies to malign Germany and the Indian nationalists in the neutral countries, further re-examination and redress have long been overdue in this area on the basis of the original German documents concerning these events. Pioneering Indian authors, who have evaluated the revolutionary nationalists and their rightful place in the history of India's struggle for freedom, have not studied the role of these freedom fighters in the round, and German archival sources, especially on the subject of Indo-German co-operation, have almost wholly been ignored. They have depended more on hearsay evidence and deficient recollections of former revolutionaries than on authentic German materials. Consequently, some of their accounts are seriously flawed because of their failure to compare and verify individual reports and recitals with authentic evidence. The fraud and charlatanry of some so-called revolutionaries and their unsavoury actions have also remained unexposed. Since Oppenheim's 'India Committee', which initiated the so-called German intrigues in India, came under the complete management and control of Indians at the beginning of 1915, these intrigues must be identified as essentially Indian intrigues supported by Germany. Therefore the Indian revolutionaries share the blame for the failures, pretentions, incompetence, and cowardice of these intrigues. Further, in mitigation, it must be added that in the face of aggressive British diplomacy, espionage, and on-the-spot hangings of suspected 'seditionists', the untried Indian revolutionaries had no chance. It is significant how C.R. Cleveland, the head of the Indian Criminal Intelligence Department, praised his men in 1917:

> The British Government has been fortunate, I think, in having in its service, or at its disposal, a number of devoted and loyal Indians who have shown as little inclination to fraternize with the seditionist as a fox-terrier with a rat. There have also been a number of British officers who have looked upon the tracking of dangerous sedition as the big game of their life.[4]

It is to Chatto's credit that in spite of the successive failures of the India Committee to revolutionize India, his personal reputation *vis-à-vis* the German Foreign Office remained untarnished, and he could still extract further material support from it for a vigorous anti-British press campaign in Sweden in an effort to internationalize the Indian question. Chatto made full use of the largely pro-German neutral Sweden. Supported by the left Socialists he debunked the pro-British-Empire 'Socialist and Labour International'. Chatto's Stockholm period also saw the first Indo-Bolshevik contacts. However, not yet converted to communism, the nationalist revolutionary Chatto failed to obtain any financial support from the Comintern for his future political work with Indians in Europe.

Debarred from entry into almost all the west European countries after the end of the War, Chatto had to remain in Germany. But he was asked to remain non-political by the German Foreign Office which appreciated the great importance of the Indian market for German economic recovery. However, to gain access to that market, Germany required the friendship of the British rulers in India and not of Indian nationalists. A secret Anglo-German plot to hand over Chatto and other pre-War Berlin Indians to the British narrowly failed. This was followed by macabre attempts by British Secret Service agents to kill Chatto in the streets of Berlin. Undeterred, Chatto continued his anti-British propaganda and fearlessly attacked the Germans as well for their commercial racialism.

During this difficult post-War period in Berlin, Chatto met Agnes Smedley (1892–1950). Although in many ways the two were alike in their characters and pursuits, living together ruined both of them emotionally. Smedley's observations on Chatto and her life with him in some of her books as also letters to her friends, Florence Lennon in America and Karin Michaelis in Denmark, have provided ample information about Chatto's private life in Germany.

Anti-imperialism and India's freedom were the twin leitmotifs of Chatto's life. However, his means and strategy of fighting imperialism progressively changed through various phases, and, starting as a national revolutionary, Chatto ended up as a communist internationalist and a social revolutionary. After Smedley left for China, Chatto became more and more involved in communism. A short fruitful friendship with Nehru, when both were involved with the League Against Imperialism, kept him happily in touch with India. But later when the League became a mere adjunct of the Comintern, Nehru left it, and Chatto lost his connection with mainstream Indian politics again. He continued to produce a great deal of polemical literature taking the Comintern line.

Anticipating a complete takeover of Germany by the Nazis, Chatto left for the Soviet Union in 1931, and spent the last four years of his six-year stay there as a distinguished academic in Leningrad. With great erudition and scholarship in the fields of ethnography, anthropology, and linguistics, and profound knowledge of the works of Marx, Engels, and Lenin, he wrote forcefully in Russian academic journals and put forward the thesis that in the Soviet Union academic writing should be politicized. This aspect of his life has also been unveiled in this work.

It is tragic that such a talented genius and a truly great patriot lost his life prematurely before the notorious firing squad of Stalin. His admirers might perhaps console themselves with the thought that his restless soul had at last found some solace, peace, and tranquility in the company of his last wife, the Russian Lidiya Karunovskaya.

6   Chatto

NOTES

1. See Indira's letter to her father from Badenweiler, Germany, on 29 August, 1935 in Sonia Gandhi (ed.), *Freedom's Daughter: Letters between Indira Gandhi and Jawaharlal Nehru 1922–39* (London, 1989), p. 214.
2. Chapter 39, pp. 286–94 of M.N. Roy's *Memoirs* (Bombay, 1964) is a glaring testimony to this fact.
3. To give an example, Samaren Roy in his *M.N. Roy: A Political Biography* (New Delhi, 1997) writes on p. 59 thus: 'Roy was keen to have Chattopadhyaya and Acharya in the émigré CPI. He wrote to Chattopadhyaya who came to Moscow in November 1922.' This is a false statement as Chatto was very much in Berlin at that time. The same author, in order to minimize the role of Chatto, misstates on p. 11: 'Champakram [sic] Pillai started the Berlin group in October 1914.'
4. Cleveland's preface to J. Campbell Ker's, *Political Trouble in India 1907–1917* (Calcutta, 1917), p. vi. Cleveland mentions here that Ker had to leave out the behind-the-scenes stories from this account.

1

The Radical Nationalist in the Making

1. Home Background

Virendranath Chattopadhyaya (Chatto) was born on 31 October 1880 in a very distinguished Bengali family of Hyderabad, at that time a princely state in South India. He was second of the eight children of Dr Aghorenath Chattopadhyaya, professor of science and the Principal of Nizam College, and his wife Varada Sundari Devi. All the children were extremely gifted, and have left their distinctive marks in their different lives. The eldest, Sarojini (Naidu), born in 1879, studied in London and Cambridge and became India's most famous poetess writing in English. She was called the 'Nightingale of India', and was a lifelong trusted lieutenant of Mahatma Gandhi during the Indian freedom struggle. Virendranath, the eldest son and the second child, whose life abroad is the subject of this study, remained in India only for the first twenty-one years of his life. After matriculating from the University of Madras, he earned his B.A. degree from Calcutta University with mathematics, Latin, and English literature. He then went to England in 1902 to appear for the Indian Civil Service examination and to study law. The third child Bhupendranath, born in 1882, became the assistant accountant-general in Hyderabad. The fourth, the second daughter Mrinalini, was born in 1883. She took her Modern Sciences tripos at Cambridge, and became an educationist and served as principal of a girls' college in Lahore. The fifth child, the third daughter Sunalini, was born in 1890, and became an artist and dancer. The sixth child, Ranendranath, was born in 1895. The youngest son Harindranath, born in 1898, became a poet, parliamentarian, actor, and writer. The youngest child, the daughter Suhasini, was born in 1901—a year after Sarojini had borne her second child, Padmaja. Suhasini became an ardent communist activist.[1]

The conglomeration of such extraordinary talent in a single famliy is attributed largely to Aghorenath's breadth of mind, lifestyle, and his method of bringing up his children. Sarojini, the most famous of Aghorenath's children, described her father to an English critic and writer thus:

> My ancestors have been great dreamers, great scholars, great ascetics. My father is a dreamer himself, a great dreamer, a great man whose life has been a magnificent failure. I suppose in the whole of India there are few men whose learning is greater than his, and I don't think there are many men more beloved. He has a great white beard and the profile of Homer and a laugh that brings down the roof.[2]

What Sarojini Naidu called 'a magnificent failure', albeit out of deep admiration, is only one point of view. The dreamer Aghorenath had also a practical side of substantial achievements. He came from a village called Brahmanagar in East Bengal and his early education was in Calcutta. Well-versed in Sanskrit and widely read in the literature of the West, the young Aghorenath not only developed a taste for many European languages but also came under the influence of the reformist school of Keshab Chandra Sen's Brahmoism.

However, Aghorenath's academic passion was in chemistry. He went abroad and took the degree of Doctor of Science at the University of Edinburgh in 1877. While in Europe, he also visited Germany for research purposes. On his return to India, he was invited to Hyderabad in 1878 to establish an English–medium school. Aghorenath also founded the Hyderabad College and was appointed its principal. Later, this became the Nizam's College. Aghorenath was also a pioneer in female education in Hyderabad. With his cooperation, the Girls' College was established there, and later became a part of Osmania University. He is also credited with playing an active role in the introduction of the Special Marriage Act of British India in Hyderabad for prohibiting child marriage.

Accounts of Aghorenath's activities as an educationist and a social reformer are also extraordinary. He was a virtual *guru* to his students and they would flock to his residence. The cultured minds of Hyderabad met in his house for discussions. Such informal gatherings crystallized into action groups as well. One such group was the *Anjuman-e-Akhwan-us-Safa* (the Brotherhood Society). Its main agenda was to consider the social and political problems of the country.[3]

No wonder that Aghorenath's family had a large circle of friends of all creeds, races and classes and, as Harindranath later wrote in his autobiography, the house was 'open to all alike'.[4] Varada Sundari's kitchen was cosmopolitan, and guests were served with exotic Hindu, Muslim, and Western preparations.[5] As for the languages spoken in the house, Aghorenath and his wife conversed in Bengali with each other, but the children spoke English or Hindustani among themselves while the household personnel used Telugu, the provincial dialect.

All this information, culled from the published biographies of Sarojini Naidu, particularly the one by Tara Ali Baig, help us understand why and how, in many respects, Chatto was so akin to his father. In his erudition and expertise in several languages—both Indian and foreign, in his cosmopolitanism and secularism, in his criticism of some of the backward Hindu religious and social practices including the caste system, in his interest in forming action groups of like-minded people for achieving common goals and, above all, in his patriotism, Chatto seems to have inherited a great deal from his father.

It is interesting to see parallels in Chatto and his father in imbibing the ardent form of nationalism that emerged in India after Curzon's partition of Bengal. The Bengalis answered Curzon's high-handed execution of partition in 1905 with the movement of *swadeshi* under the leadership of Bipin Chandra Pal, Aurobindo Ghosh, and others, and from the Deccan came the cry of *swaraj* under the leadership of Bal Gangadhar Tilak. These two movements were the first truly nationalist movements in India. Aghorenath, who had taken an interest in the INC since its inception in 1885, was also close to the Bengal movement of swadeshi and boycott. Baig, quoting several sources, tells us how Aghorenath, with Abdul Qayyum and Ramachandra Pillai, helped the *swadeshi* movement to gain ground in Hyderabad.

Abdul Qayyum was an officer in the Survey and Settlement Department of Hyderabad State, and he risked his career, as did Aghorenath, to bring the new movement from Bengal to Hyderabad. A large number of young Bengalis, with no more than one set of clothes to change, began to move about the countryside with *dhotis*, matches, soaps, buttons and other India-made goods which they encouraged patriots to buy.[6]

According to a contemporary eyewitness, Aghorenath, sponsor to the movement, presided over many small private meetings.[7]

Thus, it is little wonder that Aghorenath found no fault with Chatto's pursuit of militant nationalism while in Europe. This can be gauged from some precious recollections of two of Chatto's younger sisters. Mrinalini reminesced in 1968, a year before her death, about an episode when Sir Akbar Hydari, then an important civil servant, told Sarojini Naidu that the family would be in great trouble because of her brother, Viren, whose revolutionary activities were beginning to alarm the authorities. Sir Akbar advised Sarojini to disown her brother. Thus prompted, she impulsively wrote a letter to Hydari dissociating herself from her brother. When this letter was published, the outraged Aghorenath refused to let his daughter enter his house.[8]

Another episode, recalled by Suhasini, shows how similar Chatto and his father were in their political thinking. Once a letter from Chatto to Mrinalini arrived from Germany. The CID surrounded the house. Suhasini was playing with her dolls when Sir Charles Teggart, Head of the Police, demanded entry and asked Aghorenath and Mrinalini to surrender the letter. Aghorenath courteously asked the police officers to sit down. Ranen, Aghorenath's third son, was chewing steadily as he played in the garden, while the men proceeded to ransack the place. When they were unsuccessful in finding the letter, Aghorenath showed Sir Charles a photograph of Viren and said in parting, "Tell them, gentlemen, that my son Viren will bring them independence!" When they had left, the eight-year old Ranen spat out the remnants of his distinguished elder brother's letter.[9] It is immaterial whether the episodes, as described above, are true in every respect. The fact remains that, in the eyes of Chatto's brothers and sisters, his father always stood by Chatto's nationalist spirit.

2. Law, Linguistics, and the 'India House' Radicalism

Arriving in London in 1902, Chatto prepared and appeared for the Indian Civil Service examination twice, but with no success. The Indian quota in the ICS was small at the time and most Indians who went to

England for the examination invariably joined one of the four inns of court to qualify as barristers. Chatto, too, enrolled himself in the Middle Temple.[10]

According to British intelligence records, Chatto's life in England until 1908 was not at all political. It is said that shortly after his arrival in England, Chatto met an English girl, and they started living together from 1903 in a lodging in Notting Hill, London, as Mr and Mrs Chatterton. The British Indian intelligence reports go on further to say that, in 1909, the Chattertons quarrelled and parted, and Chattopadhyaya then made friends with one Miss Reynolds who was affluent enough to contribute to Mrs Chatterton's maintenance.[11] However, Chatto, even at this time, was not merely a playboy. Besides his law studies, he was deeply interested in languages, philology, and ethnography, and during 1908–13, contributed various notes and small articles to professional journals in London, Edinburgh, and Paris, and even edited a journal called *Orient Review*. He was also engaged in teaching and popularizing Hindustani, writing books on the subject for the English and other European enthusiasts.[12]

Circumstantial evidence also shows that even before 1908 Chatto did not remain uninfluenced by the new nationalism of India. At the beginning of 1905, Shyamaji Krishnavarma (1857–1930), the wealthy Indian scholar and patron saint of Indian revolutionary nationalism in Europe,[13] started his Indian Home Rule Society in London, along with its mouthpiece the *Indian Sociologist*. Shyamaji's variety of nationalism aimed at the emancipation of India from foreign rule as soon as possible. He founded some scholarships for Indian students and leaders devoted to the cause of Indian independence and bought a house in Cromwell Avenue, Highgate, London, to be used as a hostel for scholarship-holders and distinguished Indian nationalist visitors. This place was named 'India House', and boasted such stalwart nationalists as Lala Lajpat Rai, Bipin Chandra Pal, Madame Cama, and S.R. Rana among its guests. In 1905, Chatto applied for one of Shyamaji's scholarships, but was rejected, partly due to his continued eagerness to join the Indian Civil Service. One of the qualifying conditions for this scholarship was that the intending scholar would forego any aspirations to serve under the British Indian Government. Besides, unlike Har Dayal and V.D. Savarkar, the two distinguished scholar patriots who had been recommended by Lajpat Rai and B.G. Tilak, respectively, Chatto did not have the support of any nationalist leaders.

Although Krishnavarma's kind of nationalism aimed at complete separation from foreign rule immediately and, if necessary, with violence, he was politically a fellow traveller with Tilak, Pal, and Rai until 1908. These three and their followers in Maharashtra, Bengal, and the Punjab gave a new twist to the Indian National Congress in the post-Curzon era (which came to be known as 'extremist', in contrast to the earlier 'moderate' phase which was preoccupied merely with praying and petitioning the British masters for reform). The new trend-setters ruled out armed revolt and welcomed boycott or passive resistance. 'We are not armed, and there is no necessity for arms either. We have a stronger weapon, a political weapon, in boycott', Tilak said after the 1906 session of the INC.[14] He then explained to his audience what he meant by boycott:

So many of you need not like arms, but if you have not the power of active resistance, have you not the power of self-denial and self-abstinence in such a way as not to assist this foreign government to rule over you? This is boycott and this is what we mean when we say boycott is a political weapon. We shall not give them assistance to collect revenue and keep the peace.[15]

However, when Tilak's disciple Vinayak Damodar Savarkar (1883–1966) came to London in June 1906 as one of Krishnavarma's scholarship-holders and started living in India House, he changed the character of the nationalism that had prevailed there until then. A native of Nasik and a graduate from Fergusson College, Poona, Savarkar was already a brilliant scholar, having written *The Life of Mazzini* in Marathi (1905). As a fervent nationalist, he had also been a leader of the 'Mitra Mela', an association connected with the Ganapati festival.[16] In no time he transformed India House into a virtual temple of ardent nationalism, making *Vande Mataram* (*Hail Motherland!*) its abiding spirit. He formed a special group of followers called *Abhinav Bharat* (Young India) and started regular Sunday meetings in which passages from his newly written book on the Indian uprising of 1857 were read and discussed. The yearly celebration of the 1857 uprising, first started by Krishnavarma in 1905, was also continued. The radically nationalistic programmes of India House were probably not unwelcome to Krishnavarma. However, since such activities gradually came to be viewed by the British public as seditious, and a question was raised in the House of Commons in July 1907, about whether the Government proposed to take any action against Krishnavarma, the latter became increasingly nervous. Finally, when Lajpat Rai and Ajit Singh were deported in May 1907 on charges of sedition, Krishnavarma left London quietly for a safer abode in Paris.[17] On Krishnavarma's departure, the India House programmes became even more radical under the control of Savarkar, and now differed totally even from those of the 'extremists' of the INC. Collecting arms and sending them to India clandestinely, learning bomb-making and practising revolver-shooting were some of the new activities of the India House group in the period 1908–9.[18]

Although never an inmate himself, Chatto, because of his friendship with Savarkar, came in touch with the most prominent young nationalists of India House during Savarkar's time. They were Har Dayal, V.V.S. Aiyar, Madanlal Dhingra, and M.P.T. Acharya. Since all four were destined to shape the future course of the Indian revolutionary movement abroad, and Har Dayal and Acharya, in particular, were to be associated with some of Chatto's further plans and programmes in Europe, a brief account of their background (until 1909) is helpful.

Academically brilliant but highly eccentric and opinionated, Har Dayal was born about 1884. After graduating from Delhi, he enrolled himself for an M.A. in English at the Punjab University, Lahore, and passed the examination with the highest credit and stood first in the first class. He was selected for a three-year state scholarship for studies in England. In 1905, he went to Oxford and joined St John's College. When the scholarship had only six months to run, he gave it up on the ground that it was objectionable to accept any favours from an alien government. He was thoroughly impressed by Krishnavarma's ideology, and received one of his scholarships. Although he lived at India House only for a short while, he became a member of Savarkar's *Abhinav Bharat*. In 1909, Har Dayal left for Paris via Geneva and then went to Algiers for health reasons. He returned to Paris in July 1910, and remained there until October when he went to Martinique, and from there to the USA in January 1911. While in Geneva, he also took charge of Madam Cama's paper *Bande Mataram*.[19]

Unlike the mercurial Har Dayal with a much higher intellect, Varanganeri Venkatesa Subramia Aiyar was more practical and a devoted associate of Savarkar. A native of Trichinopoly and a B.A. of Madras University, after passing his law examinations, Aiyar practised for two years as a pleader in his native town and then went to

Rangoon in 1907. The following year he went to England and became a close associate of Savarkar at India House. He was a member of the *Abhinav Bharat* and also of the revolver practising group.[20]

Madanlal Dhingra was born circa 1884 in a Punjabi Kshatriya family of Amritsar. His father was a landlord and a physician. Dhingra was sent to London to study engineering, and he successfully completed his course at the University College, London. While in London, he became a member of Savarkar's *Abhinav Bharat*, participating in the shooting training as well.

Mandayam Parthasarathi Tirumal Acharya was born in Madras about 1887. From August to November 1907, he was registered as the printer and publisher of the Tamil newspaper, *India* of Madras. When the press was moved to Pondicherry in July 1908 after the arrest of the editor, Acharya signed papers as proprietor until he left for England in November 1908, where he was closely associated with the *Abhinav Bharat* group and participating in their rifle-shooting programmes.[21]

The fact that all these four men of very different character were equally attracted to Savarkar speaks volumes for Savarkar's personality. M.P.T. Acharya had this to say about Savarkar: 'His [Savarkar's] charm was such that a mere shake-hand could convert men as V.V.S. Aiyar and Har Dayal—not only convert but even bring out the best in them.'[22]

The radicalization of the India House programme during 1908–9 was also influenced by some of the events in India around this time, such as the anti-partition agitation in Bengal, the spread of Bengal's *swadeshi* and boycott movements to Madras and Tilak's Shivaji and Temperance movements in the Bombay presidency. Similarly, some acts of political terrorism in India at this time were associated with the radical Indians in Europe. On the morning of 30 April 1908, the Bengal group of revolutionary nationalists caused a bomb outrage at Muzaffarpore, then a part of Bengal, and killed two English ladies by mistake. The real target of the bomb had been D.H. Kingsford, the district judge, who had tried and convicted persons connected with the nationalist papers *Jugantar*, *Bande Mataram*, *Sandhya*, and *Navasakti*. The details of the event, known as the Maniktala Conspiracy Case, revealed that Hem Chandra Das, the man who had brought the technology of manufacturing bombs from Paris, had connections with both India House and the Paris groups of Indian radicals.[23] Then came the verdict of the Nasik Conspiracy Case on 9 June 1909, convicting

Savarkar's elder brother Ganesh and sentencing him to transportation for life for authoring two books of patriotic songs. Savarkar, whom the Benchers of Gray's Inn had just refused to call for the current term because of the propaganda in India House, was driven to a policy of violence. In the next Sunday meeting of India House on 20 June, he repeated his vow to wreak vengeance on the British.[24] The intense anti-British feeling among the Savarkar circle at this time resulted in the assassination of Sir Curzon Wyllie, political aide-de-camp at the India Office, at the Imperial Institute on the evening of 1 July 1909. Madan Lal Dhingra committed the act as a revenge against the conviction of Ganesh Savarkar. In December the same year, the district magistrate of Nasik was shot dead by a youth named Anant Lakshman Kanhere with one of the twenty Browning pistols procured and sent to India by Savarkar. The pistols had, however, been bought in Paris with the help of S.R. Rana.[25]

India House had already been under severe scrutiny. On 14 June 1909, the *Sunday Dispatch* had published a sensational article about it entitled 'House of Mystery', denouncing its seditious atmosphere.[26] Now, as a consequence of the Nasik murder, Savarkar was arrested on 13 March 1910 and sent to India on 1 July for trial. Shortly after this, India House ceased to function as a revolutionary centre as most politically active Indians associated with Savarkar moved to Paris and elsewhere by the middle of 1910.

3. Krishnavarma, Chatto, and the Revolutionary Ideology

Chatto was one of Savarkar's close friends in London. Biographers of Krishnavarma and Savarkar speak of this friendship.[27] From the middle of March to the end of June 1910, when Savarkar was lodged in Brixton jail, Chatto and V.V.S. Aiyar visited him frequently.[28] Yet it is also clear that Chatto was not involved in the Curzon Wyllie assassination plot. Nor did he belong to the group practising revolver shooting. In fact, during 1908-9, he was closely associated with Bipin Chandra Pal in London, and like Pal he believed in the evolutionary path to Indian independence. Chatto even quarrelled with Krishnavarma in public for the latter's incitement to violence while himself avoiding any direct participation.

Soon after the anniversary celebration of the 1857 uprising in India House on 10 May 1908, India was flooded with a leaflet entitled *Oh*

Martyrs, which the British Indian government considered seditious. When the British press charged Krishnavarma for this leaflet, he came out with a strong denial, saying he had never written anything anonymously or under a *nom de plume*.[29] He, however, added that it did not prevent him from frankly admitting that he was in full sympathy with the main objective of the leaflet, namely, the overthrow of British despotism in India. In another long letter to *The Times* in February 1909, replying to some attacks made against his paper *Indian Sociologist* and India House, Krishnavarma argued that the charge of 'incitement to crime' levelled against him and India House might not look like that at all if one saw it from a different angle. He wrote:

> I ask why Englishmen have just celebrated the tri-centenary of 'Milton the Regicide', and secretary to the 'Archtraitor' Cromwell, honoured, as they both are by tombs in Westminster Abbey, the 'Archtraitor', whose statue still graces the Houses of Parliament, having been buried with Royal honours. It cannot be effectively contended that Milton is commemorated not as 'regicide' or as secretary to Cromwell, but as poet and writer.[30]

Then, coming to the charge that India House lately celebrated the killing of two defenceless English ladies in the Muzaffarpore bomb outrage, he came out with brutal frankness to make this comment:

> Much stress is laid by your correspondent upon the fact that the deeds of some of the Indian martyrs causing death of two defenceless English women are commemorated in England by monuments and scholarships, but he forgets that the death in the case was quite accidental and incidental. It was mere accident that these two ladies were killed, the attack having been originally attempted, according to all reports, for a Calcutta magistrate, who had made himself unpopular; but supposing for arguments' sake that they were killed deliberately, it would only prove that those who habitually live and associate with wrongdoers or robbers (and Indian nationalists regard all Englishmen in India as robbers) do so at their peril. Incidents in common life afford ample proof to that effect. The near relations and others who are dependent for their livelihood upon a culprit justly sent to gaol for a crime often starve and die miserably for no fault of their own... Yet society does not make any special provision for their maintenance. Constituted as human beings are, such contingencies cannot be effectively avoided.[31]

Since Krishnavarma had already left England, there was no personal danger to him. But his letter put all Indian nationalists in England connected either with India House or Savarkar in grave danger. Thus angered by Krishnavarma's letter, Chatto sent a rejoinder to *The Times*

The Radical Nationalist in the Making 17

which published an extract from it. Keeping in mind the principles of the so-called 'extremists' in the INC who had rejected armed violence and ignoring, for the time being, the principles adopted by many of his own friends and colleagues in England and India, Chatto attacked Krishnavarma by saying that he deliberately uttered a falsehood by identifying himself with the party that stood for the principle of Indian nationalism.[32] Chatto continued:

> He [Krishnavarma] may call himself by whatever name he pleases, but he is not, in any sense of the word, a nationalist. He has never been accepted as a leader even by a small minority in India, although during his 17 years' residence in this country he has striven by 'patriotic gifts' to take part in a great movement that absolutely and categorically refuses his guidance.

Chatto then ventured to define an Indian nationalist:

> The principles that entitle a man to be called a nationalist have been very clearly laid down by such popular leaders as Bal Gangadhar Tilak, Bipin Chandra Pal, Lala Lajpat Rai and Aurobindo Ghosh. In their speeches and writings the blindest of men may see how ardent is the nationalist desire for a peaceful evolution, how deep is their horror of murder and assassination.

Almost as a matter of necessity to behave properly towards the host country and to undo some of the harm Krishnavarma might have already done to British-Indian relations, Chatto wrote:

> Mr Krishnavarma talks unmitigated nonsense when he says that Indians look upon Englishmen as 'robbers' and that Englishmen submit to the 'risks of war when they go out to India'. We are bound to accept historical facts as such, and there is no sane person who looks upon the British occupation as anything but a necessary phase in the advancement of our country.

Chatto asserted once again that 'All nationalist leaders have repeatedly declared that resistance is not only justifiable, but a positive duty, provided that it is passive and does not transgress the limits of the criminal law.'[33]

Krishnavarma did not allow Chatto to escape with impunity for his remarks. His reply came at once. 'I think it is right you should know who Mr Chattopadhyaya is', he wrote to the editor of *The Times*.[34]

> He is a disappointed man. He applied to me in April 1905 for help under my scheme of Indian Travelling Fellowships, the indispensible condition of which was

that each Fellow 'shall solemnly declare that after his return to India he shall not accept any post under the government or serve under the British Government'. There were numerous candidates whose claims were far superior to his, and I had therefore to pass him over.

With a simpler and a more acute definition of nationalism Krishnavarma added:

Surely every one acquainted with Indian politics knows that nationalism in the case of India means complete separation from England and that Indian nationalists' desire is to shake off the foreign yoke. I am, of course, a nationalist in that sense.

As a credential, Krishnavarma cited Bipin Chandra Pal, one of the four 'popular leaders' Chatto had referred to, who in the September 1905 number of his paper *Free India* had praised the nationalism of Krishnavarma.[35] Detecting the disguised and misguided purpose of Chatto's letter, he laid bare the home-truth in the last part of his rejoinder:

...there are some Indian Nationalists who are at heart really with me, but owing to their residence in British territory are obliged to say and do things quite contrary to their convictions. They think that by attacking me publicly they raise themselves in the estimation of their foreign masters, but they deceive no one, and make themselves only ridiculous in the eyes of the English public.[36]

Krishnavarma's reply put Chatto in an awkward situation. Considering it as 'a charge of dishonesty and hypocrisy' levelled against him, Chatto became more eloquent about his own notion of nationalism in his next letter to *The Times*:

I have never made any secret of my political views. I ardently believe that British rule in India must be put to an end and that the intellectual, moral and economic prosperity of my country can only be secured by her complete independence of foreign control.[37]

However, there was a proverbial 'but' to follow:

But Mr Krishnavarma has since gone much further and has begun to preach secret political assassination as one of the justifiable methods of the nationalist. He has condescended to abuse Englishmen in the same manner as some of them abuse us...I yield to no one in loyalty to the cause of Indian independence, and neither my residing in British territory nor any other consideration will ever terrorise me into cowardice or hypocrisy...The day that I feel convinced of the necessity of political assassination and underground work I shall cease to write. I shall return to my country and put my theories into practice. But I shall certainly not seek a safe retreat within the hospitable walls of a European city.[38]

As will be seen soon, it was a vain claim; for even Bipin Chandra Pal, Chatto's political guru at the time, lived in London in order to avoid arrest in India. Pal, too, charged Krishnavarma for dragging his name unnecessarily into his quarrel with Chatto.[39]

Krishnavarma, in his reply, first reminded Pal that it was Chatto, and not he, who had dragged him into the debate and then told his readers that Pal had twice received high honorarium from him for propagating his political education programme to achieve Indian independence and that he had been discarded lately (September 1908) for his apostasy.[40] A reputable Sanskrit scholar himself, Krishnavarma then entered into a philosophical discussion based on India's sacred books to contradict Pal's assertion that 'secret associations have no sanctions in our political philosophy, and are repugnant to the moral instincts of our race.'

Krishnavarma also reminded Pal of the celebration of Guru Govind Singh's birthday in December 1908 at Caxton Hall which Pal had presided over and let readers know that Guru Govind Singh composed the soul-stirring 'Hymn to the Sword' which was recited in all solemnity at the meeting. He concluded:

...but every fresh measure of British aggression and repression restricting, for instance, the liberty of the press, freedom of speech, and right of public meeting as proved by the recent enactments of the Indian Legislatures and by the operation of the Regulation of 1818, imposes on Indian patriots a corresponding duty to make futile the exports of the alien despotism by employing all such means as may advance the cause of Indian Independence. As a well-known Irishman has put it, Indian nationalists cannot be fastidious as to the methods by which that cause may be promoted.[41]

Krishnavarma's letters and articles published during this time in the *Indian Sociologist* resulted in his being debarred by the benches of the Inner Temple. The Herbert Spencer Fellowship which he had endowed to the University of Oxford was discontinued by the University management.[42] After the murder of Curzon Wyllie on 1 July 1909, he became a suspect even in the eyes of moderate Indian nationalists. In July 1909, he wrote in *The Times*:

Even one of my own countrymen, Mr Surendranath Banerjee, now a delegate to the Imperial Press Conference in England, is reported to have said: 'If any one is to be blamed for instigating the crime, that man is Krishnavarma'.[43]

The killing of Curzon Wyllie put both Pal and Chatto in a difficult position as Savarkar was Pal's paying guest at that time, and Chatto was Savarkar's friend. Savarkar made himself a suspect when, at the condolence meeting of Indians in England which took place at Caxton Hall, London, on 5 July 1909, he was the only person to raise a voice of dissent against the condolence resolution.[44] An anonymous report in *The Times* of 11 July 1909 pointed to Savarkar being Pal's paying guest for a while and connected the murder with Pal's 'extremist' politics. Pal wrote back to say that the political ideal of Indian nationalism had always been and would continue to be to work out peaceful changes in the constitution and that the Indian nationalists condemned the recent murders not only on the higher grounds of ethics and religion, but considered them even as suicidal to the cause of real national freedom.[45]

Since a reporter of *The Times* had mentioned an appeal of a new journalistic venture called the Hind Nationalist Agency, of which Chatto was named an honorary secretary, Chatto felt it necessary to free Pal from any adverse criticism for the appeal[46] he had written with Pal's approval:

I cannot imagine anything so grotesquely ignorant as the suggestion that Bepin Chandra Pal, of all people, is to be connected even remotely with the recent outrages. It is notorious that he has no place whatever in the councils of those who advocate violence, and though I do not share his old world optimism, as regards a 'practical revolution', I am constrained to say that on no occasion, whether at a public gathering or in the secret intimacy of his own circles, has he ever countenanced violence of any description.[47]

Already watering down his earlier stand on the evolutionary development of Indian nationalism with British rule as a necessary phase in India's development, Chatto now, forced by circumstances, came nearer to his inner self and declared:

We do not accept as crime every act which our foreign rulers in their own interests choose to call a crime. It is no crime, for instance, to boycott British goods or the British service or British ideas or British men (and women). It is no crime to produce a moral and mental attitude in the peoples of India which will deprive our rulers of their moral support. And so long as we allow ourselves to hurt or kill no one and to create no breach of the peace, we are justified in carrying on our work of bringing about such co-operation among the people of India as shall render the further existence of the British government unnecessary.[48]

The assassination of Curzon Wyllie provoked so much hostile reaction against Indian nationalism in England, that not only 'extremists' INC but also gentle 'moderates' were virulently attacked in the British press. Some retired British Indian officials—men like Bampfylde Fuller and Charles Elliott—used the columns of *The Times* to assail moderates like Surendranath Banerjee, whom they called 'Sir Henry Cotton's hysterically loyal-tongued lot', as not only sponsoring *swadeshi* which resulted in the boycott of British goods but also helping anarchy indirectly.[49] Banerjee defended himself in the column of *The Times* by enumerating his various deeds among Indian students who condemned violence.[50] But his voice was feeble and defensive. At one of the many meetings of Indians in London at this time, he even praised the British-made *zamindari* system of Bengal. He said that he was first a Bengali and then an Indian and that the permanent settlement in Bengal had produced a leisured class of public-spirited, patriotic, devoted men.[51] As to British despotism in India, he kept silent. It was left to the good old Sir Henry Cotton, a British member of the INC and a member of the House of Commons, to set the record straight by mentioning the contribution of the despotic British government in India to the recent burst of terrorism:

> No one would wish to minimize the gravity of these offences, but no calm and judicial person would jump to the conclusion that they establish the existence of a general or widespread conspiracy. If these outrages constitute a system of terrorism on the one hand, it is indisputable that spies and informers and fake and tutored witnesses constitute an equal system of terrorism on the other. I do not know what could have influenced the wretched murder of Colonel Wyllie—that will no doubt come out at the trial; but I protest against the unwarranted assumption which without any proof in support of it connects this crime with a conspiracy in India.[52]

The way the British press tarred the Indian nationalists, both 'extremists' and 'moderates', in the aftermath of the Curzon Wyllie murder made it clear that men like Chatto, revolutionaries in the garb of extremists, would not be treated kindly. This is evident from Chatto's last letter to *The Times* in which he bitterly attacked the British government in India. Since this letter had his address as Middle

Temple, it gave the Benchers of the Middle Temple a *prima facie* cause to expel him as someone with seditious views. Partly angered at this and partly inspired by Dhingra's sacrifice of life for the cause of Indian nationalism,[53] Chatto discarded the outward veil of pacifism he had worn until then and turned into a complete revolutionary. In the second number (December 1909) of Madame Cama's journal *The Talvar* which he edited,[54] Chatto violently attacked the British practice of labeling Indian aspirations for independence anarchist:

> But if it is anarchism to be thoroughly ashamed of being ruled by a handful of vile alien vandals, if it is anarchism to wish to exterminate them with the noble desire of establishing our national freedom upon the basis of popular sovereignty, of justice, of mercy, of righteousness, and of humanity, if it is anarchism to rise for the sanctity of our homes, the integrity of our life, and the honour of our God and our country, and to slay every individual tyrant, whether foreign or native, that continues the enslavement of our great noble people, if it is anarchism to conspire ceaselessly to take human life with the only object of emancipating our beloved Motherland, then we say, cursed is the man that is not an anarchist! Cursed is the man that sleeps in his bed or carouses merrily in halls of wine, women and song, while alien parasites live and grow fat upon the scarlet sweat of our brows, and blood-suckers are raging over the land and slowly, silently, and 'peacefully' draining away the life-blood of our nation.[55]

The January 1910 issue of *The Talvar*, devoted to the Nasik murder, was equally virulent:

> The city of Nasik would have been false to her traditions and title as *Dharmakshetra* if she had failed to send forth a *Dharmavira* at the present crisis of our national existence. Both Sri Ram and Sri Ramdas, the great master and the great disciple, have stored up their *Tapas-tej* in that holy place and it is without much surprise that we learn today that Nasik has claimed the honour of being the first city in India to successfully strike down an alien foe...Jackson is the first victim that the War-goddess [Kali] has claimed, and Kanare the Martyr devotee who purchased it at the cost of his own life.[56]

The April–May 1910 issue was devoted to the execution of the convicts of the Nasik conspiracy case. Here Chatto's article was an open incitement to rebellion in India. It can also be taken as an announcement of his own political course in the immediate future:

> On the morning of the 19th April, 1910, three of the most beloved sons of Hindustan, Kanare, Karve, and Deshpande, bore witness to the faith that was

consuming their hearts and expired on the scaffold erected by the enemy... How then shall we weep for them? How can we mourn their death? One thing alone there is which we ought to do for them, and which we will do for them, and that is to avenge them. We shall carry on the work that they started, we shall not lower the flag they raised on high, we shall push on with the war until our enemies are confounded and Hindustan emerges, as in the past, the greatest nation of the world.[57]

Chatto and V.V.S. Aiyar matched such fiery printed words with continued propaganda for revolution in the regular Sunday meetings of India House which they continued to hold after Savarkar's arrest. At the meeting on 17 April 1910, death sentences were passed on two former inmates of India House for giving evidence for the prosecution in the Nasik Conspiracy Case. A letter to this effect, written by Aiyar, was sent to India.[58] As London became too dangerous for them, both Aiyar and Chatto had to leave for Paris soon. Aiyar left on 19 April, after receiving information that a warrant had been issued for his arrest. Chatto left on 9 June.

Thus Krishnavarma's assumption about Chatto proved right. That was not all. While still in London, Chatto wrote a letter to Krishnavarma on 11 April 1910, and practically apologized for his earlier unseemly attack on him:

It was just over one year ago that I attacked you and your propaganda in the columns of the enemies' leading journal: but though at the time we misunderstood each other there has been, I hope, an entire change of our relations during the last few months. My attack arose out of no sinister motive...but out of a genuine, though thoroughly misguided antagonism to your view...Our Deshbhakta Dhingra brought about the much needed change.[59]

At the same time, Krishnavarma offered Chatto a scholarship as the first lecturer in Hindi in England to show his appreciation of the change in their relationship.[60] A year later, Chatto's old mentor, Bipin Chandra Pal, also moved politically to almost the opposite direction—once again exactly as Shyamaji had visualized. In September 1911, Pal left England for India, and, on his departure, informed his followers that in view of the Coronation Durbar he did not anticipate any trouble with the authorities and that he himself was no longer an extremist. Despite his declaration, Pal was arrested at once on arrival in Bombay on 6 October 1911 on the charge of sedition. Pal pleaded guilty to the charge.[61]

24 Chatto

4. The Paris Years: 1910–14

When Chatto arrived in Paris in June 1910, he found himself among the small group of Indians devoted to the cause of revolutionary upsurge in India. S.R. Rana and Madame Cama were the long-standing pillars of this group and had also been supporting the activities of the India House group in London. Lately, Krishnavarma had also started living in Paris. He continued to publish his journal *Indian Sociologist* and kept in close touch with the Irish and Egyptian nationalist movements. Har Dayal was off and on in Paris, editing Madame Cama's paper *Bande Mataram* mostly from Geneva. He left Paris in September 1910 for California. After the murder of Curzon Wyllie, Aiyar too had gone there and remained closely associated with Madame Cama until he quietly left for India in October 1910. Chatto was the last to come to Paris. Since Rana and Madame Cama were practically the sustainers of the Paris group, a brief background of their lives is useful.

Sirdarsinghji Rewabhai Rana was born in about 1878 in the ruling family of the state of Limbdi in Gujarat. He went to Europe after obtaining his B.A. degree from Bombay in 1898. Next year, while still pursuing law at Gray's Inn in London, he took up a job at the firm of Jivanchand Ottamchand Jhaveri, pearl merchants of Paris and Surat. He soon left London to look after the firm's business at 56 rue Lafayette, Paris. Rana's business in Paris was flourishing, and, in 1905, he joined Krishnavarma's venture of sponsoring scholarships to Indian patriots by offering three Travelling Fellowships of 2000 rupees each. One of these was enjoyed by Savarkar. Rana was befriended by Hem Chandra Das when the latter came to Paris to learn the technology of bomb-making.[62]

Bhikaji Rustom Cama, popularly known as Madame Cama, was probably born between the late sixties and early seventies of the 19th century[63] in a well-to-do Parsi family of Bombay. Cama, who married a Parsi solicitor, left India in 1902 to spend a year each in Germany, Scotland, Paris, and London. After visiting America in 1907 and London in 1908, she settled down in Paris in the middle of 1909. Here she was pre-occupied with preparing and forwarding revolutionary literature to India in the form of newspapers and leaflets. Besides being behind the publications of the journals *Bande Mataram* (first published in September 1909) and *The Talvar* (first published in November 1909), her other two significant contributions to the cause of Indian nationalism were her participation at the Congress of the Socialist International in Stuttgart in August 1907, where she raised the issue of Indian independence, and the use of her influence with the French Socialist circle in the Savarkar case which I will discuss shortly.

While still in London, Chatto had worked with Madame Cama by editing her paper *The Talvar* which appeared as a tribute to Dhingra's martyrdom. The last issue (June–July 1910) of the paper appeared when Chatto was in Paris. In that issue, as already quoted in the last section, he spoke of carrying on the war with the foreigners until India's freedom was achieved.

As if to translate his words into action, the first thing Chatto did in Paris was to plan the smuggling of firearms to India. On 19 June 1910, he wrote a letter to Srikishen Balmokand of Hyderabad, on Madame Cama's letterpad, with her full address on it. Balmokand, the son of Rai Balmokand, a judge in Hyderabad State, had studied at the Nizam's College and had moved to England in 1908 to study for the bar. In London, he became a regular visitor to India House and a close friend of Chatto with whose sister Mrinalini he had already been in regular affectionate correspondence. Srikishen returned to India in June 1910 at the behest of his father who disapproved of his contacts with the London revolutionaries. In his letter to Srikishen, Chatto instructed him not to go to Calcutta and wait for his next detailed letter in a week's time. The promised letter arrived in a figure cipher, the key of which had already been indicated in the previous letter. Both the letters fell straight into the hands of the British Indian intelligence which easily deciphered the second letter, part of which reads as follows:

There was no letter from last week. Most anxious here. Before you go to Calcutta write to me and let me know how things are getting on in Hyderabad. When you go to Calcutta please see my friend Bejoy Chandra Chatterji who will be introduced by Gannu [Chatto's sister Mrinalini]. Speak to him privately about affairs and ask him to introduce you to Sukumar Mitter, son of Krishna Kumar Mitter. Tell him, that is Sukumar, that I am prepared to send rifles from here, but it is necessary to start a secondhand furniture shop in Calcutta or in Chandernagore. We could then keep sending pieces of furniture for a few months containing nothing, but afterwards containing the required articles. As regards money that [will?] be sent to Madame Cama, and as regards all instructions it would be best to send them by some trusted friend who may be coming here. As for myself and Rau [Aiyar] we had to run away because warrants are out. When you go see Gannu, she will tell you all.[64]

Chatto's Shivaji-like plan fell through completely. As a result of this letter, the houses of K.K. Mitter and Dr Aghorenath Chattopadhyaya were searched on 16 August 1910 but no further treasonable correspondence was discovered. A considerable number of letters from Srikishen to Mrinalini were found, but many recent letters had evidently been destroyed. In the opinion of the British Indian intelligence, which had until then considered Chatto 'all talk and no work', this scheme was the most feasible Chatto had devised so far.[65]

Almost immediately after this mishap, the whole Paris group of Indian revolutionaries became involved with the event known as *L'affaire Savarkar*. Savarkar, who was considered a suspect in the Nasik murder case, had gone to Paris from London on 6 January 1910. Suspecting danger, Krishnavarma advised him to remain in Paris. Unfortunately, however, Savarkar did return on 13 March and was arrested on arrival at Victoria Station under a warrant of the Bombay High Court demanding his extradition to answer charges of conspiracy with his brother and others in Nasik. After being kept in Brixton Prison, Savarkar was sent to India by the P & O Liner *Morea* on 1 July 1910. The ship arrived at Marseilles on the evening of 7 July, and, early on the morning of the 8th, Savarkar pushed himself through the open port-hole of a lavatory and escaped. Swimming ashore, he reached the quay and ran. Two marine gendarmes chased and captured him after he had run more than 300 metres into French territory and brought him back to the ship. Unable to speak a single word of French, the poor fugitive could not ask or cry for political asylum and the ship sailed away with Savarkar on board.[66]

The Paris group of Indian nationalists spent days thinking how best to tackle the problem. They discussed the matter with Monsieur Jaures, the renowned socialist leader and other French politicians. In the eyes of French socialist leaders, a serious error was committed by the Marseilles police and they resolved to compel the French government to officially demand the return of Savarkar to the free soil of France.[67] As a result, a diplomatic negotiation took place between the French and British governments, and ultimately the case was referred to the Hague International Tribunal where the British won. Maitre Jean Longuet, *Advocat à la Cour d'Appel de Paris*, a well-known young socialist, was particularly helpful to the Indians, not only through his legal intervention on their behalf but also through signed articles on Indian independence in the socialist press—particularly in *l'Humanité*.

This newspaper held that the submission of Savarkar's case to arbitration in the first instance was a tactical error on the part of France.[68]

For Chatto, the Paris years were also important for international experience. In September 1910, he became a member of the French Socialist Party. In an autobiographical speech in Leningrad in March 1934, Chatto was to recall his introduction to socialism in Paris thus: 'We met in circle *l'Humanité* of Jaures, Longuet etc. Today it seems strange to me that comrades Mikhail Pavlovich and Charles Rappoport, whom I very often met at Paris did not even mention Lenin at that time.'[69]

In Paris, Indian revolutionary nationalists also had close contacts with Egyptian nationalists who were greatly inspired by Dhingra's daring act. The startling news in Europe at the beginning of 1910 was that of the assassination in Cairo of Butrus Ghali Pasha, the Egyptian prime minister, by a nationalist patriot, Ibrahim Nassif el Wardani on 20 February. This act led Krishnavarma to think in terms of a pan-Asian union in Paris. When el Wardani was sentenced to death, Krishnavarma sent a telegram to the Khedive of Egypt: 'Your Highness's own interest and humanity, enslaved by England, imperatively demand royal clemency favouring martyr Wardani.' The telegram was published in *l'Humanité* and perhaps drew the attention of freedom-loving people.[70] Wardani's last words, as he mounted the scaffold in Cairo, were comparable to those of Dhingra.[71] As Yajnik writes, it was partially due to Krishnavarma's propaganda that Dhingra and Wardani were linked up in a spirited song by a famous Egyptian poet, El Ghayati, who was duly punished for sedition by the Egyptian government.[72]

An indication of the close relationship between the Paris-based Indian and Egyptian nationalists is evident from a handwritten manuscript by Chatto, 'Some Unpublished Facts on the Egyptian National Movement', found among his private papers.[73] According to this manuscript, the Muslim extremist student who assassinated Butrus Ghali Pasha for his alleged intention to sell Egypt's share in the Suez Canal to Britain, had been inspired by Dhingra's 1909 terrorist act in London. Chatto and Har Dayal were not only the friends of many young Egyptian nationalists but also their advisers. When this Egyptian nationalist group[74] organized a congress in Brussels in September 1910, in which J. Keir Hardie, the British Independent Labour Party leader spoke, the main paper on the 'Future of Egypt' read by the secretary of the congress Ataily, had in reality been written by Har Dayal. Another paper on the 'Army of Occupation' was written by Chatto although read at the congress by Rifaat as his own. At the Brussels congress it was decided that close contact be maintained between the Egyptian, Indian, and Irish nationalist movements. A committee consisting of Rifaat (Egypt), Dryhurst (Ireland), and Chatto (India) was formed for the purpose.[75] This happened during WWI when the Berlin India Committee functioned in the Middle East and the USA.

Soon after the Savarkar case, the Paris group started disintegrating. First, there was a financial crisis. The Savarkar case required money and there arose a problem not only of raising the necessary sum but also of using it in accordance with all the legal constraints imposed by Madame Cama.[76] Then there were conflicts arising out of individual idiosyncrasies, predilections, and private preferences. Krishnavarma was particularly disliked for his egotism and cowardliness. Not just Chatto but even Har Dayal, who had been closer to Krishnavarma than most, found him increasingly vain, greedy, selfish, and egotistic.[77] Then Dayal, who was editing *Bande Mataram*, had to be away for health reasons. Aiyar, the most active of them all, left quietly for India in October after spending six months in Paris. Chatto, the newest member, was so preoccupied with his private life, that from the spring of 1911 he was practically lost to the Indian revolutionary cause. During that spring, Chatto was visited several times in Paris by Miss Reynolds, whom he later married in early 1912.[78] While still in England, Chatto's private life had already distracted him from the Indian revolutionary cause. In 1909, Dayal, then in Algeria, suggested to Rana that Chatto take over the editorship of *Bande Mataram*:

> I have asked Madam Cama and Mr Aiyar to ask Chattopadhyaya to undertake it. He will agree that maintenance of the journal is necessary, as it is a useful institution of the party. He [Chatto] wields a facile pen: so four pages a month will not be any trouble to him. Rather he should be glad to do the duty. I have not written to him directly as I don't know him well at all. He is Mr Aiyar's friend and Mr Aiyar can arrange the matter easily.[79]

Dayal heard from Rana about Chatto's private preoccupations, and was surprised that Chatto had not had time even for *The Talvar*. Har Dayal wrote back, 'But now that I know the truth, I shall try my utmost to keep up *Bande Mataram* consistently with my other duties.'[80] So hopeless became the condition of the Paris group at the beginning of 1912 that Rana wrote to Aiyar in Pondicherry in January, 'We are under great depression for the present. All comrades do not show or continue the same vitality. It cannot be helped.'[81]

During 1912, two incidents lowered the estimation of Indians in the eyes of Parisians. Govind Amin, a former India House inmate who had lately started a pearl business in Paris, was charged by some Indian merchants, including S.R. Rana, with theft of pearls and precious stones worth several thousand francs. The Indian denouncement to the police led Amin to commit suicide. And, in November, a Hindu gems dealer was prosecuted for selling fake pearl necklaces as genuine.

In spite of these mishaps, the anniversary celebration of 1857 took place as usual on 10 May 1913 in Paris, and later that year copies of postcards from Paris arrived in India bearing on one side the photograph of V.D. Savarkar and on the other the complete oath of his *Abhinav Bharat*. No other records are found of the Paris group. Shortly before the declaration of war against Germany in 1914, Krishnavarma left for Geneva where Dayal had also returned from the USA. Madame Cama and Rana were both interned. In the second week of April 1914, Chatto left for Germany. According to a friend of his at the time, he was registered at Halle in Germany, enrolled as a student for a doctorate degree with philosophy, with Sanskrit and Arabic as additional subjects.[82]

NOTES

1. For details of Aghorenath Chattopadhyaya's family see Tara Ali Baig, *Sarojini Naidu* (New Delhi, 1974), pp. 10–11.
2. Sarojini Naidu, *The Golden Threshold*, p. 15, quoted in Tara Ali Baig, *op.cit.*, pp. 1–2. The Englishman was Arthur Symons. See also Padmini Sengupta, *Sarojini Naidu* (New Delhi, 1974), p. 7.
3. Tara Ali Baig, *op.cit.*, pp. 7–8.
4. Quoted from Harindranath Chattopadhyaya, *Life and Myself*, p. 15, by Padmini Sengupta, *ibid.*, p. 8.
5. *Ibid.*
6. Tara Ali Baig, *op.cit.*, p. 10, with reference to P.C. Roy Chowdhury, in *Amrita Bazar Patrika*, 25 November 1967.
7. *Ibid.*, referring to Damodar Satvalekar's reminiscences.
8. *Ibid.*, p. 12. The present author also heard the story from A.C.N. Nambiar in the early 1970s in Zurich. According to Nambiar, who had lived together with Suhasini, Chatto's youngest sister, in Berlin in the late 1920s, Aghorenath disowned Sarojini in retaliation.

9. *Ibid.*, The episode described here happened perhaps in 1910 as on 16 August in that year the police searched Aghorenath Chattopadhyaya's house hoping to discover some treasonable correspondence from Chatto to his sister Mrinalini. However, no objectionable material was discovered. See for this incident J.C. Ker, *Political Trouble in India* (Calcutta, 1917), p. 199.
10. J.C. Ker, *Political Trouble in India* (Calcutta, 1917), p. 407. Chinmohan Snehanobis in his book (in Bengali) *Rus Biplab O Prabashi Bharatiya Biplabi* (Russian Revolution and Indian Revolutionaries Abroad) (Calcutta, 1973), p. 61, writes that Chatto left India for England on 31 October 1901.
11. *Ibid.*, p. 206.
12. The meagre Chattopadhyaya papers left with his Russian wife L. Karunovskaya contain a list in his own hand, although very sketchy, of Chatto's publications during 1908–13. According to it, in 1908, he edited and published a journal called *Orient Review*. Moreover, during 1908–10 he contributed many philological notes in *Notes and Queries*, London. In 1911 he wrote various small articles on Indian languages and literature in *People's Encyclopaedia*, Edinburgh. The same year he published an article called 'Etymology of Coffee' in the journal *Revue Linguistique*, Paris. In 1913, Chatto revised the book *Grammar of Hindustani Language* (London), and published the book *Hindustani* in three editions—English, German, and French. A copy of this list was preserved in the erstwhile Dimitrov Museum in Leipzig.
13. The standard work for the life of Krishnavarma is Indulal Yajnik's *Shyamaji Krishnavarma: Life and Times of an Indian Revolutionary* (Bombay, 1950).
14. Ram Gopal, *Lokamanya Tilak* (Bombay, 1965), p. 256.
15. *Ibid.*
16. Ganapati or Ganesh is the elephant god in Indian mythology and popular Hindu religion. The 'extremist' leader Tilak of Maharashtra used the festival relating to this god politically to arouse the inert masses against the British.
17. J.C. Ker, *op.cit.*, p. 174.
18. In June 1908, there was a lecture at India House on 'The Making of Bombs'. In November of the same year, Savarkar talked about how to procure arms. In May 1909, revolver shooting was practiced regularly at a range on Tottenham Court Road. J.C. Ker, *op.cit.*, pp. 177–8.
19. J.C. Ker, *op.cit.*, pp. 196–7. For Dayal's later activities during the war, see chapter II and also Nirode K. Barooah, 'Har Dayal and the German Connection', *The Indian Historical Review*, VII (1–2), July 1980–January 1981.
20. *Ibid.*, pp. 200–4.
21. J.C. Ker, *op.cit.*, p. 442.
22. Quoted in Dhananjay Keer, *Veer Savarkar* (Bombay, 1966), p. 33.
23. See J.C. Ker, *op.cit.*, pp. 142–3. See also Indulal Yajnik, *op.cit.*, pp. 255, 262.
24. Yajnik, *op.cit.*, p. 267.
25. For details of the Nasik murder and the Browning pistols procured by V.D. Savarkar, see J.C. Ker, *op.cit.*, pp. 181–2.
26. Yajnik, *op.cit.*, p. 263.

27. See Yajnik, *op.cit.*, p. 263; Dhananjay Keer, *op.cit.*, p. 30.
28. J.C. Ker, *op.cit.*, p. 187. According to one account, Chatto visited Savarkar in that jail as many as 15 times. See Harindra Srivastava, *Five Stormy Years: Savarkar in London* (Bombay, 1983), p. 18. This may well be a fact, although the author's other accounts of Chatto's activities are extremely faulty.
29. 'Indian Sedition', *The Times*, 29 June 1908.
30. 'Indian Anarchism in England', *The Times*, 20 February 1909.
31. *Ibid*.
32. 'Indian anarchism in England', *The Times*, 1 March 1909.
33. *Ibid*.
34. 'Indian Anarchism', *The Times*, 10 March 1909.
35. *Ibid*. Praising Krishnavarma's view of Home Rule for India, Pal had written: 'Whatever loyal patriots of the old school might say or representatives of the ruling bureaucracy in India might try to represent, there is absolutely no question that the rising generation of our educated countrymen in every province are in sincere sympathy with the movement for the promotion of Home Rule Autonomy in India, of which Pundit Shyamaji Krishnavarma is the founder and principal spokesman in England.'
36. *Ibid*.
37. Chatto's letter under the broad heading 'Indian Anarchism', *The Times*, 19 March 1909.
38. *Ibid*.
39. Pal's letter under 'Indian Anarchism', *The Times*, 11 March 1909.
40. Krishnavarma's letter under the general heading 'Indian Anarchism', *The Times*, 19 March 1909.
41. *Ibid*.
42. Krishnavarma's letter in *The Times*, 30 March 1909, under the heading 'Indian Anarchism'.
43. 'Mr. Krishnavarma in His Defence', *The Times*, 17 July 1909.
44. 'The murder of Sir Curzon Wyllie: The Indian Meeting', *The Times*, 6 July 1909.
45. 'The Extremist Attitude', *The Times*, 12 July 1909.
46. The appeal was concerning the forthcoming fortnightly called *Swaraj*, which Pal and Khaparde had launched. The first issue appeared on 27 February 1907. See J.C. Ker, *op.cit.*, p. 192.
47. A letter from Chatto under 'The Extremist Attitude', *The Times*, 12 July 1909.
48. *Ibid*.
49. 'Indian Loyalty', *The Times*, 12 July 1909; the letter by Bampfylde Fuller. Banerjee's answer to charges made against him by Sir Charles Elliott.
50. *Ibid*.
51. Speech of S.N. Banerjee in the report on the meeting of the Indian Union Society, *The Times*, 19 July 1909.
52. Henry Cotton's letter under 'Indian Loyalty', *The Times*, 12 July 1909.

53. See below Chatto's letter to Krishnavarma, 11 April 1910.
54. The first issue put the place of publication as Berlin but, in fact, it was printed by The Rotterdamsche Art and Book Printers of 61, Haringvleit, Rotterdam. The first issue of the paper came out on 20 November 1909, and the last was the June–July issue in 1910.
55. As quoted in J.C. Ker, *op.cit.*, p. 118.
56. *Ibid.*
57. See J.C. Ker, *op cit.*, p. 119.
58. *Ibid.*
59. Yajnik, *op.cit.*, p. 264 fn.
60. *Ibid.*, p. 265 fn.
61. J.C. Ker, *op.cit.*, pp. 191–2.
62. J.C. Ker, *op.cit.*, pp. 197–8.
63. Bulu Roy Chowdhury in a booklet called *Madame Cama* (New Delhi, 1977), p. 2, puts the date of Cama's birth at 24 September 1861. This does not seem to be correct considering the youngish look of her photograph about the time of the Congress of the Socialist International in Stuttgart in 1907. British Indian intelligence puts the year of her birth as about 1875.
64. *Ibid.*, p. 198.
65. *Ibid.*, pp. 199–200.
66. *Ibid*, p. 183; Yajnik, *op.cit.*, pp. 287–88.
67. Yajnik, *op.cit.*, p. 289.
68. *Ibid.*, p. 292; J.C. Ker, *op.cit.*, p. 209.
69. A speech delivered on the international day of MOPR on 18 March 1934. Andrey Nikolayevich Dalskiy, *Vospominaniya*, Ms., Leningrad, 29 March 1962, p. 7. For Dalskiy, see also Chapter 9.
70. Yajnik, *op. cit.*, pp. 281–2, 284.
71. Wardani solemnly declared that 'God is One and that Mahomet is the prophet and that liberty and independence is a saying of God.' Dhingra had spoken thus: 'As a Hindu, I feel that wrong done to my country is an insult to God. Her cause is the cause of Shri Rama. Her service is the service of Shri Krishna. Poor in wealth and intellect, a son like myself has nothing else to offer to the Mother but his own blood and so I have sacrificed the same on Her altar.'
72. Yajnik, *op. cit.*, p. 285. Krishnavarma reeived an excellent photograph of martyr Wardani, together with a brief appreciative notice: 'The friends of Wardani send you a copy of his portrait and his handwriting. Those who give their lives for their native land will never be forgotten.'
73. From the microfilm of the original manuscripts in Chatto's own hand formerly preserved at DML. No date.
74. Among the members of the group were: Mohammed Ferid, Dr M. M. Rifaat, Hamid-el-Ataily, Loutifi Jonmah, and Abdul Hamid Said, *Ibid.*
75. *Ibid.* Dr M.M. Rifaat later founded the organ of the Egyptian Emancipation Movement entitled *La Patrie Egyptienne* in Geneva in March 1914.

Krishnavarma published many articles from the pen of Dr Rifaat in his paper *The Indian Sociologist*. See Yajnik *op.cit.*, p. 310.
76. See J.C Ker, *op.cit.*, pp. 208–9.
77. Dayal to Rana, Albergo Isola Bella, Lago Maggiore, 1909, NMML Har Dayal Papers. Acc. No. 185.
78. J.C. Ker, *op.cit.*, p. 206.
79. Dayal to Rana, Algiers, 24 May 1909, NMML, Har Dayal Papers, Acc. No. 185.
80. Dayal to Rana, no date, NMML, Har Dayal Papers, p. 125.
81. J.C. Ker, *op.cit.*, pp. 206–07.
82. *Ibid.*, pp. 210–11, 213. See also Abinash Chandra Bhattacharya, *Europey Bharatiya Viplaber Sadhana* (Preparation for the Indian Revolution in Europe) (Calcutta, 1958), p. 132.

2

The Enemy of Our Enemy is Our Friend

1. WORLD WAR I AND GERMANY'S THREAT TO INDIA POLICY

The German assessment of the British Indian situation towards the close of the Bismarckian period revealed something very significant for the Germany of Kaiser Wilhelm II. The Kaiser believed that an uprising would inevitably occur against the British in India in the event of a British reverse in a major war. This belief inspired, intrigued, and solaced Wilhelmian Germany throughout the years leading to World War I. Wilhelm II showed a keen interest in Indian developments, personally vetting most of the political despatches concerning India and commenting upon them. German officials in India, while truthfully reporting the fears and forebodings of the Anglo-Indians, never failed to see the realities of the situation that the British had a favourable position in India.[1] Nevertheless, the Kaiser and, to some extent, the German Foreign Office (AA) in Berlin came to hold exaggerated notions of British India's insecurity, such as the possibility of a Russian invasion, the internal disaffection of the Indians, the Turkish influence on the Indian Muslims, and Japanese imperialism.[2] At first, Berlin hoped that these potential dangers to British India would act in Germany's favour in exacting concessions from Britain. But the conviction that Anglo-Russian reconciliation was impossible and the caution imposed by the so-called danger period before the navy was built seem to have led Berlin merely to expect things to turn in its favour. There was no effort to evolve a policy either alone or in conjunction with Russia to profit from Britain's Russophobia in India. As a result, when the era of this Russophobia ended in 1907, Germany did not reap any diplomatic advantage. Germany's pro-British neutrality in the Boer War did not result in any benefits in the area of economic expansion as expected from reciprocal British goodwill. Curzon, then Viceroy of India, was responsible, directly or indirectly, for thwarting some German hopes in this direction.[3] Immediately following the Anglo-Russian Convention of 1907, there was an opportunity for Germany to hinder the growth of Anglo-Russian friendship by taking advantage of dissatisfaction in Russia with the limitation which this Asiatic settlement placed upon further Russian expansion in Central Asia. But Germany missed this opportunity and 'the easiest way by which Great Britain and Russia could be kept apart was ignored'.[4]

In the post-1907 period, when the German world-power policy was heading for a collision with Britain, which was no longer suffering a Russian 'pressure on India', the Kaiser and the AA seem to have counted upon anti-British Indian revolutionary elements as possible allies in the event of a final clash with Britain. Some evidence of 1909 shows how Professor Schiemann, the influential commentator of the *Kreuz-Zeitung,* was regularly fed exaggerated news of Indian revolutionary preparations by George Freeman, an Irish Sinn Fein leader in America connected with the Indian revolutionary nationalists abroad. Such news seems to have convinced some influential people connected with the AA as well as the Kaiser of an inevitable anti-British uprising in India in case Britain engaged in war with Germany.

However, even in the post-1907 period, German diplomats and other consular officials in India never considered the British position in India weak at any stage or ever thought that British India could be dangerously threatened by a foreign power. German officials not only looked down upon the extremist nationalists but also the Indian national movement as a whole. The burden of the whole socio-political tradition of imperial Germany stood in the way, and they failed to appreciate the Indian demand for independence and democracy. Anti-parliamentarianism, hostility to Western liberalism, disregard of the modern importance of the fundamental rights of man, and the consideration of aristocracy as a socio-political system superior to democracy were some of the chief characteristics of the conservative tradition[5] of the German officials. Even the German liberals of the time were not concerned much with the individual rights of man; they were votaries of the German power-state for the sake of which they readily accepted social Darwinism and 'illiberal imperialism'.[6] The influence of Gladstonian liberalism among some of the British officials in India, the Indians' agitation for decentralization, representative government, and the rights of man based on the principle of equality, were subject to perpetual condemnation by pre-War Germans in India. Racialism also saturated their minds. In the post-1907 period, at a time when political terrorism was quickening the tempo of Indian nationalism, the sympathy of some liberal and socialist politicians in England for some of the political aspirations of the Indians was enough to enrage the Kaiser and the German officials. Political terrorism was also no help to German commerce in India. In these circumstances, there could hardly be any thought of mutual understanding between Indians and Germans on close political cooperation.

With the political agitation of one section of the Indian people—the Indian Muslims—the German officials had, however, no quarrel. There were two main reasons for this. First, being under the spiritual influence of Turkey, Indian Muslims formed a part of the so-called German Orient policy. Germany counted upon their support in any policy undertaken jointly with Turkey. Second, the Muslims, frightened at the possibility of being submerged under Hindu domination in case of a full parliamentary democracy in India, remained mostly outside the pale of the primarily Hindu-directed reform-cum-liberation movement. So the politics of Indian Muslims was not ideologically repugnant to the Germans. Besides, its Turkey-oriented aspect, it was thought, could only be an asset to the German power-state policy. Naturally, after the Balkan wars, when the traditional Muslim support for the British was eroding in India, the German officials, at the threshold of a war with Britain, pondered whether it was not time to activate the tacit German interest in Indian Muslims by egging them on against the British. To this thinking Enver Pasha's idea of a Turco-German pan-Islamic expedition to Afghanistan to induce her to invade India came as a most welcome suggestion to Berlin at the outbreak of the war.

Until 1913, however, the German officials in India had not believed in the Turkey-oriented Indian Muslims' power to threaten the British internally. But in the summer of 1913, seeing how the growing disaffection of the Indian Muslims was causing great concern even to the experienced British and in view of the impending war between Germany and Britain, Count von Luxburg, the German consul general in India, advised Berlin as follows: 'Despite a desirable slow rapprochement between Germany and Britain for the time being we have no reason to make it easier for the British to rule India.'[7] The hopes that the growth of pan-Islamism in India aroused in Luxburg in 1913[8] gave authenticity to what had already been assumed in some quarters of the German military circles. As early as October 1911, General Friedrich von Bernhardi published his widely circulated book *Germany and the Next War* where, while advocating a war with Britain, he tried to show how the precarious conditions prevailing could lead to German advantage. 'England so far, in accordance with the principle of *divide et impera* has attempted to play off the Mohammedan against the Hindu population', wrote Bernhardi. 'But now that a pronounced revolutionary and nationalist tendency shows among the latter, the danger is imminent that Pan-Islamism, thoroughly roused, should unite with the revolutionary elements of Bengal. The co-operation of these elements might create a very grave danger, capable of shaking the foundations of England's high position in the world.'[9] Gradually the German newspapers began to print information about the revolutionary nationalists abroad.[10]

On the eve of WWI, these developments in the internal Indian scene were reassuring to Wilhelm II who, irrespective of the views of others, had long been convinced of Turkey's hold on the Indian Muslims and of their power to bring disorder to British rule in India. Thus on the night of 30 July 1914, when he read a report from the German Ambassador at St Petersburg stating that, according to Sazonov, Russian mobilization could not be reversed and, therefore, inferred that war was inevitable, he wrote, in the excitement of the moment:

Now our job is to show up the whole business ruthlessly and tear away the mask of Christian peacemaking and put the pharisiacal hypocrisy about peace in the pillory!!! And our consuls in Turkey and India, agents, etc. must get a conflagration going throughout the whole Mohamedan world against this hated, unscrupulous, dishonest nation of shopkeepers—since if we are going to bleed to death, England must at least lose India.[11]

The Kaiser was not alone in thinking in terms of revolutionizing the Islamic world. When the war ultimately came, General Helmuth von Moltke, Chief of the German General Staff, wrote to the AA on 2 August, 1914, the day of the treaty between Germany and Turkey, emphasizing that:

> If Britain becomes our opponent, attempts will have to be made to instigate a rebellion in India. The same has to be tried in Egypt...Persia must be called upon to make use of the favourable opportunity to throw off the Russian yoke and, if possible, to act together with Turkey.[12]

In this connection the military importance of the Baghdad Railway also came to the forefront. General von der Goltz spoke forthrightly about its connection with British India. In his view, to force Britain to her knees, an invasion might become necessary either in Egypt or India, and in both cases the Baghdad line was needed. On 26 February 1915, Goltz assessed the importance of the speedy construction of the Asia-Minor Railway. A march on India, Goltz declared, was not a 'fairy tale adventure' by any means; for what Nadir Shah of Persia had accomplished in the 18th century and others like Alexander the Great and Tamerlane before him, could certainly be done 'with the perfect means of the modern age'. Indeed, a carefully prepared campaign against India would constitute a 'worthy and decisive conclusion' to the present world conflict.[13]

Once the instigation of a revolution in the Muslim world became a military necessity, German diplomatic agents immediately became busy finding ways to do so. In fact, it was already too late to organize a pan-Islamic movement, as the German ambassador in Turkey, Baron Hans von Wangenheim, was to comment towards the end of August 1914. Only by quick and determined action could Germany now, in his view, make up for the blunder of omitting such preparations in the pre-war period.[14] The man who took the lead at the beginning in organizing the pan-Islamic movement on behalf of the AA was Baron Max von Oppenheim.[15] Oppenheim, who has been credited as the spiritual father of the Kaiser's famous Damascus speech of 1898[16], and who had been informing himself about the Indian Muslims for quite some time[17], wrote to the German Foreign Office on 18 August 1914:

> Britain knows that once she is pushed out of India she may never get India back again. If there were deeper unrest in India Britain would be forced to send a major

portion of her fleet to Indian waters to protect the numerous British interests, the British people there, and the British world position. British public opinion would also want it and thus Britain would have to conclude an early peace favourable to us...[18]

The concrete shape of Germany's threat-to-India programme, however, came from an idea of Envar Pasha whose great wish it was to see a group of German military officers, dressed like Muslims, accompanying a group of Turkish officers to the Amir of Afghanistan who, according to him, was only waiting for encouragement to attack India.[19] Wangenheim informed Berlin about Pasha's wish, and the AA was ready to cooperate. Oppenheim worked enthusiastically in selecting the German group, and he was able to inform Pasha before the end of August 1914 that 15 people were ready to participate in the Afghan expedition.[20] Information from the Swedish explorer Sven Hedin, that the Amir of Afghanistan 'was burning with desire to attack British India' gave further impetus to the venture.[21] The preparatory work from the German side was put into the hands of a commission.[22] On 4 September, Wangenheim recorded that, in the Turkish war ministry, a central office for the Islamic movement had recently been formed.[23] Ali Bey Bashhamba of this office, known as *Tashkilat-i-Mukhsusa*, and Fuad Bey of the Turkish Secret Service were the contact men for Indian revolutionaries in Turkey. In Constantinople an Indian, Abu Said el-Arabi, was also given editorial charge of the Urdu portion of the pan-Islamic journal *Jehan-i-Islam*.[24]

2. CHATTO AND THE FORMATION OF THE BERLIN INDIA COMMITTEE

The German interest in the Indian revolution on the eve of the War encouraged Indian revolutionaries abroad. It had so far been only a pipe dream. As far back as February 1910, Har Dayal in *Bande Mataram* considered that Berlin was 'the capital of the country which at present is most hostile in spirit to England' and gave his opinion that 'the cultivation of friendly relations [by Indian revolutionaries] with the powerful German nation will be of great advantage to the cause of Indian independence.'[25] It was also in a German journal in March 1911 that Krishnavarma's views on Indian nationalism and unrest appeared.[26] In 1912, Mohamed Barakatullah, a pan-Islamist who worked hand in hand with Indian revolutionary nationalists in the USA and Japan, in a glowing tribute to the Kaiser in his paper *Islamic Fraternity*, remarked:

...In case there be a conference of the European powers [over Tripoli] or a European war, it is the duty of the Muslims to be united, to stand by the Khalif with their life and property, and to side with Germany. Germany's word alone is reliable; while the others blow the trumpet of independence, integrity, civilization and progress, but they at the same time go marching along through bloodshed, desecration of holy places, rapine and plunder.[27]

In April 1913, yet another Indian nationalist from Europe wrote an anonymous article in the *Leipziger Neueste Nachrichten,* inviting Germans to take greater interest in India, particularly trade. The author also assured Germans of the great love and respect Indians had for them.[28] While forwarding a copy of the article to the AA, the paper's editorial office did not disclose the name of the author, introducing him only as a member of the Indian Nationalist Party living in Europe.[29] Circumstantial evidence, however, shows the piece to be the work of Chatto and Abinash Bhattacharya.[30] Thus, when WWI finally broke out, it was only natural that those Indian revolutionaries in Europe who intended to remain active would contact the Germans and try to turn England's difficulty to their advantage. In this case it was the turn of Chatto to start a new phase in Indian revolutionary activities abroad.

At the beginning of the War, Chatto and Abinash Bhattacharya were at Halle in Germany.[31] Chatto, as already mentioned, was enrolled as a student at the University of Halle.[32] Bhattacharya had been there longer, having arrived in 1910 to qualify himself as a chemist.[33] By the middle of August 1914, both of them were in touch with one Mrs Simon, the widow of a county court counsellor at Halle, who happened to have good relations with Helmuth Delbrueck, a nephew of Clemens von Delbrueck, the minister for the interior in the Prussian government. On 22 August, Mrs Simon sent a cable to Stettin asking Helmuth to use all his influence to arrange an interview for Chatto with minister Delbrueck so that he could make some 'important proposals' connected with the War and India.[34] Helmuth Delbrueck seems to have had earlier contact with Bhattacharya for he wrote to his uncle immediately, introducing Bhattacharya as his friend.[35] These efforts were successful, and before long Bhattacharya was informed by Mrs Simon that the matter was in progress. On hearing this, Bhattacharya himself wrote to Dr Delbrueck with great excitement at the prospect of a German victory in the War about which he had no doubts. To him, the German victory also meant freedom for India.[36] As a result, Bhattacharya and Chatto were soon in Berlin, and, before the month was out, they became associated with the existing German plans concerning India.[37]

In the early months of the War, German patriotic feelings went hand in hand with the patriotism of the Indian nationalists. Ex-missionaries with past Indian experience, and those who had recently returned with fresh knowledge of India at the outbreak of the War, offered themselves for propaganda work.[38] The press not only reported news of the British Indian situation but also published the expression of Indian sympathy for the Germans.[39] Those people in Germany who saw this War as one forced on them unjustly by Britain saw new significance in the Indian situation for Germany. An educated young man from Lueneburg—no other than the future famous philosopher Professor Fritz Heinemann—for example, wrote very enthusiastically to the Berlin police:

A little while ago German newspapers carried expressions of sympathy by the Indians for Germany. In this connection I should like to ask you to send addresses of some Indians living in Berlin or in other German towns... It could be of greatest importance for the development of the European situation if now India would get *true* news about the situation of England; the Indians are almost 300 million people and are thirsting for liberation. England would get heavy blows by difficulties in her most important colony and would soon be forced to peace with Germany.

To emphasize the importance of the work he further added: 'I should be grateful if you would answer my letter soon. Quick action is necessary and could be of great value for Germany.'[40]

Envar Pasha's information about the Afghan Amir's eagerness to join any venture against England and Russia was already very inspiring. It was followed by various false and misleading rumours and reports of outbreaks of revolt in India and of England seeking Japan's help at a heavy price to save India. On 25 August 1914, Quadt, a former German consul general in Calcutta and now the German minister at Athens, transmitted to Berlin the information he received from a German national, who had recently returned from India, that India would send no more troops to Egypt, for, in the event of war between Turkey and England, unrest among the Indian Muslims was an absolute certainty. In another report from Teheran to Wangenheim on 27 August Kardorf, the German minister, mentioned what he heard from British sources that the Indian expeditionary force was being ordered to return from Muscat because of the state of siege prevailing in Bombay and Karachi. On 4 September, the Admiralty staff received news of an Indian revolt in a message from China. Six days later, came the news via Sweden from the Washington Embassy that Japan had officially confirmed to Chinese quarters the outbreak of revolution in India and that Japan was asked for military support by England which she promised under the following conditions: a) free immigration to British possessions in the Pacific; b) a 200-million dollar loan; and c) a free hand in China.[41]

The Indian revolutionaries did not believe the report of the outbreak of Indian revolution to be true. Har Dayal, in Constantinople, considered it improbable.[42] But as a result of these reports, the Berlin-sponsored programme for India acquired new dimensions. In its search for Indians in Germany, Austro-Hungarian territories, Switzerland, America, and in the Ottoman Empire, the German Foreign Office traced all the leading Indian nationalists in these countries. The veterans of Indian revolutionary propaganda in Europe were, however, not available for active help. Krishnavarma, who was living in Geneva at the time, showed his sympathy with the Germans but was reluctant to play any active part in any programme because of his old age.[43] The patrons of the Paris group, Madame Cama and S.R. Rana, had already been interned in France.[44] Berlin was, however, successful in getting the active support of the most important of the Indian revolutionaries whose political aim coincided with the German plan of an Indian invasion. This was Har Dayal, whom Lajpat Rai described as 'an advocate of open rebellion.'[45] Har Dayal had just returned to Geneva after having spent about three and a half years in busy revolutionary propaganda on the Pacific Coast, where he had founded the Yugantar Ashram in San Francisco, and had launched its revolutionary mouthpiece, *Gadar*. On 26 March 1914, he was arrested by the US authorities for deportation as an undesirable alien. But when released on bail, he absconded to Switzerland.[46] Dayal was first mentioned in Wangenheim's report of 1 September from Constantinople. He gave Dayal's Geneva address where he was staying with the Egyptian, Dr M. Rifaat, and suggested that the Foreign Office should contact this man 'who could be of valuable service to us'.[47] On 3 September 1914, the consul general in Geneva, Geissler, contacted Har Dayal. Geissler was impressed by the intelligence and energy of this young man of thirty years who was already experienced and influential in revolutionary activities. In order to bring about an Indian outbreak of disturbance

Dayal recommended the invasion of India from Afghanistan and Baluchistan and said that he would be ready at any moment to go to Constantinople to help in preparing an Afghan expedition.[48] On the night of 5 September, Dayal left for Constantinople under the assumed identity of a German East African merchant, Romalingam Das, born in Dar-es-Salaam. In Constantinople he was to stay with his friend Abu Said.[49]

Meanwhile, besides Chatto and Abinash Chandra Bhattacharya, the only Indians in Germany with a solid revolutionary nationalist background, many other Indians who had just finished their studies, gathered in Berlin from various parts of Germany to work in what was then known as Oppenheim's India Committee. Dr Wilhelm Mertens and Professor Salomon in Heidelberg were responsible for bringing them in one place. Later, Chatto too made a round trip of Germany and Switzerland to assemble Indians.[50] The Indians thus brought together were: Abder Rahman, A. Siddiqui, Mansur Ahmed, Maharaj Narain Kaul, Dr M. Prabhakar and Hormusji Kersasp.[51] They were joined by Champakraman Pillai from Switzerland, who was then engaged in Indian nationalist propaganda from Zurich, issuing a sporadic paper called *Pro-India*, and Dr J. C. Dasgupta, a chemist working in a firm in Basel.[52]

Baron Oppenheim was the chief adviser and supervisor of the Indian work, acting as the liaison man between the Indians and the AA. Three other persons who also acted as links between Indians and the AA were Ernst Jaeckh[53], H. K. Regendanz[54], and Herbert Mueller.[55] Once the Afghan expedition commission had selected the German team for it, Oppenheim had little to do with its conduct, which was to be directed from Constantinople. As a member of the commission and as an expert on the Muslim world, he was to choose appropriate Indians for taking part in the expedition from Berlin. It was also Oppenheim's official duty to coordinate and conduct the activities of the Indians in Berlin. The propaganda work proposed among the Indian soldiers recently sent by the British to Egypt; propaganda among Indian prisoners of war in Germany; exploring ways to send money to Indian revolutionaries at home and in the US; receiving Indians and attending to their problems; collecting authentic information about the situation in India; sending 'true' war news from Europe to be circulated in India; arranging contact men in various parts of the world for Indian work; purchasing, collecting, and sending weapons and explosives to

India; collecting articles, translations, etc. from the Indians to be used by the 'Information Service for the Orient'. All these activities came under the general supervision of Oppenheim. He performed these tasks enthusiastically and dutifully, paying attention to the various suggestions of the Indians. He knew that a huge sum of money was to be sent to India by various means. Early in September 1914, he was busy finding means of sending small sums of up to 10,000 marks to Lahore, Calcutta, and Bombay. He consulted many big German firms as to whether they could help in sending even bigger sums to India. He also contacted the Hamburg Nobel Dynamit Co. to address the Indians' request for explosives.[56] The two earliest Indian messengers sent to India with small sums of money were Professor Satyendra Sen and one Dr Joshi, in the middle of September. A couple of days later, another two persons were sent likewise.[57] In the second half of September, Oppenheim was trying to send 250,000 mark to India through a Hamburg firm via Java. The money was to be paid to various persons in India in instalments, as advised by Chatto.[58] Oppenheim also suggested to Zimmermann that the Indian students in Germany who desired to continue their studies should be helped by paying some fixed sum per month irrespective of their attitude to England, and this money should be paid as a lump sum.[59] Meanwhile, as arrangements were made for sending money to India, Oppenheim had already opened an office for the Indian activities in mid-September 1914 in Berlin-Friedenau, Meinauer strasse 2, with Dr H. Mueller as the manager.[60] He asked the AA to inform Constantinople that a committee of highly suitable Indians from Germany and Switzerland for the Indian work had been established.[61] In November, when Dr J.C. Dasgupta from Switzerland was preparing for a business trip to India representing his firm, the AA arranged 60,000 marks to be sent with him for the cause of the Indian revolutionaries.[62] Towards the end of December, Chatto suggested the buying of diamonds which people going to India could take with them, the British not permitting money to be brought from outside. Oppenheim took prompt action on this too.[63]

The opening of a separate office for these activities signified the importance given to the Indian work. But, just when everything seemed to have gone off well with the Indian programme both in Constantinople and Berlin—both sides exchanging enthusiastic and encouraging news[64]—on 15 October came the news of Har Dayal's sudden departure from Constantinople to Geneva. He took a Turkish passport as Ismail Hakki Hassan and left Constantinople without even consulting or bidding farewell to Wangenheim.[65] Wangenheim suspected the reason for Dayal's sudden departure to be Hindu-Muslim animosity.[66] In a belated clarification, however, Dayal gave a different set of reasons. He said that his whole idea of going to Constantinople had originated out of his meeting with Geissler. After the meeting, he had given to Geissler, in his capacity as 'General Secretary of the Hindustan Gadar Party',[67] a project for provoking a general uprising in India through an invasion of the country from Afghanistan. 'As India is a vast plain, and England holds the seas, and the semi-independent states have no modern armies', suggested Dayal, 'an effective military movement against England can be started only with the help of Afghanistan, a mountainous country of brave soldiers, membering 5,000,000 who hate England and Russia.' He had also suggested how to put the project into practice: an unofficial group of priests and notables, bearing letters from the Shaikh-ul-Islam (the highest religious dignitary at Constantinople), should visit Afghanistan and persuade the court at Kabul to attack the British forces in Baluchistan. At the same time, efforts should be made to organize the tribes in southern Persia and Baluchistan where only a few British regiments were stationed.[68] Meanwhile, the Indian Nationalist Party would concentrate its whole strength on the state of Kashmir. As Kashmir had only a few irregular troops that could probably be won over, and it being a mountainous region, Dayal thought that the Nationalist Party would be able to resist the British forces for a long time. He emphasized that initial success was indispensable for the accomplishment of his plan. He expected Germany to help Afghanistan, southern Persia, and the Indian Nationalist Party with officers, arms, ammunitions, bombs, aeroplanes, and wireless apparatus.[69] His optimism regarding Kashmir was due to this reason: 'Apart from the general unrest in India among all classes,' Dayal wrote, 'we have 10,000 Hindus in the United States and Canada and about 100,000 in China and the Malay Peninsula. The nationalist paper *Gadar* circulates among them, and they are just now very much agitated over the Indian question in British Columbia. At least a few thousand will respond to an appeal for immediate action, if German support is assured.'[70]

Dayal's scheme also included acts of terrorism in various parts of India by 'young men ready for any sacrifice.' The success of the invasion, he oddly thought, 'would let loose the forces of revolt all over

India, especially in the states of Hyderabad and Nepal.' He also stressed the necessity of establishing communication by cable letter or messenger with Hindus in China, the USA, and East Africa. He himself would 'be successively at Constantinople, Mecca, Baghdad and Kabul to help the execution of this project, if it is accepted.'[71]

Geissler at the time did not send Dayal's complete letter to the AA, only the gist.[72] He later denied that he had told Dayal of Berlin's acceptance of his plan in its entirety. According to Geissler, he had only informed Dayal of Berlin's great interest in it.[73]

Justifying his sudden departure from Constantinople, Dayal said he had gone to Constantinople with a two-fold objective: propaganda among the Indians living in Turkey and Persia, and the establishment of a revolutionary centre at Kabul with German cooperation.[74] He said he had failed to achieve his objective for four reasons: first, the Germans in Constantinople did not wish to spend money; second, they did not know how to deal with men; third, they did not trust the Indians; and, fourth, they did not wish to encourage his independent initiatives.[75] To prove his point, Dayal gave some examples. Regarding German parsimony, he said that when he told Wassmuss that several thousand Indians could be brought from the USA with proper encouragement, Wassmuss, to his surprise, enquired whether they could come on their own. Similarly, when the first batch of the expedition had left for Aleppo, it failed to take the most experienced Indian, Dawood Ali (real name P.N. Dutta), on financial grounds. As to his second charge, Dayal complained that Wassmuss did not treat him as a responsible and trustworthy colleague. As an example of his third charge, Dayal said that while he was organizing the Indian group, he was kept utterly in the dark about the other activities of the expedition, so much so that he did not even know when the first batch of the Turco-German expedition left Constantinople. Moreover, when he asked to send information to Berlin about the needs of Indian helpers, the matter was treated in a half-hearted manner. Lastly, Dayal objected to Dr Weber's and Wassmuss's reluctance to allow any scope for his independent initiatives while insisting on the acceptance of their own ideas.[76]

Wassmuss, who seems to have annoyed Dayal most, was the leader of the German contingent of the Turco-German expedition to Afghanistan in accordance with the earliest plan. Compared to the rest of the group of utterly inexperienced Germans whom he was to lead,

Wassmuss, by reason of his post as German *chargé d' affaires* at Bushir, had some knowledge and personal experience of the part of Persia through which the expedition was to march. Yet accounts of the ill-fated Turco-German expedition and its German participants reveal that due to his fanciful and visionary character, Wassmuss was unable to inspire his subordinates with trust and respect.[77] That Wassmuss was obsessed with his own egotistical plans is also admitted by his otherwise sympathetic English biographer.[78] Dr. Weber, who also came in for Dayal's criticism, was connected with this expedition as a dragoman in the German embassy at Constantinople.

Dayal as a leader had limitations similar to those seen in Wassmuss. Like Wassmuss, Dayal was given to egotistical assertions and was consequently disliked by his colleagues and subordinates. Besides, Dayal lacked tenacity of purpose, something in which Wassmuss excelled. Dayal had based his charges on the violation of the alleged conditions under which his services were accepted by Geissler as representative of the AA. It is likely that Geissler had assured Dayal of the cooperation of the German leadership of the Turco-German expedition in organizing the Indian group and preparing it for an invasion of India. It is also likely that in the midst of the multifarious initial problems of the inept German contingent[79], there was hardly any time for the German leaders to give thought to the ultimate aim of the expedition, the invasion of India. In any case, there was no strong refutation of Dayal's charges from the official side, except for the question of money. Responding to the charges from the AA, Wangenheim wrote back on 27 November:

You will not mind if I do not refer in detail to the four accusations against the German Civil Service. They are mainly based on wrong understanding and conclusions and most of them could have been solved satisfactorily here had Har Dayal spoken out more precisely. So in particular the money question, which has now become a matter of complaint, arose only because Har Dayal himself declined to accept any means when asked. According to Har Dayal's own instructions the Indians who were to be called from the United States were to have sufficient money with them. His plans could have been supported financially from here if they were initiated. But instead, Har Dayal suddenly left Constantinople thereby causing—particularly among the competent Turkish quarters—the suspicion that he might be a traitor.[80]

Wangenheim persisted in what he had earlier said to be the reason for Dayal's departure:

In reality, however, I think that Har Dayal's main reason was the fear that because of the Turkish-Islamic character of the propaganda initiated here with German support the Hindu element would be neglected and that he himself would not play the role he had hoped for.[81]

There is no doubt that Dayal resented having to play a lesser and subordinate role in Constantinople. He had made it clear in the letter quoted earlier. Referring to Weber and Wassmuss' treatment of him, he wrote:

They knew that I had asked Indian colleagues to come from Berlin, London and America and yet they would ask me to leave Constantinople as an ordinary member of the party. They did not seem to understand that I had come to Constantinople to organise action on behalf of the Indians, that I had a definite plan of work, and that I did not need their advice but cooperation.[82]

Dayal argued that, if the ultimate purpose of the Afghan mission was to bring about a revolution in India, Indians should be sufficiently represented. 'The whole object of the mission would be frustrated,' he wrote, 'if a few Indians accompanied a large expedition as ordinary members, without any position or authority formally recognized by the German or Turkish government...I was appointed to organize the movement for India and the Indians: other men did not know the situation of our party and could not judge what should have been done.'[83]

The Har Dayal issue[84] brought the whole future of Indo-German cooperation into question both among Indians and at the AA. This cooperation was in any case based on shaky foundations. The Indians in Berlin were not happy to work under the direction of any middleman liaising between them and the AA. Although they were yet to meet the AA personnel, they seem to have already conveyed their dissatisfaction with the existing system. Not that Oppenheim treated them badly or was insincere.[85] Oppenheim strictly adhered to the principle that the AA should under no circumstances come into direct contact with the Indian revolutionaries. This was just what the Indians disliked. There were many influential Germans who had their own schemes for an Indian revolt and who met the Indians privately to this end. With one of these men, Professor Rudolf Otto of Goettingen, who himself disliked Oppenheim, some of the leading Indians had very good relations, and they discussed their problems with him. The fact that

Chatto and Kersasp wrote to Professor Otto on the day (8 December) after their first talk with the AA personnel, in which they complained about Oppenheim's control over them, reveals that the Indians had discussed their grievances with Otto before contacting the AA directly. It was because of his prior knowledge of Oppenheim's method of working with the Indians that Otto, while submitting his own scheme of Indian work to the Foreign Office on 8 November, put the following condition: 'I would be ready to work in cooperation with Herr Baron von Oppenheim, provided there shall be complete mutual frankness and cooperation, but not under his direction.' It is also clear that when Oppenheim insisted on the Indians' not meeting any private persons other than those to whom they were recommended, he had men like Otto in mind.[86] The problem the Indians faced particularly was that they were not able to guide policies regarding matters which primarily concerned them. The Dayal issue showed this problem in yet another dimension: what would be the position of the Indian revolutionaries, cooperating with the German government, if, at any point, they and their cause were to be suddenly abandoned by the Germans? This question was left out of consideration in the beginning, because the Indians had no bargaining strength at the time.

Chatto seems to have so far been unaware of Har Dayal's presence in Geneva.[87] But by the end of October, Chatto and Siddiqui were in Switzerland to meet him. It was during their stay in Geneva that on 2 November Dayal wrote a strong report detailing all his experiences in Constantinople and giving his reasons for leaving abruptly. The letter was handed to Geissler by Siddiqui.[88] Prior to this, Dayal had already written two letters to Geissler on 19 and 24 October, but in neither did he use such strong language. In response to Geissler's efforts to persuade him[89] previously to go to Berlin or return to Constantinople, Dayal had very politely rejected the idea by pointing out the ineffectiveness of the existing plan:

It is a great privilege for us Oriental revolutionists to work in co-operation with the great and powerful German Government, but I am afraid that the ideas according to which this part of the work is being carried on will lead only to failure and my visit will not change matters. I am rather sad, but I must state the situation as I see it in the light of my judgement.[90]

He was somewhat sharper in his next letter of 24 October:

I also notice that while you and the authorities in Berlin wish me to follow your plan in every particular, you do not wish to accede to my requests in any matter...I therefore desire to be excused from repeating the experiences of Constantinople.[91]

According to Dayal, the only practical and mutually helpful undertaking was a mission to Afghanistan, and until he met Chatto and Siddiqui at the end of the month, he had no respect for the work that was being done by the Indians in Berlin. As a postscript to the letter just quoted Dayal mentioned:

I have no desire to go to Berlin for the petty and unimportant work that is being done there by the Indians. My presence is not necessary for such work.[92]

At their meeting in Geneva, Chatto and Dayal seem to have compared notes about the conditions of work for Indians in Constantinople and Berlin. They seem to have also settled their old personal differences, and agreed to a joint effort if Chatto could secure better working conditions and terms from the AA. As Chatto was not able to make any headway in this direction, Dayal gave no final answer to Geissler about coming to Berlin. On 17 November, Geissler wrote to Berlin that

after getting a letter from Chatto, Har Dayal wrote to me that neither now nor ever after is he going to come to Germany. I have a feeling that he does not think the Berlin job to be fitting for his ambition.[93]

We do not know what exactly was the content of the letter from Chatto, but circumstantial evidence suggests that Chatto may have referred to the same difficulties that he was soon to bring to the notice of the AA.

On 7 December, Chatto, Dr Mansur Ahmed, and Kersasp met the legation secretary, Dr Otto Guenther von Wesendonk[94], who personally looked into the Berlin-sponsored programme for helping the various nationalities under Russian and British subjugation. The purpose of their visit was to submit a plan of action and to know whether they could, in future, deal with the AA directly rather than through liaison men like Baron von Oppenheim, Dr Mueller, or Dr Jaeckh. According to the Indians, these liaison men were not well-informed about the Indian situation and Indian people. As they themselves were actively engaged in the Indian propaganda work, they saw no reason why they should not be in direct contact with the AA.[95] They emphasized that, as far as Indian conditions and people were concerned, they were better informed than any European.[96]

The memorandum that Chatto and others submitted to Wesendonk painted a very rosy picture of the prospects of an Indian revolution and their contribution to the task so far. They said that since nearly the beginning of the war, an organization of Indian nationalists in Germany and Switzerland had been functioning in Berlin to provoke a great uprising in India with the help of German authorities. They stated that their Committee had sent about 12 members to India to get in touch with the leaders of various secret and public organizations to explain their plans personally. These members from Berlin were all trained in the production and use of explosives and would in turn select and train suitable Indians for revolutionary purposes. Moreover, they would issue instructions to their followers and the leaders of the revolutionary organizations, in the event of a declaration of war on Britain by the Amir of Afghanistan, to mobilize their forces on the borders, stage great uprisings, destroy telegraph and railway lines, blow up bridges and monuments, and attack and destroy the British everywhere.[97] Their plan also included propaganda in India in December among political and social organizations at their annual meetings. They mentioned, in particular, the Indian National Congress, the Indian Industrial Conference, Indian Social Conference, the Indian Educational Conference, and the All India Muslim League.[98] The Indians were hopeful of success particularly because of the discontent of the overseas Indians (especially in America, Canada, and South Africa). Exploiting the incident of the *Komagata Maru*,[99] as a result of which many people were killed, they said that the plight of Indians in Canada had caused 3–4000 emigrants to return to India, through whom it would be easy to stir up the soldiers and the masses.[100]

The time Chatto chose to get rid of any German middlemen between the Berlin Indians and the AA was significant. It was no secret that a successful revolt in India could be attempted only through the help of the Gadarites of North America, and yet Chatto and his earliest Indian colleagues on the India Committee had no direct information of the Indian situation in North America. The Committee, therefore, sent two members, Dhirendra Sarkar and Narayan Sadashive Marathey, to the USA with sufficient money at the end of September. While Sarkar was to select trustworthy and experienced Indians in New York,

Chicago, St Louis, and San Francisco, Marathey's task was to explore the possibilities of buying arms.[101] The venture paid off. As a result, several proclaimed revolutionary nationalists like Jatindra Nath Lahiri, S.C. Mukherji, Akhil Chandra Chakravarty, Taraknath Das, Heramba Lal Gupta, M.P.T. Acharya, Kedar Nath, and Rishi Kesh Latta arrived in Berlin by the end of November, and some like Bhupendra Nath Dutta were on their way to Berlin at the time of Chatto's meeting with Wesendonk on 7 December.[102] The presence of these revolutionaries from America undoubtedly emboldened Chatto. Detailing the Berlin Indians' ensuing programmes, his memorandum mentioned that two of these gentlemen would be sent back to the USA from where they would work to establish two revolutionary centres in Shanghai and Batavia for the purpose of transporting arms. Similarly, messengers would be sent to India to negotiate the delivery of the smuggled weapons with revolutionary parties.[103] The memorandum stressed the importance of propaganda among the Indian pilgrims in Mecca and among Indian soldiers in southern Persia, Basra, the Persian Gulf, and in France.[104]

3. 'India Committee' in Indian Hands

Wesendonk forwarded the complaints of the Indians and their plan of action to Arthur Zimmermann, the under secretary of state for foreign affairs, and asked him what reply he should give. Zimmermann raised no objection to Wesendonk's negotiating directly with the Indians.[105] Being young, immensely energetic, skilful, and professionally ambitious, it is probable that Wesendonk wished to handle and direct the course of Indian activities himself. Legation secretary Wesendonk is actually more known as the promoter-in-chief of revolution among the peoples of the border areas of the Russian Empire. His role as regards the suppressed nationalities of the British Empire is largely unknown. In the Russian sphere of influence, the letter of thanks that the Baltic Baron Uexkuel, whom the AA had commissioned to organize the League of Russia's Foreign Peoples, wrote to Wesendonk on 8 May 1916, is an eloquent testimony to his momentous work. The Baron said that the German Reich ought to erect two monuments in recognition of his services: one on the northernmost point of Finland and the other on the southernmost point of the Caucasus.[106] Be that as it may, as a result of the Chatto-Wesendonk direct talk on 7 December, Oppenheim's

India Committee came largely under the control of Indians themselves with Chatto as its prime figure.

Since the work of Oppenheim's *Nachrichtenstelle fuer den Orient*[107] frequently overlapped with the India Committee's, as long as he remained in Berlin, news and reports concerning Indian activities continued to come to Oppenheim. But at the beginning of 1915 he was transferred to Constantinople and the India Committee established itself firmly under Indian leadership. It also acquired a new office of its own at Berlin-Charlottenburg, Wielandstrasse 38.[108] The Indians were happy to work under the friendly Wesendonk.[109] In the middle of January 1915, Chatto met Dayal in Geneva again and persuaded him to come to Berlin and join the India Committee's leadership.[110] Both devised plans to contact Indian soldiers in Marseilles and revolutionaries in Paris.[111] From Switzerland, Chatto let Professor Salomon in Heidelberg know that Dayal would arrive in Berlin soon.[112]

While in Switzerland for the second time in January 1915, Chatto also met Mahendra Pratap, a 28-year-old visiting Indian landlord from Hathras in the Aligarh district of the United Provinces. Son of the late Ghansham Singh Bahadur of Mursan (a feudal possession with 4500 inhabitants, between Aligarh and Agra) and supposed brother-in-law of the ruler of Jhind, Pratap had left India on 18 December 1914 for a short tour of Europe and had arrived in Switzerland after visiting Italy.[113] Pratap, who affixed the title of Kunwar Raja to his name, claimed to have good relations with many of the princely houses of India, most particularly those of Nabha, Jhind, and Patiala. In fact, he gave Chatto to understand that the rulers of these princely houses had asked him to find out the genuineness of the German interest in Indian freedom. Long in search of a notable personality with access to the Indian princes, Chatto requested Pratap to come to Berlin to head the Committee's proposed mission to Afghanistan.[114] A fantast and adventurous eccentric by nature,[115] albeit with undoubted nationalist zeal, Pratap accepted the proposal under the condition that he have an audience with the German Emperor. The condition was readily accepted by the AA, and Chatto returned to Geneva to fetch Pratap to Berlin. Thus Chatto succeeded in winning both Dayal and Pratap for the Berlin India Committee. Dayal arrived in Berlin as a German East African (alias Ramdas) on the morning of 27 January, and Pratap (Mohamed Pir) arrived with Chatto (Mohamed Djafar) on 9 February. On arrival Pratap was received as a government guest and lodged at the Continental Hotel.[116]

On a visit to Berlin from Constantinople in February 1915, Oppenheim saw the change in the method of working with the Indians, and warned Zimmermann that, in the interest of both the Indians and Germany, direct contact of the AA with the Indians should be avoided, and that the AA should revert to the policy maintained by him until December 1914.[117] The AA apparently took no notice of this warning.

NOTES

1. For the views of official German representatives in India before World War I see N.K. Barooah, *India and the Official Germany 1886–1914* (Frankfurt/ Berne, 1977), pp. 11–90, 93–148.
2. India does not seem to be the only area about which Berlin, in the pre-War years, held a different opinion from the authentic judgment of its accredited agents. See Sir H. Nicolson, *Diplomacy* (London, 1963), 3rd ed., pp. 148–9.
3. See Barooah, *op. cit.* pp. 59–72.
4. R.P. Churchill, *The Anglo-Russian Convention of 1907* (Iowa, 1939), pp. 343–4.
5. Cf. H. Kohn, *The Mind of Germany* (Boston, 1957), pp. 273, 277.
6. Discussing two leading German liberals of the time, Hans Kohn points out the impact of social Darwinism on Max Weber who countered an attack on Prussia's policy against her Poles thus: 'We alone made out of the Poles human beings.' Similarly, in Friedrich Naumann's eyes Karl Peters' inhumanity was insignificant compared to his services to German expansion. See ibid., pp. 283, 288. For Weber, see also R. Dahrendorf, *Society and Democracy in Germany* (New York, 1967), p. 57.
7. Count von Luxburg to Bethmann-Hollweg, Simla 29 July 1913, AABI, 50.
8. See Barooah, *op. cit.* p. 90.
9. General F. von Bernhardi, *Germany and the Next War* (London, 1911), p. 96.
10. See, for example, *Leipziger Neueste Nachrichten*, 1 April 1913 and *Berliner Tageblatt*, 6 March 1914, for Dr Johannes Tschiedel's article 'Englands indische Sorge'.
11. DD (1927), II (401), p. 120; the English version from Balfour, *The Kaiser and His Times* (London, 1964), pp. 351–2.
12. DD, (662), pp. 133–6. On 5 August 1914 Moltke repeated this request. DD, (876), pp. 94–5.
13. AA Tuerkei 152, Vol. 79, quoted in U. Trumpener, *Germany and the Ottoman Empire 1914–1918* (Princeton, 1968), p. 291.
14. Wk 1, p. 39, Wangenheim to AA, Therapia, telegram 26 August 1914. Wangenheim got full encouragement from the Foreign Office to go ahead with any action against British colonial possessions. *Ibid.*, p. 40. Zimmermann's reply to Wangenheim 27 August 1914.

15. Dr Max Adrian Simon Baron von Oppenheim (1860–1946): 1883 doctorate in jurisprudence (Goettingen); 1896 attached to the consulate general, Cairo; extensive study tours in Islamic countries, mainly in the Arab world, emerging famous as an archaeologist through is expedition to the Chad Lake area; 1896–1910 attaché, consulate general, Cairo; 1910 designated as 'Minister resident' but left Foreign Office of his own accord: 1911–13 engaged in archaeological excavations in the Hittite city of Tel Halaf; August 1914 in Foreign Office again; founded the Nachrichtenstelle fuer den Orient (Information Service for the Orient) in Berlin; 1915 attached to the embassy in Constantinople to organize an information and propaganda centre. See also W. Caskel, 'Max Freiherr von Oppenheim 1860–1946', *Zeitschrift der Deutschen Morgenlaendischen Gesellschaft* (Wiesbaden, 1951), vol. 101; W. Treue, 'Max Freiherr von Oppenheim—der Archaeologe und die Politik', *Historische Zeitschrift*, (Muenchen, 1969), vol. 209, I, pp. 37–74.

16. See Fritz Fischer, 'Germany's Aims in the First World War' (New York, 1967), p. 123. Professor Wilhelm Treue, who happened to be also the keeper of the Records of Bankhaus Oppenheim in Cologne, refutes Fischer's assertion that Oppenheim submitted to Kaiser Wilhelm II his thesis of the world political importance of the pan-Islamic movement. But Professor Treue does not rule out Oppenheim's indirect influence on the Kaiser's speech and even says that Count Metternich, who accompanied the Kaiser on his Orient trip, might have presented Oppenheim's papers to the Kaiser; see W. Treue, 'Max Freiherr von Oppenheim, der Archaeologe und die Politik', in Historische Zeitschrift, Vol. 209 I (Muenchen, 1969), pp. 37–74.

17. From Cairo on 20 February 1909, Oppenheim sent a report to the Imperial Chancellor Buelow on the contemporary Indian political situation after meeting the Aga Khan. On 16 May of the same year, he submitted a report on the close relationship between the Indian Muslims and the Egyptians. AABI 44.

18. Wk 11, 1, p. 32. Oppenheim to Bethmann-Hollweg, Berlin, 18 August 1914.

19. U. Gehrke, *Persien in der deutschen Orientpolitik waehrend des I. Weltkrieges* (Stuttgart, 1960), p. 23, n. 8 and 9.

20. Ibid., p. 23.

21. Wk e, 1, Reichenau to AA, Stockholm, 25 August 1914.

22. The commission consisted of: von Holtzendorf, director, Hamburg-America Line; H.R. Mannesmann, firm Mannesmann-Roselius; Naval Captain Loehlein, Reichsmarineamt; minister resident Baron von Oppenheim; Dr Ernst Jaeckh, Orient publicist; and legation secretary von Prittwitz, deputy of Dirigent Baron Langwerth in the Foreign Office. Wk e, 1, Prittwitz's note on the sitting of 4 September 1914.

23. Wk 1, 4 September 1914, p. 64.

24. For details of the war-time activities of Indians in Turkey see Chapter 3 in this volume.

25. *Bande Mataram*, February 1910, extracts in Ker, *op. cit.*, p. 114.
26. Yajnik, *op. cit.*, p. 300.
27. The ungrammatical language original. Quoted in Ker, *op. cit.*, p. 261.
28. 'Gute Aussichten für Deutschland in Indien', *Leipziger Neueste Nachrichten*, 1 April 1913.
29. The paper's letter to AA, Leipzig, 4 April 1913, AABI 49.
30. Abinash Bhattacharya (1883–1967) was a friend of Aurobindo Ghose and a leading revolutionary in Bengal. He was the author of *Bartaman Rananiti* (The Modern Art of War) and one of the founders of the revolutionary paper *Jugantar*, published from Calcutta. He had first-hand experience of the terrorist and conspiratorial underground activities that had been going on in Bengal since 1907.
31. Weltkrieg 1914. Unternehmungen und Aufwiegelungen gegen unsere Feinde; Indien (from now on Wk 11f), 2, pp. 52–5; 67.
32. Ker, *op. cit.*, p. 213.
33. A.C. Bose, *Indian Revolutionaries Abroad 1905–1922* (Patna, 1971), p. 253.
34. Wk 11f, 1, p. 20.
35. Wk 11f, 1, pp. 15–16.
36. Wk 11f, 1, p. 18. Bhattacharya to Dr Delbrueck, no date. For more details about Bhattacharya's letter, see Barooah, *op. cit.*, p. 186 and fn. 68.
37. Wk 11f, 1, p. 46. Legation secretary von Prittwitz's note, 31 August 1914.
38. See Wk 11f, 1, pp. 1–3. For more details see Barooah, *op. cit.*, p. 186, fn. 70.
39. See for example 'Das Geheimnis der indischen Aufstandsbewegung', *Deutsche Montagszeitung*, 21 September 1914, AABI 51.
40. Wk 11f, 1, p. 102. Dr Fritz Heinemann to the Berlin police, Berlin, 31 August 1914.
41. See AABI 51, 25 August 28 August and 12 September 1914. Wk 11f, 1, p. 63, Wk 11f, 1, p. 5.
42. Wk 11f, 2, p. 33. Wangenheim to AA, 13 September 1914.
43. Wk 11f, 1, p. 107. Romberg to AA, Berne, 8 September 1914. See also Wk 11f, 1, p. 117 and Wk 11f, 6, p. 112.
44. Ker, *op. cit.*, pp. 213–14.
45. Lajpat Rai, *Young India* (New York, 1917), p. 199. Later, when Dayal was asked by the AA why he wanted Indians from the USA to come to Constantinople instead of going straight to India (which would be cheaper), Dayal told Wangenheim that it was not the question of sending help to India; it was the question of recruiting a good number of determined young Indians for the planned invasion of India so as to encourage rebellion in India. Wk 11f, 3, p. 24. Wangenheim to AA, Therapia, 26 September 1914.
46. Ker, *op. cit.*, pp. 234–8.
47. Wk 11f, 1, p. 53.
48. Wk 11f, p. 56. Romberg to AA, Berne, 3 September 1914, enclosing Geissler's telegram.
49. *Ibid.*

50. Wk 11f, 1, pp. 44, 120; Wk 11f, 3, p. 17; Wk 11f, 6, p. 89.
51. Wk 11f, 1, p. 144, Oppenheim's note to Baron Langwerth, 7 September 1914; Wk 11f, 2, p. 57, Oppenheim's note, 15 September 1914.
52. Wk 11f, 1, p. 116, Romberg to AA, 8 September 1914; Wk 11f, 2, p. 124, Romberg to AA 23 September 1914; and Wk 11f, 1, p. 60.
53. Ernst Jaeckh was an expert on the Balkan and Middle East problems at the AA in Berlin from 1912. At the outset of the War, he worked with Matthias Erzberger in the Nachrichtenstelle für Auslandsdienst (Information Office for Foreign Countries) which was founded for propaganda purposes. He was in Constantinople many times on special missions. About Jaeckh's importance and influence during the War in Germany, see F. Fischer, *Germany's Aims...*, p. 124.
54. Regendanz was the liaison-man in general between the Imperial Colonial Office and the banks, and the chief mover behind the scenes of policy in Morocco. It was Regendanz who as early as August 1914 devised an ingenious plan of sending a mixed group of three persons—a German, an Italian, and an American—with Naval Captain Loehlein to India as travelling salesmen of luxury goods of an American firm. According to this plan, the first two were to act as political agents and meet the native princes and help in preparing proclamations to be circulated among the local people, while the American was to be kept in the dark about the real motive of the mission. See Regendanz to Langwerth, 20 August 1914; Wk 11f, 1, pp. 9–12.
55. Dr Herbert Mueller, later a Sinologist and journalist, was soon to be the treasurer of the Berlin Committee. See also H. von Glasenapp, *Meine Lebensreise* (Wiesbaden, 1964), p. 71.
56. Wk 11f, 1, p. 131, Oppenheim to AA (Wesendonk), 9 September 1914; Wk 11f, 3, pp. 20, 76–7, Egmont Hagedorn Co. to AA, Hamburg, 26 September and 30 September 1914.
57. Wk 11f, 2, pp. 79–101. These four persons were paid 3400 marks in English, French, and German currencies, a part in gold.
58. Wk 11f, 2, pp. 130–2, Oppenheim to Wesendonk, 21 September 1914.
59. Wk 11f, 4, p. 56, Oppenheim to Zimmermann, 17 Octtober 1914.
60. Wk 11f, 2, p. 58.
61. *Ibid.*, p. 67; Wk 11f, 3, p. 32.
62. Wk 11f, 5, p. 1, AA to Deutsche Bank, 1 November 1914, with Wesendonk's and Zimmermann's notes.
63. Wk 11f, 7, p. 47, Wesendonk's note, 29 December 1914.
64. In one of Wangenheim's reports of this period, a draft telegram from Dayal to be sent to New York was enclosed wherein Dayal asked Chakravarti to send 'largest possible number of Hindu boys from California for work in Constantinople.' Dayal also added that they should come on their own and with six months' expenses with them. Wangenheim to AA, Therapia, 21 September 1914; Wk 11f, 2, p. 117. As to Berlin, Oppenheim was planning

to send Chatto to Constantinople where he was to join Dayal for the onward journey to Afghanistan and Baluchistan (where they would make preliminary preparations for the military invasion of India). Oppenheim's draft telegram to Constantinople, 16 September 1914; Wk 11f, 2, p. 67.
65. Wk 11f, 4, p. 21, Wangenheim to AA, Therapia, 15 October 1914.
66. Ibid.
67. Wk 11f, 5, p. 44, Dayal to German consul general, Geneva, 2 September 1914. Geissler, however, did not send this letter to AA until 2 November 1914 along with Dayal's subsequent letters to him.
68. Ibid.
69. Ibid.
70. Ibid.
71. Ibid.
72. Wk 11f, 5, pp. 42–3, as Geissler wrote to AA on 2 November 1914.
73. Ibid.
74. Wk 11f, 5, pp. 42–3, Dayal to Geissler, Geneva, 2 November 1914.
75. Ibid.
76. Ibid.
77. U. Gehrke, *op. cit.*, p. 25, n. 27.
78. C. Sykes, *Wassmuss; The German Lawrence* (Leipzig, 1937), pp. 42–4, 66.
79. See Gehrke, *op. cit.*, p. 24, n. 22.
80. Wk 11f, 6, p. 59, Wangenheim to AA, Therapia, 27 November 1914.
81. Ibid.
82. Wk 11f, 5 (in packet), Dayal to Geissler, Geneva, 2 November 1914.
83. Ibid. By 'our party' Dayal meant his Gadar Party in America as general secretary of which he signed this letter to Geissler on 2 November 1914. It was expected of him to bring Indians from America to Constantinople or to India for revolutionary purposes.
84. For Dayal's relations with the German officials, see N.K. Barooah, 'Har Dayal and the German Connection', *The Indian Historical Review*, VII, July 1980, pp. 185–211.
85. Horst Krueger in his 'Har Dayal in Deutschland' (1964) has arrived at some false conclusions about Oppenheim by reading a couple of documents absolutely wrongly and mixing persons. His a *priori* judgments were enthusiastically taken by Dayal's biographer Emily C. Brown in her *Har Dayal: Hindu Revolutionary and Rationalist* (New Delhi, 1976), pp. 184, 187. For the details of these false assumptions on Oppenheim see N.K. Barooah, 'Har Dayal and the German connection', op. cit., pp. 186, 189–90.
86. See Barooah, *op. cit.*, p. 198 and fn. 115.
87. Chatto did not even mention Dayal in his earlier correspondence with the AA. Similarly, Dayal did not name Chatto in his list of Indian revolutionary nationalists in Europe.
88. Wk 11f, 5, Geissler to AA, Geneva, 2 November 1914.
89. From the moment the AA came to know of Dayal's sudden return to

Geneva it constantly asked Geissler to persuade Dayal to come to Berlin. The fear that Dayal might divulge the German conspiracy had vanished after Wangenheim's report that the original Turkish suspicion of betrayal on Dayal's part was utterly baseless. Lately, the AA also came to realize the importance and influence of Dayal among the revolutionary Indian nationals in America, some of whom had already arrived in Berlin. Geissler was somewhat annoyed at Dayal's letter of 2 November, and wrote to the AA that if Har Dayal was no longer considered useful, his letter should be returned to him as unacceptable on account of its 'improper form'. The AA, however, did not intend to blow up the incident and considered it safe and useful to have Dayal in Berlin. *Ibid.*, and AA's comment on it. Wk 11f, 4, pp. 63, 76–8.

90. Wk 11f, 5, Dayal to Geissler, Geneva, 19 October 1914.
91. *Ibid.*, Dayal to Geissler, Geneva, 24 October 1914.
92. *Ibid.*
93. Wk 11f, 5, p. 87, Geissler to AA, Geneva, 17 November 1914.
94. Dr Otto Guenther von Wesendonk (1885–1933): 1903–8—studied in Bonn, Berlin, and Heidelberg (Dr of jurisprudence); 1908—joined the Foreign Service and was attached to the German embassy, London; 1910—a short spell each at Brussels and Constantinople; 1911 –at Berlin; 1913—legation secretary at Tangiers and another doctorate in Politics from Wuerzburg; January 1914—had to leave Foreign Service for having married a Portuguese; 10 August 1914–April 1919—at Berlin, attached to the political department; 1922—consul general, Tiflis, also D. Phil from Bonn; 1927 (over and above the Foreign Office assignment)—general secretary of the International Elbe Commission at Dresden.
95. As examples of their difficulties, they mentioned Oppenheim's demanding from them a report on Hindu-Muslim relations in India, and Dr Jaeckh giving an uneducated Indian, Caderwail, the leadership of Indian propaganda activities at Constantinople. Wesendonk's official note on the meeting of 7 December 1914. Wk 11f, 6, pp. 44–5.
96. Wk 11f, 6, pp. 44–5, Wesendonk's note, 7 December 1914.
97. Wk 11f, 6, pp. 48–9.
98. *Ibid.*, p. 50.
99. *Komagata Maru* was a ship chartered in Hongkong from a Japanese firm by one Gurdit Singh, a Sikh from Punjab, to take Indians intending to emigrate to Canada. The purpose was to challenge the recent immigration restrictions introduced especially against the Asiatics. On 4 April 1914, the ship sailed with 165 Punjabis from Hongkong. When it arrived at Vancouver on 23 May, there were 375 Punjabis on board, including 25 Muslims. They were not allowed to disembark and were compelled to return. The British authorities brought the ship back to Calcutta where it was moored at Budge-Budge on the Hooglly river on 29 September. The passengers were directed to disembark, and proceed to the special train which was to take

them to Punjab. The Sikhs, however, decided to march to Calcutta, 15 miles away, and on their way encountered European police. A riot broke out resulting in indiscriminate firing with 22 casualities. See J.C. Ker, *op. cit.*, pp. 239–45; *Sedition Committee Report* (Calcutta, 1918), pp. 103–4.
100. *Ibid.*, pp. 50–1.
101. Both Sarkar and Marathey were given 5000 marks each for travel expenses. An extra 20,000 marks were placed for Sarkar at the German Consulate in New York. Both left for the USA from Rotterdam on 27 September 1914. See Wk 11f, 1, p. 137, Oppenheim's and Wesendonk's notes 9 and 10 September; Wk 11f, 2, pp. 110–23, 139; Wk 11f, 3, p. 40.
102. Most of these Indians came under false passports as German East Africans by French, Italian, and Greek steamers. For the dates of their arrival see Wk 11f, 5, pp. 20, 41, 55, 113, 114, 149, and Wk 11f, 6, p. 121.
103. Wk 11f, 6, p. 53.
104. *Ibid.*, pp. 54–5.
105. *Ibid.*, p. 45. Wesendonk's note on 7 December. In the beginning there was a possibility of Professor Otto replacing Oppenheim. See Wk 11f, 7, pp. 6–7, Chatto and Kersasp to Professor Otto, 24 December 1914.
106. Fritz Fischer, *Germany's Aims in the First World War,* p. 125, also pp. 145, 558–9 for Wesendonk's work in the Russian borderland.
107. *Nachrichtenstelle fuer den Orient,* which was founded by Oppenheim in mid-August 1914 and renamed *Deutsches Orient-Institut* after the War, collected news from the countries of the Middle and Far East to use for propaganda purposes. It also looked after the Orientals living in Berlin. Besides Germans, it had co-workers from various countries. It produced a prisoners' newspaper in the various languages of the prisoners of war (after due censorship by Wesendonk of the AA and Capt. Nadolny of the general staff). It also issued frequent bulletins which were periodically compiled into a quarterly called *Der Neue Orient.* Among its German co-workers were Dr Herbert Mueller; Heinrich Jacoby, general secretary of Persische Teppich-Gesellschaft AG; Ferdinand Graetsch, a missionary with Indian experience; Professor Eugen Mittwoch, Orientalist; and the young Indologist Dr Helmut von Glasenapp. See H.V. Glasenapp, *Meine Lebensreise,* Ch. IV.
108. About the formation and later changes in nomenclature of the Berlin India Committee see Barooah, *op. cit.*, pp. 205–6 and appendix III, pp. 227–8.
109. The documents of the War years clearly show the extremely good relations between Wesendonk and the Indians throughout the War period. The Indians were also invited to private parties at Wesendonk's house.
110. Wk 11f, 7, p. 81; Wk 11f, 8, p. 110, Romberg to AA, Berne, 13 and 26 January 1915.
111. Wk 11f, 7, pp. 125, 139, Romberg to AA, telegram, 13 January 1915.
112. Wk 11f, 7, p. 178, Geissler to Oppenheim, Berne, 13 January 1915.
113. Wk 11f, 8, pp. 8–9, 83–4, Wesendonk's note on Pratap, 16 and 22 January 1915; notice in the *Times,* 24 November 1915; notice about Pratap missing

in *The Times of India,* 15 July 1916.
114. Wk 11f, 7, p. 178, Geissler to Oppenheim, telegram, 13 January 1915, giving Chatto's message.
115. This is clear from Pratap's subsequent life. Also interview with Hentig with whom he maintained a lifelong friendship.
116. Wk 11f, 9, p. 87; Wk 11f, 9, p. 107, Romberg to AA, telegram, 8 February 1915.
117. Wk 11f, 10, pp. 55–7, Oppenheim to Zimmermann, Berlin, 25 February 1915.

3

Attempts at Revolutionizing India

The three original and connected programmes of the German Foreign Office to bring about insurrections and rebellion in India were: a) to send an expedition to Kabul in order to persuade the Amir of Afghanistan to invade India with the military and financial backing of Turkey and Germany; b) to make propaganda among the British Indian soldiers stationed in Mesopotamia, the Persian Gulf, and Suez Canal area, and recruit other Indian nationals in the Ottoman Empire for an Indian expeditionary force to invade India; and c) the shipping to India of a large quantity of arms and ammunition and as many Gadarites from America as possible to ensure the success of the projected rebellion. When the Berlin India Committee came under the management of the Indians themselves, these programmes remained intact, although with an increased emphasis on Indian interest as seen by the Indian revolutionaries themselves.

1. MISSION TO AFGHANISTAN

Since the first Afghan expedition, which had scant respect for the Indians' interest, had failed for all practical purposes, the initiative taken by Chatto and Har Dayal to send Mahendra Pratap to Afghanistan on a new mission was highly welcomed by the German Foreign Office (AA). Besides an audience with the Kaiser, Pratap met the Chancellor, Theobald von Bethmann-Hollweg, who gave several signed letters addressed to the Indian princes at his request.

On 9 April 1915, accompanied by an AA representative, 29-year-old Lieutenant Werner Otto von Hentig, and Dayal, Pratap left for Constantinople. Hentig was to bring Pratap and the other members of the mission safely to Afghanistan through Turkey, Iraq, and Persia, and represent the German government in any eventual political or economic understanding with Afghanistan. Pratap, on the other hand, was to hand over the personal letters of Kaiser Wilhelm II and Sultan Ghazi V to Amir Habibullah and persuade him to join hands with pan-Islamic and revolutionary nationalist forces to liberate India. Dayal was to stay in Constantinople to guide the Berlin Committee's programme in the Ottoman Empire. At Constantinople, the Turkish government approved the Afghan mission, and Envar Pasha, the war minister, showed great enthusiasm for it. Pratap was presented to the Sultan as well. At Constantinople, the Pratap-Hentig mission was joined, among others, by Kazim Bey, a Turkish officer; Muhamed Barakatullah[1]; Dr Becker, a military surgeon; and Walter Roehr, a German who had lived many years in northern Persia. Later, in Persia, Captain Oscar von Niedermayer, who had escorted Prince Peuss, the German Ambassador-designate to Teheran, also merged his group with this mission.[2]

At the beginning of May, the most difficult part of the journey for the party started with many natural hazards and encounters with British spies. Northern Persia was dominated by Russian troops and the south by the British. Therefore, the only available route was the difficult central one through the great salt desert of Kevir.[3] Hentig proved a very able guide and, in spite of the fact that the British had prior knowledge of this expedition and had tried in every way to thwart it, the mission safely arrived in Kabul in early October 1915. The British had obtained an assurance from the Amir that the mission members would be arrested and interned on arrival in Afghanistan. However, they were not arrested but quartered on the outskirts of the capital at the Afghan government's expense. To all intents and purposes, it was a virtual house arrest. As Pratap later described: 'Food was plenty. View was fine. We could see and enjoy green valley below and high mountain in the distance. But we were not allowed to go out of our four walls... We were state prisoners (and) this thought began to prey upon us.' Only after several protests, including a threat of hunger strike, could the party receive two interviews with the Amir at Paghman, in the middle of October 1915.[4]

Amir Habibullah was an expert at playing the diplomatic game. He saw clearly that it was not in his interest to exchange the existing British subsidy for a mere promise of help in future from the Central Powers (Germany, Austria-Hungary, Turkey, and Bulgaria). Under pressure from the party at the court, led by his brother, Nasarullah, the Amir agreed to sign only a draft treaty of friendship with the Germans in January 1916. On the basis of this treaty, consular relations would be established between Germany and Afghanistan in 1926. But the treaty did not alter the Amir's fundamental attitude towards the British in the absence of ready supplies of German arms and finances. One of the members of the mission, Dr Walter Roehr, after the war, stated: the Amir would have joined any of the warring nations if he had known who was going to win in the end.[5]

Convinced that the Amir would go no further than this, the Germans left Afghanistan to the great relief of the British. While returning they split up into various parties. In early July 1916, Hentig with a small group including Roehr went to China via the Pamirs and Chinese Turkestan. This made the British nervous since they were well aware of his powers of persuasion. The British tried their best to persuade the Chinese to arrest Hentig. They were infuriated with what Hentig wrote to Sir George MaCartney, the British Consul General at Kashgar, professing his intention to respect neutrality but oppose force with force[6]—a fact the India Office considered 'a fine piece of insolence'.[7]

After the Germans left, Pratap and Barakatullah remained in Kabul until the Russian revolution of 1917. An interesting sideline of their mission was the formation of the provisional government of India in Afghanistan in December 1915. Pratap was made President, Barakatullah Prime Minister, and Ubeidullah, another pan-Islamite Indian present in Afghanistan at that time, the Minister for Home Affairs. The idea of a provisional government of India was the brainchild of Barakatullah, who had long experience in political agitation and had also been a Gadarite leader. Before joining the Berlin Committee, in a letter to Dayal from New York dated 24 November 1914, Barakatullah considered the crucial importance of capturing a piece of land and establishing a provisional government, and then seeking recognition from European powers. He thought that it would facilitate war loans from England's opponents.[8] It is significant that the idea was later taken up by Subhas Chandra Bose during World War II. Be that as it may, in 1917 Pratap returned to Germany via revolutionary Russia with letters from the Amir to the Kaiser and the Sultan of Turkey.

2. ACTIVITIES IN THE OTTOMAN EMPIRE

The Berlin India Committee's other pan-Islamic programmes in Constantinople and other areas of the Ottoman Empire also failed in spite of the ardour and dedication of some of the Indians involved. Towards the end of January 1915, Chatto and Barakatullah decided to send three groups to Turkey besides the one for Afghanistan. Two groups, the so-called Baghdad and Suez Canal missions, were to work to dissuade Indian soldiers stationed in those areas from fighting for the British, and raise an Indian volunteer army consisting of potential deserters from the Indian prisoners of war and of local Indians. The third group was to remain in Constantinople. Dayal, living in Constantinople, was to supervise the work of all the missions.[9] Wesendonk immediately sanctioned 250,000 marks, and it was decided that one Kalisch, a German, was to accompany the two groups to Baghdad.[10]

The Baghdad group consisted of five members belonging to the Parsi, Hindu, and Sikh communities, but they all had Muslim aliases. The group was under the leadership of the Parsi H. Kersasp (Hassan Ali Khan). The other members were Kedarnath (Syed Kadar Ali), Basant Singh (Abdul Aziz), Rishikesh Latta (Shaikh Zea-ud Din), and Chet Singh (Jan Mahamed). Kersasp and Rishikesh were provided with revolvers in Baghdad. Later, A.C. Sharma (Mubarak Ullah), Kandubhai Nayik (Ali Bin Hassan), and Pandrerang Khankhoje (Khan Khoja) were added to the party.

Even before the declaration of war against Turkey, the British had sent an Indian expeditionary force to Iraq to protect the Abadan oil installations, cover the potential landing of reinforcement, and reassure the Arab potentates.[11] A brigade of the 6th (Poona) Division arrived at Bahrayan in the second half of October, and, after a fortnight, moved northwards up to the Persian Gulf to seize the fort at Fao, at the mouth of the Shatt-el-Arab. Later reinforced, it captured and occupied Basra in November 1914.[12] Emboldened by the feebleness of the Turkish resistance, the British military command intended to advance this force further with the ultimate aim of capturing Baghdad itself. By the time the Berlin Committee's members began their activities in Mesopotamia, the expeditionary force, now reorganized as a corps, operated within the triangle of Fao-Amara-Masiriya to control the major tribes on the Tigris and the Euphrates.

Arriving in Baghdad in early May, the Baghdad group worked earnestly. They set up a press, and issued a weekly paper in Hindi and Arabic to reach the readership of Indian soldiers. Their enthusiasm was appreciated by the local German officials, and, in July, Wesendonk received the first report of their excellent work in Mesopotamia.[13] But it was soon clear that they faced insurmountable difficulties in various directions. The Turkish military authorities had always been cool towards the activities of the Indian nationalists with their Muslim names and German money. Additionally, local Turkish civil authorities in distant parts of the Ottoman Empire were under the strong influence of Anglophile Arab notables of the areas, and it took the German officials a great deal of effort to protect the Indians from persecution and continuous police harassment. There were also internal differences between the Turkish army and the German officials. Again, it was not easy to influence the diverse Indian troops in Mesopotamia, among whom there were very few Muslims, the majority being Sikhs and Gurkhas. Hesse, the German consul general at Baghdad, regretted that even in the face of the promising work of Indians, the supreme commander of the Turkish army stopped the Indian work on the battle front. He said the fact that the Berlin Indians were not really Muslims and yet fought for pan-Islamism with German money aroused the mistrust of the Turks. Finally, the jealousy and intrigues of the local Indian Muslim inhabitants made an already difficult situation even more difficult. Consequently, in September, the Baghdad group dissolved itself, and some of them, such as Rishikesh Latta, Chet Singh, and Basant Singh, left for Persia.[14]

A month after the dissolution of the Baghdad mission, the group of Indians that had gone to Egypt with a similar purpose also had to wind up their activities. Included in the Suez Canal mission were the leaders M.T.P. Acharya (Muhammed Akbar), B.N. Dasgupta (Ali Haidar), L.P. Varma (Hussain Ali), Taraknath Das (Bahadur Khan), Rajab Ali, and an Egyptian Ismail Husni. Although some of these men were intellectually more advanced than their colleagues in the Baghdad mission, the Suez Canal (or Damascus) mission was a dismal failure from beginning to end. Its primary aim was to make propaganda among Indian troops in Egypt, but this was completely dependent on when and with what determination the Turks would commence their offensive from the Sinai desert against the British forces. The mission remained completely idle, and only rarely succeeded in sending messages to the Indian soldiers through the Bedouins.

After the failure in approaching the Indian soldiers in Egypt, the Indians considered shifting their work to the holy places of Hadj in Arabia. The idea was to win over the Indian pilgrims coming to Mecca and Medina, and, through them, establish communications between India and Southern Arabia.[15] Both Hohenlohe, the German ambassador in Constantinople, and Oppenheim, based in Damascus, understood the desire of the Indians to be useful in some way to the German and Indian causes, but they had substantial reasons to dissuade the Indians from any such involvement. First of all, in their opinion, the number of Indian pilgrims would not be large, and the British would not allow them to proceed without some screening measures. Second, all propaganda in the holy places was banned except with the permission of the Grand Sheriff of Mecca, and in accordance with an agreement reached between him, Enver Pasha, and Baron Oppenheim, it had already been stipulated that no propaganda of any organization, except the Sheriff's own, would be permitted during Hadj.[16] Oppenheim, therefore, advised the Indians to be active in the Sinai area.[17] But the intense heat and the resulting forced idleness of the place made the Indians go the way of their colleagues in Baghdad. The first to leave the group was Taraknath Das whose planned destination was Japan.

In Constantinople, where Dayal was appointed to supervise the Berlin Committee's activities in the Ottoman Empire, things took a scandalous turn for the Indians, for which Dayal was mainly responsible. Through his overbearing manner, he made himself at once unpopular among his colleagues, one of whom, a Gadarite himself, found him boastful, arbitrary, and an 'intriguer of intriguers'.

As a matter of fact, Dayal himself seems to have very quickly lost interest in making propaganda from Turkey. This is apparent from his failure to make any contribution to the Baghdad and Damascus missions as also by his secretive and mystifying behaviour. In April, he informed the Committee in Berlin that, in future, he would stop writing detailed reports but abstained from giving any reason.[19] Whatever he planned or proposed in the subsequent months until his departure from Constantinople had nothing to do with the propaganda work in the Ottoman Empire. To give some examples of his messages at the time: he enquired from Chatto whether Miss Howsin could go to India 'for an important work' and if so whether she could meet him in Sofia[20]; he wanted a Swede named Stiller to come from America but would not inform the Committee of the reason[21]; he made deals with the American Jack (Benjamin Harrison) Sloan, interned in Germany, and the Berlin Indians suspected to be an English agent (whom even Ram Chandra considered at best 'a scoundrel')[22]; and at the end of August, he himself suddenly left for Budapest with no plans to return.[23] None of these actions were in any way related to the work in Constantinople. As one of the serious-minded Berlin Indians in Constantinople, Taraknath Das, rightly said: 'Mr Har Dayal did not want to have anything to do with anybody but was engaged in doing what he pleased.'[24]

After leaving Constantinople, Dayal confessed that, during his days in Turkey, he hesitated to undertake any elaborate programme because he feared the war might end in September or October 1915.[25] In a letter to a high-ranking official of the AA in May, Dayal said that he was only working for the future, 'for I foresee that perhaps we shall not be successful in chasing the British out of our country during this war'.[26] In this rather rambling letter, written in French, Dayal further wrote:

> We Hindu nationalists try to do everything possible to stage a serious uprising in India. But work has to be done particularly for the future. Germany had prepared for forty years for this war and Germany is a free, wise and mighty state and so how can one expect that those Hindus, servile and ignorant, would rise against the British who are the rulers of sea and diplomacy, without any advanced preparation, namely moral and intellectual preparation, extensive propaganda [and] discipline.

In order to avoid sounding too disparaging of the German officials, Dayal added:

> I am ready to talk with any important person to convince the German statesmen that it would be in the German interest to work toward a policy of sympathy for the national Hindu movement.[27]

The obtrusive use of the word 'Hindu' in the above letter shows how little he understood the primary task and focus for which he was sent to Constantinople by the Berlin Committee, namely, to win over the local Indian Muslims to its cause. Dayal found these Indians at loggerheads with the Berlin Committee members, and, instead of trying to reconcile them, he introduced new elements of conflict. Arrogant and insensitive beyond belief, he named the Committee's Constantinople office '*Bureau du Parti National Hindou*', and, in his very first letter to Berlin, proposed that the pan-Islamic paper *Jahan-i-Islam*, sponsored by the Turkish War Office and edited by Abu Said, an Indian Muslim, be taken over by the Indian nationalists along with its government subsidy.[28] The idea was ludicrous and unfeasible. As Schabinger, one of Wesendonk's assistants at the *Nachrichtenstelle fuer den Orient* (News Service for the Orient) pointed out, the paper already had too well-established a reputation and readership among the pan-Islamites to allow it to change its character overnight and become a patently nationalist publication. Moreover, since the Germans provided the finance, the transformation was bound to create a tension in Turco-German relations.[29]

However, the AA placed some 10,000 marks at Dayal's disposal for his press work,[30] in order to prevent him from antagonizing Abu Said and other Indian pan-Islamites. It was his own disinclination rather than the lack of financial resources that led to Dayal's failure to make common cause with the Indian Muslims of long standing in Constantinople. Records do not show the existence of an outstanding person among this group of Indians for nationalist propaganda. In addition, the reports of Wangenheim and Oppenheim indicate that the Berlin Indians were suspicious of anyone outside their own group; which in turn made others suspicious and mistrustful of the Berlin Indians.[31]

The fact that the Berlin Indians, with assumed Muslim names and abundant German funds, were engaged in pan-Islamic propaganda, a cause dear to the Muslim heart, should have pleased the Indian Muslims in Constantinople. But the opposite happened. Their leader, Abdul Jabbar Kheiri, a native of Delhi, was one of those contacted by the Berlin Committee at the earliest stage of its formation.[32] Kheiri was never at ease with the Committee led by the Hindus. In May, he came to Berlin and complained to the AA against Dayal's strident Hindu bias.[33] Later, he unsuccessfully tried to obtain German funds for his separate propaganda.[34] Limited though his intellectual horizon was, Jabbar had the persistence of a fanatic and was also an ardent Hindu hater.[35] By November, Jabbar and his brother Abdus Sattar formed a society *Hind-Ikhwat-ul-Islam Anjumani* (Society of Indian Muslim

Brotherhood) which is supposed to have been supported by some influential Turkish people. According to Taraknath Das, the society established its headquarters in a very decent house, and succeeded in starting a weekly paper *Ikhwat* (brotherhood). Jabbar also managed to obtain an appointment as 'professor of Urdu' at the University of Constantinople.[36]

However, what Jabbar wanted most was German patronage, which he failed to receive because of the Berlin Committee's opposition[37] and Wesendonk's low opinion of him.[38] Nor did Jabbar have much success in maligning the Berlin Indians so long as Dayal remained in Constantinople. But, on the day after Dayal left, Jabbar's campaign against the Indian nationalists intensified. At the time of his departure from Constantinople, Dayal neglected to destroy some of the correspondence from the Berlin Committee, including a confidential letter Chatto had written from Sofia. Jabbar gained hold of it, and used it to malign the Committee.[39]

Summing up the Berlin India Committee's rather fruitless activities in Constantinople, Hohenlohe nevertheless advised the AA against ending the Indian activities abruptly in order to stave off a bad impression. He suggested that someone with talent should be put in charge to prevent the situation from deteriorating further.[40]

Accordingly, on 12 November 1915, the India Committee selected Abdul Wahid, Dr Mansur Ahmed, Ata Mohammed, and the Afghan Hafiz for Constantinople in the hope that these Muslim members would retrieve some of its lost prestige. Some local Muslims were also included in the Committee. The India Committee also acquired 200 revolvers for the members to take along with them.[41]

In Constantinople, the new group called itself the Young Hindustan Association, and was recognized by the Turkish government. The second Baghdad mission under the leadership of Dr Ahmed was also formed. Wahid, who was knowledgeable about conditions in Turkey, was to run the Constantinople office. The new Baghdad team left for their destination in February 1916, and counted among its members apart from Ahmed, Acharya, Dasgupta, Varma, Rajab Ali, and Maqbul Hussain.[42]

However, no sooner had the group at Constantinople started their work than several external and internal problems sapped their energy. Jabbar's magazine started an onslaught on the Indian nationalists and, as before, Ali Bey Beshhamba of *Tashkilat-i-Maksusa*, the department of the war ministry dealing with the Indians, from whom the Indians had to obtain permission for their activities in the Ottoman Empire, remained indifferent to the Indians' proposals. To make matters worse, internal dissensions broke out among the Muslim Indians. Wahid was disliked by the Turkish officials, and the Indians charged him with embezzlement of money to the tune of several thousand marks. Ata Mohamed sided with Jabbar and branded the Berlin Committee members German agents who were working systematically against the Turkish interest.[43]

Arriving at Baghdad on 7 April 1916, the new Baghdad team, whose sole object was to revive the earlier plan of forming an Indian volunteer corps out of the deserters, Indian prisoners of war, and local Indians, found intense opposition from Turkish army officials. Although Envar Pasha was willing to give Mansur a chance, the local Turkish military was opposed to the Indians playing any political or military role. Mansur also made himself unpopular among his Indian colleagues by his aloofness and personal aggrandizement.[44]

Persisting with his intractable plan of building a troop of 10,000 men, Mansur asked for 750,000 Turkish pounds and 10,000 complete uniforms and weapons from Germany.[45] Forwarding Mansur's letter by the end of June 1916 to Berlin, German officials both in Baghdad and Constantinople came to the conclusion that in the light of the existing situation in Mesopotamia and Persia, no useful purpose would be served by the activities of the Indians, and would only exacerbate the Turkish situation. Hesse also wrote from Baghdad about the Turkish mistrus of Mansur because of his closeness to the British.[46]

By the time Mansur's request reached Constantinople on its way to Berlin, Chatto and Bhupendranath Dutta had already arrived there (in the last week of June). The German Embassy in Constantinople told them that they considered Mansur's plan most unrealistic. Chatto and Dutta agreed that, in the previous seven months, although more than 30,000 marks had been spent nothing substantial had been achieved. They thought it would be futile, in the absence of any tangible results, to engage in further disputes and discussions with the Turkish authorities, and decided to close the Young Hindustan Association and proceed to organize the India Committee's affairs afresh. Their most intractable problem was the resurrection of the credibility and reputation of the now almost-defunct India Committee. They held on to the idea of the Indian volunteer corps, and decided to speak with von Lossow, the German military attaché at Constantinople. They sought his objective opinion, and hoped he would not consider the scheme too utopian and impracticable. Chatto argued that if the participation of Georgian, Tartar, and Arab legions was valued, the involvement of an Indian military component should be considered more significant because of the positive political impact it would have on India and other countries.[47]

Accompanied by Birendranath Dasgupta, Chatto and Dutta visited the Indian prisoners at Konya and Eskisehir in Turkey to see their condition first-hand and assess the possibility of propaganda among them.[48] They then submitted a report to Ali Bey Bash Hamba, in which they tactfully praised the Turkish authorities' care for the Indians and suggested the removal of some of the other difficulties the prisoners still experienced. They blamed some of the local Indians of damaging the cause of the Indian nationalists by their conduct. As part of a new project, Chatto proposed to circulate two newspapers in Turkey, one in English from Berlin for the Indian prisoners of war and the other, in French, meant for Constantinople. These newspapers were to appear twice a month, in 3000 copies.[49]

Meanwhile, the German officials in Constantinople lost all faith in the usefulness of any further Indian activities in the area. Metternich, from the German Embassy in Constantinople, wrote to the AA in Berlin that it was not that the Indians lacked goodwill and enthusiasm, but that a favourable atmosphere for their activities simply did not exist. In this very down-to-earth report, Metternich mentioned that, although the Committee members endeavoured to make propaganda from the Turkish military lines in the hostile camps at Suez and Basra, there was no measurable success. Moreover, the Turkish government would not allow Indian propaganda in the holy places of Arabia. Field Marshall Colmar von der Goltz, the German adviser to the Turkish army, and Rudolf Nadolny, the Foreign Office's liaison officer in the German general staff, were not in favour of financing the Indian volunteer corps. They would confine Indian activities in Turkey to Indian prisoners only, and place the Turkish military lines beyond their scope. As far as establishing contact with Indian political activists through Turkey, Persia, and Baluchistan—was concerned, the chances, according to Metternich, slim at best, had become even more difficult, if not totally impossible.[50] To make matters worse, Hesse reported from Baghdad Mansur's tactless and insulting remarks about the Germans.[51]

In view of the difficulties outlined above, Chatto and Dutta decided to keep only minimal activities in Constantinople under the direction of Champakraman Pillai.[52] The earlier organization (the Young Hindustan Association) was abolished, and the new one was simply called Indian National Party. Varma and Acharya remained with Pillai, and Mansur returned to Berlin with Chatto. The prisoners' camps at Eski Shehir and Konia for Muslim and Hindu officers, respectively, were to be looked after by Abrahim Adam, Birendra Nath Dasgupta, Kandubhai Nayik, Hardas Singh, and Mirza Abbas. Chatto and Pillai asked for 2450 Turkish liras for this purpose, covering four months' expense (November 1916–January 1917). The AA asked the chargé d'affaires at Constantinople to pay the Indians the whole amount immediately.[53] Wesendonk tried to soothe the German officials in Constantinople by saying that news from India showed that the activities of the nationalists were having some effect, as a direct result of which new recruitment for the British army in India had become much more difficult. Further, it was also hoped that the prisoners would eventually join the revolutionary programme after they had been thoroughly influenced by the nationalists.[54]

However, within a month, a new problem cropped up among the Indians. Radowitz, the chargé d'affaires in Constantinople, informed Berlin in late October about Pillai's genuine complaint that although he was the leader, the Berlin Indians preferred to correspond only with Dasgupta. Radowitz appreciated Pillai's sincerity and determination for good work, but he did not know the background of the Berlin Committee's sudden change of heart for Pillai. The Committee had come to know by mid–October 1916 that, although Pillai's patriotism was unquestionable, one of his friends in Switzerland, Dr E.E. Briess, was a British spy. Just at that time, Pillai received a letter from Briess inviting him to Zurich for a talk. Although there would seem to be a link between this invitation and the reason why Indian friends like Dr Abdul Hafiz, Chatto, Mansur, Rifaat, Dayal, and others had abandoned him,[55] Pillai himself was unaware of Dr Briess' real identity. The Turkish authorities, on the other hand, were determined not to allow any Indian activities among the Indian prisoners of war whereupon the German military attaché advised that all Indians be sent back to Germany. The general German official opinion in Constantinople was that the result of Indian propaganda was very poor compared to the huge investment involved. However, they still believed that it would have been helpful if the prisoners programme had gone ahead, but the Turkish authorities had been uncooperative in this area.[56]

Eventually, by 20 November 1916, the Berlin India Committee decided to withdraw from Turkey. Dasgupta was immediately recalled to Berlin; Acharya and Nayik were to remain for some time in Constantinople and Aleppo, respectively, while Mansur and Pillai were debarred from further work even in Berlin.[57]

The situation for the Berlin Indians in Turkey had come to such a pass that they were not even able to quit Turkey gracefully. Ali Bey Bash Hamba and Fuad Bey, the representatives of *Tashkilat* and *Amaniat-i-Umumia*, respectively, asked the India Committee to clear up all the existing problems between the Turkish government and the Turkey-based Muslim Indians before wrapping up their activities. The complaints were related to various financial matters and other accusations made by the Muslim Indians hired in Turkey.[58] This required Chatto's presence in Turkey where, in February 1917, he proceeded after prior assurance from the Turkish for his safe return. He had to deal with a tricky situation. On the one hand, he faced criticism from the Turkish, and, on the other, he received no support from the German officials based in Turkey. Blaming the Turkish government for the unfortunate plight of the Indian Committee, Chatto, with the help of Wesendonk, finally managed to close the Committee's work in Turkey by the first half of March. On 10 April 1917, he returned to Berlin with the last two original Committee members, Acharya and Nayik.[59]

3. Problems of Arms and a Failed Revolution: Activities in New York, Chicago, San Francisco, Shanghai, Batavia, and Bangkok

As in the case of the first two pan-Islamic programmes of the India Committee, their third programme included purchase of arms and ammunition and gathering of Gadarites and other expatriate Indians from all over the world in order to send them to India to engineer a revolution. The AA and its diplomatic representatives in the USA, Shanghai, Batavia (present-day Jakarta), and Bangkok tried in good faith to respond to the Indian request. But owing to unforeseen mishaps, some treacheries, the inexperience of the participating Indians, and aggressive British diplomacy and espionage, all efforts to bring about a revolution in India failed miserably. Chatto himself never visited these places, and provided direction and advice only through Wesendonk and the Committee's representatives in the US. Although gun-running had been initiated before the Berlin Committee came under his control, it would seem necessary to refer to it briefly for a proper assessment of his role.

Even before the Berlin Committee's representatives, Sarkar and Marathey, arrived in the USA, the Gadar Party in San Francisco had already enquired at the German consulate if Germany would help with weapons and officers for a revolution in India. When Berlin came to know of this in early October 1914, it asked its embassy in Washington to buy 20–30,000 rifles with large quantities of ammunition and arrange to send them to India.[60] Within five days, Berlin learned that several large American firms were willing to sell weapons worth at least $ 60,000 and send them to India by neutral ships.[61] Some experts in the German Admiralty, however, considered that weapons worth $ 60,000 would be insufficient for India, and that between one to three million marks would be required to buy a useful quantity of arms, apart from the cost of transport.[62] Meanwhile, after receiving the first message, Captain Franz von Papen, the military attaché of the German embassy in the US, quickly bought in the American market, through the Krupp American representative, Hans Tauscher, 11,000 Springfield rifles of Spanish American War vintage with four million cartridges, 250 Mauser pistols, and 500 Colt revolvers with ammunition at a total cost of $ 140,000.[63] In justification of his quick decision to buy the weapons, von Papen explained that since France and England had been buying arms frantically in the American market, he thought soon there would be no weapons available in large quantities.[64] The German eagerness to help the Indian revolutionaries was exceptional. Believing that India was ripe for revolution, Bernstorff on 19 December telegraphed Berlin that, if necessary, some 25,000 Mauser rifles with 30 million cartridges could be obtained through a South American agent at a cost of $ 2.5 million.[65] When he received this news, Wesendonk immediately wanted to meet Chatto for discussion.

Although the procuring of arms in the USA was one of the themes in Chatto's memorandum of 7 December to Wesendonk, he was unprepared for the news of Papen's quick purchase. Indeed, Chatto somewhat worried when Wesendonk told him of the possibility of acquiring even more arms. This was because he was not aware if, apart from preparing a group in India to receive the arms, the Berlin

Committee had yet formed a trustworthy team in the USA to handle the transport of the arms. Therefore, when he met Wesendonk on 20 December to discuss the arms purchase, Chatto suggested that the arms already bought should be sent either to Shanghai or Java and kept under German supervision until the India Committee found two or three capable men to smuggle them to India.[66]

Chatto was more concerned about the lack of proper German war propaganda in India, which lack, in his opinion, had dampered enthusiasm for rebellion in India. The immediate revival of this enthusiasm, according to him, was to be given top priority. To this end, he proposed that the India Committee would now spread the 'real information about the war situation' from America. In a document containing his proposals for America, Chatto wrote:

It is evident that correct news of the war and German victories are studied by and carefully kept away from the Indian public. The English are spreading false news, which has undoubtedly the most damaging effect, and it is beyond question that the dissemination of correct news among the people of India is of vital importance, without which the success of any revolution in India would be almost an impossibility.[67]

The India Committee soon selected its man for America. It was Heramba Lal Gupta who had just arrived from the States, one of the Indian nationalists selected by Sarkar and Marathey. Born in Calcutta in 1884, Gupta had first gone to the USA a few years before the war. Chatto told Wesendonk that, besides sending war information and money to India in small sums, Gupta would select people in the USA from among both students and labourers. Additionally, he would deal with the arms transport, explore the possibility of instructing Indians in the use of explosives, and supply the Gadar Party with funds for sending people to India. Chatto asked for 100,000 marks for the work in the USA, half of which was to be kept with the German consul in New York and the other half with his counterpart in San Francisco.[68]

Gupta arrived in New York on 20 January 1915, and thereafter went to Boston and Chicago—where the educated Indians, mostly Bengalis, were to be found. By the time he arrived in the USA, the AA had already advised its embassy in Washington to give Gupta enough money for his work in the USA, China, and the Dutch East Indies. The embassy put aside an equivalent of 150,000 marks granted by Berlin for the purpose.[69] Bernstorff informed Berlin that for the Indian work in

Shanghai, Batavia, and Bangkok, consul general Knipping had already opened a central office in Shanghai.[70]

As for the transportation of arms, Papen, after about six months of consultation with Peking (present-day Beijing), Shanghai, and San Francisco, entrusted the job to Frederick Jebsen, a German-American shipping agent in California. On 3 March 1915, Papen informed Berlin that Jebsen had sent the arms from San Diego to Tapolo Bampo in Mexico in a schooner, the *Annie Larsen*, under the Mexican flag, and that from there another ship would reload the cargo and proceed to Bangkok or any other place the Indians chose.[71] Jebsen adopted this course for fear of coming under the surveillance of the British agents. The other ship, an old oil tanker, the *Maverick*, which Jebsen bought for Papen for $ 55,000,[72] was to take the cargo of the *Annie Larsen*, and proceed to its Indian destination. But the buying of the ship took a long time because, as Papen said, obtaining permission from the Admiralty to purchase from their fund was a lengthy process.[73] Thus, in early March, when the *Annie Larsen* was waiting at the uninhabited island of Socorro off the Mexican coast for the *Maverick*, the latter had yet to start. When the *Maverick* eventually arrived at the appointed place on 29 April, the *Annie Larsen* had already been forced to sail to Acapulco twelve days earlier because Socorro had run short of water. To make matters worse, the *Annie Larsen* could not return to Socorro because of strong adverse winds and had to dock, by the end of June, in a small port near Seattle where its cargo was impounded by the American authorities. The *Maverick* sailed away to Batavia, and arrived without weapons on 19 July to the great disappointment of Narendranath Bhattacharya (whose assumed name was Martin), the representative of the Bengal revolutionaries waiting there.[74]

Even if the *Maverick* had been able to receive the *Annie Larsen's* cargo the arms would probably not have reached the Indians because of the treachery of a Baltic German using the alias 'Oren'. He offered to sell important information concerning the *Maverick* to the British consul general in Batavia, W.R.D. Beckett, in a letter dated 28 June 1915. Oren's information alerted the British into taking vigorous measures against such German ventures,[75] and to round up the Bengal revolutionaries who were preparing to store German arms in the Sunderbans. The leader of the Bengal revolutionaries, Jatin Mukherji, was killed.

Before the *Maverick* adventure ended in a fiasco, Heramba Lal

Gupta had suggested to Papen that another 8000 rifles and 2000 revolvers be bought and shipped to India.[76] Gupta became acquainted with a German in Chicago, Jacobsen, and through him came to know an antique art dealer, Albert Wehde, also from Chicago. He suggested that Wehde be used to channel money to India via Bangkok and Manila.[77] It was decided that Wehde would proceed to Bangkok with another German American, George Paul Boehm, an elderly ex-German soldier who wanted to do something for his country during the war. While Wehde was to finance Indian revolutionary groups from Calcutta, pretending to purchase Oriental antiques for the Chicago museums, Boehm and another German, Sterneck (alias Schulz), were to train Indians in the Thai jungles and lead them to Burma.[78] Wehde received $ 3000 for travel expenses and $ 20,000 as the first instalment of the money to be given to the Indians.[79] Boehm also received $ 1500 to travel to Bangkok.[80] When they arrived in Manila they saw the possibility of arming even the Gadarites. There were two interned German ships in the Manila harbour, the *Sachsen* and the *Suevia*, which had been carrying arms to Shanghai. When the war broke out, they were forced to take refuge there. In early July 1915, the cargoes of the two ships were transferred to a motor schooner, the *Henry S* which Papen had recommended for purchase at a price of $ 17,500[81] The idea was to take the weapons to Bangkok and from there to Chittagong. However, the British agents pressured the American customs to refuse clearance to the vessel. The Germans were so discouraged they abandoned the enterprise altogether.[82] Wehde returned to Shanghai, and was later betrayed by Sterneck who revealed every detail of his secret assignment.

As suggested by Gupta, Papen was actively engaged in procuring arms for the revolutionaries. In May 1915, he informed Berlin that he had bought 7300 Springfield rifles of 45/70 calibre, 2000 Colt army revolvers of 45 calibre, and 10 Colt Gatling machine guns with a large quantity of ammunition at a cost of $ 123,000, without freight. He thought of shipping the arms by the regular Holland-America steamship *Djember* on 15 June either to Batavia or Padang using the trusted agent Denniger. In Padang the cargo could be taken over by the *Maverick*. Papen said it would take about 40 days for the cargo to arrive in Batavia.[83] But this whole venture also failed. The British consul general in New York, Sir Courtenay Bennett, was informed about this large cargo of arms by some of his many secret agents. Bennett passed this information on to the Holland-America line, and the latter refused to take the arms as cargo. Tauscher told the authorities that the arms were bound for China and that he had taken them in good faith.[84] Meanwhile, Papen was informed by the German consul general in Shanghai that since May more than 250 Browning pistols with 36,000 cartridges had been sent to Bangkok and a further 200 with 20,000 cartridges would be sent shortly.[85]

However, the failure of the above-mentioned ventures did not dissuade the AA from making further attempts to send arms to India. On 10 June, Berlin informed Washington that a further sum of one million marks had been sanctioned lately for Indian work.[86] On 12 April 1915, one George Vincent Kraft (born in Amsterdam in 1888 of a Dutch father and German mother, who had been a German planter in the Dutch East Indies before being wounded in fighting as a volunteer in France), showed interest in revolutionizing British India from the east coast of Sumatra. Nadolny, the AA representative in the general staff contacted Wesendonk[87] who consulted Chatto. Since the India Committee found Kraft's proposals 'extremely useful and practical', he was asked to come to Berlin for consultations. It was arranged that during his stay in Berlin he would receive 50 marks weekly.[88]

When Kraft laid out his plan,[89] Chatto was very favourably impressed, and, following his meeting with him, wrote enthusiastically:

> The most suitable place in the Dutch Indies for our work is not Java but the East or residential coast of Sumatra. The vast majority of Indians live in that part, it is much nearer India and the communications are better. The population is in general anti-European, but with careful work, a purely anti-British movement can be built, thus avoiding conflict with the Dutch Government. Most of the smaller tradesmen, e.g. bakers, commercial travellers etc. are Indians...The Hajis are good material to work on...The whole East coast of Sumatra is full of marshes and is situated with uninhabited islands. These islands could be used as depots for arms and ammunition. Coastal fishing boats ply regularly between Sumatra and Indian (chiefly Bengali) coast...There are about 250 Germans in the district of East coast of Sumatra alone, and hundreds more in Java and other parts. These could, perhaps, be organized into a volunteer corps, and could enter India secretly to help the revolutionaries in the event of a general insurrection.[90]

The AA asked Kraft to go to Batavia immediately and report to Windels, the consul general. It was arranged that he would receive 1380 marks monthly, paid in advance. However, to the great misfortune of the German Indian programme, Kraft's intention was not to render service to his country but to act as a double agent and sell information to the British. Thus, before coming to Berlin to meet Wesendonk and Chatto, he went to Amsterdam, and offered to work for the British. When he arrived in the Dutch East Indies in July, he reported to the British consul at Medan. After meeting Windels and Martin (later M.N. Roy), Kraft went to Shanghai to meet Knipping, and on the way, in Singapore, arranged his own arrest by the British in order to fool the Germans and gain their confidence. The British consul general in Singapore, Major-General Dudley Ridout, fully realized Kraft's value as a double agent and paid him two pounds a day before Kraft proceeded to Shanghai, where he hatched a plan of raiding the government of India's penal settlement in the Andaman islands by a group of trained Germans. Having convinced Knipping of the soundness of his plan, Kraft returned to Singapore and again stage-managed his fake arrest and eventual escape from the British.[91] Thus, Kraft proved invaluable to the British in foiling the projected German supply of arms to the Indian revolutionaries.

It was some time before the Germans in Batavia and Shanghai discovered Kraft's game. Dr Gehrmann, Diehn, and Jessen—the last two had escaped from Shanghai prison with Kraft—were chosen by him for his Andaman raid. They failed to impress Windels.[92] Moreover, the AA informed Knipping at the end of February 1916 that the German navy viewed the Andaman plan as impracticable, and it was, therefore, not to be executed.[93] However, this did not stop Kraft from concocting new schemes till the late autumn of 1917.[94]

While Kraft was busy pushing his plans, with the Germans blissfully ignorant of his spying, another plan was in progress in Siam (present-day Thailand) with the blessings of Knipping to help the Gadarites bring about a revolution in India through action on the Siam-Burma border. This Gadar plan was supported by the German consul general in Siam, Dr Erwin Remy. Like all pre-war German officials in India, Remy, who had been German vice-consul in Calcutta (1909–12), was absolutely convinced of the unshakeable supremacy of the British in India. But under instruction from Berlin, he had to go along with the Gadar plan just like Voretzsch, the German consul in Singapore, who had also served as vice-consul in Calcutta (1901–4).[95] In August 1915, Voretzsch and Remy discussed ways and means of supporting Knipping in the Indian endeavour.[96]

Briefly, the plan was that Remy would establish a base in the jungles near the Burmese border, where the Gadarites, both local and those arriving from China and Canada, would receive military training. Remy was a little encouraged when Atma Singh, whom he had sent to Bengal, Madras, and Punjab in early 1915, came back with cheerful news that the British had constant fears of an uprising in India. Bhagwan Singh was the early proponent of the plan, but instead of coming in person he sent Sohan Lal to be the leader. Knipping sent three courageous Germans from the Peking Embassy, W. Haensing, Ecks, and Jaehnigen. However, Remy only used the help and expertise of Haensing and sent him to the operation centre at Pakho.[97] Knipping also arranged the supply of arms in beer cases through an officer of a Norwegian ship plying between Swatow and Bangkok. In July 1915, the last five Indians, including Jodh Singh, arrived in Bangkok making the group sizeable and armed enough to cross over to Burma. But by this time the British had been alerted. They had managed to infiltrate the Gadar camp through an Indian spy posing as a revolutionary, and had obtained all the vital information. Three high-ranking officers in the Siamese police were British, and they too had kept an eye on the movements of the Indians. Herbert Dering, the British minister at Bangkok, contacted the cooperative Siamese foreign minister, and soon investigations and trials followed in Burma resulting in the hanging of several participating Gadarites, including Sohan Lal. David Petrie of the Indian Criminal Intelligence Department had also arrived at the scene to assist the investigation.

Thus ended probably the only promising attempt to bring about an insurrection in India. The Germans were playing for high stakes, and it is no wonder that Windels was very bitter about the ultimate result. According to the Bangkok Germans, the Indo-German revolutionary events in Siam played a major role in Siam's declaration of war against Germany. Windels commented that German commerce in Siam, with nine beautiful commercial ships, had long been a thorn in the British side, and that the German loss obviously constituted a great gain for the British.[98]

When the project of transporting arms to India by sea failed, some thought was given to the land route via China to the Indo-Afghan border. But in October 1916, Knipping wrote that this would be possible only by giving proper information to the Chinese government, which was, however, under great pressure from the Entente countries to join them. Like Windels, Knipping too was by then completely disenchanted with the Indians, including Martin and Bhagwan Singh, 'who stir up their countrymen sitting themselves at safe hiding places without making any personal sacrifices themselves.' He pinpointed one constant problem in working with the Indians:

> As the past has proved, it is not the [German] authorities in China who are helpless and powerless to help the Indians, but the Indians themselves. As soon as they do something on their own initiative, they get into dangerous difficulties from which they can only be rescued with the help of the consulates.[99]

4. The Berlin Committee in the USA after the Arms Debacle

At the time the Siam plan ended in a fiasco, in August 1915, Heramba Lal Gupta found himself in Japan exploring the possibility of cooperation between Indian revolutionaries and Japanese ultra-nationalists on a pan-Asiatic platform. He was soon joined by Rash Behari Bose (whose assumed name was Thakur) from Shanghai. Both of them were closely observed by British intelligence from the moment of their arrival in Tokyo. The British ambassador pressed the Japanese government to hand over the Indians to the British. However, Thakur and Gupta were successful in influencing a section of the Japanese press into highlighting the British high-handedness. The *Yamato Shimbun* of Tokyo took the lead and published some articles under the heading 'A message to England'. But the British succeeded in obtaining deportation orders for Thakur and Gupta. In order to prevent the implementation of these orders, Toyama Mitsuru, the powerful 'political boss', at Sun Yat-sen's suggestion, kept hiding the Indians for five months until Gupta could leave Japan safely.[100]

During Gupta's stay in Tokyo, the Berlin Committee chose in his place Dr Chandra Kanta Chakravarty as their USA representative. On 29 December 1915, Chakravarty arrived in Berlin for a few days[101] and returned to New York with the new programmes of the India Committee.

The new programmes seem to be in part Chakravarty's own brainchild, and were largely unrealizable. He planned to send agents from the USA to the West Indian islands to induce Indian immigrants to return to India and organize revolt. He had a similar plan for the Indians in British Guyana. He also wished to send agents to Java to consult with Kraft about the Andaman invasion, arrange the printing of all the Committee's propaganda literature in the USA, and send a secret Oriental mission to Japan. For these projects the Committee asked for 20,000 marks to be paid to Chakravarty immediately, and another $ 10,000 to be kept reserved for him with the German consulate in New York.[102] The AA granted the whole sum immediately, and directed its Washington embassy to ensure that Gupta and Dhiren Sarkar were to work under Chakravarty.[103]

When Gupta returned from Japan, Count Johann von Bernstorff, German Ambassador to Washington, informed him of the India Committee's decision. Gupta, however, was not willing to work under Chakravarty but on his own. This was not allowed. But Bernstorff reimbursed Gupta $ 3000 which he said he had to borrow in Japan. In consideration of Gupta's good work until then, Bernstorff, on his own initiative, decided to pay Gupta, from the old funds, $ 100 per month as living expenses.[104]

The Calcutta-born Chakravarty was about 30 years old at that time. He had gone to the USA in 1910, after having had some connection with the Bengal nationalist agitation of the post-Curzon era. At the time of becoming the chief representative of the Berlin Committee in the USA, he was living with a German named Dr Ernst Sekunna in New York who was again connected with Wolf von Igel, Papen's assistant who functioned as liaison between Indians and the German consulate. This is the same Chakravarty against whom George Freeman had already warned the India Committee.[105] Chakravarty furnished the Berlin Committee with spurious accounts of his work, sometimes in private code, arranged between him and the Berlin Committee. Each and every letter from him invariably contained a request for more money.

A few examples of the contents of Chakravarty's reports to the India Committee and the latter's indulgent attitude can be cited. In April 1916, at a time when Chakravarty had not even formed a USA subcommittee or visited the West coast to meet the Gadar leaders and rank-and-file to reinvigorate the organization, his preoccupation seems to have been the acquisition of German money. Sensing the straining diplomatic relations between Germany and the USA because of the von Igel case[106], and thinking this might cause Count Bernstorff's departure (and that his successor might not be as indulgent) Chakravarty requested another $ 30,000 in advance. The Berlin Committee supported the request saying:

The credit asked for will not be considered large, when it is remembered that the U.S., the West Indian Islands, British Guyana, Manila and Japan are included in the field of work of our comrades in America.

Wesendonk recommended a grant of 150,000 marks for the Committee's American work and, as usual, his suggestion was readily accepted.[107]

The two recurring themes of Chakravarty's reports were the fostering of relations between India and Japan through various publications and the sending of Indians from the West Indies, British Guyana, and some other places with large Indian immigrant settlements to India to create unrest. The first of the two themes, although important for the future, was not urgently connected with producing a revolution in India, and the second was simply a bogus venture for obtaining easy money. In a letter Chakravarty wrote in April 1916 to the Berlin Committee, he said:

...A Pan-Asiatic League has also been organized so that some of our members can travel without arousing any suspicion... I have had talks with one of the directors of Yamato Shimbun of Tokyo... It would be necessary to buy off these papers as they understand it is mutual interest of Japan and India... They have also decided to attack the Anglo-Japanese treaty as being antagonistic to their national interest. To carry on the work, it will be necessary to put at the disposal of the Committee over here $ 25,000... X is to send the people from Trinidad to India. X has men whom he wants to send off in 2 or 3 batches. They are from Madras and Bombay. Their contracts are over and there can be no suspicion if they return. It will cost $ 200 for each man.[108]

In a letter written in code to the India Committee which they forwarded to Wesendonk in complete text on 7 May, Chakravarty wrote:

We arranged everything to control two Japanese dailies for 14 thousand dollars, but the Embassy says that there is no need for it.[109]

At the beginning of June 1916, Chakravarty wrote:

The men I sent from Trinidad have reached their destination. The other batches sent off before have perfected their organizations. They believe, they can start an insurrection successfully as soon as they receive moderate supplies of arms... I have not yet received any direction from you nor any sanction of the money which is urgently needed for the continuation of the work.[110]

A week later Chakravarty wrote:

> We are sending 20 more men from that place [Trinidad]. The first batches have reached their destination. Their reports are very encouraging...The organization [in India] has almost been completed. Many of our old members are active and free. They are only afraid if arms are not available soon, there may be a premature uprising in Madras, Punjab and Bengal. Some of our men [in India] who are maturing the plans are being accused of personal cowardice.[111]

Chakravarty's correspondence is dominated by requests for more and more money. Only in September 1916, seven months after his arrival in New York, did Chakravarty think of forming the USA sub-committee and going to California to meet Ram Chandra who, he said, was willing to conform 'to our party policy.'[112] On 25 October 1916, Chakravarty spoke of his endeavours to collect arms:

> We have not succeeded in sending more than 200 rifles and some three thousand cartridges in the last six months through the Pacific... Need 15 thousand dollars for expenses.[113]

In an early correspondence, Chakravarty also referred to the possibility of bringing about an uprising in the West Indies itself. In a letter of 7 November, Chakravarty seems to have let his imagination run riot:

> Our preliminary work has been completed in the British West Indies. We are waiting for your final decision. We can muster nearly 70 to 75 thousand men, and if they are properly officered and directed, we can easily control the situation, unless the present British garrisons are strongly reinforced and supported by the powerful reserves of munitions. In that case, as there are no fortifications in those islands, and for want of necessary artillery, we will be compelled to cross the border and enter Venezuela. That part of the country is at present in an unsettled condition, and we have the assurance of receiving the support of the Gonzalla party... The Venezuela government would herself be unable to do anything without military help of either America or Britain...[114]

Chakravarty was given to both lying and exaggeration. In his year-end report on 29 November 1916, he begged:

> We brought about a secret understanding with Japanese and Chinese Governments. We have created an atmosphere in which we can exist in future with their passive sympathy. In America the name of England has been made synonymous with tyranny and odium.[115]

Although avaricious himself, Chakravarty was niggardly towards others. Whatever may have been Ram Chandra's shortcomings, there is no denying that it was his Gadar organization which had first brought about German-Indian cooperation for the supply of arms to India, and that it was individual Gadarites who actually extended practical service to the cause of revolution in India. And yet Chakravarty could not stand the Gadar party also receiving recurring grants from the Germans. It is remarkable that Chakravarty, who had received $ 75,000 till 3 March 1917[116] for doing practically nothing, should have written thus:

Gupta got 28 thousand dollars, and is still getting a hundred dollars monthly; Gadar got 32,000 dollars, and is still getting an uncertain sum monthly as encouragement. The sum is big and the result is very poor. *It should be a cardinal principle of our work to show some result in relation to Germany.*[117]

It is strange that the Berlin Committee, run mainly by Chatto and Bhupendranath Dutta, concurred with Chakravarty and recommended that the recurring grants to Ram Chandra and Gupta be stopped if they failed to cooperate with Chakravarty.[118]

Chakravarty sank so low that he did not even shrink from dragging the name of Nobel laureate Rabindranath Tagore in the mud and tarnishing his reputation. Tagore arrived in New York on 18 November 1916 to lecture at the Carnegie Hall. On 10 January 1917, Chakravarty reported:

...He [Tagore] was introduced to the proper authorities and [he] declared his opinion that if Germany had established a connection two years previously to the war, everything would be ready now. We have given him 12,000 dollars.[119]

Tagore was never offered money by Chakravarty or any other German agent. Chakravarty's statement was baseless—a 'lying calumny' in Tagore's words. On 19 April 1917, the AA informed the Berlin Indians that contrary to Chakravarty's information, there was no money transaction between Herr von Skal and Tagore.[120]

In the small hours of the morning on 6 March 1917, Chakravarty and Sekunna were arrested for violating the neutrality laws of the USA. Chakravarty acted like a coward and readily confessed that he had been sent from Berlin and went on to reveal the identity of his associates.[121] Soon many other Indians in Chicago and San Francisco, including Gupta, were taken into custody for violating American neutrality, and the main trial began in San Francisco on 20 November 1917, the so-called Hindu Conspiracy Case.

5. Chatto's Leadership Until the Failure of the Revolutionizing Attempts

The Berlin Committee's activities in Afghanistan, in the Ottoman Empire, and in the USA had been planned before the Committee came under the management of the Indians themselves. But when the Committee came to execute its plans roughly from the beginning of 1915, the Indians had taken over, and, without their consultation, the AA did nothing as far as India was concerned. Only the task of buying larger quantities of arms and transporting them to India was left completely in the hands of the German officials in the USA and China. Even on this matter, sinch the request for arms initially came from the Gadar party of Ram Chandra, the German officials in the USA kept, the Gadarites and later, the Berlin India Committee's representative in the USA, Heramba Lal Gupta informed about every development. The role of the Indians in the so-called German intrigues in India was deliberately suppressed by the British in order to influence the neutral countries against Germany. It was later ignored by most Anglo-American writers depending heavily on British Indian intelligence reports. The 48 basic volumes at the AA concerning the incitement of rebellion in India during WWI make it absolutely clear that the initiators of all the actions in the so-called German intrigues in India were Indians. It is also true that due to Wesendonk the AA was extremely obliging to the Indians' requests. What Wesendonk recommended was invariably approved by Arthur Zimmermann, under-secretary of state for foreign affairs until 1916 and later foreign secretary from 1916–17.

As part of an assessment of Chatto's management of the Berlin Committee, it is essential to bear in mind how his opinions and judgements were valued, accepted, and carried out by Wesendonk and the AA.

It is obvious that the Berlin India Committee, throughout its existence, suffered from the lack of a regular link with any revolutionary group in India, not to speak of a nationally organized revolutionary party. This was not Chatto's fault for, unlike Dayal, who boasted to the Germans with exaggerated statistics of the revolutionary potential of

Indians at home and abroad and even spoke of a nationalist party in India ready for revolution, Chatto's optimism about a rebellion in India was based only on what the India Committee had achieved by way of preparation until the first week of December 1914 (as outlined in his memorandum to Wesendonk). Chatto never claimed the existence of a nationally organized revolutionary party in India; he only hoped that, with German help, it might be possible to bring together the various revolutionary groups in the Punjab and Bengal. His inspiration was the aftermath of the *Komagata Maru* episode.

There was, however, the image question of the Berlin India Committee and the name recognition of Chatto in India. A more distinguished personality in place of the lesser-known Chatto as the head of the Berlin India Committee might, perhaps, have helped bring about a broader-based revolutionary party in India by enhancing the Committee's prestige in the eyes of Indians. The two leading names that came to the fore were those of Krishnavarma and Lajpat Rai. In fact, during the earliest phase of the India Committee, the German ambassador at Constantinople, Wangenheim, had informed Berlin about Krishnavarma saying that even the Turks were interested in him. However, Chatto dissuaded Oppenheim from inviting Krishnavarma. Oppenheim accepted Chatto's warning and wrote to the AA:

My Indians, who know Krishnavarma very well, warn against him, saying that he is a cowardly man of low mentality and is concerned with his own material and personal benefits, and would never take part in any revolutionary activity. No Indian nationalist would like to have anything to do with him as he has until now only discredited the nationalists, and, through his indiscretions in many ways damaged the nationalist cause.[122]

Chatto can be squarely criticized for putting his personal quarrels and preferences ahead of the nationalist cause. It was not true that no nationalist would have liked to work with Krishnavarma. In fact, Dayal for one, recommended just about this time, that Krishnavarma be invited. Chatto soon realized that, to enhance the image of the Committee, a nationally known person was necessary, and asked Harish Chandra and Heramba Lal Gupta to persuade Lajpat Rai to come to Berlin (although Rai had publicly asserted his dislike of revolution and foreign aid). Rai refused to join the Berlin Committee because he had 'absolutely no doubt that the Germans would grab India and would suck the life blood out of her, even more mercilessly than the English

Attempts at Revolutionizing India 89

had done.'[123] Not daunted, even as late as in September 1916, Bhupendra Nath Dutta wrote to Tagore, then in Japan, to bring Japan to India's side and influence Rai to come to Berlin.[124]

Chatto seems to have had his apprehensions about Dayal. They were justified in the light of Dayal's strange, vainglorious, and generally unhelpful behaviour towards the Berlin Committee in Turkey and elsewhere. No doubt the changed relations between Turkey and Germany during the war had much to do with the failure of the Berlin Committee's Afghan mission and their activities in the Ottoman Empire. Dayal's aloofness, secretiveness, and intrigues contributed no less, not only to the inner dissensions among Indians but also to the loss of prestige of the Committee in the eyes of German and Turkish officials in the Ottoman Empire. Chatto did what he could to salvage the Committee's reputation under the existing circumstances.

As far as the buying and shipping arms is concerned, a great deal of mishaps and mismanagement occurred for which Chatto cannot be held responsible. Papen's inefficient management of arms shipping, the fruitless voyages of the ships and delays took away the surprise effect from the event, gave rise to many rumours, alerted the British, and provided a fertile ground for treason, treachery, and espionage. India did not have a large British Indian army at this time,[125] and the British, facing their greatest danger in India from the revolutionaries, took effective steps to malign Germany, the revolutionaries' ally, in the neutral countries. Through intensive propaganda, aided by treachery of some of the volatile Indians themselves, they achieved their goal first in the USA and then in Siam and China.[126]

However, to compensate for all the previous failures, Knipping, Windels, Remy, and Voretzsch, against their own better judgments, made a last-ditch effort to help the Indians achieve a modicum of success. They not only arranged arms but also military training for the Indians. But aggressive British diplomacy and espionage foiled the German effort. Those Indians who were arrested proved cowardly and were only too ready to reveal their secrets, to the detriment and embarrassment of the German diplomats. The diplomats were naturally embittered.[127]

Chatto was shamed by the cowardice of the Indian revolutionaries. In a face-saving letter he wrote to Wesendonk:

...lots of inexperienced and untried men have been used by the Californian party and other revolutionary centres. This use of untried men has led to various misfortunes. These men have been enthusiastic in their work, but, when arrested betrayed much of what they know. Many of these men are unknown to the representative Nationalists. Much of the misfortune is due to men picked up in a haphazard fashion for the work.[128]

Since the Siam-Burma plot was mainly a Gadarite venture, Chatto was afforded a chance to vindicate his decision against supporting Ram Chandra and the Gadar party. But the fact is that all the Indian 'revolutionaries', and not just the Gadarites, were untried men (although there were evidently more courageous people among the Punjabis of the Californian group than in the Indian groups of New York and Chicago).

It is difficult to understand this streak in Chatto's thinking under the influence of Chakravarty, who excluded the Gadarites completely from his plans. At a time of repeated failures at revolution, one would have expected him to unite and not divide nationalist Indians for future work. From this point of view, his consistent opposition to Ram Chandra is indiscernible. He stopped the AA's financial grant to Chandra and even to Gupta just because the two refused to work under Chakravarty. It is also strange that Chatto should have had faith in Chakravarty's wild and fanciful projects of enlisting men in Trinidad and sending them to India to foment a revolution. What is more, Chatto said nothing in criticism or rebuke following Chakravarty's betrayal immediately after his arrest. Perhaps this aspect of the Chatto-Chakravarty relationship will remain obscure for ever. Chakravarty, however, left an eloquent tribute to Chatto in his book:

He [Chatto] never lowered the national dignity and self-respect as a representative of India. He associated with the German Foreign Office as an ambassador and an ally to render mutual assistance during the war.[129]

The tribute is, no doubt, apt. Chatto's task, as the head of a revolutionary organization whose centre was situated far away from where the revolution was to take place, was not easy. It was well-nigh impossible to prevent cheats, charlatans, and spies creeping into the organization pretending to be genuine patriots. Like his German partners Chatto too was duped and deceived massively. An incident that took place in December 1915 shows eloquently how loyalty and treachery, faith and perfidy, trust and betrayal, success and failure went hand in hand in these uncertain times. In December 1915, Harish Chandra, the former secretary of Mahendra Pratap, had gone to England and France to influence high-ranking Indians to take part in revolution and send German money to India, returned to Berlin with a success story. According to him his contact man, Raja Kushal Pal Singh, the former representative of the Talukdars of Oudh in the Supreme Legislative Council in India, had informed him that some Indian princes and nationalist leaders had lately joined together and decided to wage war against the English with the aim of establishing an independent national government, provided Germany extended moral and material help in the form of arms and ammunition, officers, financial loans, and, eventually, recognition to the provisional government that might be established. On 17 December 1915, Chatto in his capacity as the 'general secretary, the Indian Independence Committee', presenting the Berlin Committee in a formal way as an organization, wrote a letter to Zimmermann. He requested him to issue a formal letter with the German acceptance of these conditions. Chatto explained the urgency of such a letter since the Raja was returning to India in January 'to enable events to be precipitated in the spring of 1916.'[130] On Wesendonk's recommendation, Zimmermann replied promptly. The following is his letter:

Virendranath Chattopadhyaya Berlin, 19 December 1915
General Secretary, Indian Independence Committee
Wielandstrasse 38
Berlin-Charlottenburg

Sir,
In reply to your letter of the 17th instant, I beg to inform you that the German Government is ready to give to the Indian Princes and to the leaders of the Indian National Movement all the material and moral assistance which is possible to render under present circumstances. Should the Indian Princes and people succeed to free India and to establish a provisional Government, the Imperial Government will be ready to recognize this Government. You may be formally assured, that Germany, the true friend of all oppressed nations, has no other than commercial and cultural interest in furthering the cause of the national independence of India. I request you to communicate the contents of this letter to Raja Kushal Pal Singh.
Believe me Sir,
Yours sincerely
Zimmermann
Under Secretary of State[131]

In Berlin, Harish Chandra said that his contacts with many wounded Indian soldiers in England and France had assured him that they would work for the Indian revolution on returning to India. Wesendonk was impressed by Chandra's achievement, and quickly granted the £ 4000 for his services, which Chandra had asked for.[132] It was not known to Chatto that on his first visit to England Chandra, like Kraft, had arranged for his mock arrest by the British and had become a British spy. Only two months before his second appearance in Berlin, Chandra had met Lajpat Rai in New York. Rai found out that Chandra had been bought over by the British and was working in the USA for them. Rai despised him as much as he despised Chakravarty.[133]

Unaware of Chandra's spying activities, the India Committee in April 1916 made detailed plans with him regarding Afghanistan, the Nizam's Hyderabad, England, Japan, Siam, and Ceylon.[134] It sent M. Prabhakar (*alias* Prager), one of the earliest members of the Berlin Committee since Oppenheim's time, to Montreux to meet him. At Chandra's request, Wesendonk also went there on 15 April to consult with him at the Hotel Eden. According to the understanding reached between them, Chandra agreed to continue influencing the Indian princes touring Europe, avoid frequent visits to Switzerland which, from the AA's point of view, was infested with British spies, and, additionally, send trustworthy agents to Europe. They also decided to discontinue attempts to kill British Indian officials in Europe, although it was recognized that a successful attempt on Kitchener's life would make a great impression on the Orientals, and agreed that the Dutch Indies should be given up completely as a base. Finally Chandra was asked to obtain photographs of the letters that had earlier been sent to the Indian princes for circulating them in the Punjab and Hyderabad.[135] Chandra received a remuneration of 80,000 marks from Prabhakar for his services.[136] Thus armed with fistfuls of German money and trust, Chandra set out for the USA to help his British masters, to the detriment of the Indian nationalist cause and German interests.

NOTES

1. Born in 1864, and son of an employee of the Bhopal State, Muhamed Barakatullah was one of the first to start anti-British propaganda in America. In 1909, he became professor of Urdu at the Tokyo School of Foreign Languages, and in early 1910, started his paper, *The Islamic Fraternity*, which

advocated militant pan-Islamism. The paper was suppressed, and in 1914, he was dismissed from his job at British instigation. Leaving Japan in May 1914, he arrived in San Francisco, where he took active part in the Gadar propaganda.
2. See Mahendra Pratap, 'My German Mission in High Asia', *Asia*, 25 (5), May 1925, pp. 382–8, 448. When the Pratap-Hentig mission arrived in Kermanshah towards the end of June 1915, Niedermayer, who had to bring the newly appointed German consul general, Prince Reuss, to Teheran, joined the Pratap-Hentig mission in July after finishing his original assignment.
3. See N.K. Barooah, 'When Afghanistan was Impenetrable and India Under Foreign Rule', *My World*, April 1980.
4. *Ibid*. See also Mahendra Pratap (Raja), *My Life Story of Fifty-five years* (Delhi, 1947).
5. Ridout, Straight Settlement, Singapore to War Office, 1 April 1919, IOR L/P & S /10/520 File 4529/2788 enclosing report on Roehr, who was captured by the British on board the *SS Atreus* en route from Shanghai to Rotterdam on 26 March 1919.
6. For the British nervousness about the possible end of Afghan neutrality and the German-sponsored insurrections among the tribes in the North-West Frontier Province of India since the activities of Wassmus, Zugmeyer and Griesinger in Central Asia, see the correspondence between Marling, the British representative at Teheran, and FO; secretary of state for India and the Viceroy of India; and between Viceroy and IO during June–September 1915. IOR L/P & S/10/473 (3443/2339, 2489, 2496, 2538, 2663, 2911, 2930).
7. Macartney to Manners Smith, the British Resident at Srinagar (Kashmir), Kashgar 10 Aug 1916 and the IO notes thereto. IOR L/P & S/10/520 (4529/4377).
8. Wk 11f, 7, pp. 73–5, Barakatullah to Dayal, New York, 24 November 1914.
9. Wk 11f, 9, p. 18, IC Resolution.
10. Wk 11f, 9, pp. 170–5, Wesendonk's note 25 February 1915; Wk 11f, 10, p. 94, Zimmermann to Dresdner Bank, Berlin, 17 March 1915.
11. See S.H. Longgrigg, *Iraq, 1900–1950: A Political, Social, and Economic History* (London, 1953), pp. 77–8.
12. *Ibid*., p. 78; Hardinge of Penshurst, *My Indian Years* (London, 1948), p. 102.
13. Wk 11f, 16, pp. 55, 67, Wesendonk's note, 10 July 1915, giving the view of Dr Schacht, a medical member of the Klein expedition.
14. Wk 11f, 21, pp. 62–3, Hesse from the German Consulate, Baghdad, to AA, 22 September 1915.
15. Wk 11f, 19, p. 34, Hohenlohe to AA, 26 August 1915; Wk 11f, 20, pp. 2–3, Hohenlohe to AA, 3 September 1915.
16. Wk 11f, 20, pp. 2–3, 62, Hohenlohe to AA, 3 and 14 September 1915.
17. Wk 11f, 21, p. 121, Neurath to AA, 23 October 1915.

18. Wk 11f, 14, p. 108 ff, L.P. Varma to Chatto, Constantinople, 14 May 1915.
19. Wk 11f, 13, pp. 148–9, Dayal to IC, 23 May 1915. The apparent reason for this decision was that he was required to submit his letters to the embassy open. But even when the AA gave the IC members the privilege of sending closed letters, no detailed messages were sent by Dayal.
20. Wk 11f, 14, p. 37, Wangenheim to AA, 13 May 1915. For more details about Miss Howsin, see Chapter IV towards the end.
21. *Ibid.*, p. 87, Wangenheim to AA, 19 May 1915.
22. Wk 11f, 19, p. 66, Dayal to Wesendonk, telegram, Budapest, 28 August 1915; Wk 11f, 22, p. 151, IC to Wesendonk, 7 November 1915.
23. Wk 11f, 19, p. 51, Constantinople Embassy to AA, 28 August 1915.
24. Wk 11f, 22, p. 144 ff, Taraknath Das, 'Report on Present State of Affairs in Constantinople' submitted to IC through Dr Weber, Constantinople, 12 November 1915.
25. Wk 11f, 20, pp. 186–9, Dayal to under secretary of state, foreign affairs, 9 October 1915.
26. Wk 11f, 14, pp. 137–42, Dayal to Georg Widel, Constantinople, 22 May 1915. Dayal met Widel (a minister by rank) at the house of Baron Langwerth before proceeding to Constantinople.
27. *Ibid.*
28. Wk 11f, 13, pp. 75–7, Dayal to IC, 16 April 1915.
29. *Ibid.*, p. 74, Schabinger to Wesendonk, 6 May 1915.
30. *Ibid.*, p. 170, AA to Constantinople, telg., 29 April 1915.
31. Wk 11f, 14, p. 3, Wangenheim to AA incorporating also Oppenheim's opinion, 3 May 1915.
32. See N.K. Barooah, *India and the Official Germany, op. cit.*, p. 191.
33. Wk 11f, 14, p. 97, Wesendonk to Berne, 23 May 1915.
34. Wk 11f, 15, p. 85, Wangenheim to AA, 23 June 1915; Wk 11f, 19, p. 56, AA to Constantinople, 28 August 1915.
35. Note, for example, the following from his statement entitled 'Moslem India in Search of a Powerful and Sympathetic Friend' submitted to the AA through the German embassy in Constantinople in February 1917: '...Now the word Hindu is of Persian origin and it means black. This name was given to the various tribes, religions, races and sects living in India. It is interesting to note that the name, which was given in hatred and derision was afterwards adopted by the non-Moslem dwellers of India. They even went still further, by giving the general name to their religion and called it Hinduism.' Wk 11f, 39, pp. 14–43.
36. Taraknath Das, *op. cit.*
37. Wk 11f, 15, p. 85, Wangenheim to AA, 23 June 1915.
38. According to Emily C. Brown, Jabbar was 'well thought of by the German foreign office.' This is not true. From the very beginning, Wesendonk considered Jabbar an intriguer and a fanatic. He wanted to remove him from Constantinople by enticing him with a job at the *Nachrichtenstelle*. It did not

work. Later, in 1916, when Jabbar planned to open a branch office of his organization in Berlin, Wesendonk remarked: 'For such a mystical and fanatical society there is no place here.' In September 1918, the Kheiri brothers complained to the political department of the German general staff that the AA continued to be completely under the influence of the Hindus, and that was why they were also against the Kheiris. Wk 11f, 20, pp. 60, 130; Wk 11f, 30, p. 137; Wk 11f, 31, p. 34; Wk 11f, 45, pp. 249–50. See also Brown, *op. cit.*, p. 191.
39. Wk 11f, 19, p. 49, Hohenlohe to AA, telegram 28 August 1915.
40. Wk 11f, 20, p. 32, Hohenlohe to AA, 14 September 1915.
41. Wk 11f, 22, p. 63; also Wk 11f, 26, pp. 97–9, Wesendonk's note, 13 November 1915.
42. Wk 11f, 26, pp. 62–4, IC to Wesendonk, 5 March 1916.
43. Wk 11f, 29, p. 18, Metternich to AA, 2 June 1916.
44. Wk 11f, 29, pp. 144–5, Acharya to Chatto, Baghdad, 19 May 1916.
45. Wk 11f, 30, pp. 3–5.
46. Wk 11f, 29, pp. 194–5, Hesse to AA, telegram, Baghdad, 20 June 1916.
47. Wk 11f, 29, p. 269, Chatto and Dutta to Hafis, Constantinople, 1 July 1916; Wk 11f, 30, pp. 13–19, 74–8.
48. Wk 11f, 30, pp. 108–12.
49. Wk 11f, 30, pp. 13–19.
50. Wk 11f, 30, pp. 30–3, Metternich to AA, Therapia, 6 July 1916.
51. Wk 11f, 34, pp. 121–35, Acharya's report, Constantinople, 23 October 1916.
52. Wk 11f, 30, p. 90, Metternich to AA, 24 and 25 August 1916; Wk 11f, 31, pp. 29–31.
53. Wk 11f, 32, pp. 79–85; Wk 11f, 32, p. 119; Chatto-Pillai plan to German embassy in Constantinople, 8 September 1916.
54. Wk 11f, 33, p. 145.
55. Wk 11f, 34, p. 31, Radowitz to AA, 8 November 1916; also Wk 11f, 33, pp. 125–6, German consul general, Geneva, to AA, 12 October 1916, enclosing Briess' letter to Pillai on the same date.
56. Wk 11f, 34, pp. 37–8, Radowitz to AA.
57. Wk 11f, 34, pp. 71–4 and pp. 100–1, IC to Wesendonk, 20 November and 1 December 1916.
58. IC to Wesendonk, 14 February and Chatto to IC, Constantinople, 10 February 1917. The Muslim members hired in Turkey were Maqbul Hussain, Inayat Ali, Ibrahim Adham, Mohamed Yussuff, Atta Mohamed, and Abdul Wahid.
59. Wk 11f, 36, p. 124, German embassy, Constantinople to AA, 3 March 1917, AA to Constantinople embassy, 5 March 1917; Wk 11f, 37, p. 88, Kuhlmann to AA, telegram, 11 April 1917.
60. Wk 11f, 3, p. 82, Bernstorff to AA, telephone, 30 September 1914; *ibid.*, p. 112; Zimmermann to Washington embassy, telegram, 9 October 1914; also *ibid.*, p. 120, AA to Washington Embassy, 11 October 1914.

61. Wk 11f, 4, p. 44, German embassy Washington to AA, 16 October 1914.
62. Wk 11f, 4, p. 56, Wesendonk's note on 18 October after talks with Captain Grasskoff and Captain Loehlein.
63. Wk 11f, 5, p. 64 and Wk 11f, 6, p. 60, Papen's message from New York, 20 October and 5 December 1914.
64. *Ibid.*
65. Wk 11f, 6, p. 119, Bernstorff to AA, telegram 19 December 1914. Papen's quick purchase of arms caught Ram Chandra completely unprepared. When asked about the destination of the cargo, Chandra, in order to save face, named Karachi although there was little or no preparation there. The delay in sending the arms saved Chandra from blame. See Lajpat Rai, *Autobiographical Writings*, V.C. Joshi (ed.) (Delhi, 1965), pp. 303–4.
66. Wk 11f, 6, pp. 124–5, Wesendonk's note on this meeting with Chatto on 20 December 1914.
67. *Ibid.*, pp. 126–9, Chatto's memorandum, 'Proposals for work in America'.
68. *Ibid.*
69. Wk 11f, 7, p. 2, AA to Washington, 24 December 1914, Zimmermann's note, 27 December 1914.
70. Wk 11f, 9, p. 31, Bernstorff to AA, 3 February 1915.
71. Wk 11f, 10, p. 5, Papen's letter in Nadolny to AA, 3 March 1915.
72. Wk 14, 12, p. 105, Nadolny forwarding Papen's letter, New York, 24 March 1915.
73. Wk 11f, 12, p. 41, Papen to AA, New York, 8 March 1915.
74. FO 371/2494, p. 281, Beckett to Grey, 2 July 1915.
75. FO 371/2494 (106706), Beckett to FO, 2 July 1914.
76. Wk 11f, 12, p. 105, Papen to AA, New York, 24 March 1915.
77. Wk 11f, 13, p. 154, Bernstorff to AA, 20 April 1915; FO 371/2784 (8266), statement of George Boehm, 16–7 November 1915.
78. Wk 11f, 14, p. 80, Bernstorff to AA, 23 April 1915.
79. Wk 11f, 14, p. 49, Bernstorff to AA, 20 April 1915.
80. Wk 11f, 14, p. 80, Bernstorff to AA, 20 April 1915, and Wesendonk's approval.
81. Wk 11f, 18, pp. 86–8, Papen's report, New York, 23 July 1915, forwarded by Nadolny.
82. Wk 11f, 22, p. 135, Papen to AA, New York, 5 November 1915; also Wk 11f, 44, p. 138, Zitelmann to AA, 14 June 1918.
83. Wk 11f, 14, pp. 174–5, Papen's report 10 May 1915, in Nadolny to AA, 6 June 1915; Wk 11f, 15, p. 72, Papen's message, 31 May 1915.
84. Wk 11f, 18, pp. 86–8, Papen's report, New York, 23 July 1915, forwarded by Nadolny.
85. *Ibid.*
86. Wk 11f, 14, p. 198.
87. Wk 11f, 13, p. 13, Nadolny to AA, 17 April 1915, forwarding Kraft's letter from Lille.

88. Wk 11f, 13, p. 73, Wesendonk's and Nadolny's comments 28, 29, and 30 April 1915.
89. Wk 11f, 14, pp. 41–4.
90. Wk 11f, 13, pp. 137–41, India Committee on Kraft's plan, 29 April 1915, in Chatto's hand.
91. FO 371/3069 (223290); 371/2495 (124971), Beckett to FO, 30 July 1915; 371/3423 (51442); 371/2495 (13663), General Ridout to FO, Singapore, 23 September 1915.
92. Wk 11f, 26, pp. 26, 39–41, Windels to AA, 4 and 5 January 1916.
93. Wk 11f, 26, p. 26, AA to Washington Embassy, 26 February 1916.
94. Kraft's last scheme was a propaganda plan costing $ 100,000. Wk 11f, 40, pp. 12–15, AA to Section Politics General Staff, 3 November 1917.
95. For Voretzsch's views on India, see N.K. Barooah, *India and the Official Germany 1886–1914, op. cit.*, pp. 111–18.
96. AA Siam 4, vol. 1, Remy's report, Berlin, 8 November 1917.
97. The other two Germans had to be left at Bangkok since they came as hunters to a place where hunting was prohibited on religious grounds and thereby made themselves suspects.
98. AA Siam 4, vol. 1, Remy to AA, Berlin, 8 November 1917. Betrifft: Die Kriegserklaerung Siams an Deutschland, pp. 108–20.
99. Wk 11f, 36, pp. 12–13, Knipping to AA, Peking, 6 October 1916.
100. Wk 11f, 35, pp. 3–7, Bernstorff to AA, 12 September 1916, enclosing Gupta's account of his work for the IC.
101. Wk 11f, 23, p. 180; *ibid.*, 24, p. 61.
102. Wk 11f, 24, pp. 109–11, IC to AA, 10 Jan, 1916.
103. *Ibid.* Wesendonk's and Zimmermann's approval, 10 January 1916. Also Wk 11f, 25, p. 45, AA to Washington, 4 February 1916.
104. Wk 11f, 33, p. 148, Bernstorff to AA, 30 August 1916; *ibid.*, 35, pp. 3–7, Bernstorff to AA, 12 September 1916.
105. Wk 11f, 10, p. 98, Bernstorff to AA, 2 March 1915, enclosing Gupta's message. It was alleged that Chakravarty was in love with one Mrs Waven, widow of an English officer and a suspected spy. But at that time, the IC, Berlin, considered Dr Chakravarty only 'rather eccentric in habit'; *ibid.* IC's resolution on Chakravarty of 6 March 1915; *ibid.*, p. 99. For Lajpat Rai's opinion of Chakravarty see Rai, *op. cit.*, pp. 217–18.
106. On 21 April 1916, the Times' New York correspondent reported that Papen's assistant Wolf von Igel's private house was searched by the US Justice Department, and 70 lbs of documents, including those about inciting revolution and acts of incendiarism in India and elsewhere, were confiscated. Count Bernstorff protested against the act claiming that since von Igel was an embassy official, his office was immune from the American justice system. The Times, 22 April 1916; Wk 11f, 27, p. 158, Wesendonk's note on 27 April warning Chakravarty and Harish Chandra.

107. Wk 11f, 27, pp. 144–5, IC to AA, 24 April 1916, and Wesendonk's comment thereto, 25 April 1916.
108. Wk 11f, 29, p. 69, Chakravarty's letter, 29 April 1916.
109. Wk 11f, 29, p. 44.
110. Wk 11f, 30, pp. 56–7, Chakravarty's report, 8 June 1916.
111. *Ibid.*, p. 58.
112. Wk 11f, 31, pp. 121–2, Chakravarty to IC, 4 September 1916. It is a little confusing because a month before, on 5 August, without a meeting with Ram Chandra, he had formed a committee consisting of Shrinivash Wagel, S.M. Pagar, R. Chandra, Leo Ling (a Chinese), a Burmese and two members from the Pacific Coast, Wk 11f, 34, pp. 221.
113. Wk 11f, 34, pp. 140–1.
114. Wk 11f, 34, pp. 157–8.
115. Wk 11f, 36, p. 168, Wesendonk underlined the last sentence and made a marginal comment: '*Wohl etwas optimistisch gesehen!*' [Seen rather optimistically!]
116. According to Wesendonk, $ 65,000 had been sent for Chakravarty until 15 December 1916, from which Bernstorff handed over to him in instalments $ 62,000. Wk 11f, 34, p. 16, Wesendonk's note. See also Wk 11f, 36, p. 138 for Bernstorff's account. At the beginning of March, Wesendonk sent $ 10,000 to Chakravarty through private channels. Wk 11f, 36, pp. 120–1.
117. Wk 11f, p. 139, copy of a letter (undated) from Chakravarty forwarded to Wesendonk by the IC on 11 December 1916. Emphasis added.
118. Wk 11f, 34, p. 159, IC to Wesendonk, 15 December 1916.
119. Wk 11f, 36, p. 83, Chakravarty to IC, 10 January 1917.
120. Wk 11f, 37, p. 130, IC. to AA, 19 April 1917, Wesendonk's note, 22 April 1917. About Tagore's reaction to the allegation, see Stephen Hay, 'Rabindranath Tagore in America', *American Quarterly*, 14 (3), 1962.
121. *Examiner*, San Francisco, 13 December 1917.
122. Wk 11f, 4, p. 104, Oppenheim to AA, 21 November 1914.
123. Rai, *op. cit.*, p. 204.
124. Wk 11f, 31, p. 110, Dutta to Tagore, 3 September 1916.
125. Seeing peace reigning in India, Viceroy Lord Hardinge released 18 regiments of cavalry, 71 and a half battalions of infantry and six artillery battalions for fighting on the Western front, Gallipoli, Mesopotamia, Egypt, and East Africa. Moreover, the Indian princes also contributed to the war with their armed forces.
126. One example is how Sir William Wiseman, the chief of British intelligence in the US, used underhand means and arranged for information about a bomb plot to be passed on to the New York police in order to get the house of Chakravarty searched. The papers seized from the house led to Chakravarty's arrest. See also Don Dignan, *The Indian Revolutionary Problem in British Diplomacy*, (New Delhi, 1983), p. 131.

Attempts at Revolutionizing India 99

127. AA Siam 4, vol. 1, Remy on German-Siam relations, Berlin, 8 November 1917.
128. Wk 11f, 40, p. 226, Chatto to Wesendonk, 14 December 1917.
129. C. Chakravarty, *New India, its Growth and Problems* (Calcutta, undated), pp. 25–6.
130. Wk 11f, 23, p. 116.
131. *Ibid.*, p. 116 d–e, Wesendonk's appreciation, 17 December 1915; IC to AA, 17 December 1915.
132. *Ibid.*, pp. 110–11, Zimmermann's approval, 18 December 1915.
133. Rai, *op.cit.*, pp. 215, 217.
134. Wk 11f, 27, pp. 68–72.
135. Wk 11f, 27, pp. 119–20, Wesendonk's note after meeting Harish Chandra in Montreux, 20 April 1916.
136. Wk 11f, 27, p. 74, Romberg to AA, Berne, 12 April 1916, Zimmermann's approval, 13 April 1916.

4

Internationalizing the Indian Question from Stockholm 1917–21

1. EXPERIENCE WITH THE SECOND INTERNATIONAL 1917

By the end of 1916, when all major ventures to provoke an unrest in India had failed miserably, largely due to aggressive countermeasures by the British, it became clear both to the German Foreign Office and the Berlin Indians themselves that no further plans for revolutionizing India could be undertaken. But it was impossible for the German government to abandon the India Committee for fear of denting its own image abroad. At a time when the prestige of the Committee was at a low and the activities of its members practically non-existent—except for infighting and mutual rivalry[1]—a heaven-sent opportunity made it possible for Chatto to make fresh endeavours in a new direction.

After the failure of the two anti-War socialist conferences in Switzerland—those of Zimmerwald (September 1915) and Kienthal (April 1916)—in which only a few groups participated and little unity was achieved, the Dutch-Scandinavian Socialist Committee, with the support of the International Socialist Bureau, the Zimmerwaldians, and the Petrograd Soviet, took the initiative to arrange an international socialist conference in Stockholm in May 1917 to give expression to their collective will for peace.[2] As the founder-leader of the Dutch Social

Democratic Labour Party, P.J. Troelstra, just before leaving Holland for Stockholm, said: 'A war serving imperialist purpose must be rejected.'[3]

Perceiving the possibility of shifting the propaganda part of the Berlin Committee's activity to a neutral country, Chatto was keen to take part in the Stockholm peace endeavours. The AA readily acceded to his request, just as it permitted various other nationality groups working closely with it, for instance, Egyptians, Persians, Irish, and various nationalities subjigated by the Russian Empire.[4]

Armed with propaganda literature of the Berlin Committee, particularly matter with critical comments on British rule in India by British socialists through the years, Chatto arrived in Stockholm on 13 May 1917, accompanied by M.P.T. Acharya, an old associate from the India House days.[5]

The city of Stockholm was, at that time, teeming with foreign political activists. Political refugees from Finland and Russia had already been active in radicalizing the Swedish Social Democratic Youth Movement. Now the secretariat of the Zimmerwald movement also moved there from Berne. Between April and May of 1917, many exiled Russian socialists of all shades, including Lenin, passed through Stockholm on the way to their homeland. Although, later in the year, compulsory passport and visa regulations were introduced, foreigners were still granted great freedom to engage in political activity.[6] No wonder that the two Indians found Stockholm most ideal for their work. 'There is not a single spy,' they wrote to their colleagues in Berlin, 'One can work here unhampered and the atmosphere for work is far more pleasant and agreeable than in Switzerland.'[7]

Chatto's first concern was to secure representation to the conference. As a rule, only socialist parties of individual countries were represented at a socialist conference, and he was told that if Indians were allowed to speak in previous international socialist congresses—as in the case of Madame Cama at the 1907 Stuttgart Congress—it was only as private individuals who had been introduced to the audience by English socialists like Hyndman and others. Chatto pleaded his case with various people responsible for the conference: Van Kol and Camille Huysmans of Belgium, who were also connected with the International Secretariat in Brussels; Peter J. Troelstra, one of the founders of the Dutch Democratic Labour Party; and Karl H. Branting and Gustav Moller, chairman and secretary, respectively, of the Swedish Social Democratic Party.[8]

Since it was almost a ritual for the European socialists to criticize the colonial expansion of European capitalist powers, especially British rule in India, the Stockholm Indians hoped they would succeed in persuading the organizers to grant them representation, enabling them to raise the question of Indian independence. In one of their brochures, they wrote: 'By reason of the very fundamental principle of socialism the Indian problem has a special interest for those who accept that creed. So long as the powers are permitted to continue in occupation and exploitation of vast territories inhabited by civilised people, there can be no world peace... India should be liberated from foreign domination and be able to enjoy the benefits of national government.'[9]

But whatever the pre-War anti-imperialist rhetoric of the European socialists, in 1917 the question of self-determination of the peoples of Asia and Africa was not seen by them as an obstacle to world peace. Not very long ago, some of these socialists had taken the view that European capitalism had a civilizing mission in the colonies, whose people were to be brought to the next higher phase of culture, from where socialism could take over the work of guidance.[10] Further, men like Branting could not be expected to offend the British government by permitting the Indians to internationalize the issue of their Independence. Branting was one of the key figures of the conference as it was through his mediation that British and French participation was expected. He had an excellent reputation with the Allied peoples and governments because of his strong opposition to German influence in Sweden and his belief that world democracy depended on the defeat of the Central Powers. As Moller told Chatto, if the British and French governments came to know of any possible propaganda against colonial rule, they might refuse passports to any socialists travelling from England and France.[11] Huysmans indicated another possible hurdle for the Indians: since they did not operate from any neutral country in Europe but from Berlin, they may be taken by some to be agents of the German government. Also, he added that even the socialists were wary of each other.[12]

Chatto's meeting with Huysmans gave him his earliest opportunity to justify the presence of the India Committee in Berlin, and rebutt the charge that the Indians were German agents. The Indians were in Berlin for the simple reason that it was a place 'where we could live most safely', he told Huysmans. He went on to say that, from his own experience, no neutral government was really neutral, that he had been expelled from Switzerland for having done less there in one year than he had done in Sweden in a week. Furthermore, he could not live in a neutral country because of attempts made by the British government to assassinate him. He also said that his colleagues were all arrested in the USA at the request of the British ambassador, and that finally 'we have our bones ready packed to be brought to the frontier any moment'. Such arguments worked, and thereafter Chatto found Huysmans sympathetic.[13]

Following his first encounter with the organizers of the Peace Congress, Chatto was able to extract some concessions from them. Moller arranged the printing of the Swedish translation of the 1910 *Manifesto of the Executive Council of the British Social-Democratic Party Regarding India* at Branting's press, and also undertook its circulation among the Swedish socialists through his office, although not before the arrival of the British delegation.[14]

However, what helped the Indian nationalists' presence felt in Stockholm was their close association with those delegates who were connected with the question of the nationality of the Finns, Poles, Hungarians, and some other national groups of the old Czarist Empire. Irakly G. Tsereteli, Georgian leader of the Russian Menshevik Party, whom Chatto called 'our friend', suggested that all these various nationalities join together to hold a separate conference of the oppressed nationalities and send a delegation to the congress.[15]

As done by the Finns, Chatto too declared at the outset that he was not so much concerned with peace propaganda as with the problem of Indian independence. While giving interviews to the foreign press, Chatto varied his tone and temper according to the purpose he wanted to achieve. For example, to the correspondent of a Budapest daily Chatto said, no doubt for the consumption of the AA, the following: 'In any case we judge war and peace in a different way than you. We believe that so long as England, the greatest robber of the world does not relinquish her colonies, there is not going to be a lasting and honest peace. That is why we do not want that Germany delivers back the territories conquered in the war so long as England, France, Russia and Italy are not forced to renounce their colonies.'[16] Similarly, his earliest contact with the famous Swedish pro-British daily *Dagens Nyheter* seems to have been a clever device for the purpose of establishing a distinct identity for the Indian nationalists. However, in order to avoid causing any offence to the AA, he wrote to his German colleagues that his connection with a paper which turned out to be not 'pro-German' was unfortunate.[17] Whatever the reason, the British minister in Stockholm, Sir Esmy Howard, was alerted by the declared mission of the Indians in Stockholm. Towards the end of May, he informed the British Foreign Office that the Indians were going to take part in a conference instigated by the Finns and various Russian nationalities. He warned them of the German hand behind the venture, which aimed at persuading 'Lenin or other anti-English Russian extremists to work for the Indian independence movement in Russia.'[18]

In the end, the Socialist Peace Conference did not take place. After various postponements from May until autumn, it was finally abandoned due to the non-arrival of the British and French socialists. With this, the question of Indian representation at the conference ceased to be an issue.

However, a series of preliminary negotiations had already taken place among the various delegates in Stockholm. It is clear that the Indians were represented like the other national groups.[19] The primary concern of the Indians was whether the Indian question would figure in the discussion of the principle of national self-determination. However, Chatto was mortified to find that the deliberations of the planners of the projected conference had failed to include the issue of subject nationalities. The German delegation had, indeed, before its return, included India, Ireland, Egypt, Korea, Tibet, Tripoli, and Morocco in their 'right of self-determination' plan[20], but this was not done on the basis of an anti-colonial stance.

As far as Chatto was concerned, he remained indefatigable throughout the episode of the abortive conference in his efforts to internationalize the Indian question. Worth quoting here is the testimony of a German diplomat, Baron Lucius von Stoedten, minister in Stockholm, who in his despatch to the AA concerning the Stockholm Peace Conference wrote: 'The Indian, Chatto, has not received much sympathy for his efforts from the Socialist Committee here. Despite this, he intends to put up an energetic campaign against England concerning the Indian question...Chatto gives the impression of being an energetic and skilful fighter for his cause, who would not give up even at the risk of his own life.'[21]

2. The First Indian Contact with the Bolsheviks 1917–18

His experience with international socialists at Stockholm seems to have made two things clear to Chatto: that the Berlin Indians had to have an office in Stockholm, and that a permanent contact should be established between them and other nationalities on the common platform of anti-imperialism.

As to the need of a permanent address in Sweden, Chatto wrote to his Berlin office—now managed by Bhupendra Nath Dutta—that having to continuously give a hotel address to people made an undesirable impression. Moreover, if Indian propaganda was to be effective, it must hide its German sponsorship: 'We lose by our propaganda being regarded as German intrigue.'[22] The AA did not oppose Chatto's proposal of establishing a branch in Stockholm. The branch opened on 7 July 1917 at Artillerigatan 28 B and was called the European Central Committee of Indian Nationalists, better known as Indian National Committee in Sweden. Financed by additional German grants, its aim, according to Chatto, was to issue regular communications to the press of all countries and send 'telegraphic contradiction of English lies'. [23]

Having attained his first objective, Chatto concentrated on the second: solidarity with other subject nationalities. The first international action of his new organization was to send a telegram on 4 September 1917 to the All Russian Muslim Council at Petrograd wishing success to their forthcoming United Muslim Congress in Kazan. Also voicing his disappointment with the Second International Socialists, the telegram ran:

By demanding from the Provisional Government of Free Russia to pursue a consistent and determined policy aiming at the recognition of equal rights and full national self-rule for the peoples of Europe as well as of Asia and Africa, the organisers had done much for the cause of mankind. It would, however, be wrong if in Russia one believed that Stockholm conference is taking up the cause of the peoples of the Orient...[24]

A great deal was expected from the new Russia of the time. In the telegram Chatto also wrote:

The solidarity of all Oriental peoples and the support of Free Russia which solemnly gave up imperialism of the Tsarist regime are bound to accelerate the process of a political renaissance of the Orient.[25]

However, it was the radical Bolsheviks, rather than the provisional government—an alliance of Mensheviks and social-revolutionaries, on whom Chatto seems to have pinned his hopes. This is discernible from another telegram sent in October on behalf of the Indian Committee to the Petrograd Soviet of Workers' and Soldiers' Deputies, dominated by the Bolshevik faction. The telegram read:

> Revolutionary Russia is striving for a durable peace on the basis of the people's right to self-determination. The instruction given to Mr Skobelov who was sent to Paris [economic Conference] does not, however, correspond to this striving as the fundamental questions of India, Egypt and Ireland were completely forgotten. The Indians, Egyptians and Irish people are convinced of their natural right to complete self-determination. The freedom movement among these peoples has developed to such an extent that lasting peace is impossible without a positive solution of their problem. In faithfulness to the ideas of the Russian Revolution and in view of the tremendous significance of a liberated India for Russia and for the whole world we ask the Workers' and Soldiers' Council to relentlessly and fearlessly fight the shameless and merciless British imperialism at the Paris Conference as well as at the peace negotiations.[26]

When this telegram was published in Maxim Gorky's *Novaya Zhizn*, a non-party newspaper close to the Russian Zimmerwaldians, the anti-Bolshevik *Rech* came out with an article entitled 'Stockholm Indians', pooh-poohing the latters' concern for all the suppressed peoples. The author of the article detected in the spirit, contents, and good Russian of the Indian telegram the influence of persons like Parvus, Grimm, Granetszky, Balabanoff, and Radek, who were then operating from Stockholm and whom the author found behaving like German agents.[27]

For Chatto, who later (in 1927) became 'the soul' of the Berlin head office of the League Against Imperialism[28], the concern for the subject peoples was certainly not disingenuous. But the article in the *Rech* was not wrong in assuming some connection between the Stockholm Indians and the Zimmerwaldians. As we will see below, Chatto had dealings with persons like Angelica Balabanoff, Ture Nerman, and Carl Lindhagam—all three members of the International Socialist Commission of the Zimmerwald Organization with its headquarters in Stockholm. Lindhagen and Balabanoff were also president and secretary, respectively, of the Third Zimmerwald conference that took place in Stockholm from 5 to 12 September 1917.[29] With Nerman and Lindhagen, Chatto even developed a personal friendship. The Left Zimmerwaldians' dislike of the 'socialist patriots' of the belligerent countries and, more importantly, the inclusion in their programme of a declaration of the political and economic independence of all colonies seem to have brought Chatto closer to them.

The Stockholm Indians' interest in the new Russia grew further when, in October, they met a Ukrainian Bolshevik, Konstantin Mikhailovich Troyanovsky, one of the earliest Russian propounders of spreading the revolution to the East, who informed Chatto and Acharya of the intense anti-British feeling in Russia, thus holding out good prospects for the success of anti-imperialist propaganda by India, Ireland, Egypt and Persia.[30] Troyanovsky believed that India in the East, like Russia in the West, was to serve as a vanguard of revolution, and of radical agrarian and other reforms; that Persia, Turkey, and Egypt were the gates to the Indian 'citadel'.[31] A few days before the October Revolution, Chatto received a draft project from Troyanovsky, to bring India and revolutionary Russia closer together.[32] In the theoretical part of the draft, Troyanovsky elaborated revolutionary Russia's automatic anti-imperialist commitment. As he explained, with the Russian Revolution 'an important link came off the imperialist chain.' Whereas autocratic Russia herself was a subject of foreign subjugation and exploitation, revolutionary Russia now wished to be neither a subject nor an object of West European (British and German) or Asian (Japanese) imperialism. But there lurked the danger of the new Russia herself becoming an object of imperialism in the near future. The financial dependence of Russia following the War might lead to her becoming a 'noble vassal' of Britain. Therefore, for revolutionary Russia, the struggle against imperialism—particularly British—was not a purely altruistic endeavour, but one born out of healthy national self-interest. The existing world situation demanded that Russian non-imperialism become anti-imperialism.[33]

Troyanovsky then suggested that Indians in their opposition to British imperialism could become a natural ally of revolutionary Russia. Being isolated, where should, he asked, Russia now seek her friends and comrades. He went on to argue that since the experience with European democracies before and during the War was disappointing, and the Second International had already broken down beyond repair, it would be in vain to look towards Western Europe. Hence a new orientation of Russian foreign policy was necessary with India and China as focal points.[34]

Since Troyanovsky, in the practical part of his draft project, underlined the importance of spreading knowledge of India in Russia, Chatto made an arrangement whereby with financial assistance, Troyanovsky agreed to publish periodically in the Russian press articles sent by the India Committee. He also promised to help establish contact between Chatto and important Bolshevik leaders.[35]

This interaction of the Stockholm Indians with a Russian extremist did not meet with objection from the AA. On the contrary, the Germans encouraged it, as it was in tune with their policy of the time to support extremist elements in Russia in order to conclude a separate peace with a government dependent upon German goodwill.[36] Wesendonk recommended the payment of 7000 kroners to Troyanovsky, as requested by Chatto, hoping that in this way, something might be achieved for the German cause through men who would otherwise avoid any contact with Germany or German agents.[37]

Things moved fast for the India Committee in this new Russian direction. On 8 November 1917, a day after the October Revolution, at Lenin's initiative, the Second All-Russian Soviet Congress issued a 'Decree on Peace' where, among other things, Allied Powers were condemned for not giving the Irish, the natives of the colonies, and India the right to decide their own political destinies.[38] Then, about a month later, on December 3, Lenin and Stalin made one of the most bitter attacks of the time on Britain in an appeal to the 'Moslems of the East', who were asked to overthrow from their native land 'the rapacious European plunderers', the 'robbers and enslavers', who had been trading there for centuries. The 'rising' of the 'oppressed' Indian Moslems was particularly singled out as an inspiring event for the Moslems of the East.[39]

Whether the Stockholm Indians were immediately aware of Lenin's passionate involvement in Indian matters is not known. But they were well updated in the daily press about the peace negotiations (December 1917–March 1918) at Brest Litovsk between Soviet Russia and the Central Powers. Point six of the Russian six-point formula, submitted on 22 December, insisted that self-determination be applied to the colonial areas and, in this respect, it was a change of the greatest magnitude from the Western programmes.[40] Then, on 29 December, in his third invitation to the Entente Powers, Trotsky, Foreign Commissar and leader of the Russian delegation at the Brest Litovsk negotiations, asked the Allied peoples and governments 'to found a peace upon the complete and unconditional recognition of the principle of self-determination for all peoples in all states giving this right to the oppressed peoples of their own states.'[41]

Particularly thrilling to the Indians in Stockholm and Berlin was the news of Trotsky's special mention of India at Brest Litovsk. Chatto, who had earlier appealed to the Russian delegation to take up the question of Indian independence, wrote to his colleagues in Berlin on 17 January 1918: 'Trotsky has already made his mind up about the Indian question as is not only shown by his two declarations on the question and his interview to the *Daily News* representative in Petrograd, but also is known to us from other sources.'[42]

The 'other sources' mentioned by Chatto must have been the latest communication from Troyanovsky, written from Petrograd on 21 December 1917, detailing his work concerning India ever since he left Stockholm.[43] In the middle of November 1917, he had submitted a memorandum on Indo-Russian Friendship (along with his draft constitution of the proposed Russian-Indian Society) to the Peoples Commissars, consisting of men like Lenin, Trotsky, and Lunacharsky. This was done through the last mentioned, Anatoly Vasilyevich Lunacharsky, an author, publicist, and educationist from Ukraine, whom Troyanovsky personally knew and who took an enthusiastic interest in the project. No wonder, within a few days, Troyanovsky saw Trotsky about the matter. In fact, he wrote the postscript of his letter to Chatto and Acharya while still sitting with Trotsky, the person responsible for giving permission to the Indians to travel to Russia. For other arrangements of the journey, Chatto was asked to contact V. Vorovsky, Bolshevik representative in Stockholm, who was to receive direct instructions from the Commissar of Foreign Affairs.[44]

Thus it is clear that Troyanovsky was behind Trotsky's utterances about India at Brest Litovsk. Chatto wrote to Wesendonk:

When Trotsky issued his proclamation to the Entente Powers and mentioned India, we felt sure that he had already been approached by our emissary. Our belief was confirmed by a letter received from him through Russian courier.[45]

Troyanovsky emphasized the overwhelming importance of Chatto or Acharya's visit to Petrograd, as a sign of a living bond between Russians and Indians. He even arranged accommodation for the Indian representative at the house where he and his wife were staying. Kurt Riezler, counsellor at the German Legation in Stockholm and running the newly-created Russian section, attached 'great significance' to Chatto's visit to Petrograd considering it 'very important for our Russian interest.' With a view to eventual collaboration with Russia, Chatto required an immediate policy discussion with Dayal; and Riezler recommended to Berlin that since a legal journey of Dayal had so far been difficult to arrange, secret means through the army political section be tried to send him to Stockholm.[46]

The formation and adoption of a distinct policy towards the Bolsheviks had become an urgent matter for the India Committee. In the winter of 1915–16, Dayal was debarred from active participation in the India Committee's activities because of his running battle with other leading members and subsequently his nervous breakdown. From then until the middle of November 1917, he recuperated in various sanatoria and guest houses. Early in November 1917, Chatto saw the prospect of some work for the India Committee in Stockholm. He, therefore, invited Dayal to patch up his differences with him in order to 'unite all our efforts and achieve something so long as there is yet time to do so.' It was thought that Dayal's earlier association with the Industrial Workers of the World in the USA and his connection with the international anarchists would be an asset in dealing with the Bolsheviks. Since Chatto wished to exploit the prestige of his name, he wanted Dayal to travel under his real name. But this made it difficult to obtain a Swedish visa, and Dayal remained in Vienna for nearly a year;[47] and when finally arrived in Stockholm in October 1918, it was not to work with the India Committee but to declare his dissociation from it.[48]

Meanwhile, the proposed Indo-Soviet collaboration was nipped in the bud because of a policy change of the AA towards the Indians. Soon after their arrival in Stockholm, the Indians, together with Irish, Ukranian, and Finnish nationalists, had been pressing the German government to declare their war aims and peace priorities and announce their support for the freedom of subject nationalities. In July 1917, Baron Lucius, head of the German diplomatic mission in Stockholm even recommended to the German Chancellor that some such 'semi-official statement' was desirable in view of the British propaganda efforts to appease the nationalists in Ukraine, Finland, and Estonia.[49]

On 30 November 1917, the India Committee from Berlin formally wrote to the German Chancellor that since the enemy and neutral countries had already been aware of German cooperation with Indian nationalists throughout the War, the German government should help the Indian cause through an official announcement of its support for the self-determination of the Indian people.[50] In the eyes of the India Committee, such an announcement was even more imperative following the Russian declaration on the subject of Indian independence at Brest Litovsk. It was evident that if the Germans failed to do at least as much as the Russians had done, Indo-German collaboration would certainly be seen as ridiculous. However, no such announcement came forth from the Germans. Instead, relieved of the war on the Eastern front, the German high command and the Colonial Office, in the middle of the Brest Litovsk negotiations, let loose their dream of 'a great African colonial empire...with naval bases on the coasts of the Atlantic and Indian Oceans.'[51] A recent British propaganda publication in Sweden, which included pre-War eulogies of the British Empire by German university professors[52], further fuelled Chatto's anger and he decided to go on the offensive. Consequently, he wrote to his colleagues in the middle of January 1918:

We have every reason to think that the Indian and allied questions have been completely given up by the German government as they have their own axe to grind in colonial politics. The only way in which the governments can be moved is by merciless exposure of all hyprocrisy in their political dealings.[53]

The language of Chatto's letter, coupled with the fact that he preferred to send such a confidential statement by ordinary mail and not through diplomatic channels, made Wesendonk suspicious of Chatto's motives. He observed that 'lack of an official German statement in favour of India, Egypt and Ireland together with certain press comments'[54] had obviously brought Chatto to the conclusion that the German government was heading towards a reconciliation with Britain at the expense of the Indians. He then concluded that, in his entire conviction,

Chatto is very close to maximalists. He will cooperate with Germany just as long as he thinks it advantageous for India. Now that he has seen that Trotsky has readily accepted his proposals concerning India, and has more than once mentioned the Indian question, according to his way of thinking, he will arrive at the very apparent conclusion that in the materialisation of the Bolshevist revolutionary ideas in the entire world, including Britain, lies the hope for India rather than in the nexus with Germany, which even shrinks from announcing officially her platonic interest in the Indian cause.[55]

Wesendonk, therefore, decided that Chatto's journey to Russia would be against the German interest. He also wished to prevent Dayal from going to Stockholm to see Chatto, for he feared that Chatto might find in Dayal, with his international anarchist connections, a powerful ally.[56]

At Wesendonk's instigation, the AA instructed their Stockholm legation that Chatto's journey to Russia was out of the question. But it cautioned great care in handling him. At the same time, it advised that Chatto be made to feel that Germany, as always, laid the greatest store by the Indian cause and that it fully appreciated his invaluable propaganda.[57]

As a result of Berlin's new policy towards the Indians, Riezler stopped further payment to Troyanovsky. Chatto, who had not revealed his financial dependence on Germany to Troyanovsky, was now in a compromising situation. Consequently, he made a bitter attack on the Germans. 'We are constrained to say,' he wrote to his Berlin colleagues, 'that this is one of those causes in which we are regarded as pawns in the German game to be used only in the moment of need.'[58]

Chatto assumed that it was a paragraph in Troyanovsky's 'Rules of the Russian Indian Society'[59], which had disturbed the AA most. Point six of these rules prohibited any Indian member of the Society from having any intimate and prolonged connection with the Central Powers, which still followed anti-democratic and imperialist aims.[60] Chatto, therefore, wrote to his Berlin colleagues:

It is true that Troyanovsky is an opponent of German imperialism. But that is really not the reason why he cannot work for the Indian cause and thus against England. Are we ourselves not against every form of imperialism? If nevertheless we work with the Germans and help them in any small matter where we can, it is because we feel that their victory will eventually be ours. We therefore think that it is an extremely short-sighted policy for the Germans to withhold support in a small matter even if it does not serve their immediate interests.

The despatch, clearly meant for German officials, ended with the following hard-hitting words:

As it is the German government which are fighting shy of the question of nationalities in general, as well as of India, in spite of the African colonies being flung in their face; and whatever statement are made, as for example, Dr Solf's are so provoking and humiliating to us that it is really a question whether the German government looks upon us as sincere patriots or merely as tools and pawns and temporary paid agents.[61]

The despatch finally convinced Wesendonk that Chatto's visit to Russia would not serve German interest at all; the AA, however, again advised their Stockholm officials to treat Chatto with the utmost tact, and assure him that Berlin considered the Indian nationalists thoroughly sincere patriots who would never be used as mere tools. But it had to be brought home to the Indians that in any political action, such as that concerning Russia, 'we can go only as far as German interest allows.'[62]

With the Brest Litovsk negotiations already going the German way, the AA wanted the Indian link with the Bolsheviks to cease as it had lost its importance to Berlin. Moreover, the Bolsheviks were very bitter at this time at what came to be known as the 'dictated peace'. As Wesendonk was convinced that Chatto had become a Bolshevik in his views,[63] it is easy to see why the Germans were anxious for the India Committee's connection with Russia to end.

But the fact of the matter is that it was not ideology which had attracted Chatto to Bolshevism. Far from being impressed by Marxian dialectics, Chatto had warned his colleagues, in March 1918, against even behaving like socialists: 'We should on no account follow the ostrich policy of believing that we are hoodwinking European political parties by pretending to be anything else but nationalists.' It is doubtful if he was anything but a revolutionary nationalist ever; although, as we will see, in later life, he tended to follow the communist line by force of circumstances. One of his close friends from the Stockholm days, the Finn Herman Gumerus, in his autobiography, portrayed Chatto as a burning anti-English nationalist.[64] Others like Professor Ture Arne, Ture Nerman, and Zato Hoglund considered that he had no political ideology but only a political goal, which was the independence of India.[65]

Thus, as a bourgeois nationalist and with German associations at that, Chatto had to literally walk the tightrope during the course of his meetings with the Bolsheviks and communists in Stockholm. The AA's objection was not the only reason for the failure of his intended visit to Petrograd. He mentioned two more to his Berlin colleagues: the uncertain position of the Bolsheviks in Russia, and the dilatory tactics of Vorovsky, Soviet representative in Stockholm, who was to arrange

114 Chatto

Chatto's journey. Chatto suspected that the dilatoriness was due to the influence of Angelica Balabanoff, who had, he said, been perpetually denouncing the India Committee for spending German money lavishly on brochures and so on. Chatto thought that Balabanoff, perhaps, frightened Vorovsky into believing that Indians might compromise the Bolsheviks.[66]

As neither Chatto nor his colleagues were sure of the positive results his visit to Soviet Russia would achieve, he seems to have decided not to estrange the India Committee's relations with the AA on the issue of the Russian connection. In his judgment, the odds were too heavily against fraternizing with the Bolsheviks. Moreover, as a recognized democratic leader, having the allegiance of his colleagues, he could not decide without consulting all the Committee members in Berlin. He therefore decided to concentrate on propaganda in neutral Sweden, opportunities for which were already available to him.

The situation in Sweden was ideal for the Indians for a variety of reasons. There was a fair amount of pro-German public sympathy. The chances of the imposition of arbitrary restrictions at the instance of the British government, as happened in Switzerland, were much less. There was also more possibility of communication with India through visiting Indians or other nationals. Communications with England and the USA were also easier, and contact with Russia was possible only from Sweden.[67] Moreover, in Stockholm, the members of the Indian Committee had already established close contacts with some other nationality groups. Finally, the Committee members could maintain links with people, like the Left-wing socialists, who had sympathy for Indian nationalism but were staunchly opposed to German imperialism. Thus, the German willingness to appease the Indian Committee through increased financial help suited Chatto, enabling him to expand his propaganda work to a new pitch of feverishness (which I will examine in the next section).

This section on Chatto's contacts with the Bolsheviks from Sweden during 1917–18 cannot be concluded without mentioning two 1918 publications by Troyanovsky in which India featured in a big way. In one of them, *Vostok i revoliutsiia: Popytka postroeniia novoi politicheskoi programmy dila tuzemnykh stran Vostoka—Indii, Persii, Kitaia* (The East and the Revolution: An outline of a new political programme for the countries of the East—India, Persia, China), Troyanovsky stated that India in the East could play the same role as Russia in the West in carrying forward the revolution.[68] In his vision India was to serve as a vanguard of revolution, and of radical agrarian and other reforms, and that Persia, Turkey, and Egypt would be the gates to the Indian citadel. For this to happen, according to him, the sparking of a revolution in Persia (by Russia) was indispensable. The Persian revolution would clear the way for revolution in India and China.[69] It is very possible that the Indian link in Troyanovsky's scheme was emboldened through his discussions with Chatto on the development of political agitations in India. It is interesting that later, on 5 August 1919, Trotsky regretted having devoted so little attention to Asia and asserted that the international situation was evidently shaping in such a way that 'the road to Paris and London lies via the towns of Afghanistan, the Punjab and Bengal.'[70]

Since his departure from Stockholm, Troyanovsky had also been working on the Indian portion of a selection of Tsarist diplomatic documents, the proposed publication of which Trotsky had announced on 22 November 1917. In June 1918, this Indian portion was published by the Peoples' Commissariat for Foreign Affairs in Moscow as the so-called 'Blue Book on India'. This 115-page volume under the editorship of Troyanovsky contained only a few telegrams and despatches written chiefly by M.M. Nabokov, the Russian consul general in Calcutta, his vice-consul, Lisovsky, and his successor Tomanovsky between 27 October 1913 and 17 February 1917.[71] There was nothing startling about these despatches relating to Tsarist Russia's relations with British India. The unmistakable purpose was, of course, to show the pro-British and anti-nationalist attitude of the officials of the then imperialist Russia, and to declare the future policy of the new people's Russia towards India. Significantly, the book's get-up and its 8-page introduction were such as to incite the people of India and Afghanistan against British imperialism and in favour the new Russia. On the flyleaf between the title and the introduction, there were three lines in large print:

"India for the Indians!"
"Down with the Imperialists!"
"Long live the International!"[72]

Troyanovsky, in his editorial, described the various exploitations of India by the cruel British imperialists and the yearning of the natives for liberation. Heavily influenced by the propaganda literature of the Berlin Committee, which he received from Chatto, Troyanovsky blamed the

British rule for India's periodic famines, the utter poverty of its masses, its militarism, and its financial ruin for having to support 100,000 English bureaucrats annually with about £14 million.[73] Troyanovsky also described the deprivation of the Indians of their country's civil services and the growth of a liberation movement in India against this oppressive foreign tyranny. To link the British determinatioin to hold on to India with all their might to the existing war, Troyanovsky said that the British brought about the World War to save their imperial holdings, specifically to check the German threat to India by way of the Turkish province of Mesopotamia.[74] As in his previous theorization on the Russo-Indian rapprochement, he again maintained that India in rebellion would be a natural ally of Russia:

...Our revolutionary path in the not distant future will bring forth joy, not only on the plane of the struggle for national liberation, but also on the broader principle of the class struggle and for the socialist order.[75]

Troyanovsky's introduction to the Blue Book provoked and enraged the British, especially when it also became known that preparations were in hand to translate the work into various European and Oriental languages.[76] The British consul general in Moscow considered Troyanovsky's introduction 'a malicious attack on British rule in India by a person who is obviously ignorant of the rudiments of the subject' and added further that it was 'the deliberate intention of the Bolsheviks...to raise against us in India, Afghanistan and elsewhere the ill-feeling of Moscow and to rouse Islam to such action as will benefit Germany.'[77]

3. CHATTO'S ANTI-BRITISH PROPAGANDA FROM STOCKHOLM 1917–21

I have already mentioned that, when Chatto left Berlin for Stockholm in the middle of May 1917, his ultimate aim was to shift the propaganda activities of his group to a neutral country while still enjoying German support and protection. Accordingly, after their arrival in Stockholm, Chatto and Acharya proceeded in a very determined and systematic way. They began by learning the Swedish language through private tuition,[78] and decided to equip themselves with a good, even lavish, reference library as soon as they found a place for their office. 'All books on India mentioned by you or in current publishers' lists are always ordered by us,' Chatto once wrote to his

Berlin colleagues.[79] Money was always in plenty, and, especially after the loss of the Russian link, the Germans were anxious to appease the Indian Committee by providing liberal finances.[80] The reference library, considered to be an 'unnecessary luxury' by a visiting emissary of the AA,[81] proved, however, to be of great help once the Indians began furnishing news and information about India to the press and other public men.

In his propaganda, Chatto endeavoured to project an independent image and whatever gain the Germans derived was an indirect one. Although the pro-German section of the Swedish press was generous in printing the Indian Committee's material, Chatto successfully remained in contact with other Swedish newspapers which had a different political bias. In fact, as mentioned earlier, the Indians' first announcement of their ensuing propaganda was published in the pro-English *Dagens Nyheter*[82] and Chatto himself was close to Left-wing socialists like Ture Nerman, editor of *Folkets Dagblad Politiken*, and his friend, Carl Lindhagen, Mayor of Stockholm. Moreover, Chatto ensured he was not seen at the German legation,[83] and kept suggesting to the AA to send money to him by means other than through its mission in Stockholm. The AA appreciated the significance of this request, but failed to discover an alternative method.[84]

The objective of Chatto's propaganda in Sweden was to internationalize the Indian question, that is, to equate the Indian independence issue with other burning problems of national self-determination then threatening world peace. This internationalization could be best achieved, Chatto seems to have thought, by giving wide publicity to the evils of British imperialism in India from authentic sources and by cooperating with other suppressed nationalities fighting imperialism. Accordingly, his propaganda covered the following aspects: (a) publishing brochures and pamphlets in Swedish and other major European languages containing criticism of British imperialism in India by prominent public men from Britain, India, and the USA, and getting them reviewed in the Swedish press; (b) issuing press releases expressing Indians' solidarity with other freedom-seeking nationalities and explaining or interpreting Indian issues; (c) contacting influential public men in order to interest them in Indian affairs; and (d) issuing public refutations of what Chatto called 'English lies' about India.[85]

Among the brochures of the Indian Committee, three were most significant, and constituted the nucleus of the whole propaganda. The first two were the so-called 'socialist brochures', introduced earlier, at the Socialist Peace Conference, though at that time only for private circulation. The first one, *Opinions of English Socialist Leaders on British Rule in India*[86] reproduced of H.M. Hyndman's 1910 *Manifesto of the Executive Council of the British Social Democratic Party regarding India* along with 24 excerpts from other published books or articles by Hyndman, J. Keir Hardie and J. Ramsay MacDonald. The second socialist brochure, *The International Socialist Congress: Speeches and Resolutions on India*[87] was a collection of the proceedings relating to India of four sessions of the Second International between 1900 and 1910. The third publication, *Some American Opinions on British Rule in India*[88], which was an answer to a British propaganda brochure of the same name, incorporated critical, and sometimes even scathing, views on the subject by many eminent Americans such as William Jennings Bryan, William Randolph Hearst, Senator Robert M. La Follette, Brooks Adams, William T. Harris, Rev. J.T. Sunderland, Mark Twain, and Andrew Carnegie. The crowning glory of the brochure was undoubtedly the 1906 indictment of 'British Rule in India' by W.J. Bryan, three times candidate for the American presidency and secretary of state from 1913 to 1915.

There were more brochures to follow such as *Roger Casement und Indien*[89]; *British Rule in India: Condemned by the British Themselves*[90]; *India and World Peace: Reflections on the Political Situation in India: How England Conquered India; India under British Rule (Illustrated); England's Perfidy in India: A Chronology of Broken Treaties and Wanton Confiscation;* and *India as the central factor in Asiatic question*.[91] In the early months of 1918, a book also appeared in Swedish about England and her suppressed peoples with special chapters on India, Ireland, and Egypt. The chapter on India was written by 'a member' of the Indian Committee. The declared aim of the book was to prove the genuineness or otherwise of Britain's war aims with examples from history.[92] Towards the end of the War, the Indian Committee also published another book in German about the freedom struggle of the Indian nationalists during 1906–17.[93]

All these works highlighted, in many different ways, the basic evils of British rule in India: extravagant militarism; crushing taxation; colossal drain of wealth from India to Britain in the name of 'Home Charges'; neglect of education; denial of higher office and civil liberty to Indians; and the 'perpetual, hopeless, grinding poverty' it brought to the Indian people. Select critical views of eminent, former British administrators in India such as Montgomery Martin, Thomas Monroe, William Digby, and Henry Cotton were used to substantiate the Indian nationalists' charges against Britain. As one brochure says it in its introduction, 'Even in perfidious Albion there have been some men in every decade...who have raised their voices in protest or confessed the truth otherwise.'[94] However, the most gripping accounts of British evils in India came from some leading politicians of England, India, and the USA. For example, in a chapter on extravagant British militarism in India in one of the brochures, Ramsay MacDonald was quoted:

On the whole, I think two charges can be substantiated against us. Our Government is extravagant, and we have behaved meanly to India. We charge the Indian tax-payer with the cost of the India Office in Whitehall—even with the cost of building it; we would never think of making such a charge against colonies; India has to pay for Aden—and for Imperial embassies in different parts of Asia; but the depth of meanness was surely touched when we tried to charge India with £ 7,000, the cost of the representatives and guests from India who took part in the coronation ceremonies of the late King.[95]

MacDonald found it ridiculous that as against this, only a little over £ 1.5 million were spent on education in India.[96]

The colossal drain of wealth from India to Britain was, of course, a recurring theme in the whole propaganda. But it was probably shown most effectively in a brochure detailing the whole atmosphere of an annual session of the Socialist International—that of Amsterdam in 1904—when it discussed the abuses of 'capitalistic colonial expansion'. Dadabhai Naoroji, then 80 years old, truly 'the grand Old Man of India', came to the dais and 'amid storms of applause and shouts of bravo' declared that 'the charge brought against England of sweating India is borne but by facts.' The propounder of the famous 'drain theory' then illustrated his point:

Of 200 million rupees which India pays in taxes, 100 millions go to pension British Officials who have served in India and who spend this money in other lands. All mines and the tremendous natural resources of the country are in the hands of the English. Two hundred million rupees a year are lost to India, they go to enrich the British capitalists and merchants. The result is that the sources of revenue are dwindling. Of the 200 million inhabitants at least one million, according to the official admission, are forced to hunger. The result is that pest and cholera rage...[97]

The brochure also reproduced the immediate reactions to Naoroji's speech. Hobson, of the Fabian Society, speaking after Naoroji said:

If one looks at the profits drawn by the English Government and the capitalist class from India one would be led to believe that India is the happiest and most prosperous land. But the millions and millions that flow from India to England are the fruits of unparalleled extortion and oppression of the natives...[98]

Van Kol, while presiding on the day's proceedings, then added, again with storms of applause: 'I hereby declare that the Congress of Amsterdam has branded England's criminal colonial policy in India with the brand of ineradicable shame!'[99]

The charge of British denial of civil liberty to the Indians came most forthrightly from the American William James Bryan and Hyndman, who, among the British socialists, was most vocal about the Indians' right to freedom. Hyndman accused the British government of arresting Indian patriots without charges and deporting them without trial; of outraging the right of defence by counsel; of suborning prejudiced witnesses; of putting down public meetings; and of suppressing the freedom of the press.[100] Even during the War, in October 1916, Hyndman asserted that 'an empire which declares that it is fighting a world war for the maintenance of national rights and national freedom cannot in decency keep one fifth of the human race in subjugation.'[101] Bryan, too, found nothing praiseworthy in the despotic British rule in India. 'Let no one cite India as an argument in defence of colonialism,' he remarked, adding that 'on the Ganges and the Indus the Briton has demonstrated, as many have before, man's inability to exercise with wisdom and justice, irresponsible power over helpless people.'[102]

Throughout the autumn of 1917 and the first half of 1918, a large number of Swedish newspapers of different political hues either reported about or quoted substantially from the major publications of the Indians. *Afton Bladet,* Sweden famous liberal organ (founded 1830), which remained generous to the Indian propaganda throughout, took the lead in introducing its readers to the critical publications of the Indians.[103] In early June 1918, the newspaper even published two extensive articles based on critical pre-War American and British views on India to be found in the Indian Committee's publications.[104] A large number of other Scandinavian papers publicized the Indian brochure and Chatto's other despatches relating to Indian events. Chatto was to write later: '...hardly a day passed without clearly revolutionary articles being read in at least some of the 50 to 60 papers to which we sent them.'[105] Some of these newspapers were: *Afton Tidningen, Appell, Folktes Dagblad Politiken, Goteborgs Aftonblad, Karlskrona Tidningen, Klockan, Nya Dagligt Allehanda, Spegeln, Stockholm Dagblad, Stockholm Tidningen,* and *Svenska Dagbladet.*[106]

With a variety of press releases issued from his office of the 'European Central Committee of the Indian Nationalists'—generally called 'Indian National Committee' in Sweden—Chatto tried to keep the issue of Indian independence alive in Sweden during the last two years of WWI. At the time of the Brest Litovsk negotiations, Trotsky's utterances about the small nationalities' right to self-determination and the Indian people's 'heroic struggle' for freedom were well-publicized.[107] Then Chatto managed to publish in the Swedish press Indians' solidarity exchanges with various nationality groups like Finns and Ukrainians.[108] Events like the annual session of the Indian National Congress in December 1917 and the British Labour Party in January 1918 provided opportunities to publicize the past, present, and possible future attitude of these organizations to British rule in India. In the case of the INC, the role of Annie Besant, the newly-appointed president and one of the leaders of the Home Rule movement, was stressed in transforming the Congress from a mere 'discussion club' into an organization of political activists handling the British rulers firmly. The non-communal character of the INC and the post-1916 ('Lucknow Pact') Hindu-Muslim unity were highlighted by the prominence of Mohamed Ali at the Calcutta session as a representative of the Muslim community.[109]

Two renowned Indians whom the Berlin Committee and their American Gadar associates had most earnestly, but unsuccessfully, tried to win over to their side during the most stirring period of their activity between 1914 and 1916 were poet-philosopher Rabindranath Tagore (who had become an internationial celebrity by winning the Nobel Prize for literature in 1913) and Lala Lajpat Rai, the ardent nationalist politician and publicist who lived in the USA throughout the War. The Berlin Indians had expected some pronouncement from the poet regarding the patriotic aspiration of the Indian youth involved in the freedom struggle.[110] Similarly, they had long been disappointed with Rai, who, in spite of being known as an 'extremist', failed to join hands with the Indian revolutionary nationalists in Berlin and the USA.[111] Now, however, selected statements of these two men on Indo-British relations were adroitly used by Chatto for his propaganda. In 1917, Tagore, in an essay called 'The great and the small', made a distinction, among other things, between 'the great' Britons of high character in their homeland and 'the little' Britons ruling India.[112] Pointing to the excessive brutality and arrogance of the latter while dealing with patriotic Bengali youth, Tagore said that since he had always denounced extremism among Indian patriots from the days of the *swadeshi* movement, he had the right to condemn with equal force the extremism in government policy as criminal.[113] He then extolled the unprecedented patriotic zeal of the youth of Bengal, who, for the sake of their country, discarded the path of opportunism and defied government oppression. He squarely blamed the policy of 'the little' Britons in handing over the youths of the country to extremists, revolutionaries, and the brutalities of the secret police.[114] Chatto prepared a report on this essay and, in the middle of February 1918, Tagore's thoughts could be read in some Swedish papers under the heading 'Nobel Prize holder Tagore about Britain in India.'[115] Here the poet was shown to be disillusioned with the then current trend in East-West relations, where the West showed interest only in dominance and exploitation, thus rendering the whole relationship unnatural and bringing it to an inevitable historic tragedy.[116] Tagore's concern about British despotism in India, which, on the one hand, had led the young educated Indians to violent opposition, and, on the other, created an atmosphere of mutual hatred between rulers and ruled, was a topic of interest for some Swedish papers. According to one report, Tagore wrote in grief to a literary friend in London that the only European sharing 'our sorrow' was Mrs Besant, for whom he expressed his greatest admiration.[117]

Since, in one respect, Chatto with his Indian Committee was working on the same lines as Rai with his India Home Rule League of America, that is, furnishing facts and reliable information about Indian affairs to the press[118], some of Rai's recent writings on India and British responsibilities there proved very handy to Chatto. Introducing Rai as 'one of the famous leaders of Indian nationalism who remained in America during the war and became the Indian representative to the League of Oppressed Peoples, founded lately in New York', Chatto distributed a brochure to the Swedish press incorporating Rai's recent views on British rule in India.[119] Here, once again, the poverty, illiteracy, unemployment, political and economic bondage, and defencelessness of the Indian people under the British were highlighted.[120]

The Home Rule movement in India since 1916, under the leadership of B.G. Tilak, Annie Besant, and Sir S. Subramania Aiyer, gave a new impetus to the Indian freedom struggle. It arose out of the growing restlessness and self-consciousness of the middle classes, therefore it was natural that the decisions and activities of the All-India Home Rule League found their place in the press releases of the Indian Committee. Besides the historical background of the Home Rule movement, about which the Stockholm Dagblad published a long article[121], the details of Indian resentment at the internment of Besant in 1917 because of her active part in the movement for Indian reform were also given. The controversy around the letter that Aiyer had written to President Wilson about British 'misrule' in India and the Indians' desire for self-government were made use of by the Indian Committee. The details of the controversy as expressed in British Parliament were reported in the Swedish press[122] as was the opinion of some leaders of the Home Rule movement that Indians be allowed to contest British Parliamentary seats.[123]

Many Indian political events, such as the general urge for reforms, including the demand of Indian women under the leadership of Annie Besant for equal rights and facilities in education and public life[124], the visit to India of Montague, British secretary of state for India, in connection with the ensuing constitutional reforms[125], the sensational conspiracy trial of Indian revolutionaries in the USA[126], and reports about the heroes of the Lahore Conspiracy Case[127], found their place in Swedish papers. At times, even items of pure cultural interest, such as the Swedish translation of Indo-Persian verses, were also not lacking.[128]

The fact that Stockholm was the venue of so many international gatherings during the period of Chatto's stay there enabled him to meet many influential people from Sweden and other countries. Mention has already been made of his contact with some of the leaders of the Socialist International and representatives of the newly-formed Soviet Union and of his fruitful relations with many newspaper editors. However, his contact with two Leftist socialists in Stockholm, Ture Nerman, editor of *Folkets Dagblad Politiken*, and Carl Lindhagen, Mayor of Stockholm, was of particular importance during the later part of his stay in Sweden, when the British not only began their counter-propaganda but also tried to influence the Swedish government against him.

I will discuss these two aspects in the next section, but here it might be interesting to point out Chatto's first public encounter with Nerman and Lindhagen.

In November 1917, a conference of suppressed Muslim nationalities which took place in Stockholm[129] was attended among other delegations from various Islamic countries by two Indian Muslims from Constantinople, Abdul Jabbar Kheiri and his brother Abdus Sattar. They were the representatives of their own organization, *Hemheq*, which they had recently established as parallel to what they called the 'Hindu Committee' in Berlin.[130] The Kheiris were considered religious fanatics both by the AA and the Indian Committee[131], and Chatto refused to join them at the conference, arguing that Indian Muslims were part of the same single struggle for national freedom. Lindhagen, who had been busy with the peace movement since 1916, helped organize this Muslim conference. On 7 November 1917, he also wrote an article in True Nerman's *Folkets Dagblad Politiken* on 'the suppressed Mohamedan tribes of India'—words which he probably borrowed from Jabbar Kheiri's speech or pamphlet at the conference.[132] Chatto wrote a rejoinder and asserted that the entire population of India and Burma, including 67 million Muslims and 248 million other Indians, with the Hindus in the majority, were all engaged in the same struggle for national freedom and self-rule based on safeguards for various religious groups, their laws, traditions, and culture.[133] Lindhagen agreed with Chatto that the diverse Indian groups were but one single people—a nation—but also drew his attention to the extensive diversity which beset the question of Indian nationality with peculiar difficulties. He emphasized his own preoccupations with the freedom of suppressed nationalities. He also referred to his efforts at the 1916 Peace Committee and to his motion in the Swedish Parliament in 1917, and suggested that a conference held exclusively on the Indian question would not be particularly helpful.[134]

There was, of course, no doubt about Lindhagen's devotion to the Indian issue. While engaged in peace work in 1916, a Berlin Committee member, Taraknath Das, met Lindhagen in Stockholm on his way to the USA, and accompanied him to Kristiania where Lindhagen organized a 'neutral conference' on peace and self-determination of the nations. Das, who maintained contact with Lindhagen until the middle of 1936, always remembered Lindhagen's understanding of the Oriental question, 'his genuine interest in India', and his 'superb courage of conviction'.[135]

Thus, Chatto's public sparring with Lindhagen only brought him closer to the Leftist socialist circle in Stockholm. In Lindhagen and Nerman, he found friends ready to fight for him and his cause. Like Das, Chatto too maintained his contact with Lindhagen long after his Stockholm days.[136]

4. BRITISH REACTION TO INDIAN PROPAGANDA IN SWEDEN

The Indian campaign in the Scandinavian press against British imperialism in India, from the autumn of 1917 to the summer of 1918, was extensive. Chatto was not at all exaggerating when, in June 1918, he wrote to Wesendonk that they had 'literally bombarded the press as well as the publicists and other influential people here with literature on India.'[137]

In the face of all this, the British government could hardly be expected to sit idle, especially when it had been particularly sensitive to what was being said about India in the neutral press. At the outbreak of the War, it primarily concerned itself with 'seditious' opinions expressed in the American and Dutch press. But from 1916, Sweden too came under its watchful eye due to a clash in the columns of the respectable *Dagens Nyheter* between Taraknath Das and Gilbert Murray, Regius professor of Greek at Oxford, then working for the British Secret Service.[138] In Stockholm for a short while in the summer that year, en route to the USA, Das came across some statements made by Murray about British India in that paper. He refuted Murray's assertions about the various achievements of the British in India and accused them of keeping the Indians deliberately illiterate. Besides, he regretted the narrow vision of the European statesmen in their search for a permanent peace and asserted that the whole European attitude towards Asia was a matter of shame for Christendom.[139]

Before Tarak's remarks reached Murray at Oxford, the British minister at Stockholm, Sir Esme Howard, took a serious view of them, and the British Foreign Office considered them very offensive.[140] Howard himself joined issue with Das and made a great effort to explain that, far from feeling oppressed, the Indians were happy making common cause with the British in the present war and were ready for even larger sacrifices.[141] From Oxford, Murray too sent a long reply maintaining once again that India was not ripe for self-government and that the allegation of British exploitation was a mere myth created by the Indians.[142] The controversy continued to rage. While Das accused the British of deliberately neglecting education in India, and called into question the loyalty of the Indians to the British Raj[143], Howard insisted that, except for a handful of anarchists, the whole of India was loyal to the British. He quoted both well-known and unknown Americans to prove that the British administration of India was a most successful political venture.[144]

By the time Das found himself in Stockholm, the British Foreign Office had already adopted a very aggressive attitude towards the Indian revolutionary nationalists abroad. So when Das left neutral Sweden, the British Foreign Office, thinking he might enter China on the Siberian Railway, advised the Russian government to arrest all Indians crossing either the Swedish or Rumanian frontier. An embarrassing episode occurred when Russia acted according to this British advice: a high-ranking official of the Indian postal service, one Frank Thomas Demoule, going to Russia to learn the language was arrested.[145] Das was saved only because he changed his plans and went to the USA first.

With this background of British reaction a year earlier, it is easy to imagine how sensitive the British government would be when Chatto and Acharya declared, immediately after their arrival in Stockholm in May 1917, that their mission in Sweden was to work for self-government in India.[146] Howard at once informed London that Chatto and his friend might take part in the 'nationality conference' which, according to rumours, was soon to be held.[147] The FO suggested to the India Office that 'as the Indians, who are reported to be going to Stockholm for nationality conference, are criminals who are wanted in India', their record sheets should be communicated to Mr Branting and other influential socialists.[148] The India Office drew up a list of six Berlin Indians likely to take part in the proposed Stockholm conference. However, they cautioned that none of them was at present a 'criminal wanted in India' though 'one of them has been convicted'.[149] While passing this to Howard, the FO regretted that the records of the Indians 'are scarcely calculated to prejudice against them.' It nevertheless advised Howard to make any use he could of the information, but instructed him, at the same time, not to give copies of the India Office records to anyone.[150]

It wasn't easy, however, for the British legation to get Chatto expelled from Sweden as long as the War continued. As Chatto revealed later, the German influence was considerable in Sweden during the War, and Swedish authorities, particularly the ministry of foreign affairs, paid special attention to the wishes of the German legation in Stockholm.[151] The British therefore had to either prevent or counter Indian propaganda in Sweden. In October 1916, the British Foreign Office had considered inducing neutral governments to prevent the publication and distribution of 'seditious' propaganda, and found that the convention concerned was the Rome Postal Convention of 26 May 1906. According to this convention, there was a ban on the dissemination of propaganda material by mail.[152] In this case, propaganda material did not enter Sweden from outside. It was propaganda in the Swedish press, produced by the Indian Committee. Hence the British decided to carry out a counter-propaganda, and keep a strict eye on the movements of Chatto and his foreign friends such as Dr Hermann Gumerus, head of the Finnish Committee in Stockholm.[153]

The India Office used the services of 'a distinguished Scandinavian scholar', W. Archer.[154] But in view of the energetic press campaign of the Indians, Egyptians, and the Sinn Feiners, the FO took up the suggestion of its legation in Stockholm in January 1918, and decided to send natives of India, Egypt, and Ireland to the Scandinavian countries. The Indian chosen for the purpose was a retired Indian civil servant, A. Yusuf Ali, then a lecturer in Hindustani at the London School of Oriental Studies.[155]

Ali was at once ready to go to Scandinavian countries provided an adequate honorarium and hotel expenses were paid.[156] A man of moderate political opinion with 'a warm appreciation of the British empire'[157], Ali was satisfied with the piecemeal reforms of the British in India. In April 1917, a mere invitation by Austin Chamberlain, secretary of state for India in the War Cabinet, to three delegates from India to advise him, prompted Ali to write an article in the *Manchester Guardian* entitled 'India in the Empire Council: A Symbol and its Future Meaning'. He regarded it as the first instalment of reforms which would culminate one day in dominion status for India.[158] In Ali's view, the two issues which concerned India directly were the Mesopotamian question and German East Africa. He believed that any solution to the first problem was bound to be unsatisfactory if it failed to take into account the wishes of 'our 66 and half million Mohamedan fellow subjects in India'. Similarly, the large Indian population in East Africa entitled India to a voice in the settlement of that part of Africa.[159]

Towards the end of April 1918, Ali arrived in Stockholm. In an interview to the *Stockholm Tidningen*, he alleged that all Indian political organizations, save a handful of anarchists, were loyal to Britain, the 'mother country'; that India had willingly contributed £ 100 million to the British war effort; and that the Indians had voluntarily joined the army in great numbers.[160] On May 3, in a lecture on the 'peoples of India', Ali extolled the virtues of British rule in India under which great advances were made in the political, intellectual, and economic fields.[161]

Chatto and Acharya suspected from the outset that Ali was a British agent.[162] The aggressive reaction of a British audience to the distribution of some handbills by the Indian Committee positively confirmed their suspicion.[163] The confrontation with Ali led to the intensification of the anti-British campaign.

Chatto made a virulent attack on Ali. He scoffed at the so-called voluntary contribution to the British war expenditure, and pointed out that since the Viceroy's Executive Council had only one Indian member, the manipulated result was a forgone conclusion. He quoted Madan Mohan Malaviya, a member of the Legislative Council, in saying that the Indian financial contribution meant a yearly increase of six million pounds in tax for 30 years for the miserably poor Indian population who would continue to be deprived of school education, agriculture, and industry.[164] It was not loyalty to the British but sheer poverty and downright necessity to escape hunger and starvation that had driven the Indians to join the army. In fact, it was a scar on civilization that 300,000 ignorant, innocent Indian soldiers had to fight in France, Egypt, Mesopotamia, Arabia, Persia, and Africa and sacrifice themselves for the imperialist aims of Britain, Chatto added.[165]

Perhaps the most interesting part of Chatto's rejoinder was his view on Indian political organizations. He commented that there were only three parties in India: a small minority of cowards and job hunters, ever ready to sell themselves and their country for some small personal gain; the moderate nationalists belonging to the Indian National Congress and the Muslim League; and the revolutionary nationalists. All political developments in India were the result of the activities of the moderates and revolutionaries. He abhorred the word 'anarchist' for the Indian revolutionary nationalist.[166] The moderates were gradually increasing their demands, and some of them had gone so far as to declare that

Home Rule could not be achieved without agitation. The revolutionaries, on the other hand, were working openly as well as secretly to overthrow British rule through an organized and armed insurrection. They believed in the possibility of awakening the 'European conscience' through involvement in international politics. It was because of the activities of the revolutionaries since 1905 that the fortunes of the moderates had improved. He declared that it would be an insult to call the moderates 'loyal' to the British. The moderates were mere opportunists, and took a moderate line because they believed that there was no possibility of escape from the British stranglehold in the immediate future.[167]

Ali's retort was to make a frontal attack on the writings of the Indian Committee in the *Afton Tidningen*. He observed that the Indian Committee had merely consisted of two anarchists, that they had no national base whatsoever, and that their operations had been sustained entirely by foreign finances and guidance.[168] He eulogized British rule unreservedly, and gave the impression of speaking on behalf of both the INC and the Muslim League whose loyalty to the British rulers was unquestionable.[169] After a private meeting with Ali, Chatto and Acharya reflected that it was 'quite hopeless and disgusting' to argue with Ali, who even 'spoke Hindustani with an English accent and believes that English should be the language of India.'[170]

The Times immediately carried a Reuters report on what had appeared in *Afton Tidningen* about Professor Yusuf Ali's demasking of 'the bogus Indian Committee' of two anarchists who 'can in no way be regarded as nationalists as they neither represent India nor are they in touch with that country.'[171]

Chatto and Acharya sensed that the times were changing for them in Sweden with a change in the course of the war in favour of the Entente. The pro-German conservative government had to make way for the pro-Entente liberal-social-democratic coalition, and, in May 1918, some commercial agreements were also concluded with Great Britain and the USA. The pro-British attitude of two Swedish dailies was only the first signal of this change.[172] The *Afton Tidningen* even refused, at first, to publish Chatto's reply to Ali on the ground that it was replete with 'abusive epithets'. Later, however, it did publish a revised version, but, by that time, Ali had left Stockholm.[173] It also published a protest letter, signed by one Mohamed Ali, criticizing Ali for his loyalty theory and for generally painting British rule in glorious colours.[174] Another paper, *Stockholm Tidningen*, for its part, published only a gist of Chatto's reply in two columns, in what Chatto called 'a mutilated form'.[175] No wonder that the British legation in Stockholm took comfort in that Chatto's reply 'was only published in extenso in one paper the *Afton Tidningen* of May 29, in extremely small print and with no headlines.'[176]

In this reply Chatto declared that the Indian Committee in Stockholm was a revolutionary body, similar to the Irish Sinn Fein, striving for the independence of India. The Indian revolutionaries were not anarchists but nationalists and 'every Indian who believes that the English dominion in India is an oppressive and unjust regime of foreign exploitation which must be put an end to, is a nationalist.' To counter the impression given by Ali of the Indian revolutionary party as insignificant, Chatto pointed out that 'one of England's aims in involving America, Siam and China in the war was to crush our revolutionary organisations, which have accomplished so much for their country during the last ten years.'[177]

Chatto then tackled the question of foreign funds and guidance. He decided to be open about the matter[178] and declared that:

This insinuation has so often been made, not only against us but also against the Sinn Feiners, Finns, Ukrainians and even against the Russian Bolsheviks, that we consider it may be of general interest to touch upon the matter. In the present war there are not only two belligerent camps, but also two corresponding camps of oppressed and subject nationalists. Owing to an entirely national natural combination of circumstances, the oppressed nationalities of the Entente desire the defeat of their oppressors, while the nationalities oppressed by the Central Powers desire the victory of the Entente. We hold that the interests of all oppressed nationalities are identical, and it is our personal opinion that there is no prospect of world peace until not only aggressive imperialism has been crushed but also the power of the capitalist and militarist classes has been broken. But under present conditions and for the moment we Indians have only one fight to fight and that is the fight for our national liberty. For this purpose we are—we mention in passing—ready to receive, and fully justified in receiving, help in any form from any government, belligerent or neutral, from any political or private organisation or individual, for the greater humanitarian work of freeing a fifth of humanity from the British yoke...Lovers of freedom of English, American, German, French, Russian and other nationalities have for many years supported our movement in various ways, and during this war we cooperate, like the Sinn Feiners and the Egyptian nationalists openly and intentionally with the enemies of England.[179]

In the last part of his reply, Chatto remarked: 'In spite of his excellent English and his pride in being a worthy citizen of that Empire, Mr Yusuf Ali must change the colour of his skin before he can be an equal of his British rulers.'[180]

Chatto's open confession of working together with the enemies of England was a valuable instrument in the hands of the British to put pressure on the Swedish government for an eventual action against the Stockholm Indians. To this extent—as rightly observed by the FO—Ali's counter-propaganda was a 'most useful piece of work'.[181] However, it is interesting to note that, although both the FO and the India Office were willing to give Ali an official letter of thanks for his services, neither office could agree as to who should sign such a letter. What is more, even the files concerning the matter were lost before any decision was made.[182] This embarrassing incident added a prophetic note to the closing remarks of Chatto's reply.

There was no immediate action against Chatto as the British would have wished. In early June, as if to give a boost to Indian propaganda in the changing situation, the *Aftonbladet*, which the British considered 'violently pro-German'[183], published two editorials on British rule in India.[184] In one, based on the Indian Committee's brochure on American opinions, the paper sharply criticized President Wilson for going back on his principle of national self-determination, particularly in the case of Ireland and India and urged the American administration to favour the Indian cause for freedom.[185] The second editorial, based on another brochure of the Committee, contained some pre-War views of British socialists. While giving the socialist movement credit for making the British policy of exploitation in India better-known in Europe, the paper wondered why the socialists in general and the Swedish 'neutral' socialists in particular should now ignore the principle of self-determination of nations, and show open sympathy for British political interests everywhere.[186]

The editorial went on to ask if it was not a flagrant violation of the principle of self-determination that the Irish struggle for freedom and democracy was described as a lawless uprising and the Indian cause found so little sympathy among the socialists.[187]

The British decided to reactivate the pro-British section of the Swedish press. Thus, on the heels of the second editorial of the *Aftonbladet*, there appeared an article in the *Svenska Morgonbladet* entitled 'England's Greatest Cultural Feat'.[188] The author, J.M. Ollen, was one of the paper's editors. He made no secret of his opposition to the Indian Committee and the *Aftonbladet*. He failed to understand why Indian revolutionaries should make propaganda for Indian independence in Sweden and why the Swedish public should be bombarded with one-sided information about India. He considered British rule in India 'a treasure house of European culture'. 'The English officials,' he said, 'are born to be leaders. Human, upright, dutiful, incorruptible, they have not only won the respect but also the confidence of the people.' He concluded that England had too much respect for enlightenment, higher education, progress, and human rights and dignity to withhold progress in India.[189]

Ollen's criticism of the Indian Committee did not go unchallenged. A fortnight later, the *Svenska Morgonbladet* published a long rejoinder in which Chatto answered Ollen's criticism point by point. He explained why the Indians were active in Sweden, and how Sweden could help India.[190] If Swedish businessmen were interested in Indian trade and commerce and the Swedish missionaries in converting the Indian people to Christianity, why should the general Swedish public remain ignorant of the actual political and economic situation of India?[191] Sweden was important to the Indians because it was a significant neutral country, free from the imperialist mania of the big powers, willing to hear the voice of suppressed nationalities and destined to play its role in the coming peace negotiations.[192]

Since Ollen tried to see a connection between the *Aftonbladet's* general pro-German views and its support of the Indian campaign, Chatto explained that the Indian Committee's propaganda was not in favour of Germany. The Indians were merely making use of the opportunity offered by the imperialists themselves. He expounded his argument thus:

Presently the imperialist powers are divided into two hostile camps and the nationalities who are suppressed by these powers naturally make use of the differences among the suppressors to obtain political advantages for themselves...It is also quite natural that each of the imperialist groups tries to make use of the suppressed nationalities for their own political propaganda.[193]

It was because of the mechanics of imperialism itself that, while, on the one hand, the pro-German publicists had embraced the cause of the Indian, Irish and Egyptian liberation, the Anglo-Saxons, on the other, had with equal enthusiasm stood up for the independence of Poland,

Bohemia, and Armenia.[194] In these circumstances, the nationalists had to adopt the slogan of '*divide et libera*' in order to counter the imperialist dictum of '*divide et impera*'. Chatto therefore argued that it was 'neither fair nor honourable, nor is it a proof of sound reasoning to suspect the patriots of any of these countries of working in the interest of the parties to the war. It is certainly not our fault if Germany takes advantage of our propaganda.'[195]

Before Chatto's reply was published in the *Svenska Morgonbladet*, Ollen's article had been reprinted by the *Social Demokraten*, the organ of the Swedish Democratic Party, with a subheading: 'A light on the so-called Indian Committee'.[196] Since the paper failed to immediately publish a rejoinder from Chatto, he had it published in *Aftonbladet* although it was addressed to the *Social Demokraten*.[197]

Obviously Karl Hjalmar Branting (1860–1925), leader of the Swedish majority Social Democrats and editor of *Social Demokraten*, went against the Indian Committee because of *Aftonbladet*'s attack on him by name in an earlier article on India.[198] The constant British pressure on him to take some action against the Stockholm Indians might have also played a role. Further, in *Aftonbladet*'s attack on the Swedish majority socialists, Branting, perhaps, saw the hand of the young Swedish Left-wing Socialists—men like Lindhagen and Nerman —with whom Chatto was associated. It must be remembered that the triumph of the Bolsheviks in Russia had raised the prestige of the revolutionary Left wing among the European socialists and further diminished chances of the revival of the Second International, in which Branting and his colleagues were then engaged.[199]

Whatever Branting's real motive, Ollen's article only added fuel to the Indian Committee's propaganda. Chatto jeered at the eulogy of British imperialism by the Swedish majority socialists. He wrote:

Whereas the English anti-German socialist patriots such as Hyndman, who even during this war characterised British rule in India as despotic and which must be crushed, the main organ of the Swedish Social Democrats makes propaganda for British imperialism...It is really tragic for the Social Democracy that the organ which should have been at the vanguard of the Indian people's fight against British oppression and exploitation, has decided to follow the same chauvinistic principles and methods as those of the *Daily Mail* and the *Daily Express*.[200]

Chatto attacked Branting and his colleagues for trying to see a sinister link between the pro-German *Aftonbladet* and the Stockholm

Indian Committee. The Committee, he said, had nothing to do with party politics either in Sweden or anywhere else; it was not the fault of the Indians that, instead of the Liberal and socialist press, it was the Conservative press which had taken up the cause of India, Egypt and Ireland.[201] And why should a couple of leading articles in *Aftonbladet*, based on the Indian Committee's brochures upset *Social Demokraten* anyway? Chatto also pointed out that one of the articles was based on a brochure of the Indian Committee, which had first been printed and distributed through the good offices of Branting himself in the autumn of 1917.[202] He therefore commented sarcastically: 'The fact that mere appearance of a few articles in *Aftonbladet* containing certain truths about India caused the Social Democrats immediately to take up a diametrically opposite attitude is a typical proof of their shattered inner balance brought about by the war.'[203]

He had already indicated to Helmut von Glasenapp, AA emissary who had gone to Stockholm to discuss with Chatto the impending dissolution of the Berlin Indian Committee, that he would stay in Stockholm. He regarded it as an ideal place for obtaining information from England and the USA and influencing Russia.[204] Freed from the restrictions imposed by the exigencies of German foreign policy, Chatto hoped to renew his earlier contacts with the Bolsheviks, albeit quietly. But this only served to bring him under stricter British surveillance.

In order to disguise his political activity, Chatto published a notice in the *Stockholm Tidningen* announcing he would give a series of lectures on Hindustani at the Borgarskole school if a sufficient number of students were available. At the instigation of the British chargé d'affaires, the Swedish minister for home affairs decided that these lectures be kept under close observation lest their character turn out to be different from the one notified.[205]

The Hindustani course came to an end after only a short duration. In March 1919, Chatto obtained a permit to stay from the Swedish police[206] which, however, placed an automatic prohibition on his propaganda activities. In June, the Swiss government condemned Chatto *in contumacism* to a fine of 1000 Francs and two and a half years of imprisonment for his alleged involvement in an anarchist plot said to have taken place in Switzerland in July 1915. He was also forbidden for all time to enter Switzerland.[207] Convinced that the Swedish authorities would, as a result, deport Chatto or he might leave of his own accord, the FO asked its Stockholm mission to find out the name of Chatto's vessel in the event of his deportation.[208] Sir Coleridge Kennard, the British chargé d'affaires, was, however, told by Swedish authorities that although Chatto would be carefully watched by the Swedish police there was no question of his being deported for the time being. But they agreed to keep him informed of Chatto's whereabouts at weekly intervals.[209]

The British were presumably unaware of Swedish extradition and deportation acts, developed during 1910–13, according to which 'extradition should be refused in regard not only to crimes, which were political, but also to crimes concurrently constituting an offence, for example, against persons and property, but which overwhelmingly had the character of a political offence.'[210]

These judicial protections made Chatto free to lay bare the facts concerning the 1919 Swiss sentence against him. He did not deny having taken part in a plot in 1915, and even confessed that he had two conversations with one of the convicted, the Italian Communist Luigi Bertoni. He, however, denied being in Switzerland in July 1915 and conspiring against the country, insisting he left Switzerland in June that year.[211]

German records substantiate Chatto's account, and also give more information about his role in the plot. While in Switzerland in June that year, Chatto—perhaps at the suggestion of some Italian anarchists—formulated a plan to assassinate some prominent Europeans and destroy the properties of some others in Italy, Athens, and in two Balkan capitals, Sophia and Bucharest. Persons to be killed in the Balkan cities included Fitzmaurice of the British legation in Sophia and Valentine Chirol, foreign editor of *The Times*, then travelling in the Balkan states as an emissary of the British government.[212] An entirely individual venture, the plan was unconnected with the Indian Committee's programme, and was disapproved vehemently from the outset by German diplomats in Constantinople, Sophia, and Berne (but connived at by Wesendonk in Berlin). The plan is not known to have ever been translated into action in any of its details. And if one is to judge by the way it panned out in the Balkans, the part which Chatto undertook to supervise himself and about which he has left an elaborate account, it was a hopeless, amateurish adventure of untried men which produced no results. In September Berlin asked Chatto to call it off.[213]

The fact, however, remains that with the help of the AA and the

German general staff, Chatto and Dr Abdul Hafiz, his technical accomplice in Switzerland, acquired a sufficient quantity of time bombs, hand grenades, and other weapons and chemicals needed for the undertaking. It was this aspect of the matter that bothered the experienced German diplomats who were asked to provide necessary help.[214] Baron von Romberg, head of the German mission in Berne, was particularly worried about German reputation being in danger in neutral Switzerland. He believed that, as the Swiss secret police was not well-organized, Hafiz and his associates would go unnoticed for a time, but would face greater danger from the enemies of Germany who had a widespread espionage system in Switzerland, and who would not refrain from using any means available to them.[215]

Romberg was absolutely right. When, in 1919, the Swiss government found Chatto and two of his associates guilty in a trial, the hand of the British secret service was clearly discernible. In fact the chief prosecution witness, Edvard Briess, admitted in court that he was a British spy, employed at the British consulate in Zurich to spy on Indian revolutionary nationalists.[216]

Romberg was also correct in observing that the enemy would employ any means to achieve its end. This is illustrated by an episode in December 1915 when Chatto's life was in danger at the hands of a British secret service agent, Donald Gullick. The incident is not known in all its details yet. But it had no connection with Chatto's Balkan plan. It involved his relations with an interned English lady. In early May 1915, Miss Hilda Margaret Howsin of Reedness Manor, Yorkshire, who had known Chatto in London during 1907, came to meet him in Montreux.[217] When she returned to London, she took back a message from an Indian friend of Chatto's (most probably Dayal) to a woman in a tuberculosis sanatorium in England, and was arrested on the order of the home secretary under the Defence of the Realm Regulations and placed in an internment camp at Aylesbury. She was charged with having hostile association, and was told that the lady who had sent her the message to come to Switzerland was a spy and implicated in an assassination plot.[218] Thereafter, Gullick came to Switzerland in October and invited Chatto to Zurich. He pretended to be engaged in efforts for the release of Howsin. He feigned great friendship for Chatto, but his real motive was either to lure him to the French or Italian border or to kill him.[219] Gullick, however, drew the attentions of the French police through his telegrams and was, as a result, followed, and subsequently arrested by Swiss police in Zurich on 18 November along with Chatto. Until early December, Chatto was kept in military custody in Berne. Since there was no case against him, it was expected he would be set free unconditionally. But due to his admission to the public prosecutor that he headed an anti-British Indian revolutionary organization, he was 'secretly' deported for violating 'Swiss neutrality'.[220] The Germans were convinced that there was a clear case of court-martial for Gullick, but due to British pressure, he was only deported on the charge of 'illicit political activity.'[221]

About the same time that Gullick was charing Chatto in Switzerland, W. Somerset Maugham, the famous English novelist, then enlisted in the British Secret Service, was also there observing the movements of the Khedive and many other Orientals.[222] Maugham too observed Chatto, and his short story 'Giulia Lazzari' is based on the above-mentioned British plot to capture Chatto (Chandra Lal in Maugham's story), dead or alive, by enticing him to cross the border between Switzerland and France during the war to meet the woman he loved. Maugham appears in the story as Ashenden, and is told by his chief that Chandra Lal from Berlin 'is the most dangerous conspirator in or out of India' and that 'he's done more harm than all the rest of them put together.' The ending of Maugham's story does not entirely tally with the end of Chatto's life, but, as Nambiar noted, in their love for women and their countries, the two characters meet.[223] However, inspite of such extensive involvement, the British Secret Service in Switzerland does not seem to have known about Chatto's deportation in 1915. If this were not so, the British Foreign Office and the India Office would not have regretted in 1917 that they were unable to place before the Swedish government any records which could strengthen the case against Chatto.

After the 1919 Swiss trial, Chatto became more cautious in his political activity.[224] In order to highlight non-political preoccupations, he started a commercial import-export venture and also established a translation bureau together with some Swedish friends. Early in 1920, he also started to transmit non-controversial Indian news to the Swedish press.[225] It was only in May 1920 that he gave the Swedish police their first occasion to complain. In that month, on the occasion of the 63rd anniversary of India's 'First War of Independence' (1857), a full-page unsigned article appeared in the *Folkets Dagblad Politiken* under the heading 'Bloody, Violent Policy of Great Britain in India' with photographs of the notorious Amritsar massacre of 1919. When asked by the police, Chatto admitted the authorship of the article and was consequently warned not to indulge in further political propaganda.[226]

The Swedish police seem to have also suspected vaguely that Chatto had secret connections with the Bolsheviks in late 1920. One secret entry in the records of the Immigration Office in 1921 mentions the visit to Stockholm in early October of a sailing boat from Lapland called *Martha* with 30 communist sailors and propaganda literature on board and its return to St Petersburg on 29 December with Chatto and Joffe as passengers.[227] The Swedish customs, however, could not confirm whether *Martha* actually visited Stockholm, but the probability was not ruled out.[228]

So far as the report concerned Chatto, it seems to have been a later reconstruction. Although it is not clear what means of transport Chatto used to get to Moscow, he had evidently obtained a return visa from the passport department of the Swedish Foreign Office.[229] The purpose of his visit was given as his trade and commercial engagements at Reval. But there is no doubt that his real purpose was to take preliminary action to organize a conference on India in the summer of 1921.[230]

One more time, in early January 1921, Chatto received a return visa from the Swedish Foreign Office to visit Germany. What is more, according to Chatto, this visa was sent to him in Germany as, due to the short notice, Swedish authorities had been inable to issue it at the time of his departure.[231] The same year in March, Chatto again left Sweden for Berlin but without a return visa. When he applied for it from Berlin, Swedish authorities refused even when he pleaded he needed it only for a short while so as to bring his activities in Sweden to an orderly close.[232] Carl Lindhagen, the Left-wing mayor of Stockholm and a member of the Swedish Parliament[233], considered this refusal an example of the Swedish government's subservience to Britain.

The issue became the subject of an interpellation in the *Riksdag* (Swedish Parliament). On 31 May 1921, after making a detailed statement quoting Chatto, Lindhagen put a four-pronged question to the Prime Minister:

(1) Why has the right of sanctuary for law and justice, which was maintained by the Ministry of Foreign Affairs during the war, been considered more or less incompatible with the true interests of our country after the conclusion of peace and after our joining the League of Nations?

(2) Why is a foreigner no longer, as before, allowed to advocate the right of self-determination of nationalities, and can we expect a change in this attitude to foreign policy?

(3) Is it diplomatic practice that a political refugee, whom the authorities cannot reasonably expel, is, at times, provided with an opportunity to make a short excursion over the border and is then, unexpectedly, refused a visa for the return trip, contrary to what he reasonably expects or to the promises held out to him?

(4) Is there any reason to hope that the exiled Indian, Virendranath Chattopadhyaya, who has been resident here for nearly four years and has now gone to Berlin for business purpose, will be given the opportunity to return?[234]

The Prime Minister, Oscar von Sydow, said, in reply on 14 June, that Chatto was not given a visa because he did not refrain from political activities of a revolutionary character despite promises to that effect.[235] Chatto was not given an assurance of reentry, and when he left Sweden at his own risk, he did not enjoy an automatic right to return just because he had stayed in the country for some time. The Swedish government was not prepared to give foreigners access to Sweden for engaging in revolutionary activities through propaganda or otherwise and whether directed against Swedish or foreign authorities. Finally, the Prime Minister categorically declared that the Swedish government would not consider Chatto's return.[236]

Intent on embarrassing the government, Lindhagen in his rejoinder charged the Prime Minister with failing to answer a part of his question concerning foreign relations and maintained that the action against Chatto was the result of the government's subservience to Britain.[237] He argued that Chatto's propaganda activities were not new. Ever since the Dutch-Scandinavian initiative for a Socialist Congress in 1917, which had allured him to Sweden, Chatto had never concealed his nationalist aims, and neither the foreign ministry nor the police had cared much about his propaganda activities during the War. As a matter of fact, the authorities had always shown a certain benevolence towards him as long as a German victory was not ruled out. So why had the Swedish government suddenly turned against Chatto, Lindhagen queried? He concluded that it was nothing but a discreditable capitulation to British pressure and that Chatto's expulsion was directly connected with the latest visit to Sweden of Baron Palmstierna, Sweden's minister in London.[238]

Since Sweden, at this time, was expecting international support for the affiliation of the Aland Islands to Sweden—already endorsed in a plebiscite there by the Swedish-speaking inhabitants—Lindhagen insisted that the Swedish government apply the same principle of self-determination to Lithuania. But he noted with regret that, in the case of Lithuania, the principle was thrown overboard. He proceeded to make a skilful connection between Chatto's campaign for national self-determination for Indians and the aspirations of the Lithuanians. He attacked these glaring inconsistencies in Swedish policy with such vehemence he had to be called to order three times during the debate at the *Riksdag*. But this did not deter him from remarking that, as far as the right of asylum was concerned, the government ministers would do well to look to the British tradition rather than the British government of the day.[229]

Although Lindhagen did not say so directly in the debate, he and Ture Nerman even believed that the Swedish government had received a promise of help from England on the Aland question at the League of Nations, provided Sweden extradited Chatto.[240] Introducing the details of the interpellation to his readers, Nerman wrote in his newspaper that the whole affair 'reveals the rascally tricks which our Authorities—the Foreign Office and the Police—made use of in this case: it gives a clear picture of how Swedish diplomacy is allowed to operate with lies and frauds, and, further, it makes clear the complete deference of our Government to the wishes and orders of the British Government.'[241] The editor's charge was echoed in letters that subsequently appeared.[242]

To prove Chatto an undesirable alien and as such not suitable for asylum in Sweden, Sydow cited two examples. On a point of information from the Social Democrat Gustav Moller, Sydow said that Chatto had once attended a political congress in the Soviet Union although he had declared he was visiting the country on business. On another occasion, he casually mentioned that Chatto had been charged in Switzerland for planning an anarchist bomb outrage and sentenced, in absentia, to imprisonment and expulsion.[243]

Even if asylum had been granted to him, it is doubtful Chatto would have chosen to stay on in Stockholm with no freedom to engage in political activities. Chatto was a political animal to the core. He exploited opportunities in Sweden and turned himself into nationalist India's chief propagandist in Europe. He was not the man to waste his time and talent in a state of limbo. When Sweden ceased to be a useful base for his political campaign, it was time for him to move on. It so happened that, just as the Swedish government was heightening control on political refugees in general and communists in particular[244], Chatto was picking up the threads of his contacts with the Bolsheviks.[245] The gulf between Chatto and the Swedish government began to widen. When the government adopted a tough attitude towards him, he made a bitter attack on Sydow in the form of an open letter in *Folkets Dagblad Politiken* in October 1921. Chatto accused Sydow of deliberately misrepresenting the facts and acting solely 'in accordance with the commands of the British Government.' Thus, he pointed out, contrary to what Sydow had said, he did not participate in any Congress in Moscow, 'not because I had anything against it but because there was no Congress to take part in.'[247] He refuted the charge of being involved in a bomb outrage in Switzerland and getting caught red-handed. Far from being involved, he wasn't even present in Switzerland either at the time of the alleged crime or at the time of the court judgement. The whole affair was engineered by the British government. The very fact that the trial took place four years after the event was proof positive that Britain was taking advantage of her victory by making her power felt in small countries like Switzerland and Sweden.[248] Chatto recalled how Sweden had been subservient to the Germans between 1917 and 1919 the same way it now deferred to the wishes of the British. Indeed, the Stockholm Indians had not only been allowed to carry on their propaganda unhampered then, but also received some official cooperation.[249]

Chatto's virulent verbal attacks did not lead to a change of heart in Sweden and he was not allowed back. However, it was not the practice in Sweden to hand over political refugees to their enemies for alleged crimes. Chatto was neither expelled nor deported, and it is possible that the Swedish government waited for a suitable opportunity which would enable it to satisfy the British government as well as protect Chatto. The refusal of reentry seemed a convenient solution.[250]

However, it should be noted that events were taking place which made the interests of Sweden coincide with those of Britain. Both countries feared the growing influence of communism. Some of the Left-wing socialists in Sweden had become communists. Chatto, too, in his letter to Sydow, declared himself a communist, although there was no true ideological change in him at the time.[252] However, the fact remains that the Bolshevik Revolution had the potential to influence the Indian revolutionary nationalists. Thus, the Swedish government at the time was as much moved by its own interests as those of the British.

This brings to an end the eventful history of Chatto's stay in Sweden. Throughout his stay, he remained an unswerving Indian nationalist. He set himself a prodigious task, but stuck to it fearlessly through all the opposition the British could muster. The British succeeded in putting an end to his stay once they had won the War. But, meanwhile, the propaganda war Chatto had waged againt them helped keep the struggle for Indian independence alive at a time when India was too weak and subservient to organize a full-scale movement to overthrow the British Raj.

NOTES

1. See N.K. Barooah, 'Har Dayal and the German Connection', *op. cit.* pp. 185–211.
2. Merle Fainsod, *International Socialism and the War* (Cambridge, Mass., 1935), p. 124. For details of the Stockholm Conference, see pp. 124–46 and also Carl Landauer, *European Socialism* (California, 1959), vol. 1, pp. 598–619; Arno J. Mayer, *Political Origins of the New Diplomacy : 1917–1918* (New Haven, 1959), ch. 4.
3. *Akten der Deutschen Gesandtschaft Stockholm, Politisches Archiv, Auswaertiges Amt, Bonn* [hereafter ADGS] 209 I (1), A 1668, Rosen to AA, The Hague, 21 April 1917, giving Troelstra's interview with the main socialist organ *Het Volk*.
4. For an overall picture of these nationality groups, see Fritz Fischer, *Germany's Aims in the First World War* (New York, 1967), ch. 4, pp. 120–54.
5. AA, Bonn, Wk 11f 37, pp. 227–30. Chatto to Berlin Committee comrades, Stockholm, 17 May 1917.
6. Thomas Hammar, *Sweden for the Swedes: Immigration Policy, Aliens Control and Right of Asylum 1900–1932*. This is the English summary of his work which bears the same title in Swedish, p. 393.
7. Wk 11f 37, pp. 227–30.
8. Wk 11f 38, pp. 50–3. Chatto to Berlin Indians, Stockholm, 30 May 1917.
9. The Indian National Committee (European Centre), *The International Socialist Congresses: Speeches and Resolutions on India* (n.d.).
10. Neil McInnes, 'The Labour Movement' in Arnold J. Toynbee (ed.), *The Impact of the Russian Revolution 1917–1967: The Influence of Bolshevism on the World Outside Russia* (London, 1967), p. 88.
11. Wk 11f 38, pp. 50–3. Chatto to Berlin Indians, Stockholm, 30 May 1917.
12. Ibid.
13. Ibid.
14. Ibid.
15. Ibid.

16. See Ferdinand Kozma, 'Indische Agitation gegen England' in *Neues Pester Journal*, 31 May 1917. Kozma, however interviewed Chatto as correspondent of *A Nap*, see Wk 11f 38, p. 59.
17. Wk 11f 37, pp. 244–5.
18. Public Record Office, London, Foreign Office Files (hereafter FO) 371/3067, File 1220 (104797), Sir E. Howard to FO, tel., Stockholm, 24 May 1917.
19. For the list of those represented at the Stockholm Conference, see G.D.H. Cole, *History of Socialist Thought*, vol. III, pp. 46–7.
20. See Fritz Fischer, *op. cit.*, p. 389.
21. ADGS 209 I (1), Lucius to AA, Stockholm, 26 June 1917.
22. Wk 11f 37, pp. 227–30.
23. Wk 11f 37, p. 236, AA to Stockholm, tel., 25 May 1917. The German Foreign Office provided the new Indian Office with a monthly recurring grant of 5000 Kroner besides additional sums every now and then for specific purposes. Wk 11f 40, p. 6, Wesendonk's note, 2 November 1917. See also Wk 11f 41, p. 4, IC to Wesendonk, 2 January 1918, and Wk 11f 46, p. 121, AA to Stockholm, 28 October 1918.
24. Wk 11f 39, pp. 54–6.
25. *Ibid.*
26. Translated from the German version of the telegram appeared in *Norddeutsche Allgemeine Zeitung*, 28 October 1917 under the caption 'Fuer die Befreiung Indiens'. AA Britische Besitzung in Asien, 2, Britisch Indien (AABI) 56.
27. Peter Ryss, 'The Stockholm Indians' in *Rech*, reproduced in *Der Neue Orient*, vol. II, 1918, pp. 276–7 under the title *Russisches Echo eines indischen Telegramms*.
28. See Margarete Buber-Neumann, *Von Potsdam nach Moskau: Stationen eines Irrwegs* (Stuttgart, 1957), p. 107. Mrs Buber-Neumann was one of the co-workers at this office.
29. See Olga Hess Gankin and H.H. Fischer, *The Bolsheviks and the World War: The Origin of the Third International* (California, 1960), pp. 674–7.
30. Wk 11f 40, pp. 22–3, Chatto to Berlin Committee, 1 November 1917. The reason behind the Bolsheviks' hostility against the Allies was the latters' attempt to stir up a counter-revolution. See A.J.P. Taylor, *The First World War: An Illustrated History* (London, 1963), p. 163.
31. Xenia J. Eudin and Robert C. North, *Soviet Russia and the East 1920-27: A Documentary Survey* (Stanford, 1957), p. 92 quoting Troyanovsky's *Vostok i revoliutsiia: Popytka postroeniia novoi Politicheskoi Programmy dlia tuzemnykh stran Vostoka—Indii, Kitaia*, pp. 29, 40–1, 47.
32. Wk 11f 40, pp. 24–30, 'Projekt Einer Russisch-Indischen Annaeherung'.
33. *Ibid.*
34. *Ibid.*
35. Wk 11f 40, pp. 22–3.
36. See Z.A.B. Zeman (ed.), *Germany and the Revolution in Russia 1915-1918*

(London, 1958), pp. VII-XI and memorandum by Dr Helphand, pp. 140–52; Fritz Fischer, *op. cit.*, p. 364 ff.
37. Wk 11f 40, p. 20. Wesendonk's note on 6 November 1917 and AA to Stockholm Legation, 12 November 1917.
38. See C. Landauer, *op. cit.* I, p. 626.
39. Jane Degras, *Soviet Documents on Foreign Policy*, vol. I (London, 1951), pp. 15–17. There is some confusion here in Lenin's use of the words 'Hindu' and 'Indian Moslems' interchangeably, as if Hindus were some sect among the Muslims. ('Moslems of the East! Persians, Turks, Arabs and Hindus.' *Ibid.*, p. 16). Nevertheless, the unconventional appeal was particularly disturbing to the British in view of the unsettling effect it could have in India. See Robert D. Warth, *The Allies and the Russian Revolution* (New York, 1954), pp. 199–200; Richard H. Ullman, *Anglo-Russian Relations 1917-1921: Intervention and the War* (Princeton, 1961), pp. 28–9 and n. 93.
40. See Arno J. Mayer, *Political Origins of the New Diplomacy 1917-18* (New Haven, 1959), pp. 296–8; F. Fischer, *op. cit.*, p. 488.
41. A.J. Mayer, *op. cit.*, p. 306.
42. Wk 11f 41, pp. 203–6. Chatto to Berlin colleagues, Stockholm, 17 January 1918.
43. Wk 11f 41, pp. 172–6.
44. *Ibid.*
45. Wk 11f 41, p. 107 ff. Indian Committee to Wesendonk on 4 February 1918 incorporating Chatto's communications.
46. Wk 11f 41, pp. 44, 97, Riezler to AA, tels., 14 and 23 January (very secret), 1918.
47. Wk 11f 40, pp. 20, 56, Chatto to Dayal, Stockholm, 3 November 1917, and Wesendonk's note, 6 November 1917.
48. See N.K. Barooah, 'Har Dayal and the German connection', *op. cit.*
49. ADGS 209, I. Lucius to Michaelis, Stockholm, 23 July 1917.
50. Wk 11f 40, pp. 166–73, Bhupendra Nath Dutta, general secretary, Indian Independence Committee, to Count von Hertling, Berlin, 30 November 1917.
51. See Fritz Fischer, *op. cit.*, pp. 586–7.
52. Wk 11f 41, pp. 203–6, Chatto to Berlin colleagues, Stockholm, 17 January 1918. The publication, called *German Judgement on British Policy* (in Swedish), contained excerpts from the writings of professors Richard Garbe, Sten Konow, Georg Wegener, and Geheimrat von Brandt.
53. *Ibid.*
54. Wk 11f 41, pp. 227–30, Chatto to Berlin colleagues, Stockholm, 12 February 1918.
55. Wk 11f 41, pp. 197–8, Wesendonk's note, 6 February 1918.
56. Wk 11f 41, pp. 336–7, AA to Stockholm Legation, Wesendonk's draft, 6 February 1918.
57. *Ibid.*

58. Wk 11f 41, pp. 227–30, Chatto to Berlin colleagues, Stockholm, 12 February 1918.
59. Wk 11f 41, p. 170.
60. *Ibid.*, p. 176.
61. Wk 11f 41, pp. 227–30. Chatto to Berlin colleagues, Stockholm, 12 February 1918. Wilhelm Solf was the minister for colonies from 1911 until October 1918 (thereafter foreign minister). Documents do not say which particular statements of Solf's Chatto found offensive. However, the German Foreign Office informed Chatto that Solf's remarks concerned colonies with a lower standard of development and not areas like India and Egypt with their own high culture. Wk 11f 41, pp. 287–8. AA to Stockholm Legation, 27 February 1918. For Solf's colonial dream at this time see F. Fischer, *op.cit.*, pp. 586–91.
62. Wk 11f 41, pp. 287–8, AA to Stockholm, 27 February 1918.
63. Wesendonk wrote: 'The fact that Chatto identifies himself completely with the Bolsheviks can be seen from the following characteristic sentence in his letter: "The only way in which the governments can be moved is by merciless exposure of all hypocrisy in their political dealings."' Wk 11f 41, pp. 197–8.
64. Herman Gumerus, *Jagare och Ativister* (Hunters and Activists), Helsingfors, 1927), pp. 343–4.
65. Stromgren to Padman, 2 April 1955 in *Stromgren Papers* concerning Chatto and Dayal at the Royal Library in Stockholm and the author's interview with Sven Stromgren in Stockholm, October 1973. In the early 1950s, Stromgren, the founder of the Swedish-Indian Society (1948), accidentally came upon about 20 boxes of books and papers which had belonged to Chatto. This led him to do some research on Chatto. Unfortunately, nothing of importance has emerged apart from Stromgren's own summary in the document cited here.
66. Wk 11f 41, pp. 227–30, Chatto to Berlin colleagues, Stockholm, 12 February 1918, and pp. 170–1, Indian Committee to Wesendonk, 4 February 1918.
67. Wk 11f 45, p. 104, Glasenapp to Wesendonk, Berlin, 5 August 1918 giving the report of his visit to the Stockholm Indians' office.
68. See Xenia J. Eudin and Robert C. North, *Soviet Russia and the East: 1920-1927* (Stanford, 1957) p. 92.
69. *Ibid.*
70. Jan M. Meijer (ed.), *The Trotsky Papers* (London, 1964), vol. I, p. 625; see also I. Deutscher, *The Prophet Armed—Trotsky 1879-1921* (London, 1954) p. 457.
71. See J. Degras, *Soviet Documents on Foreign Policy*, vol. I, pp. 8–9; R.H. Ullmann, *op.cit.*, p. 21; British consul general, Moscow, 17 June 1918 (FO 371/3339). See also Adolf Koch, *Das Russische Blaubuch über Indien* in *Der Neue Orient*, supplement to vol. III (11–12), pp. 589–99.

72. Ibid.
73. In his pro-British and anti-communist work, *Soviet Russia and Indian Communism*, (New York, 1959) pp. 14–16, David N. Druhe mentions some Troyanovsky's charges. Druhe, however, had no knowledge of Troyanovsky's connection with the two Stockholm Indians and his earliest theorization on India.
74. The Russian *Blue Book*, p. 11, as described in D.N. Druhe, *op. cit.*, p. 15.
75. Ibid.
76. Wardrop to FO, Moscow, 17 June 1918, FO 371/3339.
77. Ibid.
78. Wk 11f 37, pp. 244–5, Chatto to Berlin colleagues, Stockholm, 20 May 1917.
79. Wk 11f 41, pp. 213–16, Chatto to Berlin colleagues, 17 January 1918.
80. The Stockholm Indian Committee received a monthly allowance of 5000 Kroner. Besides, there were always separate grants for specific work like the printing of brochures. About the money spent in Stockholm, Chatto later reflected: 'Stockholm was then the centre of work and agitation. We spent a great deal of money in meeting all kinds of people.' Wk 11f 47, Chatto to Berlin colleagues, 24 March 1919. On another occasion, he said, 'During the three and a half years that I have lived in Sweden, I have paid out on behalf of the Indian Committee at least Kr. 100,000, and printers, publishers, booksellers, typographers, and journalists etc. have had the advantage of these disbursements.' Extracts from the *Folkets Dagblad Politikenm*, 2 June 1921, in Barclay to Curzon, Stockholm, 9 June 1921, FO 371/6954 (6870).
81. As expressed by Dr Helmut von Glasenapp in December 1918, while on a fact-finding visit to the Stockholm office of the Indian Committee on behalf of the AA. Wk 11f 46, p. 108, Glasenapp to Grundherr, Berlin, 7 December 1918.
82. Wk 11f 37, pp. 244–5.
83. ADGS Nr 110/1, Chatto to Kierlin, Stockholm, 17 May 1917.
84. One of Chatto's suggestions was that the AA should send money through some commercial organization connected with India. Chatto argued that otherwise, in case of a challenge in the press, he would have no evidence to show that his money did not come from the German Foreign Office. ADGS Nr. 110/2. Lucious to AA, Stockholm, 2 September 1918; Wk 11f 45, p. 110, Glasenapp to Wesendonk, Berlin, 27 July 1918.
85. Wk 11f 46, p. 108, Glasenapp to Grundherr, Berlin, 7 December 1918; Wk 11f 37, pp. 227–30, Chatto to Indian colleagues, Stockholm, 17 May 1918.
86. Indian Nationalist Committee (European Centre), *Opinions of English Socialist Readers on British Rule in India* (Berlin, 1917), 24 pp. The excerpts are from H.M. Hyndman's *Bankruptcy of India, England for All*, 'The Awakening of Asia' in *Fortnightly Review* (London, 1916); J. Keir Hardie's *India: Impression and Suggestions* and J.R. MacDonald's *The Awakening of India*.

87. Indian Nationalist Committee (European Centre), *The International Socialist Congress: Speeches and Resolutions on India* (Berlin, 1917), pp. 13. The sessions included were those of Paris (1900), Amsterdam (1904), Stuttgart (1907), and Copenhagen (1910).
88. The Indian Nationalist Committee (ed.), *Some American Opinions on British Rule in India* (Stockholm, 1917), p. 68, including an 'Introduction' (February 1917) and 'Postscript' (April 1917).
89. Published by European Central Committee of the Indian nationalists (Stockholm, 1917), p. 32.
90. Published by the Indian National Party (London, 1915), p. 68.
91. The author has not seen the last six brochures. They are, however, mentioned in Chatto's correspondence and in various printed handbills issued by the Indian Committee office in Stockholm. According to the handbills, the brochures were freely available to interested individuals in English, Swedish, German, and French. See ADGS 81, 110/1 for the handbill.
92. *Vidrakningen med an Vardsmakt: En bok om England och Dess Undertryckta Folk* (A Book about England and Her Oppressed People) (Stockholm, 1918). Besides 'a member of the Indian national Committee', the following contributed to the book: Prof. Rudolf Kjellen, Dr Hjalmar Haralds, Prof. Erik Bjorkman, Georges Chatterton Hill, Dr E. Eloui, Herman Arris Aall, Prof. Karl Weule, and Baroness Annie Akerhjelm. The British found the book more or less violently anti-English and its authors pro-German. See also FO 395/190, Howard to Balfour, Stockholm, 30 March 1918.
93. *Der Freiheitskampf der Indischen Nationalisten: Die Arbeit eines Jahrzehntes 1906-1917* (Berlin, 1918), p. 323.
94. *British Rule in India: Condemned by the British Themselves*, op. cit., p. 10.
95. *Opinions of the English Socialist Leaders*, op. cit., p. 14.
96. Ibid.
97. *International Socialist Congress*, op. cit., p. 8.
98. Ibid.
99. Ibid., p. 9.
100. *Opinions of English Socialist Leaders*, op. cit., p. 5.
101. Ibid., p. 18. For the original article, 'The Awakening of Asia', see *Fortnightly Review*, (London, October 1916).
102. *Some American Opinions*, op. cit., p. 33.
103. See 'Om missfochallndena i Indian' (About the abuses in India), *Aftonbladet*, 6 October 1917; 'Englands herravalde i Indian: Skarp Kritik fran Socialisthall' (English Rule in India: Sharp Critique from the Socialists), *Aftonbladet*, 27 November 1917; 'Vidraknigen med en vardsmakt: Ein bok am England och dess undertryckta folk' (Settling Account with a World Power: A Book about England and Her Suppressed People), *Aftonbladet*, 24 March 1918.

148   Chatto

104. *Aftonbladet*, 2 and 10 June 1918. The articles were entitled 'Violence and Suppression against India' and 'Englishmen and Despotism in India'.
105. *Folkets Dagblad Politiken*, 13 October 1921.
106. In the following pages we will cite various Swedish newspaper items of the time about India. But for some select reviews or reports about the books and brochures of the Stockholm Indians—other than those that appeared in *Aftonbladet*—see: 'The exploited India', *Appell*, 10 November 1917; 'How the British rule India', *Spegeln*, 2 December 1917; 'Uttalanden av engelska Socialistic dare om Englands herravalde i Indien' (Statements of English Socialist leaders on British rule in India), *Appell*, 1 December 1917; 'A book on England's oppressed people', Stockholm Dagblad, 21 May 1918.
107. See *Aftonbladet*, 23 January 1918; *Stockholm Dagblad*, 24 January 1918: *Stockholm Tidningen*, 17 January 1918.
108. See *Aftonbladet*, 14 January 1918, *Nya Daglit Allehanda*, 14 January 1918, *Folkets Dagblad Politiken*, 15 January 1918; *Svenska Morgon Bladet*, 15 January 1918; and *Svenska Dagbladet*, 15 January 1918 for the message to the Finns and Wk 41, pp. 181–93 for messages to Ukrainian organizations and personalities. For Ukrainian voice for Indian freedom see 'En rost for Indiens frihet', *Afton Tidningen*, 11 January 1918.
109. See *Aftonbladet*, 26 January 1918 for a long report on the message sent by Chatto to the Labour Party Congress at Nottingham, and *Nya Daglit Allehanda*, 18 and 26 January 1918 for reports about Annie Besant's efforts and the Calcutta session of the Indian National Congress.
110. The allegation at the time of the San Francisco Conspiracy Trial that Tagore was given money by a representative of the German government during his visit to America in 1917 was, of course, baseless—a 'lying calumny' in Tagore's words. On 19 April 1917 the AA informed the Berlin Indians that, contrary to Chandra Chakravarty's information, Herr von Skal had only spoken to Tagore in the USA and that no monetary transaction had taken place. However, the fact remains that the Berlin Indians expected to hear Tagore's voice against British atrocities vis-à-vis Indian patriots. Wk 11f 37, p. 130, IC to AA, 19 April 1917; Wesendonk's note, 22 April 1917. About Tagore's reaction to the allegation, see also Stephen Hay, 'Rabindranath Tagore in America', *American Quarterly*, 14 (3), 1962.
111. Lajpat Rai had been approached by various Indians connected with the Berlin India Committee since his arrival in New York in November 1914, but he did not have any faith in the Germans and 'did not believe in the deliverance of India with their help or through their agency.' Among the people who met Rai on behalf of the India Committee in various places in the USA were: Benoy Kumar Sarkar, Chandra Chakravarty, Maulvi Barakatullah, H.L. Gupta, Ram Chandra, and Harish Chandra. It is strange though that, in spite of his great distrust of Germany ('I had absolutely no doubt that the Germans would grab India and would suck the lifeblood out of her, even more mercilessly than the English had done'), he had no qualms

Internationalizing the Indian Question from Stockholm 149

in accepting from Ram Chandra what was undoubtedly German money for the publication of his book *Young India*. See Lajpat Rai, *Autobiographical Writings* (ed. V.C. Joshi) (Delhi/Jullunder, 1965), pp. 197–206.
112. 'Choto O Boro' in *Rabindra Rachanavali* (Collected Works of Tagore) in Bengali, vol. 24, pp. 272–93.
113. *Ibid.*, p. 284.
114. *Ibid.*, pp. 286–7.
115. *Stockholm Dagblad*, 17 February 1918; *Nya Dagligt Allehanda*, 16 February 1918. See also Stromgren Papers for the original typescript of the article in Chatto's Stockholm bureau.
116. *Ibid.*
117. 'Den bittiska depotisme i Indien', *Nya Dagligt Allehanda*, 5 February 1918.
118. For Lajpat Rai's American activities of the period, see Diwakar Prasad Singh, *American Attitude towards Indian National Movement* (New Delhi, 1974), pp. 174–9.
119. The leaflet accompanying the brochure 'The Political Situation in India' by Lajpat Rai. See Stromgren Papers. I have, however, found the leaflet only and not the brochure.
120. See 'England's Tyranny in India' in *Spegeln*, 13 January 1918.
121. 'Den indiska home rule rorelsen', *Stockholm Dagblad*, 3 August 1918.
122. 'The British Rule in India: A letter from a renowned Indian Judge to President Wilson', *Nya Dagligt Allehanda*, 22 June 1918. The report, based on the material supplied by Chatto, dealt with the publication in *The Times* in May 1918 of Sir Subramania Aiyer's letter to Wilson and the House of Commons' debate on it an 3 June 1918.
123. 'Indians want to be in British Parliament', *Nya Dagligt Allehanda*, 31 July 1918.
124. *Klockan*, 8 and 28 February 1918; *Stockholm Dagblad*, 21 May 1918.
125. 'Constitutional Reform in India', *Stockholm Dagblad*, 7 June 1918.
126. *Nya Dagligt Allehanda*, 13 May and 3 August 1918
127. 'Indian War Songs', *Goteborgs Aftonblad*, 22 September 1917 about the patriotic songs of Lal Chand Falak, one of those convicted in the Lahore conspiracy.
128. *Stockholm Dagblad*,? December 1917, reporting (with Swedish translations) on Inayat Khan's collection of Indo-Persian verses. Wk 11f 40, p. 184.
129. For later reminiscences of this conference, see Oscar Wieselgren, 'Varldspolitik vid Tunnelgatan' (World policy in Tunnelgatan), *Svenska Dagbladet*, 28 March 1953.
130. Wk 11f 39, pp. 79–81, for Abdul Jabbar Kheiri's statement about his *Hemheq*. For more about the Kheiri brothers, see N.K. Barooah, 'Har Dayal and the German Connection', *op. cit.*
131. Wk 11f 39, pp. 99–100, AA to Constantinople (Wesendonk's draft on Abdul Jabbar Kheiri), 9 October 1917; Wk 11f 40, pp. 255–8a, I.C. Berlin to AA, 18 December 1917 for Chatto's opinion of the Kheiris. For Abdul

Jabbar Kheiri's relation with the other Indians, see also N.K. Barooah, 'Har Dayal and the German Connection', *op. cit.*
132. 'Det untertryckta Indien' (The suppressed India), see *Folkets Dagblad Politiken*, 13 November 1917 for Chatto's letter to the editor on Lindhagen's article of 7 November, 1917 and Lindhagen's reply to Chatto.
133. *Ibid.*
134. *Ibid.*
135. Taraknath Das to Lindhagen (Berkeley, USA), 28 August 1916; (US Federal Prison, Leavenworth, Kansas) 12 November 1918; New York City, 17 June 1936, *Carl Lindhagen Papers*, Brevsaml/Inkomna brev (Collection of letters/ Incoming letters) D 15. Taraknath Das (1884–1958) came to Berlin from the USA in November 1914 to join the India Committee. He returned to the USA in 1916 via Stockholm. Later he went to China and Japan.
136. In the late 1920s, when Chatto was one of the secretaries of the League Against Imperialism, Berlin, official correspondence with Lindhagen was maintained. See *Carl Lindhagens samling*, vol. 131.
137. Wk 11f 45, pp. 3–4, Chatto to Wesendonk, private, Stockholm, 24 June 1918. On another occasion, in 1921, he said that during the last two years of its existence the Stockholm Indian Bureau had despatched thousands of copies of their publications to 'every member of the Government and Riksdag, to all papers in Sweden, to all large publishers, journalists, university professors, teachers, naval and military people and to libraries. Besides this, hardly a day passed without clearly revolutionary articles being read in at least some of the 50 to 60 papers to which we sent them.' *Flokets Dagblad Politiken*, 13 October 1921.
138. About Murray's propaganda service for the British Government in Sweden, see Francis West, *Gilbert Murray:A Life* (London, 1984), p. 151.
139. 'An Indian Voice on India: Answer to Professor Murray's English Viewpoints', *Dagens Nyheter*, 8 June 1916. The paper introduced Das as 'a significant Indian politician'.
140. FO minute on seditious propaganda signed by S.G. and H.M., 30 October 1916, Public Records Office, London (hereafter PRO), FO 395/56 (229193).
141. 'A British Voice on India: A British Minister answers the Indian Politician', *Dagens Nyheter*, 10 June 1916.
142. 'Professor Murray on England and India: Reply to the Indian national's accusations of British Politics. India is not yet fit for self-government.' (in Swedish), *Dagens Nyheter*, 6 July 1916.
143. 'England and India: The Indian politician answers the British Mininster' (in Swedish), *Dagens Nyheter*, 9 August 1916.
144. 'England and India: A response of the British Minister to the Indian politician', *Dagens Nyheter*, 23 August 1916. Among the persons quoted by Howard were Theodore Roosevelt and Sherwood Eddy. The latter praised the high quality of the school system in India.
145. FO to Buchanan, 7 June, 1916; Buchanan to FO, Petrograd, 27 and 28 June

Internationalizing the Indian Question from Stockholm   151

1916. PRO, FO 371/2787/211 (110561) (123078) (124226).
146. Wk 11 37, pp. 244–5, Chatto to IC, Stockholm, 20 May 1917. Chatto's declaration was reported in *Dagens Nyheter*.
147. Howard to FO, Stockholm, 24 May 1917, PRO, FO 371/3067, 1220 (104797).
148. FO to IO (India Office), 28 May 1917, FRO, FO 371/3067, 1220 (104797). The suggestion was from Lord Robert Cecil.
149. IO to FO, 1 June 1917, ibid. (109622). I have been unable to trace the list of these six Indians. However, there can hardly be any doubt that the names of Chatto and Acharya, who were already in Stockholm then, were included. The person mentioned as convicted in India must be Bhupendranath Datta. In 1907, he was sentenced to one year's imprisonment as editor of *Jugantar*.
150. FO to Howard, 2 June 1917, *ibid*.
151. Chatto's open letter to the Swedish Prime Minister M. von Sydow, Moscow, 15 July 1921, published in *Folkets Dagblad Politiken*, 13 October 1921. See also enclosures, Barclay to Curzon, Stockholm, 15 October 1921, FO 371/6954 (11898).
152. Minute on publication and distribution of German-Indian Islamic seditious propaganda, 3 October 1916, FO 395/56 (229193).
153. In early November 1917, Howard informed London what he gathered from the French minister about Chatto's close connection with Gumerus. Since before the War Gumerus had lived in Rome, where his wife had leased a villa. His brother was also residing in Rome. The British feared the Indians might use Finns to pass messages through Russia and Persia. Howard to FO, Stockholm, 2 November 1917, and Sir R. Rodd to FO, Rome, 7 November 1917, FO 371/3067, 1220 (104797).
154. IO to FO, 12 February 1918 (secret), FO 395/190 (27456).
155. Howard to Montgomery, Stockholm, 17 January 1918, FO memoranda, 12 and 18 February 1918, FO 395/190, 11623 (12465) (27436).
156. FO notes, 4 March 1918, FO 395/190, 11623 (27456).
157. *Times Literary Supplement*, 5 September 1918 reviewing Yusuf Ali's three lectures in Denmark. 'Troek af Indiens Kultur'. *Ibid*. (240442).
158. *Manchester Guardian*, 13 April 1917.
159. *Ibid*.
160. 'India's attitude to England. Answer by the Indian National Committee', *Stockholm Tidningen*, 2 May 1918.
161. *Afton Tidningen*, 4 May 1918.
162. Wk 11f 44, pp. 164–8, IC to Wesendonk, Berlin, 22 June 1918, giving excerpts from Chatto's letter to them.
163. Chatto described the scene created by the British spectators thus: '...as the audience consisted chiefly of English and Anglophile people, there was considerable excitement outside the hall when the fly-leaf was put into their hands. One Englishman took down the number of the messengers; another cried out that it was unlawful to distribute matter without the printer's

name; an Englishwoman seized a number of the little sheets and tore them up in great rage, and a good few who were probably not pro-English stood by and laughed.' IC to AA, 22 June 1918 giving extracts from Chatto's report. WK 11f 44, pp. 164–8, *Afton Tidningen* 4 May 1918 reported that the leaflets merely contained a list of Indian Committee publications, offered gratis.
164. *Stockholm Tidningen*, 2 May 1918.
165. *Ibid.*
166. See N.K. Barooah, *India and the Official Germany*, *op. cit.*, pp. 179–80 for Chatto's pre-war denunciation of the term.
167. *Stockholm Tidningen*, 2 May 1918.
168. 'Indian National Committee demasked', *Afton Tidningen*, 8 May 1918. The same contents were published in *Stockholm Tidningen*, 1 May 1918.
169. *Ibid.*
170. Wk 11f 44, pp. 164–8, Chatto to IC in IC to AA, 22 June 1918.
171. *The Times* (London), 11 May 1918 See also Wk 11f 44, pp. 164–8.
172. Wk 11f 44, p. 68 and pp. 164–8, IC Berlin to AA, 16 May and 22 June 1918. See also *Anhaltischer Staatsanzeiger*, 12 May 1918 for Northcliff's propaganda against the Indian Committee of Stockholm.
173. *Afton Tidningen*, 29 May 1918.
174. *Afton Tidningen*, 12 May 1918. This letter, too, seems to be Chatto's work.
175. *Stockholm Tidningen*, 18 May 1918. Wk 11f 44, pp. 164–8, IC to AA, 22 June 1918.
176. Howard to Balfour, Stockholm, 14 June 1918, FO 395/190, 11623 (114239).
177. *Afton Tidningen*, 29 May 1918.
178. Chatto said he wanted to 'take the bull by the horns and state clearly Indians' cooperation with England's enemies.' Wk 11f 44, pp. 164–8, IC to Wesendonk, 22 June 1918, giving extracts from Chatto's letter to them.
179. *Ibid. Stockholm Tidningen*, 18 May 1918.
180. *Afton Tidningen*, 29 May 1918.
181. Note of S.G[iselle], 9 September 1918, FO 395/190, 11623 (240442).
182. *Ibid.* (111239).
183. Howard to Balfour, Stockholm, 14 June 1918, FO 395/190, 114239 (111239).
184. *Aftonbladet*, 2 and 10 June 1918.
185. *Aftonbladet*, 2 June 1918.
186. *Aftonbladet*, 10 June 1918.
187. *Ibid.*
188. *Svenska Morgonbladet*, 11 June 1918.
189. *Ibid.*
190. 'England and India: Answer of the Indian National Committee', *Svenska Morgonbladet*, 26 June 1918.
191. *Ibid.*

192. *Ibid.*
193. *Ibid.*
194. *Ibid.*
195. *Ibid.*
196. *Social Demokraten,* 12 June 1918.
197. *Aftonbladet,* 22 June 1918.
198. *Aftonbladet,* 10 June 1918.
199. For Lenin's criticism of Branting and his praise of young Swedish socialist leaders like Hoglund, Lindhagen, etc., see Fainsod, *op. cit.,* p. 150 n.
200. *Aftonbladet,* 22 June 1918.
201. *Ibid.*
202. *Ibid.* Chatto said that Tidens-Verlag printed and distributed 700 copies of the brochures with the knowledge and approval of the secretary of the Swedish Social Democratic Party.
203. *Ibid.*
204. Wk 11f 45 and 46, pp. 100–11 and 107–15, respectively, Glasenapp to AA, Berlin, 27 July and December 1918. Glasenapp visited Chatto in July and November 1918. On the latter occasion, Chatto expressed his desire to keep the Stockholm bureau in the old form until spring 1919.
205. State Foreigners Commission (SUK), Sweden, H II 125, home ministry's note, 27 January 1919. Until 1916, SUK was concerned with foreigners in Sweden. After 1916, the office for foreigners came to be known as Immigration Office (Statens Invandrarverk). For this information and the material concerning Chatto in this office, I am grateful to Dr Tomas Hammar of Stockholm University, who kindly allowed me (in 1973) to consult his notes on Sweden's immigration policy.
206. *Folkets Dagblad Politiken,* 2 June 1921, statement of Chatto in Lindhagen's interpellation in Parliament concerning the refusal of reentry visa to Chatto, in 1921. See also enclosure to Barclay to Curzon, Stockholm, 9 June 1921, FO 371/6954 F 6870.
207. *Folkets Dagblad Politiken,* 14 October 1921. Chatto's open letter to Sydow. Moscow, 15 July 1921. 'A dagger, a revolver, a bottle of chloroform as political weapons! British Governments' methods against Indian revolutionaries.' See also enclosures to Barclay to Curzon, Stockholm, 15 October 1921, FO 371/6954 F 11898.
208. FO to Stockholm chargé d'affaires, telg., 24 June 1919, FO 371/4244 F 117 (93600).
209. Kennard to FO, Stockholm, 27 June 1919. *Ibid.* (94841).
210. Hammar, *op. cit.,* p. 392.
211. *Folkets Dagblad Politiken,* 14 October 1921. The second part of Chatto's open letter to von Sydow, Moscow, 15 July 1921.
212. Wk 11f 21, Geheim (hereafter called 'acta retenta'), Chatto to Wesendonk, 'private and confidential', Berlin, 20 February 1917. See also N.K. Barooah, 'Har Dayal and the German Connection', *op. cit.*

213. *Ibid.*
214. 'Acta retenta', Wangenheim to AA, Pera, 9 July 1915; Hohenlohe to AA, Pera, 21 July 1915; Michahelles to AA (secret), 29 July 1915; Nadolny to German Legation, Berne, 14 August, 1915.
215. *Ibid.* Romberg to AA (secret), Berne, 12 August 1915.
216. *Folkets Dagblad Politiken*, 14 October 1915. Briess had earlier cunningly crept into the pre-War 'Pro-India Committee' of Champakraman Pillai in Zurich.
217. Wk 11f 13, Wesendonk's note, 3 May 1915. See also 'The Interned Lady—Miss Howsin's Release Refused—The Meaning of Hostile Associations', *Manchester Guardian*, 17 July 1917 also Wk 11f 38, pp. 208–9, Romberg to AA, Berne, 17 July 1917.
218. *Manchester Guardian*, 17 July 1917. In July 1917, after 22 months of internment, Howsin's case was still shrouded in mystery, her lawyer failing to get both the meaning of 'hostile associations' and the writ of *habeas corpus* from the court.
219. Wk 11f 23, pp. 10, 59–62, Romberg to AA, Berne, 9 December 1915, with enclosures. According to contemporary German accounts from Switzerland, Gullick was after the 100,000 Francs reward for delivering Chatto, dead or alive. According to Chatto's account of the event, the Swiss police found in Gullick's pocket a dagger, revolver, bottle of chloroform, saying and a note he was to get £ 5000 'to get him out of the way'. See *Folkets Dagblad Politiken*, 14 October 1921.
220. *Ibid.*
221. *Folkets Dagblad Politiken*, 14 October 1921.
222. Wk 11f 23, pp. 136–7. Romberg to AA, Berne, 14 December 1915, enclosing Jacoby's report.
223. See W. Somerset Maugham, *The Complete Short Stories of W.S. Maugham*, vol. II (London, 1952), pp. 753–86. The author's interview with A.C.N. Nambiar, one of Chatto's close associates in Berlin during 1921–31, on 27 September 1972 in Zurich.
224. *Folkets Dagblad Politiken*, 13 October 1921. *Ibid.*
225. The name he gave to his commercial enterprise was Den Allmanna Handelsbyran (The General Trading Bureau), and the translation bureau was called Den Universella Overstottningsbyran (The Universal Translation Bureau). Stromgren to Padman, 2 April 1955, Stromgren (Chatto) Papers, Royal Library, Sweden.
226. SUK H II 16, Promemoria, 21 May 1920. Chatto, however, mentioned that the editor made some change in the article and that the unchanged version would appear in *Aftonbladet* on 23 May.
227. SUK H II 16, Promemoria, 23 April 1921. Adolf Joffe had been the leader of the Russian delegation to the Brest-Litovsk negotiations during the first phase.
228. *Ibid.* See the entry of 26 April 1921.
229. Chatto to Sydow, Moscow, 15 July 1921, in *Folkets Dagblad Politiken*, 13 and

Internationalizing the Indian Question from Stockholm 155

14 October 1921. See also Barclay to Curzon, 15 October 1921, FO 371/6954 F 11898.
230. Ibid. M.A. Persits, *op. cit.*, p. 171.
231. Chatto to Sydow, Moscow, 15 July 1921, in *Folkets Dagblad Politiken*, 13 and 14 October 1921.
232. Ibid. Tomas Hammar, *Sverige at svenskarna: Invandringspolitik: utlanningskontroll och asylrat* (Sweden for the Swedes: Immigration policy, Alien control and Right of Asylum) 1900–32, p. 294. Hammar dates Chatto's expulsion year as 1920 but it should be 1921.
233. Lindhagen was the mayor of Stockholm 1903–30, member of the Lower House of the Swedish Parliament 1897–1917, and of the Upper House 1919–40.
234. *Riksarkivet*, Sweden, Parliamentary proceedings of the First Chamber, 1921. No. 31/5, pp. 144–9; no. 14/6, pp. 38–56. See also extracts of *Folkets Dagblad Politiken*, 2 June 1921 in Barclay to Curzon, Stockholm, 9 June 1921, FO 371/6954 F 01694.
235. Ibid., proceedings of 14 June 1921, no. 48, pp. 38–56; *Folkets Dagblad Politiken*, 2 June 1921; *Stockholm Tidningen*, 15 June 1921.
236. Ibid. See also Barclay to Curzon, Stockholm, 21 June 1921, FO 371/6954 F 7348.
237. Ibid.
238. Ibid.
239. Ibid.
240. As revealed by Ture Nerman to Sven Stromgren long after the event, Nerman also said that British assistance was received after Chatto's expulsion. The author's interview with Sven Stromgren, Stockholm, October 1973.
241. *Folkets Dagblad Politiken*, 2 June 1921 in Barclay to Curzon, Stockholm, 9 June 1921, FO 371/6954 (6870).
242. *Folkets Dagblad Politiken*, 4 June 1921, published under the heading 'Passskandalerna I' a letter by Otto Grimlund in which the Swedish government was criticized for withholding the right of entry to Chatto because of 'the order from England' and 'high politics', ADGS 110/2.
243. *Stockholm Tidningen*, 15 June 1921.
244. Hammar, *op. cit.*, p. 396.
245. See the following chapter.
246. *Folkets Dagblad Politiken*, 13 and 14 October 1921. The letter was dated Moscow, 15 July 1921. See also Barclay to Curzon, 15 October 1921, FO 371/6954 F 11898.
247. Ibid.
248. Ibid., 13 October 1921. Chatto named several secret agents, such as Lorichs, who worked for the British and always tried to entrap him. Chatto also said that he had handed over Lorichs to the Swedish police.
249. Ibid.

250. The British government knew in advance what the Swedish Prime Minister's statement in Riksdag would be on Chatto's reentry issue. On 9 June 1921, Barclay from Stockholm wrote to FO: 'The Prime Minister, I understand, intends to uphold the refusal of the visa and in the Riksdag tomorrow will reply in that sense to Lindhagen.' FO 371/6954 (6870). The reply was, however, given not on 10 June, but on 14 June 1921.
251. In 1921 the Left-wing Socialist Party was reorganized into a communist party, a section of the Comintern, under the leadership of Zeth Hoglund. However, there soon occured conflicts between the Swedish party and the Communist International. Later some members, including Lindhagen, returned to the Social Democratic fold. Tomas Hammar, *op. cit.*, p. 395.
252. Even after his return from Russia in September 1921, where he had gone along with his Berlin colleagues to discuss Indian activities with the Roy group, he wondered how the doctrine of class struggle would fit into the Indian situation. In his eyes, the Indian revolutionary movement was nationalist in character, including both the bourgeoisie and the proletariat. See N.K. Barooah, 'The Berlin Indians, the Bolshevik Revolution and Indian Politics 1917–1930'; *op. cit.*

5

Missing the Comintern Link

1. SEEKING A COMINTERN LINK

While Chatto's Left-wing social-democrat friends in Stockholm were fighting against his extradition from Sweden in 1921, both in Parliament and in the press, Chatto himself was in Moscow along with his Berlin colleagues, exploring the possibility of cooperation between the Comintern and his group on the common ground of anti-imperialism. It was exactly three and a half years after Troyanovsky had wanted them to be there. Meanwhile, as we will soon see, much had happened to obliterate the old rapport.

It was at the beginning of 1920, while still in Stockholm, that Chatto decided to reestablish contact with the Bolsheviks. He was still an ardent nationalist, determinedly against British imperialism with no firm commitment yet to communism. Not that the years of experience and the changing times had left him unaffected. He had discarded terrorism as a means of achieving his political aims, and was edging closer to a 'Soviet' model of government for India with emphasis on education and other social reforms. Considering British imperialism to be the common enemy of both the Soviet Union and Indian nationalists, he thought a *modus vivendi* would not be difficult to find for both to work in collaboration.

Chatto, however, did not make a direct proposal to any of the functionaries of the Comintern. Instead he wrote a letter on 8 January

1920 to Mohammad Barakatullah, Kumar Mahendra Pratap, M. Acharya, and Abdur Rab, all of whom had then arrived in the Soviet Union from Afghanistan. This letter was translated into Russian and sent to Georgi Chicherin, commissar of foreign affairs, along with an accompanying letter addressed to him, through the Russian diplomat Maksim Maksimovich Litvinov (1876–1951), who lived not far from Chatto.[1] In his letter, Chatto had asked the addressees for suggestions about the new orientation of their common organization against British imperialism and for Indian freedom. He suggested that care be taken not to make future propaganda too Islamic or north-India oriented. Although the Punjab ought to be given special importance, the new propaganda should have 'a communist character'. This propaganda and the building of 'a social state structure based on communism' would require money and disciplined work.

The main purpose of the letter was to sound the Comintern (through the Soviet Foreign Office) about the Berlin Indians' readiness to collaborate. The letter was discussed in the Eastern Department of the Soviet Foreign Office. One of the remarks made was that, if the Soviet Union decided to get involved in a revolutionary programme in India, the main stress should be on non-Muslims. Another remark, unflattering to Chatto, was that he was suspected of having been spoilt by German money and a European lifestyle.[2] Unaware of this adverse comment, Chatto pursued his idea further and, by the end of 1920, arrived in the Soviet Union for preliminary talks.

There are various reports about this trip but with conflicting dates. As mentioned in the preceding chapter, the Swedish police vaguely suspected that this visit took place via a sailing boat in the closing months of 1920. According to an American agent, close to the American consul general's office in Stockholm, Chatto, whom, he said, the British classified as 'an old bird and difficult to catch', left Stockholm for Moscow on 12 October 1920.[3] Yet another source, the British Foreign Office documents, give January 1921 as the time for Chatto's first visit to Moscow, organized with the help of Victor Kopp who in 1920 became the informal Soviet diplomatic representative in Berlin.[4] According to Russian scholars, writing on the early contact of Indians with the Soviet Union, Chatto visited Moscow in November 1920.[5] Many years later, on 18 March 1934, on the International day of MOPR, Chatto gave a speech in the hall of the Academy of Sciences, Leningrad, reminiscing about his earlier visit to Moscow. He only mentioned that on his previous visit in the summer of 1921, his desire to see Lenin had remained unfulfilled. He made no mention of any earlier visit in the autumn 1920.[6]

Being closest to the original archival sources, the Russian scholars' dates of Chatto's first visit in Moscow can be taken as accurate, especially when they agree, more or less, with Stockholm sources. However, the Russian scholars have not provided much detail about the visit, saying merely that on this visit a decision was made to convene a conference of Indian revolutionaries abroad in Moscow in 1921. British official documents also do not say much about Chatto's first Moscow visit. However, British documents do give an interesting account of the antecedents of the 1921 Moscow conference of Indian revolutionaries. According to them, the Soviet government sent an agent to Berlin in early March 1921 to inform the Indians that in order to receive support, they would have to show they had a substantial following in India. The Berlin Indians explained that it would be difficult to document their support in India, and asked the Bolsheviks, that if they could believe Roy in Moscow, why could they not trust the Berlin Indians?[7] The argument seems to have worked. Eventually, at a meeting between Kopp and the Berlin Indians, Chatto suggested the following points for Moscow's consideration:

1) Moscow should help Chatto financially to establish an Indian Revolutionary Society in Berlin on a sound basis;
2) Money is especially needed for the publication of an Indian newspaper for circulation among Indians living in European countries;
3) Funds are also required for the purchase of two printing presses for the publication of pamphlets, proclamations, etc., to be sent to India;
4) Russian Bolshevik agents in India, Persia, etc., should be put at Chatto's disposal as propaganda agents for Indian nationalism;
5) Moscow should allow Indian nationalists and other revolutionary elements in India to use Bolshevik couriers travelling between India and Russia to communicate with the Indian Revolutionary Society in Berlin;
6) Moscow should give financial help to Indian students in Europe, and to Indian students in India an opportunity to learn practical work in engineering, etc., in Russia.[8]

According to British information, Kopp apparently agreed to these points and couriered them to Moscow. In the meantime, Chatto left for Stockholm. During the third week of March, the Russian agent who had visited Berlin sent news from Moscow that the Soviet government could not help the Berlin Indians because of Roy's protest, who branded them as a set of bourgeois who had extracted money earlier from Germany and now wished to do so from Russia. Chatto was, however, requested to visit Moscow again for further discussions.

When these communications arrived, Chatto was not in Berlin. When he returned, Kopp requested him to go to Moscow alone. Chatto declined to go without his colleagues In April, when the Russian agent returned with agreeable news, Chatto and his colleagues left for Moscow with false passports belonging to various nationalities.[9]

British secret service reports about Indian revolutionaries are not always accurate. However, when official despatches tally with them or official actions prompted by them, they have to be taken seriously. In this particular case, of the Berlin Indians' visit to Moscow in 1921, the reports of different British secret service agents seem to have given a coherent picture of the event. On the basis of these reports, the British even decided to accuse the Russian government of violating the Anglo-Soviet Trade Agreement of March 1921.[10] Coming as it did, at the time of the opening of Roy's centre in Tashkent to train Orientals, the Soviet contact with Berlin Indians alerted the British. The Soviet Foreign Office was worried. The British Foreign Office even detected a certain nervousness on the part of Chicherin, worried that Soviet relations with the Indians might be discovered. The British, therefore, decided to confront him personally with the information at the Genoa Conference.[11]

With danger to diplomatic relations looming large, it was unlikely that Moscow would aggravate the situation by accepting the plan for propaganda work by the Berlin Indians, especially when the report about them was already unfavourable. But it seems that Chatto being the first Indian ever to take a keen interest in the activities of the Bolsheviks—even before the October Revolution—some high-ranking personalities of Moscow, who had contacts with Chatto earlier, decided that his views should at least be heard.

2. The Berlin Indians in Moscow

The planned meeting of the Indian revolutionaries was to begin on 5 April 1921, but the Berlin Indians arrived in Moscow only between the end of April and the beginning of May 1921.[12] The seven-member delegation led by Chatto consisted, besides him, of Bhupendra Nath

Dutta (1880–1961), Gulam Ambia Khan Luhani (1892–1938), Pandoram Khankhoje (1885–1967), Nalini Gupta (1890–1957), Birendranath Das Gupta (1888–?), and the American Agnes Smedley (1892–1950).[13] In Moscow, the delegation was accommodated in Hotel Lux with other foreign visitors who had arrived for the Third Congress of the Comintern to begin on 7 July.

The Berlin Indians desired to present their views to Lenin personally but, even after a long period of waiting, the expected interview did not take place. They ended up instead at the office of Karl Radek. Radek had recently taken over the secretaryship of the Comintern from Angelica Balabanova. According to Roy's *Memoirs*, Radek, seeing that the Berlin Indians' views went contrary to Roy's, warned the Berlin group that the Comintern was bound by the thesis of the Second World Congress (meaning here not Lenin's but Roy's supplementary thesis), and if they wanted to see that policy altered, they would have to assert it in the forthcoming World Congress, although not as delegates but as observers. Radek advised the Berlin Indians to contact the Central Asiatic Bureau which was in charge of promoting revolutionary activities in the East.[14] The day-to-day business of the Comintern was conducted by the so-called Little Bureau with four or five members of the executive committee of the Comintern living generally in the Soviet Union. The Little Bureau first brought the Berlin Indians to a meeting with the other Indians, including those belonging to Roy's group. However, this first meeting ended in squabbling. According to Dutta, Chatto accused Abani Mukherjee (1891–1937) of being 'a spy', and Mukherjee in turn called the Berlin Indians 'German agents'.[15]

Later, the Comintern placed the matter of the reconciliation of the various Indian groups in the hands of a commission consisting of Mikhail Borodin (Russian), Tom Quelch (British), and J. Rutgers (Dutch), the last mentioned being the chairman. At this second attempt to reconcile differences, Rutgers called upon the Berlin Indians to give their views one by one. Perhaps, not expecting such regimented proceedings, Chatto objected, saying he did not represent any individual but a group. According to Dutta, Rutgers retorted that 'we do not recognise any group but will select individuals after discussion and start work.' At this, Chatto threatened to boycott the commission, and Rutgers concluded the Berlin Indians were uncooperative and reported this to the Comintern.[16] After three months of deadlock a new commission was formed. This delay was perhaps due to the Third

World Congress of the Communist International which began on 7 July 1921 and lasted a month. The chairman of the new commission was James Bell (Britain). The other members were: M. Borodin (Russian), K. Troyanovsky (Ukrainian), August Thalheimer (German), and Matias Rakosi (Hungarian). Rakosi, who was one of the secretaries of the Comintern, worked as the secretary of the commission.

When the newly-constituted commission met, with all the Indians present, Smedley and Dutta, from among the Berlin group, presented a separate written statement each, and Chatto, along with Luhani and Khankhoje, presented a joint statement about possible Indian work with the Comintern's assistance. Chatto and Luhani also submitted a memorandum. M.N. Roy (1887–1954)[17], who was present at this last session, presented a printed paper which in substance was the same as his earlier statement on the colonial question at the Second Congress of the Comintern in 1920. He also spoke about the Indian Communist Party (Tashkent-based) which he had already founded.[18]

Smedley, in her statement of 5 August 1921[19], gave a brief account of her past Indian work in the USA which had included activities like defending Indian political activists against attempts of expulsion to India or imprisonment, spreading knowledge about the Indian situation among the Americans, sending propaganda literature and weapons to India through Indian seamen, and so on. She said that, although she had been a member of the International Workers of the World and upto 1918 a member of the American Socialist Party, she had never joined any of the communist parties. She had left the USA in December 1920 in order to join the Berlin Indian revolutionaries' mission to Moscow with the hope 'that we will found the first organization of the Indian revolutionary movement on an international scale.' Smedley stated that everywhere among the Indian national revolutionaries there existed a general desire to cooperate with Soviet Russia. She emphasized that she herself felt 'as an Indian revolutionary' who would soon go to India to spend her life there.[20] Bhupendranath Dutta submitted his thesis on the character and objective of the Indian revolutionary movement on 23 August.[21] Dutta's views were basically the same as Chatto's (these will be discussed in the next section). The only point where Dutta's views differed from Chatto's was his visualization, in his future work for Indian independence, of the presence of communist groups working simultaneously for social revolution.[22]

3. CHATTO AND THE 'THESIS ON INDIA AND THE WORLD REVOLUTION'

The detailed and analytical views of the Berlin Indians were presented to the commission in a joint statement by Chatto, Luhani, and Khankhoje.[23] The 'Thesis', which starts with an introduction is neatly divided into three parts: a) actual situation within India; b) British imperialism and world revolution; and c) the task of the Communist International.

Visualizing a Communist International committed, for the first time, to recognizing the struggle of the enslaved world proletariat for emancipation and the final assault on capitalism, the Thesis highlighted how vital the Indian sector would be internationally on all fronts: 'It cannot be denied that in its urgent and serious importance to the proletarian world revolution, India transcends other parts of the Asiatic and African continents now under the sway of world capitalism.' The Thesis, however, cautioned that precisely because of this significance and for reasons of geographical distance, ready acceptance of vague generalizations about India ought to be avoided.[24] A clear-cut demarcation between peasants and working classes was not possible in India since land-holding peasants from the countryside also worked in factories for part of the year and returned to their far-off village with the season's earnings. The permanent nucleus of the industrial proletariat could not be fixed at more than five million in a population of 315 million. Then again, this category of industrial workers was only loosely organized in labour unions whose preoccupations did not go beyond the conventional demand for the increase of wages and shortening of working hours. The development of class-consciousness among the working classes was retarded not only by the absence of technical facilities but also by the strong counteraction of a complex variety of causes, including the ignorance of an essentially conservative proletariat weighed down by age-old and entrenched authoritarianism.[25]

The industrial proletariat proper was an unknown quantity in India in its broad connotation since here 'feudalism, medieval guild-organization of small industry and modern large-scale industrialism existed side by side in a curious medley.' Thus, obstacles to the growth of class consciousness in India were too great: 'Indian society, like societies everywhere, has been implicitly divided along horizontal lines of cleavage between the exploiting and the exploited classes. But these lines of horizontal cleavage—so sharp and clearly drawn in the industrial West—have, in India, been intersected, from the very inception of its history, by exceptionally strong vertical lines of social division and, latterly, of religious antagonism.'[26] The caste-system of the Hindu society, for example, inhibited members of the same economic class from grouping together if their castes were different. Again, the antithesis between Hinduism and Islam, one with 240 million devotees and a conflicting variety of religious and philosophical ideas and the other with 20 million adherents and a monotheistic creed and democratic social constitution, prevented exploited Muslims and Hindus from joining together in a class-conscious union.[27]

The difficulty was further aggravated by British imperialism which kept alive, if not actively fuelling, such inherent Indian conditions to retard class-consciousness. Since the history of British imperialism in India was intimately connected with the beginnings of industrialism in England, it had been 'a settled imperial policy of England to keep India in an industrially backward condition.' The British working classes were told that the industrial development of India would deprive England of the raw materials drawn from India.[28] 'Undoubtedly it is this obtrusively foreign direction and control of the process of exploitation that explains the volume and intensity of response which the Indian masses make to the appropriately-worded appeals for political independence' coming from the liberal bourgoisie and the national revolutionaries of India.[29]

Working class solidarity under the liberal bourgeoisie against foreign aggression wasn't purely an Indian phenomenon either, the Thesis claimed. 'It is historically true that the exploited working classes of all countries, most of all in Europe, have been made to feel and fight by the side of their own bourgeoisie against foreign economic and political aggression.'[30] This is why, giving national independence priority over class-consciousness, the Thesis stated: "Wherever there has been a politically unfree country, its exploited classes have not been able to come to a clear perception of the existence and nature of the class struggle.'[31] Citing examples from Italy, France, England, Germany, Czechoslovakia, Ireland, and Egypt, the Thesis pointed out that 'so long as the economic exploitation of a given vast area by and in the name of a foreign political entity is a concurrent dominating factor in the economic exploitation of one class by another, the revolutionary class-consciousness of the proletariat remains merely potential.' This being so, it concluded that 'the Indian proletariat can take its rightful place in the ranks of the world proletariat in its struggle against the bourgeoisie after supervening British imperialism has been withdrawn.'[32]

Considering British imperialism in India as one of the main obstacles to the growth of class-consciousness in India, the Thesis, in its second part, tried to show that British imperialism, drawing as it did, its strength from Indian wealth and services, was the foremost obstacle not only to India but also to the world. 'As the world-revolutionary situation develops, British imperialism—with its undoubted military strength reinforced by the mercenary man-power of its dependencies—becomes more and more intolerant of remotest approximation of any part of Europe to the regime of proletarian dictatorship.' The Thesis cited the share of British imperialism in sabotaging the proletarian revolution in Hungary and its power to block, any day, the dictatorship of the proletariat out of existence in Germany, France, Italy and the Scandinavian countries.[33]

Further, the argument continued, within England itself, the inherent necessity of its imperialist expansion had effected a curious reversal of the whole process of the growth of class-consciousness, a phenomenon which had escaped the attention of the theorists of the class struggle. On no other soil, it claimed, 'has the seed of the proletarian revolution been strewn so broadcast as on the soil of industrial England; yet no other soil proved itself so sterile.' Why was it so? And why was it that the instrument of the proletarian revolution in England—the British Communist Party—was one of the weakest of the constituent bodies of the Communist International? This wasn't, the Thesis asserted, mere accident. The reason was that, although primarily called into being by a historical process of bourgeois exploitation, the British working classes—in contradistinction to the proletariat of continental Europe—lived and moved in an atmosphere of relative prosperity created by an efficient and successful capitalist imperialism abroad. Indeed, among the economically better-placed workers in England, a class intermediate between the down-trodden proletariat (unskilled and agricultural labourers) and the bourgeoisie had arisen.[34] This 'Labour Aristocracy' invested their meagre savings, either individually or collectively through their huge trade unions, in stocks and government loans. As a consequence, they had come to have the well-developed sense of a stake in the capitalist order of society while maintaining, in their relation to revolutionary class-consciousness, a kind of sub-bourgeois mentality. So the British proletariat might rise to a sense of solidarity with the proletariat of continental Europe but not with the wretched proletariat of England's Asiatic and African dependencies.[35] British imperialism was putting the British proletariat through a rapid process of transformation into an exploiting class itself *vis-à-vis* the workers of India and other dependencies.[36] Thus, within the fabric of capitalism, circumstances were arising, due directly to British imperialism, to convert class cleavage into race cleavage.[37] The Thesis further warned that 'British imperialism, more than any other bourgeois coalition in existence today, is a permanent military menace to the security of Soviet Russia and its preservation as a world revolutionary centre...'[38]

Therefore, in its last part, the Thesis suggested that the destruction of British imperialism should be the first and foremost duty of the Communist International.[39] It defended the idea of cooperation with the bourgeois-democratic and nationialist revolutionary movements of political liberation in the East, and criticized those Leftist communists (termed 'rigid Communists') who would oppose any such movements. It remarked, somewhat harshly: 'Mere academic objections, on rigid Communist grounds, to giving assistance to, and collaborating with, bourgeois-democratic and nationalist revolutionary movements of political liberation show a pathetic and stupid detachment from *realpolitik* of the world situation.' It dismissed any notion of the Indian bourgeoisie settling down to the exploitation of the proletariat in the aftermath of a British downfall by saying that, along with the destruction of British imperialism, world capitalism would fall like a house of cards.[40]

Another document, called 'Memorandum', submitted to the commission by Chatto and Luhani on 4 August, criticized the communist party founded by Roy in Tashkent. According to it, this party consisted mostly of people who were communists only by intention and not by conviction, with no clear idea of what actually attracted them to communism. It said further that a party founded in Europe and forced on to the Indian proletariat was an unnatural way of forming an organization. Only the class-conscious part of the Indian proletariat was to form the party and, therefore, any talk of an Indian Communist party was premature. Chatto and Luhani believed that, with Comintern help, an apparatus for carrying out propaganda and organizational work in India could be initiated on communist lines, and this apparatus could develop into a communist party more naturally.[41]

4. The Failure of the Moscow Mission

Chatto's Thesis failed to make any impact on the communists in general, and the Leftists in particular, as it concentrated heavily on bourgeois-democratic movements, and almost completely left out some basic Marxist-Leninist principles. Moreover, his belittling of the British proletariat and the British Communist Party was certainly not palatable to the commission's British chairman. Indeed, one wonders if the Berlin Indians were not purposely hardhitting because of the treatment meted out to them (for example, the delays and lack of courtesy attending their visit, making them feel unwelcome).

There is no doubt that the Thesis was a clever way to avoid Marxism-Leninism altogether. No wonder, Troyanovsky, old acquaintance of Chatto's and a member of the commission, termed it 'a nationalist thesis'.[42] It could not have been otherwise, as Chatto had not been converted to communism yet. Just before he left for his first Moscow visit in 1920, he candidly told an American acquaintance in Stockholm that India was not ripe for Bolshevism and, in fact, the feeling in India was 'so strong against Bolshevism that should a Bolshevik army attempt to penetrate India, the inhabitants would rise in arms against it.' However, he said that Bolshevism was the thing which British capitalists in India feared most and, therefore, the threat of Bolshevism was the strongest card for his nationalist party. For the future development of India, Chatto emphasized education more than class struggle.[43] There is no doubt, therefore, that when Chatto talked of the Marxist theory of classes and class struggle in his Thesis, he completely denied class community of the proletariat on an international scale, and, consequently, rejected the Marxist-Leninist slogan: 'Proletarians of all countries and suppressed nations, unite.' Considering national liberation as the most important task of the Indian people, Chatto's Thesis ignored the direct interests of the working classes which, seen through Marxian eyes, was one of the core forces of the Marxist struggle. As a Russian Marxist-Leninist scholar points out, the development and success of the liberation movement depended directly on whether or not, in the course of its progress, the tasks of agrarian and other social changes for the benefit of the people were carried out.[44] In Chatto's Thesis, such tasks were to be overridden by the supreme goal of national independence. In this respect, his Thesis shared a common platform with the bourgeois-nationalist wing of the liberation movement of India.

Latter-day Soviet Marxist scholars have pointed out that, although Roy might have been hasty in founding a communist party in Tashkent, the vehement criticism of his action by Chatto and his colleagues showed they had not understood the Marxist-Leninist thesis that socialist ideology was to be brought into the working classes from outside, since the proletariat by themselves could not develop this socialist awareness. Therefore, the creation of a communist party consisting of a small number of communist-minded representatives of the intelligentsia was a primary factor in uniting the workers' movement with socialism.[45]

There were other weak points in the Thesis as well which the Marxists did not fail to see. It underestimated the organizational and political apparatus of the communists, presupposing that the liberation of India from the British yoke would be equivalent to a socialist revolution. The Thesis also laid undue emphasis on India as the keystone of British imperialism. Similary, it unduly equated British imperialism with world capitalism.

Lenin apparently was not satisfied with the theses presented by Dutta and Chatto, although in Dutta's case he liked the emphasis on the peasantry.[46] As mentioned before, while emphasizing a united struggle against the foreign enemy, Datta also spoke of simultaneous work on social change.

During the four months that the Berlin Indians spent in Moscow they were made to feel that a Left-wing communist clique in the Little Bureau of the Comintern—particularly Radek[47] and Bela Kun[48]—was working against them. Radek, Kun, and also Balabanova had met Chatto in Stockholm during the War, and seem to have circulated rumours about Chatto, depicting him as one spoiled by German money and a fancy lifestyle. It is possible that the opinion of Chatto in the Eastern section of the Soviet Foreign Office, before his visit, was a result of these rumours. They seem to have affected Chatto's former relations with Grigori Zinoviev, the president of the Comintern and an enthusiastic protagonist of world revolution[49] and Georgi Chicherin, the foreign minister who had earlier asked him to come to the Soviet Union. Although Chatto found Chicherin still 'benevolent' to him, he has not elaborated on this benevolence. Perhaps Chicherin could not have helped much anyway, being nervous, as the British noticed, because of the Anglo-Soviet Trade Agreement. Unlike Chicherin, Zinoviev was in an ideal position to intervene on Chatto's behalf. At the time of the Anglo-Soviet Trade Agreement, the Russian attitude towards Germany was also changing, and Russia was thinking in terms of Soviet-German relations in a context other than that of revolution. Zinoviev, as head of the Comintern, did not wish further interference with the established programme of world revolution, and worked very hard for a proletarian revolution in Germany as well.[50] And yet Chatto was not able to see Zinoviev.

On his return to Germany in September, Chatto told an official of the German interior ministry candidly that his mission to Moscow had failed mainly due to Radek and Kun, staunch supporters of Roy (therefore averse to him). They also prevented him from meeting Zinoviev, he noted.[51] To the same German official, whom he had approached for the extension of his stay permit in Germany, Chatto gave three reasons for the failure of the Moscow mission:

1. The Indian Communist Party under the leadership of Roy and Abani Mukherji wanted the Indian work to be under their control and the Little Bureau of the Comintern was influenced by them;
2. Radek and his comrades would tolerate only Communist propaganda in the entire Orient solely by agents whom they themselves selected, without taking into consideration the realities of the situation in these countries;
3. Chatto and his comrades had been suspected as German agents apparently because of the intrigues of Roy and Mukherji, although they had themselves cooperated with the Germans in Batavia, Mexico and Singapore during the War.[52]

Chatto had gone to Moscow rather late—at least one and a half years too late—despite being the first Indian to contact the Bolsheviks. Meanwhile, the Comintern had found its man for Indian work who, unlike Chatto, was not only a communist but also one with creditable international experience in communism. Moreover, Roy had already made a name for himself in his debate with Lenin on the colonial question at the Second Congress of the Comintern.

Chatto was unhappy with many other developments he saw in Moscow which concerned India. He said his interest in Moscow was only in a programme of revolutionary activity against British imperialism and not necessarily a communist one. Roy, on the other hand, considered the formation of communist cells in India through agents—

a task which Chatto considered impracticable. He called Roy's Indian Communist Party an opportunistic venture of privilege-seekers. In his judgment, a communist movement in India at that time was out of the question. The revolutionary movement in India, according to him, was a national one, including both the bourgeoisie and the proletariat.[53]

As in his Thesis, Chatto criticized the British Communist Party in general and its representatives in Moscow in particular. In his eyes, the British communists were no different from British Liberals as far as India was concerned. The British communists, he said, had never actively tried through their press to persuade British citizens not to join the Indian army. In fact, they aspired to take control of the revolutionary movement in India as and when it took place. Despising this attitude of guardianship, Chatto suspected some of the British communists in Moscow to be spies of their government.[54] Suspecting each other to be spies seems to have been an occupational hazard in international communist gatherings in Moscow at the time. As Smedley wrote from Moscow to a friend, Florence Lennon, in America, 'Everybody calls everybody a spy, secretly, in Russia, and everybody is under surveillance. You never feel safe.'[55] Smedley herself was not spared either. There were people who considered her a British spy. Smedley continued in her letter:

...the Indians [Roy and Mukherji] opposing our plan did such dirty work as to call me a *British* spy! Think of it—not even an *American* spy—but a British one... If I had not been a member of a large delegation I suppose I would have been locked up... If I'm not expelled or locked up or something, I'll raise a small sized hell.'[56]

5. Roy and Chatto

It would be wrong to blame Roy for the Comintern's rejection of Chatto for the Indian work with Moscow's help. Although there was no love lost between Roy and the Berlin Indians, Roy can be blamed only for the extreme Leftist posture he took when he tried to persuade the Comintern to turn away from the bourgeois national liberal movement in India. His objective was that Lenin's resolution on the national and colonial question, adopted at the Second World Congress, be abolished and the legitimacy of his leftist-revolutionary connections be confirmed.[57]

However, in this posture of Roy's, a hidden purpose is discernible.

When Moscow showed interest in encouraging revolution in India, the ambitious Roy, who had already been converted to communism, immediately dashed to Moscow to be the first to start Indian work from the Soviet Union and to form a communist party of India in Tashkent with the *Khilafat muhajirums* as its rank and file. He knew that only in this way, by becoming a *bona fide* communist, could he claim superiority over Chatto who was, otherwise, the doyen of Indian nationalists in Europe. Besides being extremely popular among colleagues for his fair dealings and well-known, to friends and foes alike, for his keen intelligence and remarkable skill, Chatto was well-versed in many European and Indian languages and had wide-ranging contacts in various countries. He was both a north and south Indian at the same time, speaking major languages of both parts of the country. He abhorred communalism, admired the egalitarian Muslim social structure, and hated the Hindu caste system. Passionately involved in the all-round progress of India and the Indians, Chatto engaged himself in furthering the education and training of Indian students in continental Europe and in helping Indian businessmen enter the European market. Contrary to what the Russians heard and thought about Chatto, he cared little for money or high living, and most of the time lived in poverty because of the inbuilt generosity of his character and his unwavering devotion to the cause of Indian freedom. These admirable qualities are the makings of an ideal leader, especially in the Indian context. If the Comintern had given him sufficient support, Chatto might have built a broad-based reformist organization to intensify the fight against imperialism and advance the cause of Indian independence.

The fact that Chatto came from a distinguished Indian family connected with the mainstream Indian liberation movement was another great asset, and this seems to have fuelled Roy's jealousy. Roy seems to have feared that, if Moscow decided to back the bourgeois national movement in India, Chatto would be the obvious leadership choice. This might be why Roy persistently stood for a purely communist-led revolution in India. The condescending or disparaging tone[58] in which Roy has described the Berlin India Committee and its members in his *Memoirs* with malice, half-truths, and blatant lies is proof positive that he could not have been as sincere and cooperative as he has portrayed himself to be in his *Memoirs*.[59] His portrayal of Chatto as a 'bully'[60] and a bossy[61] man 'unable to prepare a well-argued document'[62] is nothing short of ridiculous. Roy also tries to denigrate Chatto by saying that the driving force of Chatto's delegation was only Agnes Smedley[63], although, with the solitary exception of this observation, his remarks about her are derogatory.[64] Some of Roy's account of the Berlin delegation is based either on fiction or a figment of his imagination. When he speaks about Lenin consulting him before his meeting with the representatives of the Berlin delegation[65], he writes: 'Having given them a polite and patient hearing, Lenin advised the representatives to see the secretary of the Communist International.'[66] The truth, however, is that a meeting between Lenin and the Berlin Indians never took place.

In his *Memoirs*, Roy has depicted himself as a selfless individual to whom nothing but the cause mattered. He writes that he told the Berlin Indians that if they agreed on a programme of work and decided to stay in Moscow to take over the responsibility of guiding the revolutionary activities, he would place himself at their disposal.[67] Coming as it does from an inordinately ambitious careerist, such a voluntary and self-effacing sacrifice rings absolutely hollow. During WWII, when at the behest of the Soviet Union the Indian communists joined the Allies, Roy, then a radical democratic leader, forcibly demanded from Lord Wavell a seat on the Viceroy's executive council and later even the prime ministership of India. Although impressed by Roy's sharp intelligence, Wavell privately mused, 'I was Viceroy and did not propose to be Vice-Roy.'[68]

NOTES

1. *Zapiska Indusa Chattopadiya (iz Bengali)* (Note from the Indian Chattopadiya from Bengal) to Mohammad Barakatullah, Kumar Mahendra Pratap, M. Acharya, Abdur Rab. To comrade Chicherin, People's Commissar for foreign affairs. Grevtirgatan 22, Stockholm, 8 January 1920. We have received a copy of the original letter in Russian bearing the seal and comments of the Russian Foreign Office through the kindnesses of the director of the Institute of Oriental Studies of the Russian Academy of Sciences, Moscow. Litvinov, a career diplomat, later became Commissar of foreign affairs during 1930–9.
2. *Ibid*. The two comments by the Eastern Department of the Soviet Foreign Office on Chatto's 'note'.
3. American vice consul Orsen N. Nielsen to secretary of state, Washington, confidential, Stockholm, 21 October 1920 enclosing the gist of conversations between Chatto and an American agent which took place between September and October 1920. I am thankful to Ms Ruth Price, Washington, for providing

a copy of the document.
4. FO 371/6844, Hodgson (Moscow) to FO, 21 April 1921 enclosing a secret SIS report 'Bolshevik Aid to Indian Revolutionaries'. About Kopp, see E.H. Carr, *German-Soviet Relations between the two World Wars 1919-1939* (Baltimore, 1951) pp. 48, 50–1.
5. Moisey Aronovich Persits, *Revolyutsionery Indii v Strane Sovietov 1918-1921* (Revolutionaries of India in the Land of the Soviets 1918-1921) (Moscow, 1973), p. 171.
6. See Andrey Nikolayevich Dalskiy, *Vospominaniya* (Reminiscences), Leningrad, 29 March 1962, manuscript, p. 6, Archive of the Institute of Oriental Studies of the Russian Academy of Sciences, St Petersburg, F. 138, Op. 1, No. 47; Lidiya Eduardovna Karunovskaya, *Vospominaniya o Chattopadhyaya, Virendranath Agornatovich* (Reminiscences of Virendranath Agornatovich Chattopadhyaya) (Leningrad, May 1970), manuscipt, p. 10, Archive of the Institute of Oriental Studies of the Russian Academy of Sciences, St Petersburg, F. 138, Op. 1, No. 48.

G. Adhikari in his *Documents of the History of the Indian Communist Parties*, vol. 1, 1917–1922 (New Delhi, 1971), pp. 85–7 writes that in the above MOPR speech of 1934, Chatto talked about his November 1920 visit, but this is wrong. Chatto talked on that occasion about his 1921 visit only. See also chapter VIII. (MOPR).
7. FO 371/6844, Hodgson (Moscow) to FO, 21 April 1921, *op.cit.*
8. *Ibid.*
9. *Ibid.* This British report gives the following names in Chatto's group: Chatto, Bhupendra Nath Dutta, Herambalal Gupta, Pandoram Khankhoje, and Agnes Smedley. German documents do not mention Herambalal Gupta but correctly mention Nalini Gupta. Besides, G.A.K. Luhani and another person whose name could not be deciphered, were included. AA, Indien, Pol.19 Sozialismus, Bolschewismus. The Soviet document tallies with the German one, and also gives the name of the undeciphered person as Abdul Khasan (most probably the assumed passport name), Persits, *op.cit.*, p. 172.
10. The British Foreign Office considered the following points as confirmation of the Soviet violation of the Anglo-Soviet Trade Agreement:
    a) the extremely intimate connection between the Soviet government and the Third International;
    b) the existence of a propaganda centre at Tashkent;
    c) the relations between Indian revolutionaries at Moscow and the Soviet Foreign Office. FO 371/8170, Hodgson to FO, Moscow, 9 January 1922. Various notes by high-ranking officials of FO.
11. *Ibid.* Note by R.A. Leeper, 18 January 1921.
12. *Ibid.*, p. 172.
13. AA, Indien Pol. 19, Sozialismus, Bolschewismus. Schotte's tel. to AA, 27 July 1921.
14. M.N. Roy, *M.N. Roy's Memoirs* (Bombay, 1964), pp. 482–3.

15. Bhupendranath Dutta, *Aprakashita Rajnaitik Itihash* (Unpublished Political History) (Calcutta, 1953), pp. 283-4.
16. Dutta, *op.cit.*, p. 285. See also G. Adhikari, *Documents of the History of the Communist Party of India*, vol. 1., 1917-1922, (Delhi, 1971), p. 254.
17. In 1915, Roy was sent to Batavia by his terrorist organization in Bengal to take delivery of arms the Berlin India Committee had arranged to obtain from the USA. He was to ship them to India. Following the failure of the venture, Roy travelled to various places in Southeast Asia, China, and Japan, with a generous amount of German money, before arriving in Mexico via San Francisco in 1916. In Mexico, he helped found the Mexican Communist Party soon after the Bolshevik revolution. In 1920, he was in Moscow representing the Mexican party at the Second World Congress of the Comintern. He made a favourable impression on Lenin, and was put on the Executive Committee of the Comintern International. Later, in 1929, he was expelled from the Comintern.
18. Dutta, *op.cit.*, pp. 292-3. Adhikari, *op.cit.*, p. 256.
19. M.A. Persits, *op.cit.*, p. 172, fn. 3. Here the author has given extracts from Smedley's statement in Russian.
20. *Ibid.*
21. *Ibid.*, p. 179, fn. 11.
22. Bhupendranath Dutta, *op.cit.*, pp. 289-90.
23. This 14-page typed document called 'Thesis on India and the World Revolution' carries the unmistakable stamp of Chatto's writing style and opinions at that time, although it was read out by Luhani at the meeting. The document was written in Moscow between July and August 1921. This author has procured a photocopy of the original, now preserved at the Institute of Oriental Studies of the Russian Academy of Sciences, Moscow. Henceforward referred to as *Thesis*.
24. 'The character of the problem demands that consideration should be lifted out of the cloudy atmosphere of vague enthusiasm and unscientific generalisation, to which there is a marked readiness to resort on account of the geographical distance and political isolation of India from the centres of world revolutionary congresses and conferences, and the consequent lack of first-hand knowledge to neutralise the extravagances of a *priori* theorising.' *Thesis*, p. 1.
25. *Ibid.*, pp. 2-3.
26. *Ibid.*, p. 4.
27. *Ibid.*
28. *Ibid.*, p. 5.
29. *Ibid.*, p. 6.
30. *Ibid.*
31. *Ibid.*, pp. 6-7.
32. *Ibid.*, p. 8.
33. *Ibid.*, p. 9.
34. *Ibid.*, pp. 10-11.

35. *Ibid.*, p. 11.
36. *Ibid.*, p. 12.
37. *Ibid.*
38. *Ibid.*, p. 13
39. *Ibid.*, p. 14.
40. *Ibid.*, p. 14.
41. M.A. Persits, *op.cit.*, pp. 176–7. In this document also, the topic 'the situation in today's India' was dealt with. Here the authors remarked: 'Take away the yoke of British imperialism and you will find class awareness clear and sharp.'
42. Dutta, *op.cit.*, p. 289.
43. O.N. Nielsen, American vice consul to secretary of state, Washington, forwarding from Stockholm, 21 October 1920, an American agent's report on Chatto (see above fn. 3). In this report, Chatto allegedly said that his party had discarded terrorist methods altogether and there was no danger of a religious war in India. He admitted that in the future form of government in India, there should be some elements of the Soviet model. Chatto stressed, however, that India ought not follow too closely in Russia's footsteps and should borrow from other constitutions as well, notably the American.
44. Persits, *op.cit.*, pp. 178–9.
45. *Ibid.*, pp. 176–7.
46. Lenin's reply to Dutta on 26 August after receiving Dutta's thesis on 23 August 1921: 'Dear comrade Dutta, I have read your thesis. We will not quarrel over social classes. I think that we must stick to my thesis about the colonial question. Collect statistical data about peasants' unions if such unions exist in India.' See Lenin, *The National Liberation Movement in the East*, (Moscow: Progress, 1974, 4th printing), p. 307.
    As to Chatto's *Thesis*, according to Chatto, Lenin wrote back as follows: 'To comrades Chattopadhyaya, Luhani, Khankhoje. I have read your thesis with great interest. But why a new thesis? I will soon talk with you about this! In a comradely way, yours V. Lenin'. It should, however, be noted that this letter is not to be found in Lenin's collected works. Chattopadhyaya also lost the original letter in one of his many hurried flights from one place to another, but remembered Lenin's lines to him and presented them verbatim in a talk he delivered at the Academy of Sciences, Leningrad on 18 March 1934. See also, Chapter 8.
47. Karl Radek (1885–1939), a Left-wing communist of long standing, was also connected with the Polish and German communist parties. He belonged, heart and soul, to the Bolshevik Party. Together with Zinovyev and Bukharin, Radek belonged to the troika which was the permanent ruling group of the Comintern at the time. He died either in a Stalinist prison or concentration camp.
48. Bela Kun, (1886–1939) like Radek, was a Left-wing communist. He was a Hungarian. Boris Souvarine, the French communist, who, at the end of WWI, was one of the three secretaries of the committee for the Third International,

later wrote how unappealing a character Bela Kun had been—a person nobody liked and respected and who, at Stalin's behest, carried out the most terrible tasks, until himself falling victim to the same treatment. He was liquidated in one of the Stalinist purges. Boris Souvarine, 'Comments on the Massacre (of Stalin)' in M.M. Drachkovitch and Branko Lazitch, *The Comintern: Historical Highlights: Essays, Recollections, Documents* (New York, 1966), p. 182.
49. E.H. Carr, *German-Soviet Relations Between The Two World Wars, 1919–1939* (Baltimore, 1951), p. 38.
50. *Ibid.*, pp. 40–1.
51. A.A. Indien, p. 19, Sozialismus, Bolschewismus, March 1921–January 1926, Klein to Geheimrat Lang, Berlin, 12 September 1921, giving Chatto's assessment of his Moscow trip. Chatto went to the interior ministry to extend his stay permit in Germany which was later refused.
52. *Ibid.*
53. *Ibid.*
54. *Ibid.*
55. Smedley to Lennon, from Moscow, 1921, Florence Lennon Papers, University of Colorado, Boulder, USA. The first six pages of this 10-page letter are unfortunately missing.
56. *Ibid.*
57. Persits, *op.cit.*, p. 182.
58. Here are some examples: 'Within a short time, they arrived to announce that the Indian Revolutionary Committee of Berlin, which alone had the authority to speak on behalf of India, had decided to shift its headquarters to Moscow.' (p. 478) 'The Indian revolutionaries took no interest in these discussions [the New Economic Policy of Lenin, being discussed on the eve of the Third World Congress]. Their only activity was to march up and down the long corridors of the Hotel Lux, button-holing other residents to tell them all about the inequities of the British rule in India.' (p. 489) M.N. Roy's *Memoirs* (Bombay, 1964). All quotations from this edition.
59. Finding many doctorates in the Berlin Committee Roy in his *Memoirs* writes: 'Chattopadhyaya approached them (Indian students studying in Germany) with the tempting offer that they could escape internment by joining him. A further inducement was the grant of doctorate degrees before they had finished their studies.' (pp. 287–8). At another place Roy writes that Mahendra Pratap 'came to Berlin to be elected chairman of the Indian Revolutionary Committee' and that he never met the Kaiser, the condition on which he had come to Berlin. *Ibid.*, p. 289.
60. 'Chattopadhyaya, who seems to have been a bully.' *Ibid.*, p. 294.
61. 'Chattopadhyaya who, backed by the Germans, bossed the show.' *Ibid.*, p. 291.
62. Luhani drafted the thesis since 'the others could not prepare a well-argued document.' *Ibid.*, p. 482.
63. *Ibid.*, p. 479.

64. *Ibid.*, see pp. 479, 487–8.
65. *Ibid.* p. 481.
66. *Ibid.*, p. 482.
67. *Ibid.*, p. 484.
68. Wavell, *The Viceroy's Journal* (London, 1973) Penderal Moon (ed.), p. 55, entry of 14 February 1944.

6

Hazards in Promoting Indo-German Relations 1921–6

I have already described in the previous chapter what Chatto told an American acquaintance in Stockholm in 1920 about the change he would like to see in an independent India. He visualized a Soviet-style centralized constitution with full cultural diversification and, instead of a class struggle, the vast expansion of education. This emphasis on education was reflected in an organization which the Berlin Indians soon founded under Chatto's leadership.

This organization, The Indian News Service and Information Bureau (INSIB), had been registered in Berlin-Halensee in the spring of 1921, before the Berlin Indians left for Moscow.[1] The Bureau had four departments: a) News Service (politics, commerce, industry, education, science, art, literature); b) Advertising Agency; c) Commercial Information Bureau and Commission Agency; d) Advisory Board for Indian Students.[2] The declared objective of the Bureau was to supply India with news of the political, economic, and cultural life of Germany free of British influence. Special divisions of the Bureau looked after the well-being of Indian students and businessmen in Germany. Besides, INSIB also proposed to publish a commercial journal.

When Chatto and his colleagues returned from Moscow, they, and particularly Chatto, had an abundance of time to work for INSIB. However, they were in danger of being handed over to the British as criminals. To understand why this was so, we must first know about the significance of the Indian market to Germans after WWI.

1. BARON RUEDT AND GERMAN COMMERCIAL INTERESTS IN INDIA 1921–3

When, following British permission to reopen the German consulate in India, Heinrich Baron Ruedt von Collenberg-Boedingheim (1875–1954) arrived in Calcutta in 1921 as the first German consul general after the War, the supreme German interest in India was to recover their old market and business reputation through British goodwill. Pre-War German trade with India had been lucrative, and future prospects were also considered rosy.[3] Before the War, Germany imported 300 to 400 million marks worth of raw material per year from India and exported back about 100 million marks worth of goods comprising dyes, iron and steel, and a variety of small manufactured goods. At that time, German ships also had direct connections to India.[4] The recovery of this lost trade and market was important for the Germans, since it was the time when the Allies pressed Germany for the proper execution of the Versailles Treaty, the terms requiring the payment of reparations according to the new schedule.[5] The Germans, for their part, accepted the policy of 'fulfilment'. Although a number of restrictions still remained in force for Germans in India[6], the British officials, both in India and Germany, offered a hand of friendship. Lord D'Abernon (1857–1941), British ambassador in Berlin (1920–6), created a good Anglo-German understanding and extremely cordial relations were established between him and the German Foreign Office.[7] Ruedt was 46 years old when he was appointed as consul general in India. It was his first important and challenging assignment in the foreign service after a stint as consul in Winnipeg (1913–18) and Constanza (1918–21). He was fluent in English and pro-British in attitude[8], qualities which helped in acquiring trade and commercial concessions from the Indian government.

Ruedt attached great importance to how the governing circle in India regarded him, and wrote elaborately about his good fortune to be received by the high-ranking officials with exceptional cordiality.[9] When Sir George Lloyd, the Governor of Bombay, received him in a friendly manner in December 1921, he was overwhelmed, as according to his information, Sir George was not easily accessible and prejudiced against everything non-English. Ruedt mentioned that the consul from

Switzerland had not had this luck.[10] Later, when Ruedt made his first official visit to the Earl of Ronaldshay, Governor of Bengal, the warmth he found was also far beyond his expectations. The way he was received, and the half-an-hour long conversation that followed, were so full of cordiality that Ruedt said it could not have been conducted in a more congenial manner even during the best period of Anglo-German relations.[11] Reporting, in general, his earliest experiences in India, Ruedt wrote to the German Foreign Office on 17 January 1922: 'How my official and personal relations in British India will develop in future is yet to be seen. In any case, I can say that since I set foot on Indian soil four weeks ago, I have not experienced the slightest uncomfortableness or lack of cordiality or politeness.'[12]

In the business world too, Ruedt was received well and found the whole atmosphere full of prospects for German business. The *Calcutta Commercial Gazette and Investors Guide*, a weekly paper for trade, industry and finance, with a circulation of 8–10,000 copies all over India, introduced Ruedt to their readers and wrote about the German trade in India as follows:

As import figures of German goods in India are daily increasing, we are getting numerous enquiries to open columns for giving information of German industry and German manufacture. A good many number of respectable merchants all over India who were formerly importing houses of German goods, are feeling interested in such particulars.[13]

Ruedt's assessment of the Indian national movement for self-rule also gave him hope that there would be no great change in the near future to hamper the smooth running of foreign trade, although some unpleasant events like boycotts and strikes might take place now and then.[14] Immediately after his arrival in India Ruedt, accompanied by vice-consul Klett, went to Ahmedabad, then in Bombay Presidency, to observe the 36th session of the Indian National Congress. The session began in the wake of a series of government repressions: the Congress and Khilafat volunteer organizations had been declared illegal; important nationalist leaders, except Gandhi, had been kept behind bars along with thousands of followers; demonstrations against the visit of the Prince of Wales (who had been brought to encourage loyalty among the people and the Indian princes) had been brutally suppressed with death and injury to many. All these developments gave a special colour to the Ahmedabad Congress which made Gandhi the supreme 'commander' of the national movement with special powers not only within the Congress executive committee but also outside. Ruedt said about this concentration of power in Gandhi that, although the British-oriented press in India compared this power to the rule of force by Lenin and Trotsky together, he did not think much would result from it. 'It would be wrong to expect,' he asserted, 'that Gandhi with more active involvement would bring about a revolutionary change in the existing situation in the immediate future.'[15] Ruedt further observed:

There is no doubt that the Non-Cooperation Movement will develop further. But according to my impression so far, I do not expect, at least not in the near future, that this movement will develop from the state of passive resistance, which the Asians love, to an aggressive action. It would be wrong to think that a general uprising will take place soon. Local unrests like the ones that took place on the occasion of welcoming the Prince of Wales in Bombay and lately in Madras have no wider significance...Therefore, we must not make the mistake of the wartime to conclude that...there exists an Indian uprising.[16]

In another despatch on the same day Ruedt wrote emphatically: 'In any case, we are still far away from an independent Indian state or even an Indian Dominion within the British empire.'[17]

Ruedt seems to have thought that Berlin might get an exaggerated notion of the Indian nationalist movement from outside reports, including those coming from Britain, and this might lead German authorities to shower undue favours on Indian nationalists in Germany, thereby endangering the Anglo-Indian goodwill so essential to the progress of German commerce in India. To drive the point home, Ruedt dwelt upon the subject of Indian nationalism again in his despatch to Berlin a month later. It was the declaration of the mass civil disobedience movement under the guidance of Mahatma Gandhi on 1 February 1922, and its sudden abandonment which occasioned Ruedt's despatch.[18] He began by commenting on two views from Britain about contemporary India, one by Lord Curzon, the foreign secretary, the other by Lord Montague, secretary of state for India. Whereas Curzon spoke about the various post-War difficulties in India, such as higher prices, trade hindrances, after-effects of the Amritsar massacre, and the growing desire for self-rule, Montague expressed full confidence in the positive effects of the Government of India Act of 1919. Ruedt wrote to Berlin that although Curzon's remarks might lead someone to think India was on the eve of a general uprising, he for one would not share such a view. He assured Berlin that the British still had a strong position in India, emphasizing again that, on Indian matters, Berlin's concentration should not be on Indians but on the British.

He stressed that any new difficulty for England would neither improve Germany's political situation nor would it serve German commercial interests in India.[19]

As regards Civil Disobedience which started in Bardoli on 1 February 1922 and came to an abrupt end in only a week, he felt justified in his earlier remark that the followers of a mass movement like Gandhi's could not be kept within the bounds of passive resistance when pitted against the police. The outbreak of mob violence attending the movement, with its demands for the elementary rights of free speech, free association, and a free press, was a case in point. He added that the termination of the movement was inevitable 'especially when fanaticism leads to an opinion that it is a good thing to suffer as a martyr under a fatherland idea.'[20]

A little more experience of the Indian scene made Ruedt cautious and less strident in his assertions. (His ego too, meanwhile, seems to have been hurt a bit. When he asked for some extra privileges during his summer holidays in Simla, in April 1922, the government of India curtly told him that it was premature to grant him any privileges outside the scope of ordinary consular duties.[21]) At the time of the next annual session of the INC at Gaya in December 1922, Ruedt wrote to Berlin that there was a danger to Indian peace in the near future only if Anglo-Turkish relations became aggravated. The agitation of the Indian Muslims over the British policy against Turkey could easily take a form which might go beyond mere passive resistance.[22] Only in September 1923, with the threat of the INC of a boycott of British products in India, did Ruedt come to take the Congress movement seriously, and tried to understand the implications of its economic programme.[23] This change in him was due to the loss of popularity of the Indian government for imposing the salt tax against the will of the majority in the Central Legislative Assembly. In this connection, he explained how German exporters should behave in case of a boycott. It would be thoroughly wrong, he wrote to Berlin, if in the event of a boycott of British products in India, German exporters decided to dictate the price and condition of delivery of their products. If they did so, they would lose all sympathy and only strengthen the resolve of the not-to-be-underestimated Indian people for whom rejection of British goods was only the first step towards the economic independence of India.[24] He added that the Congress Party would like India to be self-sufficient and free from dependence on foreign imports whether from Britain, Japan, or Germany. In the interest of German commerce in India, Ruedt, of course, wanted peace in India, and peace could be promoted, in his opinion, through the programmes of the British Liberal Party which believed in further developing the reforms of 1919 with additional influence for the Indian parliament.

Ruedt could not have failed to see a general Indian preference for German goods. Keeping this in mind, the man who only two years before had considered 'dominion status' a far-fetched idea, now remarked: 'An Indian dominion will undoubtedly take a different [favourable] attitude to Germany than to Canada and Australia.'[25]

It was clear to Ruedt from the moment he set foot in India that the fortunes of German trade in the country depended first and foremost on the policy and mood of the British Indian government, and then on the attitude of the British professional classes in India. Indian nationalism was a factor only in so far as the chaos it could produce from time to time in parts of the country affected the peaceful atmosphere needed for trade to flourish. As far as the British Indian government's attitude to German commerce in India was concerned, Ruedt found it very positive. This was a natural extension of Britian's general policy in central Europe in contrast to France's. In the autumn of 1923, the British attacked the French attitude to Germany on the reparations question. France was against any moratorium on reparations, which Germany had sought, and threatened to occupy the Ruhr if Germany failed to meet France's demands. In the event, France did occupy the Ruhr straining Anglo-French relations. When France finally withdrew her troops, Britain was delighted[26], because the British policy was to allow Germany to profit enough from her foreign trade so as to be able to pay the war reparations as scheduled. This is what the British Prime Minister meant when he said in the British Parliament that the Ruhr occupation would be disadvantageous for the trade between Liverpool and Calcutta.[27] Ruedt added in the same vein that, as long as German exports continued to face all sorts of obstacles, Germany would only have limited ability to buy foreign products. This limitation in turn would restrict India's ability to bring her products to the German markets and earn enough money to buy British products—primarily textile goods.[28]

Explaining the significance of German trade to the Indian economy, Ruedt pointed out that even the most short-sighted observer could not fail to notice the strong decline of Indian exports to Germany from 100 million rupees in April–September 1922, to about 72.5 million rupees during the same period in 1923. The decline was due to Germany's lack of purchasing power.

However, in India, the British official opinion about Germany did not always tally with the opinions of the British business class or the British Indian press. The main centre of British business was Calcutta, and here anti-German feeling was the strongest. Similarly, when the question of opening a German consulate in Bombay came up, British business circles in Bombay, fearing German competition, took an anti-German position. The influence of the Calcutta Chamber of Commerce, a conglomerate of many big British business houses, was very significant, to the extent that even the government was afraid to take steps to make concessions to the Germans. Because of the unfavourable economic situation, British business houses in Calcutta faced considerable losses and a number of firms survived only with great difficulty. In view of these problems, every prospect of German import to India either through the opening of a consulate or the reestablishing of pre-War German firms spelled an increased danger to them at a time when the Indian nationalists' boycott of British goods was becoming more vociferous. Ruedt also concluded that the centre of anti-German feelings was not Bombay but Calcutta, and here the *Statesman*, the widely-read newspaper among the expatriate British, took an outspoken anti-German stance. He wrote that this paper's views on Central Europe were so pro-French as to prompt a reader to ask if the editor was a Frenchman.

Ruedt, however, did not fail to see the attitude of the Anglo-Indian papers towards Germany changing to one of friendliness. He reported that other big British newspapers like the *Times of India*, the *Englishman*, and the *Pioneer* criticized French power politics which seemed to be aimed at ruining central Europe and harming England. The *Times of India*, which Ruedt found to be the most objective of all the papers, went so far as to state in a September 1923 article that the future of Germany was a matter of vital interest to India.[29] This made Ruedt hopeful for future prospects of German trade in India despite the antipathy of some British business houses. He hoped that it would gradually be understood in India that a German consulate in Bombay would not only help in importing German goods to India which India needed, but also promote the export of cotton and other products from Bombay for which Germany had a good market.[30]

By the middle of November 1923, Ruedt was able to give more favourable news about the positive attitude of the British Indian press. The *Englishman* of Calcutta received some material from Ruedt about Ruhr and the question of reparations which the paper hoped to incorporate in subsequent articles.[31] The *Times of India*, in an article in the 13 November 1923 edition, called France's Ruhr policy 'most foolish', and took to task those in Britain who considered any interference with this policy unnecessary on the ground that the prevention of the complete recovery of Germany actually aided British manufacturers. The paper even criticized Sir William Johnson Hicks, a cabinet minister, for implying agreement with this argument.[32] The minister had warned Germany that it should not attempt dumping Ruhr steel in the British market. Calling the statement 'nonsensical', the paper pointed out that the fact of the matter was that there was no such big surplus of steel at all in the Ruhr since France had already seized a great proportion of the small surplus with the objective of destroying the steel industry of the Ruhr area. According to the paper, it was France, and not Germany, where the dumping policy had originated.[33] The *Pioneer* of Allahabad, a paper popular with British Indian civil servants, also criticized France about the same time for behaving hysterically on the return of the ex-crown prince to Germany. The paper attacked France for being vociferous in her appeals for the restoration of Allied military control of Germany. It went on to say that in the intervals between the recurring fits of nervousness, France pursued her aggressive policy of militarism regardless of its effects on the Allies or the rest of the world.[34]

In spite of occasional problems, Ruedt was happy to discover an underlying sympathy for German economic recovery in the British business world, the British press in India, and among British officials. He found the British position in India stronger than the British themselves sometimes believed. He did not think much of Indian nationalism, which in his opinion was a hindrance rather than a help to German trade in India. With a single-minded devotion to progress of German trade in India, Ruedt, even early in his stay, proposed a recipe for the rapid recovery and flourishing growth of this trade. He wanted Berlin to concentrate on cultivating good relations with the British and to refrain from encouraging Indian nationalists, who, in the unlikely event of the achievement of its goal of 'dominion status', would, in any case, go on treating Germans better than other British dominions.

2. THE ANGLO-GERMAN PLOTS AGAINST THE BERLIN INDIANS 1921–4

Baron Ruedt's opinion of the British in India and Indian nationalism was music to the ears of the officials of Department III at the German Foreign Office.[35] This Department was headed at the time by ministerial director Carl Theodor von Schubert (1882–1947). He was assisted by Baron Herbert von Richthofen (1879–1952) and Curt Pruefer (1881–1959). Like Ruedt, Schubert and Richthofen were thoroughly pro-British and were determined not to harm German trade in India by showing any sympathy to Indian nationalists, particularly Berlin's old War-time Indian nationalists. They were encouraged in this attitude by information the German Embassy received in London from the India Office that it would take at least 100 years before India could be handed over to the Indians.[36]

Among the above-mentioned officials, Pruefer was the only one who had some first-hand knowledge of Indian nationalism by virtue of his stint with the Berlin Indians in Constantinople and in Berlin during WWI as head of the News and Information Service for the Orient, an adjunct to the German Foreign Office.[37] Because of this, Pruefer had some sympathies for at least Chatto and Dutta, the two veterans among the Indians. But the changed situation brought about by the German need for trade benefits seems to have persuaded him as well that British goodwill for Germany in India had to be reciprocated. Both the India Office in London and the British Embassy in Berlin expected that Germany would, as a matter of reciprocity, remove the War-time anti-British Indian revolutionaries from Berlin and make it harder for other Indians in the country to continue anti-British propaganda. Lord D'Abernon, the British ambassador, was primarily concerned at this time about the probable Bolshevik influence on the Indian nationalists.[38] The concern was partly justified. Although the Berlin group of Indians that had gone to Moscow returned disappointed, some in August and others in September 1921, after their consultations with the Comintern functionaries, M.N. Roy was still busy building an Indian communist group in Tashkent with revolutionary aims. Roy also came to Berlin as a Comintern agent and stayed there off and on between

August 1922 and August 1924 under various false names. From Berlin he despatched to India copies of his two propaganda publications, *The Vanguard of Indian Independence* and *India in Transition*.[39] Since some of the Roy-trained revolutionaries had infiltrated into India just at this time, the government of India was very sensitive to any possible Bolshevik conspiracy in India.[40]

However, it was arch nationalist Chatto, whose activities in Berlin through INSIB were considered most annoying by the British. Chatto was the most anti-British and uncompromising Indian nationalist abroad and had been pursued by the British since WWI. The combined efforts of the AA and British secret service agents made Chatto's life extremely hazardous ever since his return from Moscow in September 1921. He had no legal passport. So when he wanted to reenter Germany, a reentry visa was issued to him only for a few days.[41] Chatto requested the interior ministry officials that the expiry date of the visa be extended to at least 20 October so he could have some time to finalize his departure for America. This request was refused.[42] Pruefer, giving the reasons why Chatto should leave Germany also hinted at the danger that might come to Chatto directly from the British. In an official note he left the following remarks:

> It would be recommendable to tell Mr. Chattopadhyaya, who is by far the most influential and skilled of the Indian revolutionaries living in Europe, that in his own interest he should not decide to settle down with his friends in Germany, at least not in the near future, since the British Government, especially lately, has shown special interest for the Indian nationalists living in Germany and therefore it has to be feared that the presence of Chattopadhyaya and his friends would cause difficulties for them as well as for us.[43]

These remarks only indicated that Germany might be forced by circumstances to succumb to British pressure, not betraying the complete helplessness of the German government to protect the pre-War Berlin Indians. As Chatto, unable to advance his plan to leave for America or to flee anywhere in Europe, decided to remain in Germany hiding and continued working for INSIB, both German authorities and British spies stepped up their surveillance of him. A private letter from Agnes Smedley, Chatto's common-law wife, to her friend Florence Lennon in America (dt. 31 December 1921) makes some astounding revelations about the German government's total submission to the British:

Of course, with Germany economically helpless, England has her own sweet way politically. It is very terrible to see the once independent Germany bending to every whim of England, or growing hopeful and happy everytime Lloyd George utters a word or a hint in favour of Germany against France...There are prominent Germans here who say they wonder how long it will be until anti-English propaganda of any sort, whether carried on by Germans or by foreigners, will be forbidden...

In an earlier passage in the same letter, Smedley wrote about the harassment she and Chatto suffered from the German police and British spies:

...My husband, being an Indian revolutionary, and a social revolutionary together, has suffered terribly for many months...and when we returned to Germany [from Moscow] he was ordered by the German Government to leave this country. The British Government demanded this of the German Government. Consequently, we have been living illegally for months—since September. Our house was raided by the honorable police, and then for weeks we lived from hotel to hotel, and from house to house, never knowing where to go from one night to the next. Generally we were working in our Bureau up until midnight, and then we would go out and find a cheap hotel. After weeks of this I gave out and collapsed, due to rheumatism of the heart. Then I came out of the hospital after a month. We were followed night and day by British spies, and by the help of friends tried to get hold of them and have them arrested for illegal police activities. My husband received warnings time and again to be careful. Then about two weeks ago a terrible thing happened to him: we drank chocolate in an Islamic restaurant with some friends, and within a short time he lay unconscious on the floor; diarrhea and vomiting started as soon as he came to. The physician we consulted said he had been given arsenic, and a large dose which fortunately caused vomiting. For days he was very ill, but recovered. But before this was complete, two English agents came with skeleton keys and tried to break into the room where we live with a little old lady. Failing, they went away and came later. The little old lady went outside to meet them and asked them what they wanted; they said they wanted to rent a room and wanted to go inside and see her rooms. She refused, saying she had no rooms to rent, and had never had in her life. She did not understand English, and said the men were foreigners and spoke a foreign language which she could not understand. But both had on high military boots and coats.

Then our wanderings started again and continue to this day. We work very hard during the day, trying to build something which will remain in Germany, and at night we go where we can...We are no longer bothered by the German police, who know all about us, but the British spies make our lives a hell.[44]

Despite all the harassment, Chatto, supported by Smedley and friends, continued his propaganda vigorously. It was characteristic of him, in adverse circumstances, to work with tremendous zeal. His Bureau published, although irregularly, two journals, namely, the *Indo-German Commercial Review* and the *Industrial and Trade Review for India* (*ITRFI*). The journals were pro-German and thoroughly anti-British. No wonder that, as soon as the news of the founding of INSIB and the first of the journals appeared in India, there was a chorus of protest and anger in the Anglo-Indian press. INSIB, while giving the raison d'etre of these journals, stated that 'India should have her own agencies abroad', especially because of the 'phenomenal development of India for political, economical and social emancipation, and the world-wide influence of Mahatma Gandhi.'[45] Quoting this, the India correspondent of the *Daily Telegraph* of London commented, 'The class of matter which such an agency would supply to the extremist press can easily be imagined.'[46] The *Pioneer* of Allahabad initially also suspected that INSIB was a purely German venture and it, therefore, ridiculed the idea that 'the influence of the teachings of Mahatma Gandhi should be put forward as one of the factors which led to this German attempt to secure a foothold in India.'[47] The *Times of India* found part of an editorial of the *Indo-German Commercial Review* extraordinarily offensive where it said:

The predilection of the Indian for the German product results not only from this antipathy against England but has its reason in the goods themselves and their quality...German and Indian people have no doubt to endure presently also politically similar conditions, whereby of itself a certain community of interests is going to be created.[48]

Here Chatto very cleverly drew a parallel between the German anti-Versailles movement and India's anti-colonialism. It was clear that the British, who were trying to convince the Germans at this time that it would take another century for Indians to be able to govern themselves[49], would not like this comparison. The newspaper commented: 'Remarks of this kind go altogether beyond the bounds of fair trade competitions.' In another edition, the paper remarked that such anti-British propaganda from Germany was most unwise when Britain was making efforts to save Germany from complete collapse.[50]

The editorials of the *Indo-German Commercial Review* and its successor, the *Industrial and Trade Review for India*, carried the distinct flavour of Chatto's biting polemics and his severe anti-British thrust. He was helped in these ventures by Agnes Smedley and later, from 1923 on wards, also by A.C.N. Nambiar who was married to Chatto's sister Suhasini. Nambiar and Suhasini were brought from London to Berlin by Chatto in May 1923.[51]

The repercussions that Chatto's propaganda caused in British circles at once alerted German officials in Calcutta, London, and Berlin to take preventive measures. Ruedt, who was so very impressed by the courtesy and friendliness with which he had been received by British officials in India[52], was of the firm opinion that new difficulties for the British in India from Indians would neither improve the German political situation nor promote German trade interests in India.[53] He also disliked INSIB[54], and was particularly irritated by the way Chatto's publications cast themselves in the role of a watchdog on the lookout for any anti-India remark by Germans, including himself.[55] He advised Berlin to inform the government of India immediately that the German government had no connection whatsoever with INSIB.[56] Berlin not only did that but also informed all its embassies and other diplomatic offices all over the world not to have any contact with INSIB. This was thought necessary because, through one of its handouts, INSIB invited Indians to Germany saying they would easily get travel documents from the German consular authorities.[57] Since the *Englishman* from Calcutta, a traditionally anti-German newspaper, condemned another Berlin publication of the time *The Indian Independence*[58], the AA investigated the matter and found it to be the work of Bhupendranath Dutta. The German Foreign Office curtly told Dutta that he would lose his stay permit unless he gave up his propaganda at once.[59]

The conflict between the pro-British officials of the AA and Chatto was a moral and ideological one. These officials wanted immediate commercial profit from India by cultivating good relations with the British and, if possible, without having much to do with the Indians. Chatto, on the other hand, aimed at the further growth of Indian nationalism by trying to free the Indian mind from British-oriented predilections in education, commerce, industry, and culture. Whereas Chatto's aim was to promote Indo-German relations through people-to-people contact and understanding, German officials, although they knew quite well their trade-commercial profit from India was due largely to the anti-British movement of the Indians, were nevertheless prepared to ignore the interest of the Indian people. In connection with a German commercial journal *The Wholesale, Poesneck, Germany: German Export Trade Journal*, which appeared in India at exactly the same time as the first issue of the *Indo-German Commercial Review* and which had been critically examined by the Anglo-Indian press, the AA remarked: 'That the Indian national movement promotes our goods is known to everybody here. But if we go on telling it publicly the Indian Government would reward us with trade restrictions.'[60]

There was, however, one incident which Schubert and Baron von Maltzan (1877-1927), state secretary of the AA since December 1922, could have used as a pretext to banish Chatto. But here, too, the information would prove too scanty or unreliable in the event of a future public debate. This was about Chatto's alleged involvement in a murder plot which Count Reventlow, a well-known German publicist of the extreme Right and a War-time associate of Chatto's, engineered with Lirau, a German courier to Moscow. The plot was to be executed by Lirau in Moscow in March 1922. In the single intercepted document concerning the plot, a message sent by one Brodovsky to Mezhinsky, the chief of the Cheka, Chatto appeared, on the one hand, as one whose advice was sought by the Germans and, on the other, as one helping a Russian Bolshevik clique. Schubert claimed at the time that he, with the help of Maltzan, then head of the Eastern department of the AA, detected the conspiracy early enough to prevent its execution and thereby saved German diplomatic reputation. At the time no drastic action was taken against Chatto in order not to cause mistrust among the Bolsheviks. Moreover, Maltzan considered that Chatto's involvement in the case was more in the German interest.[61] Schubert, however, continued to be after Chatto. In December 1921, he concluded that Chatto's Bureau received subsidies from Moscow and considered it a sufficient ground to take action against him. But a private letter from Wesendonk, former head of the War-time India Programme of the German Foreign Office, to Curt Pruefer, a Senior Counsellor of Legation under Schubert, clarified that although Chatto's group had gone to Moscow for consultations and financial support, their Bureau was not financed by Moscow but by private sources. Wesendonk also emphasized that the Bureau's main aim was to provide the Indian press with information about Germany free from British influence, and to look after Indian students in Germany.[62] Schubert was not convinced, and believed the INSIB's harmless facade hid a communist-inspired revolutionary objective[63], although he had no evidence to substantiate his belief.

Unable to satisfy the British with any direct action either against

Chatto or INSIB, Schubert in August 1923 accepted a suggestion from Lord D'Abernon for a full and frank exchange of information between the two governments regarding the Berlin Indians.[64] As a starting point for discussion, the British Embassy sent the AA a dossier on INSIB which had been prepared by the India Office.[65]

Two days later, the AA gave British authorities all the information they had about INSIB and thereby also corrected some wrong assumptions of the India Office.[66] The British authorities were assured that INSIB was not politically active and as its founders had been radically anti-British they had been warned not to indulge in politics. The AA also made it clear that the German consul general in India had been against INSIB from the very beginning. When, after several exchanges of information, Lord D'Abernon and Schubert met on 25 October 1923, Schubert lost no time in pointing out that he had long been disgusted with the continuous 'intrigues' of the Indians and considered it important that the British knew the German authorities' thoughts on the subject.[67] Schubert's inimical attitude towards the Berlin Indians seems a belated reaction to the freedom the Indians had enjoyed from the AA during the War.

Schubert was happy he could convince Lord D'Abernon that the German government had no links with INSIB. However, one assumption of the India Office about the high social prestige enjoyed by INSIB in some administrative quarters in Germany proved correct. The India Office believed that Indian students in Germany who needed permits of residence from the police, or to enter college or educational institutions, or to secure training with business firms, often gave INSIB as a reference.[68] On investigation, the AA found this was really so, and it immediately gave directions to the police not to accept INSIB's recommendations in matters of residential permits. Further, the AA agreed to warn the Prussian cultural ministry and the universities against the activities of INSIB.[69] With all these restrictive measures taken against INSIB in Berlin, Ruedt was able to pacify authorities in India, assuring them that the home authorities in Germany—especially the education and police departments—would no longer take kindly to INSIB. He even added that, being bankrupt, INSIB might even discontinue its activities.[70]

The British government fully exploited the extremely obliging attitude of Schubert and his colleagues at the AA. In October 1924, Joseph Addison from the British Embassy wrote to Schubert that, according to information received by the India Office, Indians residing in Berlin had addressed a petition to the foreign minister, Stresemann, regarding the treatment of Oriental refugees in Germany. In case the information was true, Addison asked for a copy of the petition together with names of the signatories.[71] Only four days after the receipt of this request, Schubert's subordinate, Herbert Baron von Richthofen, visited the British charge' d'affaires on 16 October 1924, and during the course of an unofficial conversation stated that German authorities would welcome any opportunity to make life difficult for the Indian agitators or to expel them. They would generally be prepared to act, as far as possible, according to the wishes of the British government to mitigate this nuisance.[72] Richthofen went further to ask whether the British would like anything more to be done, for instance, to arrange for close police supervision of any or more of the individuals concerned.[73] Taking advantage of such a generous offer, the British Embassy conveyed, a little later, to Maltzan, that they would not object to the removal of the Indian agitators from Germany provided the Germans securely deported them on a German ship to India with prior intimation to the British. The British could then take measures to prevent the escape of any person on the way, for instance, to Egypt.[74] The British gave a list of wanted Indians, and Maltzan promised that if and when these persons were expelled due intimation would be given.[75]

This understanding was macabre in the extreme considering that the Indians, whom the German government was now prepared to abandon and throw to the wolves, had been their close allies during WWI. However, by the end of 1924, Berlin realized that it was not so easy to bring the Indians to British justice. Berlin informed London through its Embassy that it was not easy to expel the Indians. First of all, they had worked in the German interest during the War. Even though none of them possessed valid passports, extradition to India would be impossible as they were all blacklisted there.[76] But the British ignored these arguments and remained persistent. In 1925, the British Conservatives had a growing antipathy towards the Bolsheviks. Although in 1924 the Labour government in Britain had made a determined attack on this antipathy, and on 8 August had signed the Anglo-Soviet Treaty, when the Conservatives came to power in 1925, they refused to ratify this Treaty.[77] The British Indian government went a step further in their communist phobia. Announcing first that they had documentary proof to show that the communist elements in China were hoping for cooperation with Indians, Sir James Crerar, the home member, further declared, in the Council of State at Simla on 3 September 1925, that the Indian communists had lately become a menace to the German government which now asked the Indian government to take back these 'undesirables' and the Indian government could not say 'no' to it.[78] He argued that if these elements were to return to India new measures would be required to keep the anarchy in check.[79]

There was no doubt that, under the excuse of communist danger, the government of India was planning additional harassment of the Indian nationalists.[80] But it is amazing how the British Indian government not only misrepresented the facts but also sought to misuse the German government for their purposes. The acting German consul general in India was surprised at the British manoeuvres, but his diplomatic position prevented him from providing any official clarification.[81] The AA, therefore, asked Dufour, the German ambassador in London, to inform the British through diplomatic channels that there was no truth in the German government wanting to expel the Indian communists and approaching the Indian government for this purpose.[82] Dufour did point out to Sir Arthur Hirtzel, undersecretary at the India Office, the misrepresentation in Crerar's words. The British government readily accepted that Crerar's was an overstatement of facts and expressed that if the German government so desired they would be prepared to issue a statement to that effect.[83]

The German government decided not to insist on a correction of the statement. In December 1924, Maltzan had gone to Washington as German ambassador and Schubert, who had been the father of the Anglo-German understanding on the Indian issue, became state secretary at the AA. He now feared that a further British clarification might expose the old Anglo-German plot relating to the Berlin Indians and portray the ex-secretary, Maltzan, and the ministerial dirigent of the Oriental division, Richthofen, in an unfavourable light.[84] He did not, of course, mention his own discreditable role in this unsavoury episode.

Although late, clear thinking and good sense ultimately prevailed among the German officials deciding the fate of the unwanted Indians. After Crerar's statement in Simla, the AA finally decided that a British directed and supervised extradition of the Indian nationalists, who had throughout the War worked on the German side against the British, would be nothing less than a mean-minded betrayal. No government worth its salt could undertake such a venture. Only with a prior guarantee of amnesty could, if at all, one think of such an extradition.[85]

The AA therefore hoped that the British would understand their latest position *vis-à-vis* the Indian nationalists, who would not be extradited but asked to shun politics as long as they remained in Germany. The British understood the German problem. As Sir Arthur Hirtzel of the India Office pointed out to Dufour, it would be much better if the Indian agitators remained under control in Germany, a country friendly to Britain, rather than left free to continue their activities in countries like Austria or Switzerland.[86]

The records of the AA do not say why it was only by the end of 1924 that the Anglo-German plot against the Berlin Indians was considered unethical. However, it seems likely that on this issue Schubert faced some opposition all along from within the AA, and when the whole affair leaked out from the British side, he being the state secretary then, feared to take such a controversial decision. There is evidence that the Berlin Indians—Chatto in particular—had some sympathizers in the AA as well as other governmental departments. Dufour, for example, wrote to Berlin once: 'It is also known in British Government circles that the German Government does not have any ground to expel these Indians since, as far as German interests are concerned, they have not behaved in any unpleasant manner. But it is also known to the British Government that some German officials have rather close contacts with these Indians which, from the British point of view, is regrettable.'[87]

3. Attacking German Racial Trade Policy, 1925

Hardly had Chatto's period of hiding in Berlin come to an end, and he began to breathe a bit freely again, when he had to put all his energy into his *Industrial and Trade Review for India (ITRFI)*, a journal through which he wanted to promote good understanding between the peoples of Germany and India. However, Germany's feverish excitement about the Indian market and the manner of conducting business in India primarily through Europeans in the same manner as in the pre-War years of racial imperialism—without caring for the political changes that had taken place not only in India but in the Weimar Germany as well—shocked and angered him. As an ardent nationalist of a subjugated land, he could not restrain himself from attacking this development.

Two events, in particular, angered Chatto in the middle of 1925. One was an editorial in an English number of a German trade magazine called *Export and Import Review* entitled 'Betrayers of the White Man's Cause'. The other was an interview given by the German consul-general in India, Ruedt, while on leave in Berlin. The main thrust of the editorial was the seeking of British help in German trade expansion in non-white areas of the world.[88] But the crude and roundabout way of putting it across with absurd logic, self-righteousness, and pathetic old-fashioned racial prejudice made the whole piece at once obnoxious and highly objectionable. Here is a sample:

> International trade has had good cause lately to be apprehensive of the future dealing and trading of the white races with the coloured races of this world. Events at Morocco, and elsewhere are, as was to be expected, but symptomatic of the logical consequences of the policy embarked upon by the British and the French Government during the war to introduce coloured soldiers on the battlefields of Europe to fight the battles of white men against white men...But since the recruiting of coloured soldiers from all parts of the world and by 29 different nations against 65 million German population consummated in fact, at least in the minds of the coloured races, in the communistic principle of brotherhood between all men on earth; and it is only natural that the perpetrators of this betrayal of the white man's cause should in the course of time reap what they have sown...That a wide fissure between the former good relations of white and coloured races has burst open as a result of the betrayal of the white man's cause by the French and English war Governments, there can be little doubt in the mind of every sane and levelheaded man. Let us hope, however, that at least the British Government will again try by a well-considered policy carried out on old traditional British lines to readjust the differences between the contending races and somewhat rehabilitate the white man in the esteem of the coloured races.[89]

The editorial provoked the ardent anti-imperialist and progressive-minded Chatto not only to denounce its contents with caustic humour but also to tell a few home truths to the Germans in general.[90] Calling it an absurd notion to make colour a basis of dividing the world commercially, Chatto first commented:

> But if the white colour is taken as the unit and the expression "coloured races" is continually used in a provocative manner, the other continents may retaliate and,

by using black as *their* unit of comparison, carry on a murderous crusade against the "bleached races of the world".

He then summed up the inner feeling of the black races pungently with a Punjabi epigrammatic verse where the poet says: 'Whereas a black spot on a white skin is considered a sign of beauty, a white spot on a black skin is regarded as a sign of disease.' Chatto also lashed out at the editor for his comment on 'the Communistic principle of brotherhood' with the following argument:

What is still more surprising to us, however, is to find the journal denouncing "the communistic principle of brotherhood between all men on earth". We always understood this to be the basis of Christ's teaching and we have been told by German and other Christian missionaries that Christianity was the only religion that brought about this brotherhood—although, in view of the open feuds between Catholics, Protestants, Presbyterians, Baptists, Methodists etc., it has always been somewhat difficult to see where Christian brotherhood lies. Nor, indeed, do we quite understand where "white solidarity" is to be found, considering that all Germans and all Frenchmen, almost without exception, are preparing again to spring at each others' throats and to shed some more of their precious "white" blood, which might better be employed for the furtherance of the "white man's cause" among the coloured races.[91]

What did the 'white man's cause' actually signify at that time? Chatto answered:

To England it means the cause of British world domination and the elimination of all rivals whether white, brown, black, yellow or red. To Germany it means hanging on to England in order to get a strip of land in the interior of Africa and be allowed to trade in India and other countries under British rule, in return for which the Germans are prepared to make *salaams* to the English and help them keep down the populations of those countries.[92]

Chatto then exposed the fatalistic attitude of hanging on to the white man's superiority theory and ignoring the different aspirations, attitudes, and values of the emerging people of the exploited areas of the world:

It shows deplorable ignorance on the part of a journal dealing with world trade, when the latter asserts that the events in "Morocco, China and elsewhere" (the mention of India is carefully avoided) are the "logical consequences" of the policy of bringing "coloured troops" to Europe. Asia and Africa have suffered enough at the hands of the "white man" to arise at last and throw out the oppressors and pirates bag and baggage. But we in Asia have hitherto confined our definition of the white man to England and if we have sympathy with Germany and respect for her tremendous scientific and cultural achievements, it is not because the Germans are white but because they are an able, hard-working and persevering people from whom we have had no fear of aggression.

Then with an eye to the official German attitude towards the awakening of India Chatto said:

If Germans in India wish to express their sense of the "white man's cause" by fraternally imbibing whisky and soda in English clubs, they must not expect to retain friendship or esteem of the people of India. The sooner the hypocrisy of Christian brotherhood and the fiction of the white man are given up, the better for the future of the Germans both politically and commercially.[93]

Chatto went further to tell the Germans how faulty and humiliating their adherence to the 'white man's cause' actually was in the commercial field:

We recognize only economic factors as determining the actions and sentiments of the peoples, and we would understand the Germans if they frankly told us that, as they are financially dependent on Anglo-America, they know they are in the position of slaves and are therefore, unable to take action at present. But, after they have been beaten, robbed and humiliated by some white races, it is evidence of the complete absence of self-respect on their part to seek cooperation with them on the ground of having the same colour. Englishmen, whom most Germans regard as their superiors in culture as well as in political wisdom, never base their trade or foreign policy on the fictitious and imaginary foundation of colour. England allied herself for years with the Japanese, while the Kaiser insulted the latter by calling them yellow monkeys.[94]

Chatto's double-edged rejoinder ended with an advice to Germany:

The war of emancipation of Asia from British imperialism is inevitable, and Germany has the best chances of securing the commercial friendship of India, China and other countries by lending her moral support to them in their struggle.[95]

This moral support for the Indians' national aspirations, which Chatto desired so much from the German officials never showed up throughout the 1920s and 30s except in the case of one or two individuals in the AA. As for the German officials posted in India, it is extraordinary that throughout this period none of them had anything positive to say about the Indians as a people inspite of their full knowledge of the love. Indians had for Germany and things German. Whatever may have been the other factors in consummating such a psyche among the German officials in India, it is difficult to overlook that racialism was one of them.[96]

Ruedt's earliest reaction to the emerging India has already been discussed. In July 1924, in a despatch to Berlin, describing the latest political situation in India, he remarked that, with the passage of time, the Indian civil servants, formerly a very exalted class, were gradually coming under the critical observation of the Indian people and the dislike of the British bureaucracy among the masses was increasing by the day. But he warned the AA not to draw a wrong conclusion:

We are not interested in the removal of British control of India which under the present inner political situation could result only in anarchy, civil war, and economic blockade against foreign countries....Free competition for all exporting countries in India with the maintenance of peace and order through British police and military force will serve the German trade in India best. Therefore, all efforts counteracting this situation, no matter whether they come from the British or the Indian side, do not receive our sympathy.[97]

The other German officials in India at the time shared this view. In the spring of 1925, Ruedt left for Germany on furlough and his deputy, Wilhelm von Pochhammer, officiated as the acting consul general in India. Although celebrated later, both in free India and the Federal Republic of Germany, not only as an authority on India but also a wellwisher of Indian freedom, Pochhammer advised the AA to fight shy of Indian nationalism throughout his career in India before Indian independence.[98] To give an example of his racial prejudice against Indians, on 25 June 1925 Pochhammer obtained his long-awaited appointment with Sir Charles Innes, a member of the Viceroy's council in charge of trade and traffic. Pochhammer pleaded for the removal of restrictions on the Germans in India imposed since the War. He particularly requested that a permanent stay permit be granted to German businessmen in India until the more basic issue of the reopening of the pre-War German business houses was resolved.[99] Reasoning why Germans should be allowed into India to handle German products and trade before the time envisaged, Pochhammer argued that the exclusion of German firms from India hit not just German products but legitimate German trade as well, and explained that, due to the absence of old responsible German business houses, unreliable Indian firms had substituted for them and brought uncertainty to the market through unpredictable and erratic prices.[100] It is not known how Innes, whom Pochhammer described as 'an elderly, extremely dry and not very friendly bureaucrat', reacted to this racial tinge in his thoughts. British officials seldom took kindly to racialism shown by foreigners in India. In 1883, when the German consul in Calcutta, Wilhelm Bleek, played a conspicuous role in the agitation of the whites against the new criminal bill, known as the Ilbert Bill, and the *Ostsee-Zeitung* reported about it, the India Office found the conduct of the German consul 'unusual' since he was a German and not a British subject.[101] In this case, we only know that Innes said that he was not in a position to give Pochhammer an immediate answer.[102]

If German officials in India had kept these ideas about Indians to themselves, there would not have been any problem. But the German business world at this time was so excited about the expanding Indian market[103] and Ruedt, too, was so busy, even on leave, selling this lucrative market to enthuastic professionals back home that, on one occasion, he let slip some derogatory remarks in public about Indians and their character. After one of his public talks[104] at the AA in Berlin in May 1925, he was interviewed by the *Industrie-und Handelszeitung* (*IHZ*), a prestigious trade journal close to the AA. Ruedt first gave the journal the good news that Germany's export to India had already reached the pre-War level, occupying third place after England and Japan, and then spoke about the great and almost unlimited possibilities for expanding this market by bringing in many other classes of German goods, particularly machinery. The problem with the export of German machinery was that it required German engineers to be stationed in India, attached to their firms, which was not possible because of the restrictions on Germans settling in India until 31 August 1926. For obvious reasons, English and American engineers could not be approached and the Indians, according to Ruedt, lacked the ability, skill, and education necessary for the purpose. But the greatest problem in India, in Ruedt's eyes, as revealed in the published interview in *IHZ* was that 'the Indian, whether he be a Hindu or a Mohamedan, is, as a rule, a very untrustworthy businessman. He looks only to the immediate profits of the day and takes special pleasure in withdrawing from all obligations that do not promise the same successful results as had been originally expected.' Ruedt said that the situation was rendered more difficult for the Europeans owing to the fact that the registration of firms was not compulsory in India, and the buyer or the agent, therefore, often left premises where his business was located and reappeared again in some other place.[105]

Ruedt then entered into very sensitive terrain, and let loose some of his pet remarks on the Indian national movement (he called it a revolutionary movement), which had so far been confined to his confidential official reports only. He said:

> As a matter of principle, the Indian is decidedly pro-German, a fact which is due partially to his hostility to England. The success of the revolutionary movement is, however, not to be expected for many years to come, and would indeed signify the end of all foreign trade relations, owing to the war of religions that would break out.[106]

Ruedt's interview, published in *IHZ* as an article in his name, naturally annoyed Chatto. After verifying the contents from the editors of the journal and vainly waiting for two weeks for a dementi from Ruedt, he published a rejoinder in *ITRFI* in June 1925. He said, 'The opinions expressed by the Consul General in this interview were, we fear, based on the information of interested persons and therefore could not be regarded either as unbiased or as final.' He then went straight to the basic question of the propriety of the consul's public statement, and raised some pertinent questions: Were such opinions voiced by a German official personage of Ruedt's position going to strengthen the friendly feelings for Germany that had hitherto characterized the educated Indian? Was it proper for Ruedt to make propaganda in favour of British rule in India? Should he spread the thoroughly false notion that the attainment of national independence would mean the end of all foreign relations in India? Had it not been exactly what the British wished the world to believe, that without the British there would be chaos in India?[107]

Chatto argued that a self-governing India would serve the German interest better and not worse. Germany's Indian trade under Britain's monopoly constituted only 7 per cent of total Indian trade, while Britain held 65 per cent. A liberated India, after a short period of adjustment, would be a far better customer of Germany than an India under Britain. So Chatto asserted that it could only be in German interest to abandon race prejudice, and advised the Germans to make up their minds once and for all to take an active part in the economic progress of India, progress which presupposed national liberty.[108]

IHZ also interviewed Chatto at the time and published a lengthy article embodying some of Chatto's proposals for the strengthening of German-Indian trade relations. Some of the suggestions were: a more efficient propaganda in the Indian languages; establishment of a non-official advisory institution in India; encouragement of Indians to come to Germany; scientific and technical training of the Indians on a large scale in German universities and factories; and the foundation of a German-Indian Association. *IHZ* also praised the *ITRFI* for working successfully on those lines, and also emphasized the necessity of bringing together all common German and Indian interests in a centralized association. The function of such an association in Berlin would be, the journal wrote with special reference to the credibility of Indian firms, to found a news service to supply interesting information from India to Germans and keep Indians informed of conditions in Germany. It was also thought advisable to establish a permanent exhibition of Indian raw produce and manufactured goods. The paper underlined the importance to Germany of the practical training of Indians in German factories.[109]

Chatto had sent his article on Ruedt to the AA, and he also received the information that it was read there. Yet there was no dementi from Ruedt who was still in Germany. Meanwhile, the press in India, particularly the *Forward*, took up the matter from Chatto's journal and other Indian sources from Germany, and Indian business people of all communities addressed letters to both the German consul general in India and to the editorial staff of *ITRFI*.[110] Only three months after the publication of the interview in *IHZ*, and that too at the behest of Pochhammer, did Ruedt write a clarification to the AA and send a dementi each to Pochhammer and to the editors of *ITRFI* in the second and third weeks of August 1925.[111] This dementi arrived too late to make it to the next issue of *ITRFI* in the second half of August, but the editors gave the news of its arrival and promised to publish it in full in the next issue. It, however, warned that the responsibility for the consequences of the interview would lie solely with Ruedt and the AA allowing allegations to stand unanswered for three months, particularly since *IHZ* was the organ of the heavy industry and was generally looked upon as a semi-official organ of the German government.[112]

Ruedt's dementi was merely a proforma piece meant to hoodwink everyone. Since the interview in *IHZ* appeared as an article under his name, he simply denied having written it. He blamed the editors of *ITRFI* for not taking the trouble of verifying whether the statements attributed to him had really come from him.[113] In the dementi that Ruedt forwarded to Pochhammer, a copy of which was attached to the letter to *ITRFI*, Ruedt denied: a) having expressed the opinion about the untrustworthiness of Indian businessmen in general; b) having said that in principle an Indian was distinctly pro-German because of his anti-English feelings.[114]

In reply to Ruedt *ITRFI* expressed their happiness in learning that those sweeping remarks did not emanate from him. However, the journal categorically denied that their action to publish the *IHZ* article was hasty when they had actually waited for more than two weeks before translating and commenting on the article in *ITRFI*. After all, the journal wrote to Ruedt, 'two weeks was a sufficient period of time for the German Foreign Office to realise either that you had committed a first-rate political blunder or that the *Industrie-und Handels-Zeitung* had been guilty of attributing untrue or indiscreet statements to a high official of the German Government.'[115]

Chatto vehemently rejected the charge that, by publishing material from *IHZ*, his journal departed from its avowed policy of promoting friendly trade relations between Germany and India. In fact, it was the alleged opinions of an official of Ruedt's position that had done infinite harm to Indian business with Germany, and had strengthened the prevailing scepticism about India.[116] Chatto then tried to explain the widely prevalent scepticism about Indians, which, as we have already seen, was also the subject of Pochhammer's interview with Sir Charles Innes. 'This scepticism', Chatto wrote, 'arose principally during the notorious period of inflation through the glaring acts of dishonesty committed by a number both of Indian as well as of German firms, has no real foundation in fact, and the chief result of it is that Indo-German business is passing more and more into British hands to the obvious detriment of both countries.' After this introduction, Chatto took a potshot at Ruedt: 'We took it for granted that you were particularly anxious not to offend the susceptibilities of the British Government, for no politically conscious German diplomat would otherwise go so far as to alienate the sympathies of a whole nation of 300 million souls.'[117] Chatto then demanded from Ruedt or the AA a dementi in the German press. In another section of the same issue of the journal he wrote:

We must, however, add that we do not intend to let the matter drop until exactly the same dementi has been published at least in the Berlin journal in which his [Ruedt's] interview appeared, as infinite harm has been done to India in German business circles where the interview has been widely circulated. The fact that hesitation is being shown in the publication of a categorical denial in the German press, seriously diminishes the value of the Baron's letters to us and to the Acting Consul General in India. We do not believe that the Baron is entitled to rehabilitation in India until the mischief that has been done by his alleged interview in Germany has been fully redressed.[118]

The main point of Ruedt's letter to the AA was that his interview to *IHZ* appeared as an article under his name, and if he had known it beforehand he would never have permitted it to happen. There was no categorical denial of the controversial remarks. In fact, he wrote that 'even though in the interest of German trade certain truths should never remain hidden, because of his position as the official German representative he should not have been named as the source.'[119] Since most of his opinions were already known to the AA, he did not have to explain more except to point out that some of his statements were highlighted in a generalized form by *IHZ* and the remark on Indian businessmen was one of them. He added that in his despatches as consul general he often warned against traffic with unknown customers.[120] It is no wonder, therefore, that Ruedt's letter to *IHZ* contained no objection to any of his reported controversial utterances as such. He merely endeavoured to explain that it was not easy for him to discuss such a wide-ranging topic as the economic and political situation of India in a short time and therefore some points appeared to have been misunderstood. He only tried to say that the freedom of India from British rule would not by itself leave India in a satisfactory situation.[121]

Ruedt's letter to *IHZ* was also not a dementi as such. That is why the paper too had no complaints against Chatto's journal except to point out that Ruedt's word 'workmen' (arbeiter) had wrongly been translated as 'servants' by *ITRFI* which showed Ruedt's statement in an awkward light.[122] This proved that *IHZ* had truthfully reproduced Ruedt's statements and there was nothing for which they had to apologize.

Since Ruedt did not appear repentant, Chatto attacked him for insulting Indians as a whole:

Because a few masons or painters swindled him out of a few hundred rupees—as we understand was actually the case—the Baron is not entitled to pass judgement on the entire working class of India.[123]

The *ITRFI* blamed the AA as well for playing a double game with the Indian people, for while the consul general said categorically that he had not made the objectionable statements, no real dementi had been received by *IHZ*.[124]

Chatto's relentless search for the truth at last alerted the AA, and although the present controversy was not settled, they took steps to avoid controversies in the future. The AA did not specifically object to Ruedt's remarks, but took exception to the fact that the remarks were printed under his name. In order to avoid such mistakes in the future, senior councillor of legation and the new head of Department III, Walter de Haas (1864–1931), decided to send a decree to all German missions abroad asking their officials to be careful if on a home visit to Germany they were approached by journals like *IHZ* for interviews. They were to make sure beforehand whether or not they would want any potentially controversial statements attributed to them published under their names.[125]

Internal investigations, in the aftermath of the Ruedt controversy, further revealed to the surprise of many officials that IHZ's relations with the AA were closer than had been generally known. There existed a separate section in the AA, called Special Section N, which even received a monthly amount of 1200 marks from the journal for giving it official information for publication. This special section therefore opposed the decree by de Haas, arguing that in practical terms the decree would be a warning to all foreign representatives of the German government. They made an alternative suggestion to persuade the chief editor of the journal to an agreement that, in future, prior AA permission would be necessary for publishing anything from official German representatives abroad.[126]

It is amazing how the AA tackled the whole issue without the slightest concern for the offended feelings of Indians both in Berlin and India. There was no attempt to heal the wounds by any other means than the legalistic interpretation taken by Ruedt, denying authorship just because he did not write the article himself. The thinking of the other German officials—Pochhammer, for example—was along the same lines, and he expected nothing more from Ruedt as he maintained exactly the same opinion and asserted it in the same way, although not in public.

In contrast to these German officials in India, some of the Berlin Indians—like Chatto, Nambiar, Smedley (not Indian by birth or citizenship but in spirit), and Pillai—worked for a deep and abiding understanding between India and Germany. At this time Nambiar and Smedley contributed to the Indian press articles not only on Indo-German relations but also on the arts, science, and culture of Germany. Pochhammer once lamented that British press agencies did not bring good German news to India. He admitted that *The Hindu*, by starting a direct 'Letter from Berlin' column, brought factual information about Germany's cultural and intellectual life, and newly-published books. Discoveries by Spengler, Einstein, Stinnes, and Miethe were also regularly reviewed.[127] But Pochhammer, rather stingy and ungenerous, recorded no praise or appreciation in his despatches for these Berlin Indians in popularizing the sunny side of German life. Neither he nor any other German official in India showed any interest in the cultural and intellectual life of India or, for that matter, in Indology except perhaps for its misuse.[128]

Thinking only of German trade interests in India, which to them primarily depended on the British, the AA gave little thought to the redress of the grievances of the Indians. They, however, persuaded some of the Indians concerned in the controversy to propagate for the German government. Since it was Pillai's letter and its enclosures[129] to the confidential councillor of legation, Dr Pruefer, which had thrown up a discussion of racial trade policy at the AA, Pruefer now asked Pillai to circulate Ruedt's dementi to Pochhammer in India.[130]

After WWI, Indian trade laws prohibited German businessmen from operating in India until 1 September 1926. There was a fear that this restriction would be prolonged if Germany failed to take steps against War-time Indians as desired by the British. Far from prolonging it, Germany's visible harassment of Chatto convinced the British to overcome their distrust of Germany and bring forward the abrogation of this restriction by one year. In this connection, the Foreign Office praised its policy towards the Indians and wrote to the Association of German Industry and Commerce that the grant of citizenship to the Berlin Indians would not be in the larger interest of German trade in India as it might give the British new grounds for suspicion.[131]

Before we conclude this part on Germany's racial trade policy in

India during the Weimar Republic, a word about the difference between the personalities of Ruedt and Chatto will not be out of place. Ruedt and Chatto were both men with their own missions and principles. Ruedt's mission in India was to win the Indian market for German manufacturers and help German import houses acquire much-needed raw material from India as smoothly as possible. The two prerequisites for him to succeed in this mission were (a) the cultivation of close relations with British ruling and professional circles in India, for which he had the built-in advantage of being an anglophile, and (b) an untroubled political situation in India congenial to trade. He would have preferred if the Indians had no aspirations for self rule, let alone a movement for independence. Since it was not to be, he made it a principle never to do anything that might even remotely be seen as helping Indian nationalism. He sought Indian help only when German self-interest required it, and advised the AA not to overestimate the strength of the Indian national movement. He could always hide his antipathy towards Indian nationalism behind the diplomatic veil, or advance the hackneyed argument that, since Germany's only interest in India was economic, it could not be involved in India's political conflict with the British.

Like Ruedt, Chatto worked in the interest of *his* country. His whole life of exile in Europe was devoted to a single goal: the development of the Indian national movement with the ultimate aim of freeing India from the British. He had been a tireless campaigner against British imperialism since 1909, and the British considered him a difficult and dangerous enemy. It was Chatto's lifelong principle not to compromise with any betrayal to nationalist India, and he had the courage to fight anybody whom he considered an enemy of Indian nationalism with every means at his disposal. It was therefore unavoidable that these two men would one day, as a matter of course, clash.

Ruedt's success with the British in India and his advice to Berlin against Indian nationalism seem to have encouraged the group around Schubert, ministerial director and head of Department III in the AA in 1923, to take the questionable abortive measures against the Berlin Indians.

4. 'INDIANS IN THE BERLIN ZOO' EPISODE, 1926–7

At a time when the German government ardently desired to profit from the Indian market while still ignoring the national sensitivities of the Indian people, there happened in 1926 a climactic event in Berlin, lasting for four months, called the 'Indian show'. The show was organized by John Hagenbeck, an adventurous planter and collector of animals for zoological gardens, who had spent long years in South and Southeast Asia.[132] It aspired to present an authentic ethnological introduction to day-to-day Indian life with the help of about a hundred Indians and Sri Lankans, performing as fakirs, street magicians, snake charmers, craftsmen, and so on. The show took place in the compound of the Berlin Zoological garden, although with a separate entrance, and since the area was generally called The Zoo, Hagenbeck thought it fit to advertise the show through posters as 'India in the Zoo'. The posters were misunderstood or misinterpreted by some, and the show came to be described as 'Indians in the Zoo'.

The Indians in Berlin at once protested against the event complaining about the manner in which Indians had been presented in the show, as if their standard of civilization were akin to that of animals. An organization called the Association of Indians in Central Europe was the first to sound the matter with the Chancellor's office.[133] In this appeal, Chatto's line of thought was discernible: since India had no representation in Germany, and the British Embassy would not take any measure against an event that only abetted British imperialism, the German government should either stop the show or at least shift its venue to another place. After all, there were no such shows depicting the people of Europe in an unflattering manner. The appeal added that, if nothing was done, it would adversely affect the future political, economic, and cultural relations of Germany with India.[134]

Going by the principle that 'what is legal is also permissible', the AA took only a legalistic view of the matter. It found out from the Indologist Professor Helmut von Glasenapp that the Association of Indians in Central Europe was absolutely insignificant as was its secretary, Kapur, who had signed the appeal. Glasenapp, who was at the mercy of the British for a visa to go to India and Britain for research purposes, said that the venue in the zoo was selected 'not to show disrespect to the Indians but to show respect to the elephants for whom there was no place in German guesthouses.'[135] The AA informed Kapur and Pillai, Indian representatives, that the German government could do as little to stop the show as it could to prevent the Indians from protesting. Moreover, German artists performed everywhere in foreign countries, and even German religious performances were held in the USA.[136]

The controversy continued throughout the duration of the show both in Germany[137] and India. There were, no doubt, comments in German papers which considered the Indian criticism of the show oversensitive. But quite a few reputed newspapers sympathized with the Indian reaction. *Berliner Tageblatt* in one of their reports on the event considered the title *Indienschau* (India Show) not only an exaggeration but also funny. It then commented, 'Really, one has to go about very carefully with the nations, and the longer the distance the more careful one should be.' Linking the show with Germany's interest in the impending second visit of Tagore to Germany, the author however added that the Indians might 'console themselves with the knowledge that not every nation can send such a representative to foreign people.'[138] Similarly, the *Dresdener Neueste Nachrichten*, in one article, commented that although the show claimed to have portrayed an aspect of popular anthropology, 'seldom has the popular aspect been so frivolously dealt with as here.' The paper, which also introduced Chatto's anxieties about the consequent deterioration of Indo-German relations if German authorities remained inactive, considered it a mistake to put such a big semi-official institution like the Berlin Zoo at the disposal of Hagenbeck. 'It is regrettable,' the paper said, 'that such a kind of anthropology should be imposed on the German audience.'[139]

The inaction of the German government led Chatto, Nambiar, and Smedley to take the matter to the Indian people through their nationalist press.

No sooner were the first two reports of the show published in *The Hindu* (Madras) and *Forward* (Calcutta) in August 1926, than Ruedt in Calcutta was alerted. He found the reports and their repercussion among the readers 'unfriendly to Germany'.[140] He asked the AA to give him details of the case with which to confront the Indian reaction. Without them, the best course according to him would be to keep silent. The *Forward* report, possibly written by A.C.N. Nambiar,[141] showed the Indians' feeling of humiliation and the hopelessness of their situation:

India is a congenial field for exploitation of the 'civilised' whites. John Hagenbeck, a German, has been described as a famous importer of animals and birds. Possibly he has come to believe that members of subject nations easily come within the definition of 'animals'. So instead of importing birds and wild animals from India, he has imported nearly two hundred Indians of poorest and most primitive class and has been making money by exhibiting them. ... It is useless, however, to condemn Hagenbeck, for the Jallianwalla Bagh massacre has created the impression that Indians are hardly better than zebras and monkeys.[142]

Reports of the Berlin show in Indian papers instigated readers' harsh reaction to the show. Ruedt, however, did not advise the AA to intervene in the controversy, and not even change the venue of the show. He was angry with the Berlin correspondents of the Indian papers, particularly the *Forward*. The articles and letters in the *Forward* were, according to him, 'conceived in a spirit of hostility to Germany'.[143] Ruedt turned to one Dr Goswami, supposed to be an investor in the *Forward*, to use his influence to prevent the publication of such articles. Ruedt told him that he had learned from reports in reputed German newspapers that the exhibition had been arranged in the form of an Indian village showing all the charms of Indian village life, the working of Indian home industry, and the skills of Indian artisans. According to the pictures published in the papers, the Indians taking part in the exhibition seemed happy, free in their movements, and well-looked after. Had it been otherwise, he continued, not just German authorities but also British diplomatic and consular representatives looking after the interests of Indian subjects in Germany, would have intervened.[144] Ruedt, no doubt, cleverly used the Berlin Indians' argument about the British Embassy's silence to German advantage. He further wrote to Goswami:

I finally leave it to you to decide whether it benefits the Indian people to loosen by such incidents the ties of friendship and consideration which have always existed between our both countries by reason of deep interest of German scholars in matters of Indian philosophy, religion and Sanskrit and by reason of the admiration of Indian educated classes for German refinement and culture.[145]

Since the articles in the Indian papers also cited critical 'fairness' by some German papers, Ruedt advised the AA to locate these newspapers and tell them that their 'fairness' might bring danger to German trade in India through a possible boycott. After all, he argued, if German criticism of the show could be used by the Indians, all his efforts to promote Indo-German understanding would be in vain.[146]

Seeing the inaction of Germans officials to stop the show and the weakness of educated Indians in pressing the British Indian government to intervene, Smedley, a lifelong crusader for the cause of the oppressed, deprived, and subjugated peoples, wrote an article from Salzburg, Austria, and sent it to *The People* of *Lahore*, edited by Lajpat Rai. The article appeared in early September under the heading 'Indians in Zoological Garden'.[147] She first gave a picture of the overbearing and arrogant character of Hagenbeck who insulted the delegation of Indians that went to see him. Then she attacked the British Indian government which issued passports freely to those going abroad to be exhibited in the animal gardens of Europe, and yet blocking Indian students intending to travel to Germany for higher studies. She saw it as utter callousness—even a deep-seated spiritual rot—when the ruling capitalist classes could buy human beings who had not money enough to refuse to sell themselves. She did not spare the Indian social background either which permitted such conditions to exist. Her conclusion was that India could do nothing against such humiliation until she became politically free.[148]

Perhaps influenced by Smedley's article, a German lady at Mahatma Gandhi's *ashram* in Sabarmati also wrote to the German President Hindenburg by the end of September 1926 regarding the Indian show and the unhappiness of respectable Indians on this account.[149] This letter was forwarded to the AA by an official of the President's office. The AA wrote to the official that even if the government tried to respect the feelings of the Indian nationals, it would not be possible to advise its consular representation to deny visa to Indian citizens, who of their own will wanted to join Hagenbeck's troupe.[150]

The only substantial protest in India came at long last from the Indian Chamber of Commerce of the United Provinces on 6 October 1926. The Chamber wrote that if the facts in the article by Smedley were substantially correct, the Chamber could not condemn the event in Germany too strongly.[151] Ruedt doubted Smedley's objectivity, and said she pursued 'a certain aim and in order to give more weight to her deductions she is undoubtedly inclined to exaggerate.'[152] Ruedt further pointed out that Hagenbeck was a private citizen, and that the 'German authorities are as unable to interfere as would be the authorities of any European country under similar circumstances.'[153] Ruedt then not only reiterated the age-long German devotion to Indology—the same passage which he had used in his letter to Goswami— but also mentioned in a rather overbearing and insolent manner the things for which Indians should remain grateful to Germany:

> The aggressive articles which in connection with the Berlin exhibition have recently been published in Indian papers in a spirit decidedly hostile to my country are a poor form of gratitude for the hospitality, asylum and education so many Indians enjoy in Germany.[154]

No doubt Ruedt thought, and not incorrectly, that Chatto and his followers were behind the writings in the Indian press, explaining his reference to asylum.

By the end of 1926, the controversy died down, and the show ended in October. Both Chatto and Smedley now became extremely involved in their own individual pursuits. Chatto was organizing a conference in Brussels which would lead to the League Against Imperialism[155], while Smedley went back to her lessons at the University of Berlin for a doctorate degree.[156] Just then Hagenbeck decided to take Smedley to court for circulating misleading information in her articles, including the account of the earnings of the Indians taking part in the show and their treatment. He claimed that what the Indians earned from him in six months, they would earn in India in five to 10 years.[157] Under public pressure, the British Indian government also enquired about the matter at last, and concluded that there was no basis for the allegation that the Indians were exhibited 'along with animals' since 'the troupe occupied a portion of the zoological gardens...railed off from the rest of the gardens.'[158] Considering that a court case would only harm Indo-German relations, the Indians involved—Chatto, Nambiar, Pillai, Smedley—decided to settle the case with Hagenbeck out of court, especially when an opportunity was offered by Dr Fritz Grobba (1886–1973), who had just returned after a spell in Afghanistan to take charge of the Asian desk at the AA. Friendly and familiar with the Asian mindset, Grobba endeavoured with Chatto and Smedley to reach an amicable solution.[159] As a result, Smedley, in a statement of apology to Hagenbeck, in early February 1927, conceded some misrepresentations or exaggerations and promised to send the necessary corrections to the journal *The People* for publication.[160]

In March 1927, *The People* published Smedley's corrections.[161] However, in the same month, after the conclusion of the Brussels conference of the League Against Imperialism, the last word on the subject came from Chatto, Nambiar, and Smedley in a joint article from Brussels to the *Bombay Chronicle*. It thrashed the British ambassador for his 'amazing attitude' in defending the show:

Indians to be shown in Europe as primitive, uncultured people is but another way of supporting the British argument that Indians are half-barbarian and must live under British yoke.[162]

That there was a substance in the Indians' argument was proved within a few years when Hitler told 5000 German students in Munich in January 1936, 'Colonies are owned by the right of might. Europe needs raw material and colonies, and because of an heroic concept of life the white race is destined to rule.' He then added that the British went to India 'to teach the Indians how to walk.'[163]

While the Indian Show at the Berlin Zoo was on (it went on till 7 October 1926), Tagore arrived in Berlin in early September for his second visit (the first was in 1921) to Germany. The utmost precaution that the AA took not to offend the British in any way while participating in some of the Tagore-related events, showed how the British in India were more important to the German officials than the Indians at this time.

In early June 1926, while in Italy, Tagore expressed to a German journalist his wish to go to Germany and visit President Hindenburg.[164] Since Tagore was a government guest in Italy, the AA thought it wise to carry out the wish of the renowned Nobel Lamreate by arranging an audience with the President and organizing a reception in his honour. But the problem was how to set about it. India was not represented directly in Germany and an official arrangement with the British Embassy would be awkward. So a plan was devised along with Loewenthal, with whom Tagore was staying at Hotel Kaiserhof, and the Hindustan Association, the leading Indian students' organization in Berlin.[165] The fact that Chatto was no longer actively associated with the Hindustan Association at this time, and that the Association had discarded political agitation lately, made the task less problematic for the AA. The AA let the Hindustan Association organize a reception with invitees both official and non-official, with its approval.[166] The other conditions were: the invitation would be issued in the name of the Hindustan Association; except for Tarachand Roy, the President of the Association, and Tagore, no other person would be allowed to speak from the Indian side; the British ambassador would be invited; and the Prussian cultural ministry would foot the bill. Additionally, the AA also consulted with Ingram, the first secretary of the British Embassy, who was fully satisfied with the arrangements. It was also emphasized to the British official that the event was not organized by the German government through its Foreign Office but by the Prussian cultural ministry.[167] Tagore considered the Indian show 'unfortunate'. Nevertheless, he praised German culture highly saying, 'Only the German civilisation is capable to save the world.'[168]

5. COLLAPSE OF INSIB

Because of the lack of resources and the combined hostility of both German and British Indian governments, Chatto's INSIB failed to survive. Since the British Indian government proscribed the *ITRFI* from circulation in India, its publisher saw no reason to invest in a journal which was banned in the very place for which it was primarily meant. A part of Chatto's good work for Indian students and Indian businessmen was salvaged by Jawaharlal Nehru when he persuaded the Indian National Congress to issue from 1928 onwards a nominal recurring grant to INSIB's offspring organization. the new organization was called the Indian Information Bureau and was under the official management of Nambiar.

Lucie Hecht, an expert stenographer and English, French, and German translator who had the honour of translating for Tagore to the poet's utmost satisfaction, during his lecture tour in Germany in 1926 worked for Chatto all through 1923–31, in all the organizations he was involved with.[169] Recalling the INSIB days 46 years later, she said the following about the organization and its moving spirit:

> The Berlin-Halensee office was the spiritual, cultural and social focal point for the Indian students and trainees, Hindus and Muslims alike. It was a tragic disaster when, because of lack of money, the work had to be abandoned. Here Chatto inspired the Indians, downcast with resignation and fatalism, to action, and he hoped that they would be helpers in the Indian freedom movement and builders of the future independent India. He radiated inspiration not only through his words but also through his dynamic personality. Unremittingly active and indefatigably energetic, he was ever ready with fresh and fruitful ideas to work for the freedom of India which was the abiding passion of his life. His political life brought him many stresses and strains. But he remained undaunted and cheerful all through his political career. If thwarted in one direction, he would branch out in another. His powerful personality and self-appointed mission attracted many friends as well as enemies. But only his close friends knew his weaknesses, although he did everything openly—sometimes perhaps too openly for his own good. He could be provoked to anger, but he always rose above pettiness, malice and underhand tricks.[170]

Hazards in Promoting Indo-German Relations 1921–6 215

NOTES

1. However, the Indians informed the AA about it only on 8 December 1921. On 19 December 1921, the AA informed the German Embassy in London about the Bureau saying that it had been established a few months before by Bhupendranath Datta and some other Indians. The address of INSIB Ltd. was Buerohaus Boerse, 27 Burgstrasse, Berlin C. 2, INSIB to AA, 8 December 1921 and Schubert to German Embassy, London, 19 December 1921, AA Pol.6. *Nationalitaetenfrage, Fremdvoelker, Indien*. At the time of registration, Chatto was most probably in Stockholm.
2. *Ibid*. The various departments were shown on a printed card.
3. 'Die Aussichten fuer Wirtschaftsbeziehungen des Reichs mit Indien nach dem I. Weltkrieg' (The prospects of economic relations of the Reich with India after the First World War); a report by consul Heyer, Amsterdam, to AA, 13 February 1918, German Federal Archive, Koblenz (Kob.). Heyer had been active in India for more than five years before the War. Later Carl Duisberg, a noted German merchant, voiced a similar opinion in his 'Critical Observation on East India' on the voyage from Rangoon to Penang, 11 January 1929.
4. The most important raw materials Germany imported from India were cotton, oilseeds, jute, furs and skins, rice, manganese ore. *Ibid*., Heyer.
5. On 27 April 1921, the Reparation Commission set German debt at 132,000 million gold marks. Only on 8 July 1932, was the German liability reduced from 25,000 million dollars to 2000 million dollars.
6. The Indian trade laws prohibited the Germans from entering India until 1 September 1926 (later allowed in 1925). The reopening of the consulate in Bombay was allowed only in 1927. The entry to the prestigious British Club was prohibited even to popular German consuls general in Calcutta, and there was also no direct German ship connection to India at this time.
7. See Martin Gilbert, *Britain and Germany between the Wars* (Suffolk, 1964), pp. 43, 72, for D'Abernon's attitude.
8. Indian nationalists of the time knew that well, too. In September 1925, when Ruedt was in Germany on furlough, the acting German consul general in Calcutta wrote to Berlin that nationalist circles in India considered German officials in India Anglophiles. Pochhammer to AA, Calcutta, 4 September 1925, AA Pol.2, *Pol. Bezieh. Indiens zu Deutschland* (2).
9. Ruedt to AA, Calcutta, 17 January 1922, AA Pol.2, *Pol. Bezieh. Indiens zu Deutschland* (I).
10. *Ibid*.
11. *Ibid*. Here also he mentioned that, according to his Italian colleague, this Governor had no special liking for private receptions.
12. *Ibid*.
13. Enclosure to Ruedt to AA, Calcutta, 6 February 1922, AA Pol.12, *Pressewesen, Indien* (I).

14. Ruedt to AA, Calcutta, 17 January 1922, AA Pol.5., *Innere Politik, Parlament und Parteiwesen in Indien* (I).
15. Ruedt to AA, Calcutta, 17 January 1922, AA Pol.3, *Pol. Bezieh. zu England und Indien* (I).
16. Ibid.
17. Schubert's note, 19 December 1921. Po. 6, *Nationalitaetenfrage, Fremdvoelker, Indien*.
18. Ruedt to AA, Calcutta, 15 February 1922, Pol.3, *Pol. Bezieh. zu England und Indien* (I).
19. Ibid.
20. Ibid.
21. Chief Secretary, Government of Bengal to the German consul general, 4 April 1922, AA Pol.10, *Deutsche Dipl. und Konsular. Vertretungen in Indien* (I).
22. Ruedt to AA, Calcutta, 12 January 1923, AA Pol.5. *Innere Politik, Parlament und Parteiwesen in Indien* (2).
23. Ruedt to AA, Calcutta, 22 September 1923, AA, Ibid.
24. Ibid.
25. Ibid.
26. Martin Gilbert, *op.cit.*, pp. 42–3.
27. In Ruedt to AA, Calcutta, 2 October, 1923, AA Pol.2, *Pol. Bezieh. Indiens zu Deutschland* (2).
28. Ibid.
29. Ibid.
30. Ibid.
31. Editor, *Englishman*, to Ruedt, 2 November 1923 in Ruedt to AA, 16 November 1923. Ibid.
32. 'Ruhrites', *Times of India*, 13 November 1923, Ruedt to AA, 16 November 1923. Ibid.
33. Ibid.
34. *Pioneer*, 15 November 1923, in Ruedt to AA, 16 November 1923. Ibid.
35. Department III was concerned with trade and politics and the regions that fell under it were: Great Britain, USA, and Turkey.
36. Sir Arthur Hirtzel, under secretary of state for India to a German Embassy official, in Dufour to AA, London, 21 December 1923, AA Pol.2, *Pol. Bezieh. Indiens zu Deutschland* (2).
37. Pruefer was the head of the information division of the German Embassy in Constantinople in 1917. From October 1918, he had been the head of the News and Information Service for the Orient.
38. Viscount D'Abernon, *An Ambassador of Peace*, vol.1 (London, 1929), pp. 187, 189.
39. Roy's movements in Berlin at this time were closely observed by the office of the state commissioner for public order under the home ministry, and the latter duly reported these to the AA (reports of 14 August and 2 October

1922; 31 October and 28 November 1923). The AA also examined Roy's literature. Curt Pruefer, senior, councellor of legation, to the state commissioner for public order, 12 February 1924, AA Indien Pol.19, *Sozialismus, Bolschewismus.*
40. This infiltration ultimately led to the Peshawar Conspiracy Case of 1923 and the Kanpur Bolshevik Conspiracy Case of May 1924.
41. AA Indien Pol.19, *Sozialismus, Bolschewismus.* Pruefer's note, 1 August 1921.
42. *Ibid.* Klein's note and remark 12 and 14 September 1921. It seems the USA was thought of since he was debarred from almost all West European countries.
43. *Ibid.*
44. Smedley to Florence Lennon, 31 December 1921, Florence Lennon Papers (FLP). In Janice and Stephan R. MacKinnon's *Agnes Smedley: The Life and Times of an American Radical* (Berkeley, 1988), pp. 76–7. This quotation appears in this book in a rather topsy-turvy manner.
45. *Pioneer* (Allahabad) quoting the first issue of the *Indo-German Commercial Review.* See also Ruedt to AA, Calcutta, 3 February 1922, AA Pol.6, *Nationalitaetenfrage, Fremdvoelker, Indien.*
46. 'German propaganda', *Daily Telegraph,* 30 January 1922.
47. *Pioneer,* 27 January 1922.
48. *Times of India,* 22 August 1923.
49. Sir Arthur Hirtzel, deputy secretary of India, told one of Dufour's assistants in London on 20 December 1923 that it would take at least a hundred years before India could be surrendered to the Indians. Dufour to AA, 21 December 1923, AA Pol.2, *Pol. Bezieh. Indiens zu Deutschland.*
50. *Times of India,* 20 August 1923.
51. Nambiar and his wife Suhasini arrived in Berlin in the first week of May 1923 with the express purpose of working for the *Indo-German Commercial Review.* They were first given permission to stay for three months. In this connection it was mentioned that the paper was in the interest of German trade. AA to Berlin's Police Office, 8 May 1923, AA Pol.12, *Pressewesen* (Indian Press).
52. Ruedt described the atmosphere of cordiality that he encountered in his first meeting with the Governor of Bengal as something which could not have been better at the best of times of Anglo-German relations. Ruedt to AA, Calcutta, 17 January 1922, AA Pol.2, *Pol. Bezieh. Indiens zu Deutschland.*
53. Ruedt to AA, Calcutta, 15 February 1922, AA Pol.3, *Pol. Bezieh. zu England. Indien.*
54. Enclosure, Schubert to Lord D'Abernon, 27 August 1923, AA Pol.6, *Nationalitaetenfrage. Fremdvoelker.*
55. Here is a later example: In August 1925, Ruedt, while on vacation in Germany, gave a talk on Indo-German trade to German businessmen at the AA where he was reported to have remarked to the *Industrie- und Handels-Zeitung* that Indian businessmen were not trustworthy people. He was also

quoted as having said that German trade in India would be ruined if India made any attempt to separate herself from Britain. The September 1925 issue of *The Industrial and Trade Review of India* forced Ruedt to come out with an explanation. Pillai to Dr Pruefer, Berlin, 6 August 1925, AA Pol.2, *Pol. Bezieh. Indiens zu Deutschland.*

56. Ruedt to AA, Calcutta, 20 February 1922, AA Pol.6, *Nationalitaetenfrage. Fremdvoelker. Indien.*
57. Schubert's note to all German diplomatic representatives of Germany, Berlin, 3 January 1923 and again 4 October 1923. The list included the countries alphabetically from Abyssinia to Venezuela. *Ibid.*
58. *Englishman*, 9 August 1923, Ruedt to AA, 9 August 1923. *Ibid.*
59. AA to Ruedt, Berlin, 23 October 1923. *Ibid.* The India Office dossier on INSIB given to Schubert in August 1923.
60. The journal in question was the first Indian number. It contained a few pages of written matter and well over a hundred pages of advertisements of German goods of all kinds. The *Times of India* commented on this journal thus: 'If future numbers are to be up to sample, it is time some notice was taken of the matter.' AA Indien 2, *Pol. Bezieh. zu Deutschland*; 'German Propaganda', *Times of India*, 20 August 1923. The German Foreign Office's comment, 19 September 1923, AA. *Ibid.*
61. Brodovsky's message to Mezhinsky, 23 March 1921 and Schubert's notes, 12 and 18 April 1921, AA Indien, Pol.19, *Sozialismus, Bolschewismus.*
62. Wesendonk to Curt Pruefer, private, 1 December 1921. *Ibid.*
63. Schubert's note, 19 December 1921, Pol. 6, *Nationalitaetenfrage Fremdvoelker Indien.*
64. D'Abernon to Schubert, private, Berlin, 25 August 1923. See also C. Howard-Smith to Dufour, London, 18 December 1925, AA Indien Pol.19, *Sozialismus, Bolschewismus.*
65. 'The Indian News and Information Bureau Ltd., Burgstrasse, Berlin C.2', British Embassy to AA, 25 August 1923, AA Pol.26, *Politische und kulturelle Propaganda.*
66. AA to British Embassy, Berlin, 'Secret note', 27 August 1923. *Ibid.*
67. Joseph Addison (British Embassy, Berlin) to Schubert, 11 October 1924. See here also aide-memoire about earlier talks between Schubert and Lord D'Abernon. Also Schubert's note on 25 October 1923, AA. Indien 2, *Pol. Bezieh. zu Deutschland.*
68. Addison (British Embassy) to Schubert, 11 October 1924, reminding the latter of the Schubert-Lord D'Abernon talk on 11 October 1923, AA Indien 2, *Pol. Bezieh. zu Deutschland.*
69. AA 'Memorandum', 19 October 1923. *Ibid.*
70. Ruedt to AA, 2 February 1924, enclosing his notes to the chief secretary, the govt. of Bengal. *Ibid.* The information about INSIB's financial bankruptcy came from a report of Curt Pruefer to Schubert on 9 January 1924, AA Pol.26, *Indien.*

71. Addison to Schubert, 11 October 1924. Ibid. 'Oriental refugees'—a term given to the old Berlin Indians. Another term applied to the same group was 'communists'.
72. Howard-Smith (British Foreign Office) to Dufour, private, London, 18 December 1925, AA, Geheimakten 1936, Ind. Pol.19, *Sozialismus, Bolschewismus*.
73. Ibid.
74. Ibid.
75. Ibid.
76. AA to German Embassy, London, February 1925. Ibid.
77. Martin Gilbert, *op.cit.*, p. 130.
78. Ibid. See also Pochhammer, acting German consul general in India, to AA, Calcutta, 4 September 1925, AA Pol.2, *Pol. Bezieh. Indiens zu Deutschland*.
79. Crerar argued for extraordinary measures thus: '...The German Government had applied to the Government of India to receive those [Communist] agents on the ground that their activities were dangerous to the German state. The Government of India were bound to receive those agents back to Indian shores, but could the government allow them to carry on their propaganda?' Pochhammer to AA, Calcutta, 4 September 1925, Pol.2, *Pol. Bezieh. Indiens zu Deutschland*.
80. Ibid. Pochhammer quoted here the Swarajist paper *Forward*.
81. Ibid. Pochhammer was told that things were to be done only through diplomatic channels.
82. DeHaas to German Embassy, London, tel., 2 October 1925. Ibid.
83. Also Dufour to AA, 14 November 1925, after meeting Sir Arthur Hirtzel at the India Office, AA, Ind. Pol. 19, Geheimakten, 1936, *Sozialismus, Bolschewismus*.
84. AA to German Embassy, London, 6 December 1925, AA Indien Pol.19, *Sozialismus, Bolschewismus*.
85. Ibid.
86. Dufour to AA, 14 November 1925. Howard-Smith to Dufour, London, 18 December 1925, AA Ind. Pol. 19, *Sozialismus, Bolschewismus*.
87. Dufour to AA, 21 December 1923, AA Pol.2, *Pol. Bezieh. Indiens zu Deutschland*.
88. As quoted in the *Indusrial and Trade Review for India*, June (second half) 1925. Enclosures in C. Pillai to Pruefer, 6 August 1925, AA Pol.2, *Pol. Bezieh. zu Deutschland*(2).
89. Ibid. From Chatto's quotation from the *Export and Import Review*, in the August (first half) 1925 issue of *Industrial and Trade Review of India*, p. 183.
90. *Industrial and Trade Review of India* August (first half) 1925. Review of the Press. Although Chatto's article carried no author name, the language is unmistakably his. Moreover, Pillai, while forwarding the papers to the AA, mentioned that Chatto had written it.
91. Ibid.

92. Ibid.
93. Ibid.
94. Ibid.
95. Ibid.
96. Interestingly, this racial prejudice was much less among the German officials in Berlin. In May 1930, the AA warned a German firm with business in India for making insulting racialist remarks about Gandhi. See N.K. Barooah, 'Germany and Indian Nationalism after World War I: Nehru-Subhas' Moves for Indo-German Cooperation (1927–1938)', *Mainstream* (New Delhi), 38(12), 11 March 2000, pp. 15–26.
97. Ruedt to AA, Calcutta, 18 July 1924, AA, Pol.5, Innere Pol., *Parlament und Parteiwesen*(2).
98. For Pochhammer, see also the author's article cited in note 96 above.
99. According to the existing British regulation, subjects of enemy states were forbidden to settle in India until 31 August 1926.
100. Pochhammer to AA, Calcutta, 23 June 1925, AA Pol.10., *Deutsche dipl. u. konsular. Vertretungen in Indien*(2).
101. The *Ostsee-Zeitung*, 8 May 1883. AA to German Embassy, London, 15 March 1883 and Munster to Bismarck, London, 24 March 1883. DZA (P) (German Central Archive Potsdam) Akten des Kaiserlichen Deutschen Konsulats in Kalkutta, October 1878–August 1887 AA 51587. The Ilbert Bill sought to withdraw the privilege held by European British subjects of being tried by judges of their own race.
102. Ibid. The British Indian government, however, allowed German firms to establish in India in 1925, i.e., a year earlier than envisaged.
103. In June 1925, Chatto wrote: 'The rapidly growing interest that is being shown by German manufacturers and commercial men in the trade with India is reflected in the very large number of articles and notices that appear almost daily in German press... majority of them believe in India as one of Germany's greatest future markets....' *Industrial and Trade Review of India*, June (second half) 1925.
104. When Ruedt arrived in Berlin in the middle of May 1925 on a few months' furlough, the AA, wishing to afford commercial German circles the opportunity of obtaining information regarding the possibilities of trade with India, announced that the Baron would receive visitors once a week at the AA. *Industrial and Trade Review of India*, September (first half) 1925, p. 245.
105. IHZ, 3 June 1925. Enclosures in C. Pillai to Pruefer, 6 August 1925, AA Pol.2, *Pol. Bezieh. Indiens zu Deutschland*(2).
106. Ibid.
107. Ibid.
108. Ibid.
109. Ibid.
110. 'The German Consul General Again' in *Industrial and Trade Review for*

India, September (first half) 1925.
111. Pochhammer's telegram to Ruedt from Calcutta about Forward's criticism of his insulting utterances; Ruedt to AA, Boedigheim (Baden), 8 August 1925; to Pochhammer, Boedigheim, 11 August 1925; to *Industrial and Trade Review for India*, Boedigheim, 22 August 1925. AA Pol.10, *Deutsche dipl. u. konsular. Vertretungen in Indien* (2).
112. German Consul General's Dementi in *Industrial and Trade Review for India*, August (second half) 1925, pp. 232.
113. Ruedt to the editors ITRFI, 22 August 1925. In 'The German Consul General Again', *Industrial and Trade Review for India*, Berlin, September (first half) 1925.
114. *Ibid*. Ruedt to Pochhammer, 11 August 1925.
115. *Ibid*. ITRFI to Baron Ruedt, 10 September 1925.
116. *Ibid*.
117. *Ibid*.
118. *Ibid*. Under 'Notice to Editors', p. 248.
119. Ruedt to AA, Boedigheim, 8 August 1925.
120. *Ibid*. AA Pol.10, *Deutsche dipl. u. konsular. Vertretungen in Indien* (2).
121. 'Augen auf Indien', *Industrie- und Handelszeitung*, Berlin, 18 September, 1925, incorporating Ruedt's explanations. AA Pol.10, *Deutsche dipl. u. konsular. Vertretungen in Indien* (2).
122. *Industrie- und Handelszeitung* to the *Industrial and Trade Review for India*, 14 September 1925, reprinted in *Industrial and Trade Review for India*, Berlin, September (first half) 1925.
123. *Ibid*.
124. *Ibid*.
125. Notice by De Haas on 24 October 1925, draft by consul Litten, AA's information to all the German Missions abroad, 25 August 1925. AA Pol.10, *Deutsche dipl. u. konsular. Vertretungen in Indien*.
126. Another note to the above. *Ibid*.
127. Pochhammer to AA, Calcutta, 28 July 1925. AA Pol.2, *Pressewesen* (Indian) (1). A.C.N. Nambiar was the correspondent for *The Hindu* in Berlin.
128. For one such example of 'Misuse of Indology' by German officials in India, see the following paragraphs.
129. One of the enclosures was Pillai's article 'Germany and Storm in the British Empire' (in German) in *Tag*, 24 July 1925. AA Pol.2, *Pol. Bez. Indiens zu Deutschland* (2).
130. Baron v. Richthofen to Pillai, Berlin, 27 August 1925. *Ibid*.
131. Consul Litten to Kastl, Berlin, 28 February 1926. AA Pol.10, *Deutsche dipl. u. konsular. Vertretungen in Indien*, Bd.2. The discussion about citizenship arose since at this time Taraknath Das came from the USA, and wished to obtain German citizenship.
132. In the same year (1926) was published John Hagenbeck's book *Unter der Sonne Indiens: Erlebnisse und Abenteuer in Ceylon, Vorder- und Hinterindien,*

Sumatra, Java und den Andamanen (Dresden, 1926). The Berlin show was on from July to 7 October 1926.
133. AA Pol.2, *Pol. Bezieh. Indiens zu Deutschland* (2) B.H. Kapur, secretary, Association of Indians in Central Europe, to state secretary of the Chancellor's office, 1 July 1926.
134. *Ibid.* See interview with Chatto in *Dresdener Neueste Nachrichten*, 14 July 1926.
135. *Ibid.* Consul Litten's note, 6 July 1926, giving Glasenap's view.
136. *Ibid.* Consul Litten's note, 8 September 1926.
137. Some of the newspaper articles in Germany were: 'Indienschau', *Die Welt am Abend*, 2 July 1926; 'Indienschau', 'Der Zoo, ein neuer Lunapark', *Die Welt am Abend*, 13 July 1926; 'Kult und Kultur', *Berliner Tageblatt*, 14 July 1926, *Berliner Tageblatt*, 17 July 1926; 'Deutschland und Indien', *Dresdener Neueste Nachrichten*, 14 July 1926; 'Indien im Zoo', *Frankfurter Zeitung*, 15 July 1926; 'Indiens Mahnruf', *Die Welt am Abend*, 12 July 1926; 'Der Indienskandal im Zoo', *Die Welt am Abend*, 7 July 1926.
138. Rudolf Olden, 'Indienschau' in *Berliner Tageblatt*, 17 July 1926.
139. Richard Freund, 'Deutschland und Indien', *Dresdener Neueste Nachrichten*. The paper introduced Chatto as one of India's most popular leaders.
140. *Ibid.* Ruedt to AA, 5 August 1926.
141. Nambiar was a regular correspondent of *The Hindu* and *Forward* at that time.
142. *Forward*, 4 August 1926.
143. Ruedt to one Dr Goswami, 13 August 1926. AA Pol.2, *Pol. Bezieh. Indiens zu Deutschland* (2) The letter to the *Forward* jointly written by Balai Chand Mukherjee, Bhudhar Chandra Mazumdar, and others, published in on 11 August 1926 under the caption 'Indians as Quadrupeds in Berlin Zoo: German Brutality exposed' had a derogatory sentence about the German soldiers in WWI, the original article (by Nambiar) had only an anti-imperialist thrust. But Ruedt considered even that as hostile to Germany. *Ibid.*
144. *Ibid.*
145. *Ibid.*
146. *Ibid.* Ruedt to AA, Calcutta, 25 August 1926.
147. *The People*, 5 September 1926.
148. *Ibid.*
149. Helene Hanssding to Hindenburg, Ahmedabad, 23 September 1926, AA, Pol.2, *Pol. Bezieh. Indiens zu Deutschland* (2).
150. *Ibid.* AA to Fritze, 25 October 1926. The letter ended with the following remark: 'This matter was touched upon when the Indian philosopher Rabindranath Tagore was here and he too had the full understanding for the Foreign Office's stand on it.'
151. *Ibid.* U.P. Chambers of Commerce, to German consul general, Cawnpore, 6 October 1926.

152. Ibid. Ruedt to U.P. Chamber of Commerce, 20 October 1926.
153. Ibid.
154. Ibid.
155. Actually from early March 1926, Chatto had been busy inviting delegates to a conference of the League against Cruelties and Oppression in the colonies, which gave birth to the League Against Imperialism. See circular letters to Hasrat Mohani and Maulana Shankar Ali AA, Pol.19, *Sozialismus. Bolschewismus. Kommunismus usw.*
156. See Janice R. and Stephen R. MacKinnon, *Agnes Smedley*, p. 116.
157. AA Pol.2, *Pol. Bezieh. Indiens zu Deutschland*(1). John Hagenbeck to AA, 4 November 1926; AA (Richthofen) tel. to consul general in Calcutta, 6 November 1926.
158. *Ibid.* From consul general's office, Calcutta, to AA, 2 December 1926, enclosing 'Indian Players in Berlin not ill-treated', *Statesman* (Calcutta), 2 December 1926.
159. *Ibid.* Hagenbeck to AA, 4 and 25 November 1926; Grobba to Hagenbeck, 21 January 1927; Grobba to Chatto, 3 February 1927; Smedley to Grobba, 11 and 16 February 1927.
160. Smedley to Hagenbeck, 11 February 1927. The three points were: a) the Indians in the show received 10 to 50 rupees per month; b) the poster 'Indien am Zoo' was not meant to be invidious; c) the Indians were better treated than by most of their countrymen in India.
161. 'Indians in the Zoo', correspondence, *The People*, 20 March 1927.
162. 'Indians in European Zoological Gardens', *The Bombay Chronicle*, 21 March 1927.
163. Reuters report of Hitler's address to the meeting on 26 January 1936.
164. AA Pol.2, *Pol. Bezieh. Indiens zu Deutschland*(1) Neurath to AA, Rome, 8 June 1926.
165. *Ibid.* Consul Litten's note on 10 September 1926.
166. *Ibid.* It is, however, to be noted that Chatto was not completely out of the picture. He was very much present with the poet. First, Loewenthal was the publisher of Chatto's journal *Industrial and Trade Review of India*, which was proscribed in India. Then Chatto also arranged, with the help of Frau Lucie Hecht, the translations into German of all of Tagore's lectures on this visit and some of his poems, which he recited. (The author's multiple interviews with Lucie Hecht and the papers she loaned to him.)
167. AA Pol.2, *Pol. Bezieh. Indiens zu Deutschland*(1). Consul Litten's note, 10 September 1926. While taking utmost precautions against British susceptibilities, the AA remembered how Professor Helmut von Glasenap was refused a visa for India because he had once addressed the Hindustan Association.
168. AA Pol. 11, Nr. 6, *Andere Personalien*. Papers from AA to the office of the German President, 13 September 1926, for his orientation about Tagore before meeting him.

169. When I first met Miss Lucie Hecht in 1972, she was over 70. I saw many statements of high praise from Tagore, Dr Zakir Hussain and various other personalities for her translation of their works. The daugther of a medical doctor, Lucie Hecht had aspirations for higher university education, but the runaway inflation of the time compelled her instead to work for a living. Gifted in languages, she chose to be a translator. Chatto engaged her for translating into German not only Tagore's lectures but also many of his poems. At the advent of the Nazis, Hecht went to England and took British citizenship. I met her many times during 1972–5. She then lived in Muelheim/Ruhr, Germany. Her memory was still vivid, and she was ever so enthusiastic about Indian freedom.

170. In an interview with the author on 19 November 1972 at her house in Muelheim/Ruhr, Germany. The author had several other interviews, and occasionally corresponded with her.

7

Chatto and Smedley: Love, Domestic Tyranny, Nervous Breakdowns 1920–6

1. SMEDLEY: HER LIFE AND INDIAN WORK BEFORE 1920

In the preceding chapters, some of the activities of Smedley associated with the Berlin Indians have been discussed. But in order to understand the intricacies of the events that followed her life with Chatto as his common-law wife, we need to know more about the early life of this born rebel, socialist, humanist, feminist, and a very determined personality, someone who had already made the freedom of India her prime political programme before meeting Chatto at the end of 1920.

Smedley was born in 1892 in Osgood, Missouri, the second of five children of an uneducated tenant farmer. She was raised in mining camps in Colorado in extreme poverty and misery.[1] Until 1911, when she entered a normal school as a special student, she had had only fragmentary high school education, having to earn her keep by doing odd jobs.[2] With an indomitable craving for learning[3], writing, and self-improvement, she seized every opportunity that came by and developed, early in her life, an intense interest in social issues.[4] In 1912, when she became the editor-in-chief of her school magazine, she reviewed the book *The Mind of Primitive Man* by the American anthropologist Franz

Boas. A short story by her called 'The Romance' was also published in the same magazine (*Normal Student*), a result of the impact that Boas's study of racial prejudice and cultural difference made on her. In the story, a mother tells her children how she overcame her own racial prejudice in order to marry a Red Indian. As Smedley's biographers tell us, shortly after writing this story, Smedley publicly acknowledged her own Red Indian ancestry and sometimes called herself Ayahoo instead of Agnes. She was merely 20 years old at the time.

At the same Tempe Normal School, Agnes took part in a debate in 1912 on women's suffrage in Arizona and spoke in favour of the motion. This event is important because here she met Thorberg Brundin, a schoolteacher from Phoenix, who had a bachelor's degree from Columbia University, and was one of the judges. Although Thorberg was extremely sophisticated and very unlike Agnes, a friendship developed between the two, eventually leading to Smedley's marriage with Thorberg's brother, Ernest George Brundin in August 1912. Thorberg and Ernest were both socialists and through them Smedley was introduced to radical groups.

The marriage between Ernest and Agnes did not go well, primarily because of Agnes's fear of sex. For the first eight months of the marriage there was no sex at all. At her first pregnancy, she opted for an abortion. In the middle of 1913, Agnes left Ernest and joined San Diego Normal School as a student. Here she helped found the school's weekly *Normal News*. She also took part in school theatre. In 1915, two interesting events took place. Smedley heard, for the first time, an anti-British speech given in the school by an Indian nationalist Dr Keshav D. Shastri. About the same time, the anarchist Emma Goldman came to San Diego to give three public lectures on Ibsen, Nietzsche, and Margaret Sanger's birth control movement. Both events contributed to Smedley's political education. Shastri's lecture introduced her to the global significance of British imperialism, and, from Goldman, she learnt the significance of birth control for poor women. Smedley started taking an interest in the programmes of the Open Forum which had sponsored Goldman's lectures.

In the spring of 1916, Smedley became a committed member of the Socialist Party believing that change for the working classes was both possible and desirable. For a short while, Smedley, together with her husband, Ernest, was in Fresno working with a commercial newspaper. She became pregnant for the second time and this time, too, the pregnancy ended in abortion, convincing Ernest that a married life with Smedley was impossible. Fresno was a centre of the Indian Sikh community in California, mostly farmers. Consequently, as a reporter, she came to learn more about the Indian national movement. In the autumn of 1916, Smedley returned to San Diego Normal School. When the school authorities learnt by chance of Smedley's membership of the Socialist Party, she was expelled from the school. By the end of that year, Smedley left for New York City.

Smedley craved financial independence and success as a writer. She realized that the road to success in both these endeavours was further education. She began attending night classes at New York University. However, she could not adjust to her classmates. Her view of the sex act as animalistic added to her emotional problem. It was in a mood of frustration and emotional isolation that she attended a lecture by Lajpat Rai at Columbia University on 10 March 1917 which moved her deeply. Smedley later met Rai privately, and he tutored her in Indian history. Her contact with him had an enormous impact on her.[5] At about the same time Smedley also met M.N. Roy, Sailendranath Ghose, and Taraknath Das. Roy and Ghose later fled to Mexico.

On the outbreak of the October Revolution, Smedley rejected Rai's moderate approach, embracing the more radical Gadar movement. Between November 1917 and March 1918, Smedley, because of her selfless devotion to the cause of Indian freedom, allowed herself to be used by Das and Ghose in a naïve project in the name of their so-called Indian National Party. The two 'careerist' Indian nationalists[6] produced documents in San Francisco that claimed to have originated in 'Tagore Castle', Calcutta. These were then sent to the President of the USA and other diplomatic representatives in Washington with covering letters written and signed by Pulin Behari Bose, the representative of the Indian Nationalist Party in the USA. Smedley played the role of Bose here.

Two fateful events quickly followed in Smedley's life in early 1918. She succumbed to a forced sexual adventure on the part of Indian nationalist Heramba Lal Gupta, which she thought would damage her standing within the Indian community. Before her worries could subside, she came to know that her activities with Das and Ghose had been duly observed all along by the Immigration and Justice Department. She had to undergo not only continuous police interrogation for two weeks but also solitary confinement. Afterwards both Smedley and Ghose were brought to Manhattan Tomb Prison and a bail was set at $10,000 for Smedley and $20,000 for Ghose.

Margaret Sanger and her socialist friends, with the help of J.H. Holmes, a leading New York Unitarian clergyman, decided to collect the bail money for Smedley, and the Socialist Party newspaper, the *Call*, asked for contributions to the defence fund. Law firms also came forward to help. On 16 May 1918, the US Congress passed the Sedition Act, authorizing heavy penalties for those who hindered the war effort. In June came a second indictment against Smedley for violating the Espionage Act in San Francisco. However, by the summer of 1918, Smedley was released to the custody of her counsel on bail. But on 1 October, she had to go to jail again and was not released before December.

After her release, Sanger put Smedley in charge of the day-to-day management of the *Birth Control Review*, providing valuable information to the American women. She was helped in this job by Kitty Marion, who had been a cellmate of hers in jail. With the help of friends, Smedley found a place to live in. Florence Lennon, the 20-year-old daughter of a wealthy Jewish merchant who was then publishing translations of letters by Maria Montessori, the Italian educational reformer, in the *Call*, agreed to accommodate Smedley in her apartment for $10 a month. Lennon was both excited and amazed by Smedley's working-class manners and habits. But they became friends. Smedley then obtained a job at the *Call* with the assistance of her socialist friends. One of her journalist friends, Robert Minor, who was interested in the Russian Revolution, went to Moscow as a special correspondent for the *Call* in early 1919 to evaluate the Russian Revolution first hand. From his reports Smedley learnt a great deal about law and order in Russia. After leaving Russia, Minor sent reports from Germany about the abortive attempt by Rosa Luxemburg, Karl Liebknecht, and others of the Left-wing German Social Democrats to bring about a revolution. There Minor was arrested on charges made by the British of spreading treasonable propaganda among British and American troops. At that time, efforts were also afoot in the USA to pass legislation to deport the interned Indians, and some of them had already been assembled for the purpose.

One of the first to challenge government officials on the deportation of Indians was the historian Charles Beard, who asked for discriminating attention to each individual case. Smedley and her American and

Official photograph of Chatto as Joint-Secretary of the League Against Imperialism

Chatto and Lidiya in their Moscow apartment
(courtesy Manisha Granthalaya Pvt. Ltd., Kolkata)

O.G. von Wesendonk

Agnes Smedley (courtesy Lucie Hecht, 1973)

Willi Muenzenberg (courtesy Lucie Hecht)

Indian friends quickly mobilized a counter-offensive, and, on 6 March 1919, formed the Friends of Freedom for India (FFI). Professor Robert Morss Lovett was the temporary president, Smedley the secretary, and the office was at 92 Fifth Avenue. Lovett was a professor of English at the University of Chicago, and the editor of *Dial*, a distinguished publication of arts and letters. He opened his magazine to a full discussion of the Indian nationalist cause. In a separate pamphlet, he wrote how Sir George Delham, the head of British police in Calcutta, had been given a free hand by American authorities to search the apartments of Taraknath Das, an American citizen, without even a warrant. It was a case in point of British interference in internal US matters. Lovett and Sanger immediately incurred British displeasure.

By August 1919, the FFI's propaganda had produced some results. Workers' unions at many places sent resolutions to the Department of Labour protesting the deportation of Indians. By mid-October 1919, Gilbert Roe finally succeeded in convincing authorities to dismiss the San Francisco indictment against Smedley and Ghose. The earlier New York indictment against Smedley remained in force though. By that time, Das, released from prison, began working for the FFI.

As the year 1919 came to a close, Smedley was depressed. Her old cellmate, Mollie Steiner, had been sentenced to 15 years imprisonment. Many of her socialist and anarchist friends had suffered similar hardships. The year 1920 was the presidential election year. On 2 January, the Justice Department made one of the country's largest mass arrests. Raids took place on 2500 supposed radicals, and deportation warrants were issued to 5000 aliens. As the year progressed, Smedley left the organisational work of FFI to Das and Ghose and busied herself full-time on the *Call*. In December, she took a job of stewardess on an old Polish-American freighter bound for Europe. It sailed on 17 December. Her immediate programme in Europe was to join the Berlin Indians' forthcoming mission to Moscow.

2. CHATTO–SMEDLEY UNION: LOVE AND INNATE INCOMPATIBILITY

In late December 1920, Smedley's freighter arrived at the Danzig harbour. Smedley received a telegram from Berlin welcoming her to the country. The captain opened the telegram and tried to prevent Smedley, who had no travel documents, from leaving the boat. But Smedley was safely ashore before the captain could take any steps.[7] The rest of the formalities, including her further journey to Berlin, were taken care of by Chatto.

To be suddenly in a strange place, very different from her familiar New York, without friends or acquaintances and unable to speak the language, made Smedley feel isolated. Significantly, her very first letter from Germany to her friend Lennon, was written in a pensive mood:

> I have thought a lot of you since I left…You are the only one who really understood and I have marked Kabir's poem, with you in mind, in which he says: "Listen to me friend, he understands who loves." I understand love now, but never before…I feel no longer the harshness toward love and even find myself looking for it in others.[8]

Smedley did not have to look for long. She felt irresistibly drawn to Chatto with whom she shared a common passion and political goal: freedom for India. Not surprisingly, love and mutual admiration developed between the two almost spontaneously. Even on the question of the personal freedom of women—Smedley's special passion—she found Chatto's views progressive. She makes Anand (Chatto) say in her autobiographical novel: 'I believe in the personal freedom of women—you know that—but our comrades do not. They are like most men everywhere.'[9] Within a few weeks, Chatto and Smedley started living together as husband and wife. They could not be formally married because Chatto's earlier marriage with an English woman (who became a Catholic nun later) could not be abrogated, since, debarred from France where the marriage had been registered, he could not go there under his real name to obtain the divorce.[10]

Chatto was by no means handsome. According to a female colleague at the bureau of the League Against Imperialism, he looked like an owl[11], a thoroughly unflattering remark. But Chatto was a man of great wit and sharp intellect, as well as a superb conversationist, who could always charm cultivated women. In Sweden, he impressed many women of the upper echelons who enjoyed his company.[12] As for Chatto's influence on women, as discussed earlier, during WWI an Englishwoman was brave enough to go to Switzerland to meet the anti-British Chatto and was interned for more than 22 months for her pains.[13] Smedley's first impressions and assessment of Chatto—some of which remained lasting—were not different from those of other women:

> Virendranath was the epitome of the secret revolutionary movement, and perhaps its most brilliant protagonist abroad. He was nearly twenty years [wrong: should be

twelve] my senior, with a mind as sharp and ruthless as a sabre. He was thin and dark, with a mass of black hair turning grey at the temples, and a face that had something fierce about it...By race the family was Hindu, by culture a mixture of Hinduism, Mohammedanism, and the best of English liberalism.[14]

When Smedley arrived in Berlin, the Indians of the old Berlin India Committee were preparing for their Moscow mission of spring of 1921. This otherwise futile visit which took more than five months, was, in a way, the honeymoon period for Smedley and Chatto. At least, as we will soon see, it was the only period in their conjugal life when they were harmoniously together without inner or outward conflict. In Moscow, they often went out sightseeing or visiting people (as for instance, Emma Goldman and Alexander Berkman, then under house arrest). They had fun together, and saw, in the midst of poverty, people like Ella Reeve Bloor, wearing lace dresses over silk coloured slips and long strings of coloured beads, rings, etc., and Earl Browder coming to the forthcoming Congress of the Third International as representatives of American miners. Once they saw a big balloon sailing high over the parade grounds in Moscow, which Smedley thought might be the only balloon in Russia. Chatto looked at it and said, 'I'll bet Mother Bloor is in that balloon.'[15]

Trouble started as soon as the couple returned to Germany in September, in fact, from the very moment of their crossing the border into Germany. As already mentioned, under pressure from the British government, Chatto was refused stay permit by German authorities. Consequently, after the expiry of his temporary permit, the couple had to live under false names for many months frequently changing their lodgings. There was constant British surveillance and even a murder plot, as described earlier.[16] Despite all these problems, Chatto continued the work of INSIB, particularly the publication of the commercial magazine. In addition, he continued to look after Indian students and visitors.

As for the revival of political work among Indians, there were hurdles on two fronts. First, the Indians were asked by German authorities not to be involved politically. Second, there emerged inner divisions among the Indians themselves, worsened by the presence of Heramba Lal Gupta, who without any qualms, divulged his earlier sexual escapade with Smedley in New York. It was particularly painful for Smedley because at about the same time, she had written to Das and Ghose praising Gupta for three things: putting an Indian boy in an aeroplane factory and securing his support for one year, having connections in Spain and France, and establishing a committee in Paris.[17] Gupta seems to have nurtured a grudge against Chatto because of his replacement from the leadership of the Berlin Committee in the USA in 1916. To make matters worse, another Bengali nationalist, the quarrelsome Surendranath Karr, who had earlier opposed Das and Smedley within the FFI in New York, arrived in Berlin. He opposed both Chatto and Smedley.[18] This made further public work with the Indians impossible for Smedley, and Chatto realized that the image and authority which he had hitherto enjoyed were permanently damaged. The first signs of the disintegration of their 'marriage' showed up as early as the autumn of 1921. This led to Smedley's physical and mental breakdown necessitating psychoanalytical help to reconcile her to marriage.[19]

Besides depression, Smedley had other illnesses too. In the spring of 1922, she was in a sanatorium in Mecklenburg where unfortunately her condition became steadily worse, and so she returned to be in bed in the home of a German lady friend. Besides nervous trouble, she also had albumin in the kidney, both of which required the 'rest cure'.[20] When she was back in her apartment with Chatto, she moved to a separate room by herself. However, her depression continued. She was thoroughly disappointed both with the Indians and 'the Indian work' in Germany. The working condition in Germany was for her a thousand times harder than in the USA. She wrote to her friend, Lennon, in June: 'The Indians here harbor harsh prejudices against women and against foreigners. As usual they are inefficient in work and jealous of efficient persons.'[21] Smedley was additionally depressed due to her financial problems because of which she could not enrol herself at the university for further studies. Since she could not read German and there were no English books available in the libraries to borrow, she felt an intense intellectual isolation. Envying Lennon who was then planning to join the University of Columbia, Smedley wrote: 'I wish my father had been a real estate agent that I might enrol at the University of Berlin this winter.'[22]

In the early months of 1923, Smedley was unwell again. In June, she was in a state of semi-consciousness. She began to feel better when she started secret visits to a psychoanalyst, a student of Freud's, off and on.[23] She also had convulsions in the throat. Her nervous collapses came at least twice a month, leaving her prostrated in bed for a week at a time. She was taking sunrays treatment as well as high-frequency electric treatment.[24]

Until June 1923, Smedley desisted from directly blaming Chatto for her deteriorating mental and physical condition. She only blamed the institution of marriage. Knowing that her friend, Lennon, had a love affair with someone, Smedley cautioned her:

Beneath the skin of every man, it matters not who he is, lies the old Adam. Scratch him and you will find that I am right. He is fine in theory, our modern man. But in practice he is a walking lie. He still judges woman by her vagina, in fact woman is nothing but a walking vagina to him, and he the sole owner of it. I assure you I am right...If you ever get married, or contemplate it, look the man in the eye beforehand and say, "I have had many love affairs; so have you. I respect your own right. You must respect mine and keep your hands out of affairs which do not concern you and with which you have nothing to do.'[25]

A couple of weeks later, broaching the same subject again, Smedley continued:

As for your finding a man who will continue to use his intellect after marriage—that I doubt! Intellect and sex aren't on speaking terms in a man. You may find a great brain; but when you marry you get a man with sex organs and primitive ancestral reactions regarding them. And he will always think you should have preserved your virginity waiting just for him and until he had finished seducing all the women of his acquaintances.[26]

It was only towards the end of this 11-page letter that Smedley betrayed that her sermons on sex and marriage were based on her own personal experience with Chatto:

I married an artist, revolutionary in a dozen different ways, a man of truly "fine frenzy", nervous as a cat, *always* moving, never at rest, indefatigable energy a hundred fold more than I ever had, a *thin* man with *much* hair, a tongue like a razor and a brain like hell on fire. What a couple. I'm consumed into ashes and he's always raking up the ashes and setting them on fire again. He doesn't believe in ashes; only in fire. Suspicious as hell of every man near me—and of all men or *women* from America. My nervous collapse has quieted him much. I told him once when I was on the verge of unconsciousness: "Leave me in peace; leave me alone personally; if I can't have complete freedom, I shall die before your eyes." But he is ever now and then blazing up again. And he is always smouldering. I feel like a person living on the brink of a volcano crater. Yet it is awful to love a person who is a torture to you...We make life a merry hell for each other, I assure you.[27]

During this time, the early summer of 1923 when Smedley was having nervous breakdowns, an Indian lady friend of hers, Lila Singh, from the USA, visited her, and finding Smedley in such a condition offered her some money for a two-months' vacation in the mountains.[28] Smedley accepted the offer, and went to the Bavarian mountains in July with a pass under the name of Mrs Violet Ali Khan Hussain. The mountain climate helped her. In the second week of August, she hoped to be well enough by September or October to take a class on conversational English on 15 October in Berlin University and her higher studies. She also planned to earn some money through small jobs, including writing for the Indian press. She was also hopeful of obtaining a passport at last under her own name, and, what was more, to live alone. She wrote to Lennon that, faced with the choice of her total destruction or with a total separation, Chatto had agreed to Smedley's idea of staying apart. Chatto also agreed to give her perfect freedom in all things, and would not make a single demand or personal request.[29]

However, her hope of returning to Berlin a freer person did not materialize, and everything she wanted to do there came to nought—her university studies, her freedom, a passport under her own name, a room by herself. The reason was that she was completely broke and had to come back and stay in her common apartment with Chatto. The money left over from the vacation was spent in paying off debts. Smedley even had to walk to her doctor's everyday, an hour and a half each way. Besides, Chatto was very bitter that Smedley was being analysed, and there was little communion or communication between them, except of a purely business nature.[30] After more than a month of daily psychoanalysis, Smedley suddenly stopped therapy on 1 December 1923 because of lack of money. She was sick of being a drain on Lennon and a burden to others. The result was that her throat convulsions returned immediately, although in a mild form, and she began to feel ill again. She was very depressed—questioning even her intellectual abilities. Having never experienced such a prolonged period of depression in her life, she was planning to return to some out-of-the-way place in the USA and bury her shame in work.[31] She was thinking of taking up a job on a ship from Hamburg and sailing either to the USA or 'to any old part in the world and clear out and try to forget my life and my "unutterable unhappiness".'[32]

This was followed by a short spell of normality but Smedley's problems, for example, her sleeplessness and 'insane spells' soon returned. 'I prefer death to these spells and to sleeplessness,' she wrote to Lennon, concluding that there was not a shadow of doubt in her mind that her life depended on analysis.[33] This led her to start analysis yet again. Two days before the new year, she suffered an attack such as she had experienced never before. It started at four in the afternoon and lasted for two days and drove her nearly insane.[34] She took a strong sleeping powder but with no effect. So her landlady contacted her analyst, Dr Naef, who immediately started the treatment, agreeing to carry her bill until Smedley was in a position to pay. To the frightened Chatto she said she would return to New York as soon as she felt better. Chatto stopped all his political and other activities, and started looking for a job to earn money. Smedley's hallucinations of him locking her door and belief that he was going to murder her terrified Chatto. However, he threatened to accompany her if she returned to the USA. Knowing full well that if he did so he would at once be arrested and probably deported to India, Smedley agreed to remain with him and continue her treatment for one more month.[35] By mid-January 1924, she felt better with the treatment. She also earned a little money by writing in German newspapers. Her doctor summoned Chatto at the beginning of the month, and spoke with him for an hour or two. She asked him to refrain from opposing Smedley in every wish which did not come from him. She asked Chatto not to dominate Smedley if he wished her to recover at all.[36]

Smedley learnt through the treatment many things about herself. Some of her problems dated back to certain ideas that developed in her early years. Her doctor told her that she was more or less dominating and masculine in mind and character. Furthermore, she had hidden, repressed and suppressed every tendency which seemed to belong to the lower strata of human nature.[37] Later she also learnt from her analyst that she was 'polygamous'. She wrote to Lennon:

I don't live polygamously, but I can't help my emotions. It's pretty hard to have said all through my life that I don't give a damn for sex and then to learn I'm polygamous. My only desire, however, is to take my polygamy out in writing instead of in bed (pardon the vulgarity).[38]

Smedley also discovered that Chatto was not without blame or responsibility for her current plight:

Chatto also has much to correct in himself. He is a person who dies if he doesn't dominate. He has largely crushed me. The first year it was not so much. His encroachments extended daily and my illness increased daily. He didn't think I was ill; he called me "feeble minded" and doing things just to disturb him. I went down and down until my own subconscious is almost master of my life. Physically strong, yet I have struck bed-rock psychically and I have experienced physical suffering and spiritual suffering of which I have never dreamed.[39]

In March, Smedley left Chatto one night, and sought refuge in a cold maid's room in the home of a friend, from where she started looking for a suitable place to stay. Not being able to live alone, Chatto appeared there one night a week later, went to bed on Smedley's couch and lay seriously ill for two weeks. Chatto had to be given morphine injections to enable him to hold out. For two weeks Smedley had to nurse him. She wrote to Lennon: 'I tried then to induce Chatto to leave me alone in my desire to live alone and I got no reply but the most bitter hostility.' Both then moved to a new house.[40]

In late June 1924, Smedley had happier news to give to Lennon. She was writing for the Indian press, counteracting British propaganda against Russia. She gave up everything at the University except one lecture a week on Indian history and her class there. She joined an action group for the study of Marxism and imperialism. She, however, still remained non-political in so far as the Communist Party was concerned and had no desire to join it. She also gave public lectures; one to a Chinese and Indian meeting attended by some 500 men, and one on Kaethe Kollwitz and her art using magic lantern slides where Kollwitz herself was present. An important article by her also appeared in *The New Masses* in America.[41]

In August, Smedley gave another piece of good news to Lennon: Chatto had agreed to undergo analysis. He was going to be analysed free 'by the most important analyst of Germany. All because he is such a wreck and is a Hindu whom they wish to study.'[42] Smedley further commented: 'It will be very hard for him, for he is 43 and his habits are bands of iron.' Deriding psychoanalysis as 'priestcraft and superstition', Chatto was an unwilling subject. But Smedley had laid it down as a condition for living with him and he reluctantly agreed. She hoped that after the analysis Chatto would lose his 'baby dependence' on her.[43]

Chatto began analysis in November 1924, two days a week, and, by February 1925, both Chatto and Smedley agreed to a separation for six months. Smedley wrote to Karin Michaelis about this in the latter half of February 1925:

> I am living alone, and I am making my own living and refusing any help from him. But we live as friends. We have come to the definite agreement that we shall live like this, without any sex entering our lives, for six months, after which time I shall give my definite answer. In the meantime he also has agreed to go into psycho-analytic treatment, is already being treated. The only condition upon which I would even wait for six months was that he should be treated. Otherwise I would have left him for good and all and never seen him again. But because he is willing to see if anything is not also wrong with him, and that the blame is not all mine, I am willing to wait.[44]

By this time Smedley had recovered from her spells of sleeplessness, hysterical fits and other illnesses, and at last felt confident of leading her life the way she wanted. The first thing she decided was to not live with Chatto any more, although the arrangement had been for only six months of separation. She had strong reasons for not taking this decision earlier. In an earlier letter to Michaelis, in April of the previous year, she had written:

> You can realize, I believe, that a love such as my husband has for me, is not to be given up lightly. There are many terrible things in that love, but I have also not dealt with our case in a sane manner, because I have been ill. I must first be well, and then if our situation does not improve, I will be justified in leaving him, and can do it without regret. But now I cannot do it. Life is a very short experience at best, and to lose love, or to deliberately give up a great love, is very difficult. There are many other men I could live with, but my knowledge of men tells me that I would suffer a worse fate at the hands of most of them than I suffer now...This is not my first experience; and it is a richer, more beautiful [experience], and has more possibilities of beauty in it, than most I have known. Furthermore, I refuse to go to America until my treatment is finished.[45]

But after being cured of her problems 10 months later, Smedley became the master of her own self. 'I have reached a stage where I speak only open and brutal truth to my husband,' she wrote to Michaelis.[46] Since Michaelis was planning to write a story around Smedley's life, Smedley thought it necessary to provide her with authentic information about her miserable childhood in a working class environment and her life with Chatto in the past four years.

As far as the problems with Chatto were concerned, there was first the economic side. Chatto-Smedley's apartment was virtually a free travellers' lodge and canteen for hard-pressed Indian students and other visitors, and Smedley had to bear the burden to keep it all together from her meagre earnings. She had to wash and iron her and Chatto's clothing, scrub the floors, cook, and wash the dishes. She was constantly borrowing money from Lennon and others, and a huge part of it went into the housekeeping. There were a chain of visitors daily who came, telephoned, and obtained postage for their mail free of cost. Chatto often brought guests at mealtime unannounced. The result was that Smedley often did not have enough to eat. In her opinion, these guests who took free service in the house for granted 'were not idealists, who had never raised a hand for any human being, and would never raise a hand to help free India.'[47]

The spiritual side of the causes of disunion and disharmony was even worse. Smedley wrote in the same letter:

Before I met my husband I had had relations with other men. I had been married once. All this I told my husband when we were married that there might be no misunderstanding. He also had lived with many women and was not only once married, but he is married to this day and his wife is an English woman and lives in England. But I thought love was bigger than all material things. After one month my husband began to accuse me of being a woman of weak character because I had had sex relations with other men. And he said that he 'got leavings from other men'! Now when a man strikes at a woman like that, in view of the fact that he is also 'the leavings from other women' it is not only unethical, but it is contrary to all laws of decency and fair play. But I was sick and I felt guilty. I therefore lived in misery for four years with him and each day heard it. He almost locked me up from the Indians, and refused to let me go into the Indian work, and he said that it was because the Indians would learn of my sex life and ruin him because of it. I asked only to be permitted to go away, but then he accused me of having left every other man and now wanting to do the same with him. For three years he refused to let me write a line. He was hostile and bitter because I wanted to write and said it was only a desire to 'show off'.

All this, Smedley wrote, made her sicker and sicker until she began to have nervous attacks—similar to epileptic fits—that led her to take stronger and stronger sleeping powders. Three times when she tried to rebel, her husband physically attacked her.

Her psychoanalysis confirmed to Smedley that she was not at fault in her relationship with Chatto. It was the other way round. She expressed her bitterness about Chatto's attacks on her mind:

I do not forget the attacks upon me. They drove the iron into the depths of my soul and if I live through all the lives in which the Hindus believe, I shall never forget them. The scars will remain on my ghost. I will never forget and I will never forgive him in all the coming lives which I may have to live because he tried to subject not only my body, but tried to destroy my intellectual life and succeeded for three years. I am bitter because he succeeded—because I was defeated. When any other human being strikes at the spiritual and intellectual life of a person he may as well drive a knife into his heart and be finished with it.[48]

Restored to health, Smedley was now emboldened to reject Chatto outright as a companion. The very thought of going back to him was repugnant to her. She wrote to Michaelis:

And I tell you, despite all your arguments, despite all your experience, despite all your loving advice to me, I prefer death to returning to my husband. If I thought that I should have to return to him now and live with him and surrender my body to him, I would drive a knife through my heart the next minute.[49]

She looked back in anger and disgust on the years of her submission and suffocation at a time when she had finally vanquished and humbled her erring husband:

After four years of long illness which pointed to insanity, I am coming back to life. And I return with a heavy debt on my shoulders. And I return facing my husband day by day who comes to me in his sadness and misery, or in anger that I have left him. And now I am very, very calm, and we look at each other across an impassable gulf. And he knows at last that he has lost the power to hurt me. That is a terrible thing to learn—that you can no longer hurt a person. Now he must search within himself and see if he was not at fault in some of these things; he must learn humility of soul; he must learn to know that he had injured me.[50]

3. The Final Parting of Ways

Smedley and Chatto never lived together again. Smedley was unshakeable in her determination not to enter into a relationship with Chatto again. She had to make up for the lost years in her intellectual endeavours to write, research, lecture, and publish. Her interest in India, of course, remained intact. She started her work with redoubled zeal as she wrote to Michaelis:

Now that I have my health back I have my intellectual work back and this work shall be my companion and my guide...I have come up from the gutter,...and I have great strength. I may sound egotistical, but I am sorry if it is so...I do not have great ability in writing—no. But I have great determination and great strength of will.[51]

Friends, particularly Michaelis, Emma Goldman, Sanger, Kaethe Kollwitz, and Tilly Durieux, helped Smedley in her pursuit of an improved and active public and private life.

In the summer of 1925, Smedley's first academic essay on India in the context of world politics appeared both in India and Germany.[52] Many articles by her, on a variety of subjects, were published through 1925–6 in German, American, and Indian newspapers and journals. For Indian readers of *Modern Review* (Calcutta), she wrote several articles on art and culture in Europe from her personal experience. Some of these were: 'Kaethe Kollwitz, Germany's artist of social misery'[53]; 'Adult Education in Czechoslovakia'[54]; 'The Prague—the City of the Czechs'[55]; 'Cultural Film in Germany'[56]; three articles on Denmark's creative women[57]; 'The Salzburg Festival Plays'[58]. In *The People* appeared her articles criticizing Hagenbeck's 'Indian Show'.[59] Her articles in German, published in Germany and Switzerland, were mostly about the social and political problems of India, and concerning women.

Smedley's visit to her novelist friend Michaelis at her home on an island in Denmark in August was a great success. She stayed with her for three months and, on an earlier advice of her analyst, attempted to write her autobiographical novel. The result was the first draft of *The Daughter of Earth*. Smedley wrote to Lennon that Michaelis found the manuscript 'excellent' and was going to translate it into Danish.[60]

While returning to Berlin in December to start her English conversational class at the university, Smedley found more welcome surprises awaiting her. She happened to have a celebrity in the person of actress Tilla Durieux as her student for private tuition in English. They became friends in no time, and Durieux introduced Smedley to a German publisher for the German edition of her book. Later, Durieux took Smedley to the Salzburg festival and to Munich, and introduced her to literature, arts, music, and the theatre—the sources of her articles in the *Modern Review* of Calcutta. Durieux also offered Smedley a monthly stipend to enable her to devote herself to studies and writing. Smedley was planning at the time a doctoral thesis on the historical and economic aspects of opium. Her other subjects were all related to the British Empire with special emphasis on India and China.[61]

Smedley's doctoral project did not come to fruition, but her journalistic writings continued unabated. During 1927 and 1928, she contributed a number of articles on Asian subjects in Lajpat Rai's journal *The People*. Some of these were: 'Indonesia's Struggle for Freedom'[62]; 'China and the Indian Press'[63]; 'Chinese Peasant Movement 1926'[64]; 'Factory Life in China'[65]; 'Indian Revolutionary Movement Abroad: An Historical Sketch'[66]; 'England's War Plans against Asia: India and the Next War'[67]. She also remained faithful to the *Modern Review*. Among the articles published in this journal during this period was one on Dr Helena Lange, the founder of the first girls' grammar school in Germany[68], and a review of Catherine Mayo's book *Mother India*. [69]

At the time of the establishment of the League Against Imperialism, in the early months of 1927, the Berlin Bureau of the League was inundated with fresh authentic news and information from China. Smedley, though not directly involved in the organization, became more and more interested in China, eventually moving the focus of her activities from India to China. Smedley's one public achievement in Germany before her departure was the commitment she obtained from responsible authorities to open the first birth control clinic in Berlin in February 1928. In early March the same year, she had to undergo an operation for the removal of her appendix. Kaethe Kollwitz was by her side in the hospital and sketched Smedley in her hospital bed. Towards the end of the year, Smedley left for China via Moscow as a reporter.

When Smedley charted a separate course for herself in 1925, her political idealism was not in the least dissimilar to that of Chatto. Both were closer to the Communists and socialists, and participated in their programmes. Chatto missed Smedley sorely, and made zany efforts to persuade her to return to him. He even went to the length of using the good offices of her recent young lover, Mirza Ali Baker, an Oxford University student, with whom Smedley was completely infatuated. It was a pathetic and comic situation in which the behaviour of both Chatto and Smedley seemed far from dignified or decorous. Indeed, the behaviour of Chatto resembled that of an emotionally immature schoolboy rather than of a seasoned political activist hardened by years of unceasing struggle for India's freedom. There is little doubt that his relationship with Smedley damaged him both emotionally and politically and in a permanent way. He lost considerable stature and prestige, and his career as India's most prominent freedom fighter and politician abroad was definitely stunted by this unseemly chapter in the story of his life, which almost seemed to unseat his reason. In an emotionally distraught condition, he wrote to Nehru in early 1929:

> My nerves are in a terrible condition...I am not working effectively. There are also a number of private difficulties of long standing which I have to contend with...[70]

However, as can be seen from the previous chapter, Chatto, although emotionally scarred, was in his mettle again in his articles in the *Industrial and Trade Review for India* of 1925, writing against German commercial racism towards India. In 1926, he helped Willi Muenzenberg found the League Against Imperialism, and influenced Nehru to participate in its many activities.

NOTES

1. Except for a sprinkling of Smedley's later reflections from her *China Correspondent* (Pandora, paperback edition 1984) and some facts from her letters to Lennon, basic information about her life before 1920 has been culled from the first four chapters of Janice R. and Stephen R. MacKinnon's remarkable biography, *Agnes Smedley: The Life and Times of an American Radical* (Berkeley, 1988).
2. 'For years I wandered from one job to another—stenographer, waitress, tobacco stripper, book agent, or just plain starving.' Agnes Smedley, *China Correspondent* (Pandora, paperback 1984 edition), p. 12.
3. 'But my mother and a red-haired woman school teacher in Tercio, a mining camp, must have regarded me with hope, for they kept urging me to get an education. Education seemed to consist in reading many books, but just which I did not know. For years I groped, reading anything between covers, often understanding hardly a sentence.' *China Correspondent*, p. 10.
4. Reflecting on her life Smedley wrote: 'The virtue of submission to injustice, of rendering unto Caesar that which Caesar did not produce himself, made no impression on me.' *China Correspondent*, p. 11.
5. *China Correspondent*, p. 13.
6. Das and Ghose had no political ideology. They seem to have been more interested in being in the limelight in the USA as leading Indian nationalists. Both ruined the Friends of Freedom for India (FFI). Das later showed fascist tendencies. About Ghose, Smedley was to write to Lennon in January 1924: 'What is this I hear of Sailen Ghose being sued in court for $3,000 because of some disgraceful dealing of his...Poor ass! He has a *rotten, rotten* soul...' Smedley to Lennon, 3 January [1924], Florence Lennon Papers (FLP).
7. Smedley to Lennon, 17 January 1921 (Smedley mistakenly put the year as 1920). Florence Lennon Papers (FLP).

8. Ibid.
9. Agnes Smedley, *Daughter of Earth* (The Feminist Press, paperback 1976 edition), p. 362.
10. Chatto wrote to Nehru from Brussels on 23 January 1929 thus: 'I am living under my own name, but find that this causes me innumerable difficulties with Governments. The French have now refused to give me visa...as I wish to go to Paris only for my divorce (I was married 18 years ago in Paris under French law), I think my lawyer, Jean Longuet will get me the necessary permission.' NMML, Nehru Papers. See also Agnes Smedley, *China Correspondent*, p. 15.
11. Margarete Buber-Neumann, *Von Potsdam nach Moskau: Stationen eines Irrweges* (Stuttgart, 1958), p. 107.
12. In the 1950s Sven Stroemgren of Stockholm collected information about Chatto from his many friends there who were then still alive. Stroemgren shared some of Chatto anecdotes with this author. One day Chatto was invited by a well-known Swedish authoress, and, as usual, he arrived too late. When he apologized for the delay, the hostess said, 'But you Indians don't consider time a reality, so I never expected you to come in time.' Chatto instantly retorted in German, 'Ja, es waere sogar ein Verrat der indischen Kultur, wenn ich zur Zeit gekommen waere.' (Yes, it would have been a betrayal to Indian culture if I had come on time!) Another story gathered from one of Chatto's many lady friends in Stockholm—wife of a former minister, whom Stroemgren considered 'a bit light-footed'—pronounced Chatto's first name as *varendra nate* which in Swedish means 'every night'. Interview with Stroemgren in October 1973.
13. 22 months until 1917. She had to undergo internment as well, thereafter. See 'The Interned Lady—Miss Howsin's Release Refused—The Meaning of "Hostile Association",' *Manchester Guardian*, 17 July 1917.
14. *China Correspondent*, pp. 15–16.
15. Smedley to Lennon, Berlin, 3 October [1921], FLP. For Smedley's other observations on Moscow during this visit, see *China Correspondent*, pp. 24–6.
16. The British constantly pursued both Chatto and Smedley. They failed, either to catch or kill them. As far as Smedley is concerned, they suspected her to be a Soviet spy even at the time of her death in London in 1950. It is interesting how the British tried to exercise power over Smedley as a British subject on the basis of her unregistered marriage with Chatto. Years after this 'marriage' ended, Smedley wrote: '...my American citizenship was twice challenged in later years by the British Secret Service, which claimed, with no good intentions, that I was a British subject. To a shocked American consular official in China I once explained the situation thus: "My husband was married to a Catholic nun and for this reason could not marry me. You may call me a concubine if you will, but not a British subject."' *China Correspondent*, p. 15.
17. FO 371/7300 1922 SIS, Far Eastern and American Summary, 18 September 1922.

18. Smedley to Lennon, 31 December 1921, FLP.
19. Smedley to Lennon, 3 October [1921], FLP.
20. Smedley to Lennon, 1 June 1922 FLP.
21. Ibid.
22. Smedley to Lennon, 11 November 1922, FLP.
23. Smedley to Lennon, 18 May 1923, FLP.
24. Smedley to Lennon, 4 June [1923], FLP.
25. Smedley to Lennon, 18 May 1923, FLP.
26. Smedley to Lennon, 4 June [1923], FLP.
27. Ibid.
28. Smedley to Lennon, 4 June [1923], FLP.
29. Smedley to Lennon, Berchtesgaden, Bavaria, 11 August 1923, FLP.
30. Smedley to Lennon, 12 November 1923, FLP.
31. Smedley to Lennon, 8 December 1923, FLP.
32. Ibid.
33. Smedley to Lennon, 8 [28?] December [1923]. This is a second letter of the same date. Smedley was extremely careless in dating her letters, so from the contents this could be towards the end of December. FLP.
34. Smedley to Lennon, 3 January [1924], FLP.
35. Ibid.
36. Smedley to Lennon, 19 January [1924], FLP.
37. Ibid.
38. Smedley to Lennon, 25 August 1924, FLP.
39. Smedley to Lennon, 19 January [1924], FLP.
40. Smedley to Lennon, 17 March [1924], FLP.
41. Smedley to Lennon, 29 June [1924], FLP.
42. Smedley to Lennon, 25 August 1924, FLP.
43. Ibid.
44. Smedley to Michaelis, 21 February [1925], Karin Michaelis Papers (KMP).
45. Smedley to Michaelis, 9 April [1924], KMP.
46. Smedley to Michaelis, Wednesday Morning [possibly January 1925], KMP.
47. Smedley to Michaelis, 21 February [1925], KMP.
48. Ibid.
49. Ibid.
50. Ibid.
51. Ibid.
52. 'India's Role in World Politics', Modern Review, 37 (5), May 1925, pp. 530–41; 'Indien als entscheidender Faktor der Weltpolitik', Zeitschrift fuer Geopolitik, 2 (6), June 1925, pp. 385–403.
53. Modern Review, 38 (2), August 1925.
54. Ibid., 39 (1), January 1926.
55. Ibid., 39 (4), April 1926.
56. Ibid., 40 (1), July 1926.
57. Ibid., 40 (2), April 1926; 40 (3), September 1926 and 40 (4), October 1926.

The creative women being Karin Michaelis, Betty Nansen, and Ingrid Jespersen.
58. *Ibid.*, 41 (1), January 1927.
59. 'Indians in European Zoological Gardens', *The People*, 3 (10), 5 September 1926. A follow-up article appeared in 1927.
60. Smedley to Lennon, 12 November [1925], FLP.
61. *Ibid.*
62. *The People*, 4 (1, 2), 9 January 1927.
63. *Ibid.*, 4 (16), 19 April 1927.
64. *Ibid.*, 4 (21), 29 May 1927.
65. *Ibid.*, 4 (26), 26 June 1927.
66. *Ibid.*, 5 (6), 11 August 1927.
67. *Ibid.*, 5 (8–9), 25 August 1927 and 1 September 1927.
68. *Modern Review*, 41 (5), May 1927.
69. *Ibid.*, 42 (3), September 1927.
70. Chatto to Nehru, Brussels, 31 January 1929, NMML, J. N. Papers.

8

The League Against Imperialism Phase and the Fateful Turn of Events 1926–31

1. WILLI MUENZENBERG AND THE IDEA OF AN INTERNATIONAL CONGRESS ON COLONIAL OPPRESSION AND IMPERIALISM

In the mid-1920s, Chatto was fairly well-known in Berlin as a veteran leader of the Indian community, a journalist, and an anti-imperialist activist.[1] Besides, through Smedley's various articles in the German press about Chatto's elder sister, the poetess Sarojini Naidu[2], who took over as President of the Indian National Congress in December 1925, Chatto seems to have acquired an added importance. For example, during the controversy over 'Indians in the Berlin Zoo', the *Dresdner Neueste Nachrichten* introduced Chatto not only as 'the most prominent Indian living in Germany' but also as a brother of Sarojini Naidu, 'the most famous woman of India'.[3] Although politically quite distant from Naidu, Chatto, being deeply interested in poetry himself[4], did not desist from talking about his illustrious sister to his friends.[5] However, it was his new political orientation that took him to his next phase of political action, where he associated himself with oppressed national groups in an organized common fight against colonial oppression and imperialism. This broadened his field of activity from a narrowly Indian focus to an international perspective without however cooling his passion for India.

Chatto's new orientation had much to do with some of the current activities of Willi Muenzenberg (1889–1940), a Leftist media baron, communist member of the Reichstag (German parliament), and the patron saint of the 'front organisations'. Renowned as an expert propagandist and organizer of aid for the Soviet Union through the *Internationale Arbeiter-Hilfe* (IAH, Workers International Relief), Muenzenberg turned his attention in 1925 to the cruelties and oppression in colonial and semi-colonial countries and founded the League Against Colonialism. Babette Gross, Muenzenberg's life companion, gives an account of this organization as follows. During 1924–25, the Comintern increasingly turned to the 'fellow travellers'. A direction published in the *Inprekorr* urging the need for communist influence in mass organizations moved Muenzenberg to take some pioneering steps.[6] As the agricultural surplus of 1924 in Russia made Muenzenberg's existing economic aid programmes for Russia superfluous, his attention turned to China. In May 1925, there was a strike in Shanghai against the Japanese textile factory, and this developed into a general strike against all foreign capitalists after military intervention by the British. A month-long trade boycott followed against the British colony of Hong Kong. The brutal methods with which the British suppressed the movement produced anger in the West and solidarity among the Chinese people. Muenzenberg then launched the League Against Cruelties and Oppression in the Colonies in early February 1926 to be run by Louis Gibarti (Wladislaw Dobos) and Lucie Peters. The earlier League Against Colonialism merged into the new organization. The purpose of this new organization was to make systematic propaganda in the imperialist countries about the evils of colonialism.

Germany, no longer a colonial power after the War, was well-suited for an anti-colonial organization for two other reasons: a) the German bourgeoisie's reluctance to show any ambition for colonies in public; and b) the presence in Berlin of some 5000 political refugees and students from various colonial countries in whom radical, and particularly communist, tendencies were clearly discernible.[7] However, the German authorities were suspicious of this organization because it proclaimed loudly: 'Germany ought not to have colonies.'[8]

Students from the various colonial countries took part in the events of the League Against Colonial Oppression. Some Asian students from China, India, Indonesia, Indo-China, and Japan, who had already come together in a pan-Asiatic league, were connected with it.[9] Chatto and his nephew Jayasurya Naidu (Sarojini Naidu's eldest son), who was then a medical student in Berlin, also became active in the programmes of this organization. Chatto, detesting the rise of Right-wing reactionary tendencies in Germany at the time, not only associated with Muenzenberg but also became his close friend.

Muenzenberg's strategy of a common action for China through the International Trade Unions Federation did not materialize. However, with the special help of Russian trade unions and the Norwegian and Austrian sections of IAH, he could still manage to collect $250,000 to buy foodstuff and clothing for the newly-built division of the IAH in Peking. Besides, he mobilized artists and authors for his China appeal, and, on 16 August 1925, even arranged a Congress in Berlin with the slogan: 'Hands off from China'. By such means, he wanted to bind, as he said, the proletariat of the West with that of the East.[10] The British government had already reacted nervously to the campaign led by Borodin, the Russian adviser of Chiang-Kai-shek, and Muenzenberg felt encouraged by this reaction.

The success of the China action led Muenzenberg to think in terms of a permanent organization which would bring together the representatives of freedom movements in the colonies and the friends of anti-colonial movements and parties in the West on a permanent basis. The energetic and quick-thinking Muenzenberg reacted swiftly and arranged a congress to discuss such an organization. The League against Cruelties and Oppression in the Colonies was put into action. Muenzenberg hardly spoke a language other than German, but had an extraordinary administrative capacity for running organizations outside Germany through prolific ideas and an ability to choose the right person for the right job.[11] Allied with Muenzenberg through ideological affinity, Gibarty was particularly helpful to Muenzenberg as a good negotiator with his command of five European languages.[12] Chatto's proficiency in English, French, German, and the Scandinavian languages was also of great assistance to Muenzenberg. But at the beginning of their working together, it was Chatto's deep involvement in Indian politics and particularly his connection with Nehru that helped Muenzenberg most, for it was through Chatto's persuasive mediation that he hoped to win Nehru over for the impending congress.[13] By early March 1926, Chatto and Gibarty were busy sending advance circular information about the congress to nationalist leaders of many colonial countries.[14] The aims of the conference were given as follows:

1. A full enquiry into the working condition in the colonial or semi-colonial countries;
2. The initiation of an international protest movement against the cruelties and oppressions committed by the military forces of the imperialist powers;
3. The organization of an international relief action in favour of the most endangered nations that were in need of moral and material support;
4. The linking up of all forces fighting against imperialism and the establishment of permanent relations between all important parties and political groups conducting this fight.[15]

Within a few months favourable responses from many countries began to pour in. On 3 August 1926, in an article in *Inprekorr*, Muenzenberg publicized the information that representatives from China, India, Egypt, Sudan, South Africa, and some other African countries had already agreed to participate.[16] The justification Muenzenberg gave for the congress was a classic communist argument, that the communists must support the suppressed nations in order to promote the development of the proletarian revolution.[17]

Considering that many of the developed west European countries were imperial powers, organizing such a congress in Europe was not easy. The original plan was to convene the congress in Paris, but this was abandoned because of obstacles placed by the French authorities. Ultimately, Brussels could be selected as a venue only because the socialist foreign minister, Emile Vandervelde, gave the green signal on the condition that the Belgian Congo would not be touched upon in the deliberations. The Belgian government offered the medieval Palace Egmont in Brussels for the purpose.[18]

Even in Moscow, there was some hesitation to accept Muenzenberg's plan when he first presented it. He was warned that such a congress might lead to ideological confusion. Roy and Codovilla particularly opposed it. Being discouraged, Muenzenberg telegraphed Gibarty to stop preparations.[19] Meanwhile, Nehru, who happened to be in Europe at the time with some family members, was persuaded by Chatto to attend the Brussels Congress. Nehru wrote home, and received the necessary permission to represent the INC at Brussels. He even showed his readiness to participate in the preparatory meetings.[20] Gibarty promptly passed this information to Muenzenberg in Moscow and it made an enormous difference, for the news made Moscow change its mind immediately. In order to help Berlin's preparations, Moscow even sent a diplomat of the Russian foreign ministry, Marcel Rosenberg. There is little doubt Moscow had a diplomatic interest in the congress. As Babette Gross points out, because of their strong involvement in China, the Russians feared an attack from England. The Russians thought that, since such a Congress would certainly have Labour representatives from England, this would put pressure on the British government. Moreover, every anti-British outburst from the leaders of India and Egypt, for example, would be helpful to Russia. Thus, there was enough ground for the Kremlin to support the Congress politically.[21]

2. INDIA AND CHINA AT THE BRUSSELS CONGRESS AND THE FOUNDATION OF THE LEAGUE AGAINST IMPERIALISM, FEBRUARY 1927

The Congress commenced at the Palais D'Egmont in Brussels on 10 February and lasted till 15 February 1927. It was international not only in spirit but also in representation. No less than 174 mandatory delegates and 300 visitors from 134 organizations turned up at Brussels from 37 countries including India, China, Syria, Arabia, Korea, Indonesia, Indo-China, Annam, Japan, South and North Africa, North and Latin America, and many European countries in spite of the short notice, insufficient press publicity and the fact that delegates had to bear the expenses themselves.[22]

The agenda of the Congress broadly fell into four categories: a) reports on imperialist oppression in the colonies by representatives of the colonies; b) support given by the labour movement and progressive parties in imperialist countries to emancipation movements in the colonies; c) coordination of the forces of the national emancipation movements with the forces of labour movements in colonial and imperialist countries; and d) the building of a permanent internatioinal organization to coordinate the forces combating international imperialism.[23]

On the opening day, 10 February, S.O. Davis of the British Miners' Association was in the chair. The prominent speakers of the evening session were Lian, representative of the executive of the Kuomintang,

Henri Barbuse, the well-known French author, Jawaharlal Nehru, Sen Katayama, the veteran Japanese communist and social worker, José Vasconcelas, former minister of education, Mexico, and Fenner Brockway, the secretary of the Independent Labour Party of England.

During the following days, situations in various parts of the world were discussed: the subtle methods of US imperialism, known as the 'policy of peaceful penetration'; the nature of the movements in Syria; Japanese imperialism in Korea; Dutch rule in Indonesia; and French administration in their different colonies. However, as was expected, British imperialism with special reference to India and China was the dominant theme at the Congress. Nehru, in a press statement on the day before the formal opening, pointed out the significance of India to British imperialism indicating also how it was shaming to the Indians. Egypt and other parts of Africa were subjected to British domination to safeguard the imperial lifeline to India. Similarly, it was a matter of shame and sorrow for Indians to see Britain despatch Indian troops to China to coerce the Chinese.[24] Speaking on the opening day of the Congress, Nehru stated that the Indian problem was an international one, since neighbouring countries like Afghanistan, Burma, Persia, and Mesopotamia were deprived of their independence by the English to safeguard their prized possession—India.[25]

Several British delegates—Fenner Brockway, Harry Pollit, George Lansbury—spoke emotionally about the shameful conditions in India and China, and castigated the British Labour government of the time. As a result, there were several resolutions concerning India and China on the last day of the Congress. One of them, moved by Nehru, gave the INC the Brussels Congress' warm support for complete freedom of India and stated that the liberation of India would be an essential step towards the full emancipation of all the suppressed peoples of the world. The resolution also hoped that the Indian national movement would base its programme on the full emancipation of the peasants and workers of India, without which there could be no real freedom.[26]

In another joint statement, the delegates from Britain, China, and India[27] agreed to: a) fight for full emancipation side by side with national forces in oppressed countries in order to secure complete independence; b) oppose all forms of coercion against colonial peoples; c) vote against all credits, naval, military, and air, for the maintenance of armed forces to be used against oppressed nations; d) expose the horrors of imperialism to civil and military populations; and e) expose imperialistic policy in the light of the working class struggle for freedom.[28] In another resolution, they: a) demanded the immediate withdrawal of all armed forces from Chinese territories and Chinese waters; b) urged the need for direct action including strikes and imposition of embargo to prevent movements of munitions and troops from India to China or vice versa; c) demanded unconditional recognition of the national government; d) the abolition of unequal treaties and extraterritorial rights; and e) surrender of foreign concessions. Finally, in the interest of trade union labour movements in Britain, India, and China, the delegates pledged themselves to immediately work for their close and active cooperation.[29]

There was yet another joint declaration made by Indian and Chinese delegates on Sino-Indian relations. Recalling the intimate Sino-Indian cultural ties existing for more than 3000 years and the history of the Opium Wars and the British stationing of Indian troops in Hong Kong and Shanghai, the delegates urgently pressed for active propaganda in India to educate people regarding China and arouse them to the necessity of immediate action to unite the two peoples again by coordinating their struggles.[30]

MacDonald's Labour government came under severe criticism for their attitude to, and political support for, the national emancipation of the colonies. Speaking on the second day of the Congress, Georg Ledeburg, a member of the *Reichstag*, said that although as early as at the Stuttgart Congress of the Second International in 1907, MacDonald had voted for the resolution on complete independence and self-determination of the colonies, now that he was the British PM he behaved completely differently. Similarly, Ledeburg criticized the Belgian foreign minister, the socialist Vanderweld, who too had been present at the Stuttgart Congress but now refused the organizers of the Brussels Congress to make a public demonstration through the streets of Brussels.[31]

The great enthusiasm of the delegates for the Brussels Congress, despite the hostility shown by imperialist governments and the press, made it clear from the beginning that they would achieve their ultimate objective of founding a permanent organization. Speaking towards the later stage of the Congress, Muenzenberg announced that after several days of deliberations the 30 delegates representing all the parties and organizations at Brussels, as a presidium, had unanimously decided to establish a permanent body to be called the League Against Imperialism and for National Independence (LAI). In broad outlines, the statute and programme of the new organization were presented and were accepted unanimously. The overriding consideration, Muenzenberg said, was that all political organizations, parties, trade unions, and individuals, who were ready to fight for the national liberty of all peoples, equal rights of all races, classes, and individuals would be allowed to affiliate to the League.[32]

A galaxy of distinguished people were attached to the League. Its honorary presidents were: Professor Albert Einstein (Germany), Henri Barbusse (France), and Mme Sun Yat-sen (China). The executive committee was formed with James Maxton, MP (Great Britain) as its president, Edo Fimmen (Holland) as vice-president, and Jawaharlal Nehru (India), Mohamed Hatta (Indonesia), Liau Han-sin (China), Mustaph Chedli (North Africa), Mme Duchésne (France), S. Saklatvala, MP (Great Britain), Dr A. Marteaux, MP (Belgium), R. Bridgeman (Great Britain), Roger Baldwin (USA), and Diego Rivera, (Mexico), as members. Some 30 others, representing various parts of the world, constituted the general council. Although the international secretariat consisted of Willi Muenzenberg and Virendranath Chattopadhyaya, the burden of the day-to-day running of the League's central office in Berlin fell mainly on Chatto. Margarete Buber-Neumann, a co-worker of Chatto's in that office and wife of the German communist leader Heinz Neumann, described Chatto as 'the soul' of that office.[33]

3. THE LEAGUE AGAINST IMPERIALISM AND THE CHATTO-NEHRU RELATIONSHIP

The Chatto-Nehru meeting in Berlin in 1926 quickly developed into a close friendship with mutual affection, respect, and admiration. The friendship, which lasted until 1930, was extremely fruitful for both of them. Through Chatto and the LAI, Nehru was introduced to the world of labour movements, manifestations, and facets of imperialism around the globe, and Marxism and other radical thoughts. 'For the first time, instead of merely condemning British imperialism, Jawaharlal had tried to understand the motives, manner and methods of its functioning. His mind had taken a big step forward.'[34] Chatto seems to have injected into Nehru some of his anti-British virus as well, making Nehru regard British imperialism in India rather more critically than his father had done. In a discussion with an official of the AA along with his father in November 1927, Nehru showed great enthusiasm for the boycott of British goods, humorously adding that, in the event of a boycott, the British might try to export their products to India with a 'Made in Germany' label as, when it came to money the British had no pride or scruples.[35]

As for Chatto, the friendship with Nehru was a great opportunity to renew and reinforce his political link with India. For more than a decade he had been fighting for India's cause in Europe and had remained totally cut off from the mainstream of Indian politics. Nehru appreciated Chatto's dedication in inviting Indian students and trainees to Germany and placing them in various universities and industries. Both Chatto and Nehru discussed the future of INSIB[36], with Chatto suggesting a selection board in India with distinguished academics to choose the right kind of students and trainees for Germany and Nehru pondering what he could do through the INC to help the Bureau financially.[37] Chatto further expected that the politically rejuvenated Nehru would hitch the Indian national movement to a radical course with complete independence as its goal.

His friendship, which was not only with Nehru but with the whole Nehru family, began at a critical time of his life. It was a homecoming and a tonic for him as it reinforced his political, personal, and emotional ties with India. It gave him great comfort and solace especially as it followed his traumatic separation from Smedley, his bouts of depression and nervous breakdowns, straitened circumstances and relentless pursuit by the British secret police that had led him to hide from house to house over several months.[38] Nehru's sister, Krishna, poignantly describes the situation:

It was here [Brussels] that I met Virendra Chattopadhya, Sarojini Naidu's brother, for the first time. He was popularly known as uncle Chatto. An exile for a great many years from his motherland, having wandered alone from one country to another without a home or financial means, he lived a hand-to-mouth existence. He had not become embittered as many might have done and did become. On the contrary, he always had a smile on his face and a word of good cheer for everybody. He was clever, gentle, charming and one of the most lovable characters I have ever met…the more I saw him the more my respect and admiration for him increased. Even when stark hunger faced him round the corner he never lost courage. Many a time when all he had for his lunch was a couple of apples, he would insist on sharing it with some poor Indian student who was also hard up. When we went to

Berlin in October 1927, we met Chatto again and saw a great deal of him. We had all become fond of him and he in turn gave us all his affection.[39]

However, it was politics, or, to be precise, an agreement on the future course of the Indian national movement, which largely determined the Chatto-Nehru relationship within the context of the LAI–INC collaboration. To begin with, Nehru and Chatto agreed that the INC should take an anti-imperialist stance, and work closely with organized workers and peasants. Thus the Nehru-Chatto collaboration within the LAI was to depend on how long the Soviet Union would allow non-communist elements in the LAI to play an important role, and, in the event of the LAI turning into a purely communist organization, what stand Chatto would take. At the Brussels Congress, care was taken by the organizers to ensure the communist delegates and visitors kept a low profile. Besides Muenzenberg, the only other communists who spoke at the Congress were the Japanese Katayama and the Englishman Harry Politt. From Latin America, Manuel Gomez, long trusted by the Russians, also spoke, but he was not known internationally. An observer from the Comintern and a representative of Komsomol, a trade union delegation, also attended but were instructed to remain inconspicuous.[40] Nevertheless, Nehru did not fail to detect, even at this early stage, that the objectives of the Congress coincided with those of Soviet foreign policy.[41] This did not bother him overmuch as he saw two direct advantages to India from the League. First, it would give the INC an opportunity to keep in touch with many Asiatic and other countries with problems not dissimilar to India's. Second, the League could be used as a very effective organ to publicize the Indian national movement. The only potential problem area he visualized was the League's idea of coordination between worldwide liberation and labour movements, as the interests of workers in other countries might not coincide with India's national interests.[42]

Still in Europe in 1927, Nehru attended two of the three meetings of the LAI's executive committee held that year.[43] He noticed that, unlike the Brussel's session, communist elements, although still a minority, were trying to dominate the committee. Nehru did not attend the third meeting that took place in Brussels on 8 December. Roger Baldwin, who attended, mentioned to Nehru the pressure that might come from the Soviet Union: 'Chatto has all the problems well in hand and he does not play up to Muenzenberg (which means the Comintern) as did Gibarti.'[44] The adhesion of the Russian trade unions was giving the

League enough steady income to make real work possible, but Chatto and other non-communists realized, even at that early stage, that it might carry certain political obligations.[45] In a follow-up letter, Baldwin expressed fear that the League's financial needs might force it to depend more and more on communists and Russian trade unions which might lead to a socialist boycott.[46]

At the meeting of the League's executive committee on 2 April 1928, the functions of the secretariat were duly regulated. It was also emphasized that the League was based on the communist movement, the social democratic labour movement, and national revolutionary movements in the colonies.[47] Neither Chatto nor Nehru were seriously worried about the communists at the time. Chatto was extremely busy building up the international organization of the League which, by the middle of 1928, had national chapters in Great Britain, Holland, France, Germany, and the USA and close contacts with many colonial and semi-colonial countries, particularly India, South Africa, and the Latin American countries.[48] For his many visits to Paris, Amsterdam, and Brussels, Chatto had to travel under different names and false passports as he was debarred from these countries ever since the War.[49] Besides, Chatto's international secretariat faced three other difficulties. First, the task of bringing together for concerted action various, often conflicting, political groups involved in the struggle against imperialism was fraught with hurdles. Second, the Labour and Socialist International and the International Federation of Trade Unions, as well as social democratic parties had been carrying on a campaign of vilification against the League. Third, imperialist governments persecuted members of the League, forbade circulation of the League's literature in their territories, and confiscated correspondence between the international secretariat and the colonial organizations. Of these difficulties, the first two had to be faced mainly in Europe and the USA, as they were caused primarily by the attitude of social democratic leaders towards the colonial question. These leaders had abandoned their own pre-War stance on the colonial question and joined the imperialist camp. It was hoped that by systematically exposing the true nature of the colonial policy of social democratic and labour leaders, the League would ultimately gain cooperation from the rank and file of socialist parties and trade unions. As far as colonial countries were concerned, the League aimed at intensifying the development of a broad-based anti-imperialist movement.[50]

The international secretariat, in its report of July 1928, viewed the anti-imperialist struggle in India under the progressive leadership of Nehru very favourably.[51] Nehru, of course, was determined to radicalize the Indian movement by campaigning for independence from the moment he arrived in India just before the annual session of the INC in Madras in December 1927 where he was successful in having a resolution adopted unanimously approving the previous year's decision of the All-India Congress Committee to affiliate with the LAI.[52] He, however, failed to push through a resolution committing the INC to complete independence, meaning full control of defence, finance, economic, and foreign policy. It was felt too radical by the old guard close to Gandhi (who was then absent). The party accepted only a resolution generally adhering to the goal of complete independence. Later, Gandhi considered even this diluted version of the resolution as one 'hastily conceived' and 'thoughtlessly passed'.[53]

The issue of independence came up again at the time of the All Parties Conference when a committee was set up with Motilal Nehru as chairman to draw up a constitution of India. His son, Jawaharlal, suggested a democratic socialist republic. But the Nehru Report published in July 1928 recommended, as already anticipated by Jawaharlal, Dominion Status for India. Jawaharlal considered it nothing more than clinging to the Empire. He, therefore, formed a pressure group within the Congress Party, the Independence for India League, to mobilize support for independence as the main goal. He toured the country extensively giving fiery speeches in favour of independence and socialism, and his League, mostly active in the United Provinces, also drew up economic and social programmes based on socialism. The boycott agitation against the Simon Commission gave Jawaharlal special impetus to mobilize people against imperialism. The demonstrations against the Simon Commission in various parts of India were lathi-charged by the police as a direct result of which Lala Lajpat Rai died on 18 November 1928, and Jawaharlal Nehru was hurt in Lucknow along with Pandit Govind Bhallabh Pant.

In December, Nehru presided over the annual session of the All-India Trade Union Congress held in Jharia, Bihar. The LAI deputed the American W.J. Johnstone to Jharia as fraternal delegate. He compared the British exploitation of Indians to the chauvinism of American capitalists and white workers. When the police came to the *pandal* to arrest Johnstone, Nehru had them turned out and made a forceful speech advising the infuriated delegates to affiliate their trade unions to the LAI as suggested by Johnstone. The next day, when Johnstone was arrested outside the *pandal*, Nehru made another speech denouncing imperialism.

The restless, roving Nehru of 1928 became very popular with the younger generation of Indian nationalists, but his raging propaganda for independence did not achieve much. What was more, when the annual Congress session, in December at Calcutta, accepted Dominion Status as its goal, Nehru, out of loyalty to Gandhi and his father, accepted— though only for a year—on the condition that the campaign for independence would be reinstated if Dominion Status were not granted within a year.

Nehru's political activities since his return from Europe were keenly followed by the LAI. The executive committee in a resolution in Brussels on 28 April first congratulated the INC for accepting independence as the goal of the national movement, as all formulas of the so-called 'freedom within the Empire' were but a camouflage for foreign domination.[54] Not surprisingly, therefore, when the Nehru Report was published in July 1928, the LAI executive committee meeting in Berlin in mid-August declared to Indian leaders that any compromise with British imperialism would be a gross betrayal of the rights of the Indian people to freedom.[55]

Chatto was particularly happy with Nehru's formation of the Independence for India League and, in early October 1928, asked if it could not look after the interests of the LAI as well in India, organizing joint events with workers' and peasants' organizations, trade unions, and cooperatives. It could adopt a social programme, the kind which the INC had neither attempted nor could. According to Chatto, the time had come for action outside of the INC. He, in fact, suggested that Nehru convert his League into a branch of the LAI.[56] Towards the end of the same month, Chatto suggested the separate development of the Independence for India League outside the INC. He stated that it could be made into a powerful organization because it met the demands of the majority of Indians whose real problem had been ignored by reactionary elements in the INC who could not be relied even regarding their moderate social and economic programmes. His suggestion was that all elements standing for absolute independence with a certain amount of 'democracy' should be drawn into the League, but the central committee should consist only of those whose integrity was beyond question.[57] Agreeing with Nehru about the lack of qualified persons, Chatto thought a school for training in social revolutionary principles and tactics could be arranged and that the LAI could possibly send European comrades, well-educated in the theory and practice of revolution, as instructors. Chatto also suggested the need for a daily or weekly newspaper on actual events from the revolutionary perspective, and expressed his willingness to offer 'moral and intellectual assistance'.[58]

Unlike Chatto, Nehru never considered a separate organization parallel to the INC. All he was trying to do was strengthen the national movement by introducing the message of socialism. He warned Chatto in a letter that his Independence for India League, although aiming to become a centre for anti-imperialist activities, had so far been more or less up in the air.[59] But before this letter reached Berlin, another bunch of revolutionary tactical advice came from Chatto, asking Nehru to rally all the anti-imperialist elements to his League and come to a clear understanding with the Workers' and Peasants' Party (WPP) for a common programme in order to obtain a majority in the INC and gear it to 'our own programme'. All elements that might produce confusion or betray the cause of independence were to be eliminated.[60]

In early December (1928), the LAI secretariat was enthusiastically observing India on the eve of the annual sessions of both the INC and the WPP. Chatto rejoiced to read in the *Times* about Nehru's injuries at the Lucknow demonstration against the Simon Commission, for, as he prophesied, it would make Nehru 'more popular with the masses'.[61] Chatto also informed Nehru about the newly drafted statutes of the LAI which had been long due.[62] When these statutes reached Nehru, he quickly referred to an unclear point in them regarding the 'affiliated' and 'associated' memberships. He explained that an affiliated organization was one that was in complete agreement with the League in regard to every matter, whilst an associated organization, like the INC, agreed generally with the objects and policy of the League though not necessarily agreeing with everything the League might do.[63] One can presume that this was a soft covert warning to the LAI in view of their various demands and pressures.

The year 1929 began for Nehru, as general secretary of the INC, with the task of reorganizing the provincial Congress committees, a task entrusted to him by Gandhi. It involved compelling the provincial branches to obey the instructions of the Working Committee and implement constructive programmes in conjunction with the Congress Volunteer Corps (Hindustani Seva Dal) and other student organizations. Not much interested in the programme of spinning, Nehru looked for dedicated youths to organize peasants and workers and create a mass consciousness, more or less in the same manner as he had done in the previous year under the auspices of the Independence for India League.[64]

The fact that this time Nehru was working and speaking on behalf of the whole Congress organization and the possibility that, without the government's announcement of Dominion Status within the year, Civil Disobedience would commence in accordance with the understanding reached between Nehru and the INC alarmed the government of India. The government also noted the recent growth of trade unionism in India and the interest some union leaders were showing in affiliating with the LAI. In August, the government publicized a letter allegedly written by M.N. Roy from Berlin advising the Communist Party of India to become affiliated with the Comintern and the WPP with the LAI.[65] The intent was to use the letter as a pretext to bring about stringent legislation for the control of unions. The object of the Public Safety Bill, introduced by the government in the Central Legislature, was primarily to secure power to expel British and other foreigners in India advocating the overthrow of the government by force. The bill was, however, defeated in the Assembly with the casting vote of the President, V.J. Patel. The government, considering the LAI a communist organization, regularly intercepted Nehru's correspondence with Chatto and others.[66] In the eyes of the government, Nehru was the meeting point for both nationalist and communist revolutionaries.[67] To tackle the communists, the government arrested all the leading trade unionist revolutionaries and communists[68] in various parts of the country, and brought them to Meerut to prosecute them for a conspiracy 'to deprive the King-Emperor of the sovereignty of British India.' Meerut was chosen in order to avoid a jury which might hinder conviction. Langford James, the prosecutor, made the Meerut case a political trial *par excellence*. In his opening speech on 12 June 1929, he vilified the communists, trying to appease the nationalists at the same time:

Pandit Motilal Nehru is regarded by them [the Communists] as a dangerous patriot. His son, Jawaharlal Nehru, is dubbed a tepid reformist. Mr. Subhas Chunder Bose is a Bourgeois and somewhat ludicrous careerist. Gandhi they regard and dislike as a grotesque reactionary.[69]

Nehru wrote to Chatto that the prime motive of the trial was propaganda: to discredit the Meerut accused in the eyes of the nationalists. By way of example, Nehru said that even the government's director of publicity had been sent down from Simla to Meerut to supervise the publicity arrangements.[70] Nehru feared that the attempt might partly succeed 'because many of the friends of the accused have a way of cursing nationalists in the most offensive language' which made many people refuse to contribute towards the funds for defence. However, the Congress was behind the accused to the hilt. It formed a central defence committee to help them and set aside, for the first time in its history, a sum of Rs 1500 for their defence.[71]

The Meerut trial failed to disjoint the Congress from the LAI. Nehru, as general secretary of the Congress, officially wrote to the LAI secretariat that, in spite of hostile propaganda that the LAI was opposed to the ideas of the INC, the Congress recognized the good work the League had done and appreciated its association with it.[72]

However, in the summer of 1929, there was a change in Soviet policy towards India. The 10th Plenum of the Executive Committee of the Communist International (ECCI) in July directed communists in India to disband the WPP and concentrate on organizing a communist party in complete dissociation from the Congress. As a matter of fact, this policy had already been suggested in a report about colonial movements by Otto V. Kuusinen presented at the 6th Comintern Congress (17 July–1 September 1928), fearing that workers and peasants not being in 'a real Communist Party' might transform themselves into petty-bourgeois parties.[73]

The second World Congress of the LAI, with a majority of communists, held in Frankfurt in July 1929, also took some drastic steps of their own. The manifesto published on the occasion announced:

One of the most fundamental tasks of the world movement against imperialism, without the realisation of which no victory is possible, is the creation of a firm alliance between the oppressed colonial peoples, the revolutionary workers of the imperialist countries, and the workers and peasants of the Soviet Union.[74]

The Comintern delegate, Dmitrii Manuilsky, attacked both the Left social democrats in the imperialist countries as well as the socialist delegates of colonial countries, for merely mouthing anti-imperialist rhetoric while remaining either completely inactive or even supporting imperialist governments. The question was raised as to whether the League would still work with the INC when the majority of which, being under the influence of the Right wing, pushed aside full independence in favour of Dominion Status as their goal.[75]

It took some time before Nehru received full official information, particularly concerning the resolutions, of the LAI's World Congress at Frankfurt. Lack of finances delayed the publication of the English translation of the proceedings of the Frankfurt Congress.[76] Nehru knew the delay was due to the government's interception of his mail, and facetiously wrote to Chatto, 'So far as you are concerned you know well how dearly the British Government loves you. How can they then miss a billet-doux from you.'[77]

However, this cheerfulness of Nehru regarding Chatto and the LAI was short-lived. Bit by bit he learnt about the metamorphosis of the LAI, first from scanty press reports, then from letters of fellow socialist colleagues, and finally from the LAI secretariat itself. The news sent by Edo Fimmen and Roger Baldwin of Einstein's resignation, Maxton's removal from the executive presidentship, and the transformation of the LAI into a communist organization troubled Nehru immensely. He wrote to Chatto that this policy 'is bound to end in the collapse of the League'. Nehru also warned that many in the TUC and INC had taken exception to certain activities of the League, and that it might not be easy to continue the INC's association with it in future. He reminded Chatto that the INC was not fully affiliated to the LAI, being only an associate member.[78] Nehru had already informed Chatto about the possibility of annulling the TUC's affiliation with the LAI.[79]

Meanwhile, Chatto's letter explaining some of this news was on its way. Chatto first dealt with the Einstein episode. At the Frankfurt Congress, there also took place a pan-Arabic Conference. Einstein resigned from the honorary presidium because he was opposed to the League's Palestine manifesto on the occasion. 'We regret the loss but we cannot possibly retain pro-Imperialist persons, however distinguished, in any organisation of the League,' Chatto wrote.[80] Chatto also said that the report Nehru had received from Reuters was wrong. About Maxton, Chatto explained that although he was undoubtedly convinced that imperialism had to be overthrown, he had done nothing whatsoever to stop the imperialist manoeuvres of his ILP (Independent Labour Party) colleagues, who had unashamedly supported the Labour government in its efforts to uphold British imperialism in India, Palestine, and Egypt.[81]

The tone and temper in which Chatto explained Maxton's expulsion must have startled Nehru. Justifying the action against Maxton, Chatto wrote:

> It is sheer Imperialist intrigue to say that Maxton's expulsion was due to the desire of the Communists to dominate the League. As a matter of fact, no sincere Nationalist can wish to be associated with persons and organisations that use radical phrases merely to deceive the subject peoples and gain time for imperialism. The National Congress, in fact, ought to greet the expulsion of Maxton as a sign that the British League and the League in general do not intend to tolerate any form of half-heartedness or hypocrisy in the struggle.[82]

Perhaps influenced by the overwhelming negative opinion about the INC in the Comintern and the LAI, Chatto again emphasized the need for a mass anti-imperialist umbrella organization in India:

> I certainly think it must be admitted that it [the INC] does not cover large sections of the population who are organised in separate bodies for specific purposes but which are nevertheless very important anti-imperialist elements. I need only to refer to the T.U.C., the Workers' and Peasants' Party, the Youth League etc…What is necessary today is to have a federation of all these organisations which would unite them all in action and give them all the same clear anti-imperialist lead…Please think over the possibilities of organising an All-Indian Anti-Imperialist Federation during the December week.[83]

Some of the latest developments in the LAI, particularly Maxton's ouster, were perhaps not misled since the organization was infused with the very spirit of anti-imperialism. Maxton seems to have sheepishly, and rather belatedly, accepted the charges against himself.[84] However, what troubled Nehru was that the communists seemed to have usurped the LAI for themselves. He felt no need to discuss the matter further, perhaps because he had already decided to withdraw the INC from the League. His earlier reminder that there was a distinction between the 'associated' and 'affiliated' membership is indicative of the direction in which his mind had been moving.

In early November 1929, Chatto again complained about Gandhi's domination of the Congress and Nehru's submission to him. When Chatto learned about Nehru agreeing to preside over the Lahore session of the INC, he wrote to him:

When the cunning Mahatmaji proposed your name for the Presidency of the Congress, it was obvious that it was a move to kill you and the opposition. The interpretation in the country was quite false. The very fact that nine votes were cast for Gandhi is the best evidence that the Right Wing elements and compromisers had the majority. In your new position of President elected on the initiative of Gandhi, your hands will be completely tied, and any action that you might have otherwise taken as a leader of the independence movement will be paralysed by the necessity of having to remain impartial inside the Congress.[85]

In the eyes of Chatto, Nehru's acceptance would have been justified if he had been able 'to expose the treacherous character of the majority of the Congress leaders and to bring about a split if necessary in order to destroy a patched-up unity and clear the way for a solid anti-imperialist movement.'[86] But even as Chatto was writing these words, the *Times* carried the news of Nehru putting his signature to the understanding between the Viceroy and Gandhi, embodied in the Delhi Manifesto, pledging the Congress to a conference, together with the Indian princes, to discuss the form of Dominion Status for India. The Delhi Manifesto promised general amnesty and the release of political prisoners. Chatto pointedly asked Nehru, 'How is it possible for any serious politician to be taken in by the deceptive promises of the MacDonald Government?'[87]

Nehru did not have any substantial argument to defend himself against Chatto's criticism, and told him that he largely agreed. However, he added that, by way of protest against the Delhi Manifesto, he had resigned from the Congress Working Committee but his resignation had not been accepted. Since at the end of the year, the Congress planned a great political offensive, he was not willing to make any fresh difficulties at this critical time.[88]

Chatto and the LAI were totally dissatisfied with this explanation, and he castigated Nehru:

Whatever your reasons may be to explain away your surrender to the traitors who are negotiating for their own class interests, I myself cannot see why you did not proffer immediate resignation. That would have rallied all the youth, the workers and peasants to your side and you would have been able to defeat easily the compromisers in the Congress...It is a fundamental error to think that unity in the Congress is more important than the vital interests of the masses. After having risen to be the undoubted leader of the youth of the country and to enjoy even the confidence of the working masses, you seem in a moment of inexplicable weakness and mental confusion to have left your followers in the lurch.[89]

As Chatto pointed out, it was indefensibly awkward for Nehru to advocate independence as president of the AITUC, simultaneously pleading for Dominion Status as would-be president of the INC. He suggested a way out of this dilemma:

> Do what great leaders have often done, namely, publicly admit a mistake and take the right line. If you do this today, withdraw your signature, and make your position as President of the Congress as an opportunity for breaking up the sham unity which is so dangerous, driving out all moderate and Dominion Status men and capturing the whole Congress apparatus for the uncompromising struggle against imperialism, you will have more than retrieved your lost position.[90]

Chatto once again repeated his earlier suggestion of an All-India Anti-Imperialist Federation on the lines of the LAI and stressed that the Congress was not the representative body of the Indian people, being only one of many organizations taking an anti-imperialist stand.[91]

Contrary to the LAI's assumption of a formidable anti-imperialist Indian working class, the labour movement in India at this time was not at all powerful. The loss of bargaining power, the Trade Dispute Act (1929), and the Meerut Trial had appreciably weakened it. Moreover, the post-Meerut, moderate section of the AITUC preferred to be affiliated with the International Federation of Trade Unions (IFTU), connected with the Socialist and Labour International.[92] Besides, to Nehru's regret, the WPP, so often referred to by Chatto as a progressive force, had refused to join the Independence League.[93] Correcting the LAI's exaggerated notion of Indian workers as solidly supportive of the independence movement and its misconception that the INC was merely a den of treacherous compromisers, Nehru insightfully answered Chatto's criticism:

> I am afraid you are often very much misled by some of your correspondents in India. I can well understand a difference in outlook. If this difference is fundamental then cooperation is difficult. If there is a fair measure of agreement then it is desirable to work together. In any event it does not help matters much by calling people with whom you may happen to disagree little traitors and the like. Perhaps if you came in personal contact with some of our most aggressive young men who pose as workers' leaders you might change your opinion of them.[94]

On the same day, 30 January 1930, Nehru officially wrote to the LAI secretariat:

I am afraid you have not the least notion of conditions in India and yet you do not hesitate to lay down the law for us. The National Congress has welcomed your League and has agreed to cooperate with you but it cannot tolerate outside interference of the kind you have been carrying on.[95]

Nehru told the LAI it was curious that they had chosen to attack the INC at a time when it was politically and socially advanced than ever before. The capitalist and *zamindari* elements had dropped out, and richer professional classes had kept aloof fearing the risks involved in a struggle for independence. The same fear had driven many old Congressmen to leave, and the Congress was gradually transforming itself into a mass organization with a socialistic outlook.[96]

This letter practically ended the collaboration between the INC and LAI. On 26 February 1930, Chatto wrote to Nehru hoping Nehru would not allow political differences to embitter him or make him 'blind to mistakes simply because these happen to be pointed out by Communists.' Nehru most probably ignored the letter.[97] By the middle of 1930, the LAI had almost become an organ of the Comintern. At the fifth Congress of the Profintern (Red International of Labour) Bohumir Smeral, a Czech activist of the LAI based in Berlin, 'somewhat unexpectedly' explained that since the Congress in Frankfurt the LAI had no longer been a fighting alliance between the national bourgeoisie of colonial countries and masses of the international proletariat but a united revolutionary mass organization.[98] When the League's executive committee met in Berlin in May 1931, the transformation was evident. Nehru and other non-communist members who had resigned were formally expelled on the occasion. In 1931, the international secretariat was moved to France, a place from where Chatto had long been debarred. He was, therefore, replaced by Clemens Dutt in the secretariat. In August 1931, Chatto left for the Soviet Union. Before his departure, Chatto, along with Nambiar, met V.J. Patel once again and the latter wrote to Nehru:

I had long talks with Chattopadhyaya and Nambiar. They feel that you are too weak. They are, I am afraid, not prepared to appreciate the practical difficulties in our way and the odds against which we have to fight.[99]

4. Chatto's Fateful Ideological Conversion

In his letter to Nehru on 26 February 1930, Chatto disclosed his adherence to communism.[100] It is significant because, throughout his political career until then, he had declared himself an Indian revolutionary. Sometimes he called himself an anarchist, but most of his Leftist friends and colleagues knew that he was only an anti-British Indian nationalist and intellectual. In 1921, while in the Soviet Union, Chatto and Smedley visited Emma Goldman, then under virtual house arrest in Moscow. Goldman wrote in her memoir, *Living My Life*:

> Chatto was intellectual and witty, but he impressed me as a somewhat crafty individual. He called himself an anarchist, though it was evident that it was Hindu [here meaning Indian] nationalism to which he devoted himself entirely.[101]

True, Chatto hobnobbed with the anarchists as well. According to Nambiar, during his post-Swedish period in Germany, Chatto worked in close contact with the anarchists, among others Armando Borghi, co-editor of the newspaper *Avanti*, and Mussolini.[102] However, until he joined the LAI, he remained primarily an Indian anti-imperialist, passionately involved in the Indian freedom movement. Even after his association with the LAI, up to the time of the Second World Congress at Frankfurt, he remained at heart a fighter for India's national freedom. In her book on Muenzenberg, Babette Gross tells us that at the Frankfurt Congress, when Manuilsky was attacking the socialist delegates and Maxton and Mohammed Hatta were trying to set the proceedings to a moderate course, Chatto told the social democrat Bjane Braatoy, a friend of Friedrich Adlers, that he was in the first place an Indian nationalist and would consequently ally himself with anyone who was anti-British.[103] Babette Gross' sister, Margarete Buber-Neumann, a communist and co-worker in the Berlin Bureau of the LAI, had this to say in her memoirs: 'From all talks with him I got the impression that Chatto was not a Communist but an Indian nationalist.'[104]

All this points to our presumption that Chatto formally converted to communism only after the Frankfurt World Congress in June 1929, although he had long been a sympathizer. He probably joined the German Communist Party as well in late 1929 or early 1930.[105] Smedley wrote many years later:

> Virendranath turned more and more to the study of Marxism as a means of gaining independence for India; and eventually became a Communist Party member. I always wondered just what new design was added to the Hindu temple of his mind

by this act. I could never imagine him being regimented by any political party or following "lines" of thought and action. His mind took the whole world as its province and drew nourishment from every age.[106]

Converting totally to communism meant that Chatto embraced the theory of class struggle and the dictatorship of the proletariat. He abandoned the policy of gradual social and economic change advocated by reformists. The three years of collaboration with the radicalized Nehru seem to have proved to him the futility of having faith in the bourgeoisie. In his judgement, the Indian bourgeoisie could at best be reformist, and at worst perpetually compromising. Consequently, a sustained and determined anti-imperialist struggle could not be expected from them.

Chatto abandoned faith in democratic processes, and accepted revolution and violence as a means of bringing fundamental change. No wonder that, during this period, Chatto was advising Nehru to start an anti-imperialist independence movement outside the Congress with the cooperation of organized workers and peasants and trained revolutionary cadres. No doubt, he was led to this position by a negative notion of the Indian bourgeoisie and an erroneous perception of an Indian proletariat ready to plunge into an anti-imperialist struggle to usher in a Soviet republic of workers and peasants. When he failed to revolutionize the INC through Nehru, Chatto advocated a campaign against the Congress itself. He accepted the Stalinist 'ultra left' policy of the time, ignoring the Leninist ideal of a united front for national liberation.

Chatto's ideological change was reflected in many polemical and propagandist articles he wrote at this time. Although tendentious, these articles are highly informative. The first, from a selection I made of them in order of publication, is on unemployment in India published in the Comintern journal in early March 1930.[107] According to Chatto, the period of boom in industrial development during and following the War had gone in the previous eight years, and industrial and agricultural conditions had worsened in India giving rise to the inevitable conflict between workers and employers on the one hand, and the educated unemployed and the foreign regime on the other. He wrote that, in spite of the low wage paid to workers, the textile industry of India had entered into a serious crisis for a variety of reasons such as the ignorance of mill-owners, technical inefficiency of the factories, disproportionately high salaries paid to managers and agents, absence of an efficient sales organization, and the inability to compete with Lancashire, Japan, and the USA. Unable to profit in any other way, the mill-owners tried to squeeze out profit from the workers directly and consumers indirectly by resorting to rationalization, attempting reduction in wages, and lobbying for anti-strike legislation. All this, Chatto said, resulted in the inevitable conflict between workers and employers, finding expression in the strikes of hundreds of thousands of textile workers under the leadership of the Girni Kamgar Union. He wrote that unemployment among the educated middle class also became intense in Madras, Malabar, the Punjab, and Bengal, and the victims started forming unions and associations. He hoped that all this would certainly radicalize India. 'The only improvement in their lot is possible by the complete overthrow of imperialism and the establishment of a workers' and peasants' republic.'[108]

Chatto was greatly excited at the general strike that broke out in the Great Indian Peninsular Railway on 4 February 1930. Besides the economic demands, Chatto saw the movement assuming a definitely political stance.[109] The organizers, according to him, realized that no improvement would be possible without the overthrow of imperialist exploitation. He saw in it the resolve to boycott the imperialist Whitley Commission and fight against the reformism of Amsterdam and Geneva and the readiness to affiliate to the pan-Pacific Trade Union secretariat and the LAI. In this article, Chatto criticized Nehru, himself a member of the executive committee of AITUC, for not helping the strikers and only advocating the reference of the 'dispute' to an arbitration board. In Chatto's eyes, the true Independence Day was celebrated on 26 January 1930, just a few days before the strike, when the workers hoisted the Red Flag all over the country.[110]

In the summer of 1930, two more articles by Chatto appeared—one denouncing the Labour and Socialist International (the Second International) for their Indian policy, the other denouncing Indian nationalist leaders for their attitude to the Indian revolution. The Second International's attitude to the colonial question had always been controversial, both before and after WWI. Its members were mostly European imperialist powers, and under various pretexts—the chief being 'the civilizing effect of imperialism under socialist regime'— desisted from taking firm action towards granting independence to even the developed colonies. Chatto noted that at the congress of the

Second International in Brussels, August 1928, the word 'imperialism' was not used at all, and the whole treatment of the colonial question was based upon the premise of the civilizing mission of capitalism. And on the question of India, it only supported the endeavours of the Indian people to attain 'full self-government', carefully avoiding the word 'independence'. The Berlin Congress of the Second International in May 1930 began thus: 'The Executive recalls the Resolution of Brussels Congress of the LSI which recognises the right of the peoples of India to self-determination.' The use of the phrase 'peoples of India' was suspect to Chatto since with this expression an impression was created of the diversity that existed in India—racial, religions, and lingual—thereby justifying the benevolent role of Britain in promoting peace and unity among the heterogeneous masses.[111] The Brussels resolution had expressed its conviction that through negotiations between 'the representatives of all sections of the Indian population' and the British Labour government the right of self-determination would be established 'under the safest and most effective conditions'. This paragraph, pointing to a Round Table Conference (RTC), was also objectionable to Chatto since it meant negotiations 'with the princes, the landlords, the industrial and commercial bourgeoisie, with the national reformist bourgeois leaders, and with those labour reformists who had been working as tools of the Labour Party to destroy the working class movement in India.'[112] In this connection, Chatto condemned Indian labour leaders, Shiva Rao, N.M. Joshi, Chamanlal, and Bakhale for cooperating with the British Labour government. Chatto also criticized Brockway and Maxton, the two Independent Labour leaders, for being party to the shameful resolution on India at the Second International session, because when Gandhi and Brockway used the word independence, they contemplated a place for India within the British Empire. Against all these fake anti-imperialists or 'the lackeys of Imperialism', Chatto declared that the Soviet Union was the only genuinely anti-imperialist state in the world.[113]

It was his total disappointment with the ever-compromising Congress leaders that led Chatto to accept communism and join the Soviet camp. He was dismayed that Congress leaders failed to choose full independence as a more desirable goal to a mere 'responsible' place within the British Empire.[114] Even in 1930, when the Congress resolved to stiffen the struggle against British imperialism by resorting to the non-payment of taxes and by intensifying the boycott of British goods,

Chatto was sceptical. The slogan of independence, according to him, was only to attract the masses and the whole thing was only a device to enter into negotiations with the government and prevent the campaign developing into a revolutionary mass movement.[115]

Chatto arrived at this conclusion by studying the recent history of the Congress and its leaders. Gandhi, to start with, had written a letter to Viceroy Irwin just before his campaign for independence, whereas 18 days after the declaration of the campaign, in the 24 April edition of his newspaper *Young India* he stated: 'The present campaign is not designed to establish independence, but to arm the people to establish swaraj.'

Gandhi's successor in the leadership of the campaign, Abbas Tyabji, according to Chatto, was one who had never declared himself for independence. When he was imprisoned and the mantle of leadership fell on Sarojini Naidu, Chatto said, 'This fact alone suffices to show the political standard of the Congress leaders', for, according to him, when the Labour Congress passed the resolution on independence, Mrs Naidu and Dr Ansari declared they considered the resolution to be against the interests of the country.[116] Here Chatto was very uncharitable to his sister:

Mrs. Naidu, however, is a mere puppet who is placed in charge of the theatrical side of the campaign, while the wiser and cleverer heads are keeping their hands free for negotiations with the imperialist government.[117]

Chatto then tackled the front leaders of the negotiations team—Motilal Nehru, V.J. Patel, and Mohammed Ali—and their pattern of negotiations that resulted in the Delhi Manifesto. Chatto said Sir Tej Bahadur Sapru, the agent of Lord Irwin, who had earlier brought pressure on Nehru to sign the Delhi Manifesto, was still working behind the scenes to sway the Congress leaders. As for Motilal, Chatto said he had never concealed his preference for Dominion Status, and, as an astute lawyer, was not unaware of the danger of a mass movement to his class.[118] Assessing the past performances of Patel in politics, Chatto remarked that he had only one object in view: 'to enhance his own popularity and importance in order to make it easier to betray the movement.' He highlighted the following statement of Patel's:

It is true that Congress has now adopted complete independence as its object, but I am not without hope, if with[out] any further delay, India is offered complete responsible government within the British Commonwealth of Nations, she would be prepared to accept it, and perhaps such responsible government is more to her advantage than isolated independence.[119]

Chatto had no kind word for Mohammed Ali either, as he too was opposed to immediate independence although clamouring for the independence for the Arab countries.[120]

Chatto found it disgusting that all these Congress leaders were due to attend the first RTC to be held in London in the autumn of 1930 to discuss with the liberals, princes, and British representatives the future of India. The news that three Indian labour leaders—N.M. Joshi, Shiva Rao, and S.C. Joshi—whom Chatto considered the enemies of the Indian working class would also arrive in London for the RTC further angered him.[121]

Realizing that the Simon Commission Report would form the basis of discussions at the RTC, Chatto studied it critically, and in another article in *The Labour Monthly*[122] focused on its mischievous parts. The British printed tens of thousands of copies of this Report and circulated it widely in many countries, even with translations into European languages. The purpose behind this wide publicity of the Report by the British was, in Chatto's eyes, its propaganda value for British imperialism. The divisions and diversities of India were portrayed in rich colours with skilful use of numbers and statistics so as to convince even the sceptics of the benefits of British imperialism: on the difficulty of constructing a constitution or government to suit a land of 320 million inhabitants with 560 native states, nominally independent, 222 separate languages, peoples with two main hostile religions (168,000,000 Hindus and 60,000,000 Muslims in British India alone), and 10,000,000 outcasts. Chatto wrote:

And the conclusion to be drawn about 'this variegated assemblage of races and creeds', this 'congeries of heterogeneous masses' that is known as India, is that the 320 millions inhabiting that extraordinarily disrupted and chaotic country ought to be thankful to British imperialism for having given them a 'common government' and protection from 'foreign invasion'.[123]

Chatto, an expert linguist, dealt with the problem of the 222 Indian vernaculars, a figure often cited by the British to show that Indians were unfit for self-government, by drawing attention to the Soviet model.

There are far more languages spoken in the vast territory of the Workers' and Peasants' Republic, and yet the Russian workers have succeeded in establishing their strong independent centralised government, while maintaining the fullest possible cultural autonomy of the linguistic and national groups.[124]

Contrary to Chatto's expectations, the Congress did become radical after the Delhi Manifesto, and, and at the Karachi session in 1931, the ratification of the Delhi Manifesto was supplemented by a clause on the fundamental rights of the people under the 'swaraj' constitution. But for Chatto, it was nothing more than a trick to draw the workers and peasants into the Congress net. In another article on the INC, he stated that the working masses and revolutionary youth of India regarded Gandhi as a traitor.[125] Chatto criticized both Subhash Chandra Bose and Nehru, the two young Left-wing leaders, for ultimately accepting the Manifesto for the sake of unity in the Congress, in spite of being thoroughly against it in principle. The new circumstances that had pacified Bose and Nehru were of no consequence to Chatto. Chatto's final judgement on the Karachi Congress betrayed that he had become a prisoner of his own obsession, aggravated by his new political orientation:

The Karachi Congress represents the final and definite transition of the Indian bourgeoisie and their agents and allies among the intelligentsia from the partial struggle against imperialism, which they had carried on for a short while, into open alliance with British imperialism against the Indian Revolution.[126]

However, British imperialism primarily remained the target of his attack. Highly informative though these articles are, some of them were written solely for the purpose of defending the Soviet Union. In early January 1931, he wrote how, in the British prime minister MacDonald's New Year's 'honours list', 'no less than eighty-two members of the Indian Police Force' were honoured, a clear evidence of imperialist policy in full swing.[127] When Britain and the USA started a campaign against 'forced labour' behind the industrial growth of the Soviet Union and tried to prevent the 'tainted' Soviet products from entering their markets, Chatto wrote an article, full of detailed information, about the brutal British exploitation of convict labour in the Andaman Islands to increase the yield of important species of timber like *padauk* and *gurjan*. The timber fetched high prices in Europe and the USA.[128] In this connection, he referred to the similar situation in French settlements as well, citing authorities. Chatto's conclusion was: 'When, therefore, any imperialist opens his mouth about forced labour in the Soviet Union, the blood-soaked timber of the Andamans should be thrust down his hypocritical throat.'[129]

Another of Chatto's articles of the period, attacking imperialism in general and British imperialism in particular was about the arming of Nadir Shah's Afghanistan.[130] Here Chatto detected British imperialism's aggressive design on the Soviet Union. He said Britain could conceal this design because some other imperialist powers like the USA, France, Italy, Japan, and the pro-imperialist Germany were also busy developing Afghanistan into an important war base to attack the Soviet Union. 'Whatever may be the mutual antagonism among imperialists themselves, they are all united in their hatred of Soviet Union and Soviet China.'[131]

The last article I will consider was written in 1930–31 is about Buddhism's role in British and Japanese imperialism.[132] Enumerating various examples of Japanese imperialism in Asia from Manchuria to Afghanistan with the help of the British, the article came to the Japanese cultural and political offensive in India and how it lured some Indian leaders and scholars with fascist tendencies. Japan's victory over Czarist Russia in 1905, which had once encouraged Indian nationalism, now led some Indian nationalists to think in terms of Hindu-Buddhist cooperation. When the Japanese import of cheap artificial silk to India was making Indian mill-owners restless, the Japanese consul general in India took the opportunity to highlight the significance of trade relations between Japan and India in a lecture at the Calcutta Buddhist Centre in June 1931. The subject was discussed in an article published from Calcutta on 17 July in *Liberty*, a periodical which served as the mouthpiece of Subhas Chandra Bose. It is interesting to note that Bose, whom Chatto had until now described as a Leftist, is called here 'the very active National Socialist (Fascist) leader.' After Taraknath Das, from the USA, contributed an appreciative rejoinder on the subject of Indo-Japanese friendship, saying that 'Indo-Japanese cooperation is essential for Indian freedom and emancipation of Asia', *Liberty* in another leading article referred to this passage with approval but added apologetically: 'It is true that in the present evolution of world politics, Japan has trod in the footsteps of the West, and plays to some extent an imperialist role.' Chatto was scandalized that an Indian could ever write these words and retorted:

These shameless words were written by members of an oppressed subject nation less than two weeks before the Japanese bandits broke into and occupied Manchuria, and in spite of the fact that Japanese imperialism has been carrying on its regime of oppression, exploitation and brutal terror in Korea and Formosa for over 22 years, and has systematically [been] violating the integrity and independence of China and intriguing and conspiring towards its dismemberment.[133]

In his capacity as the executive secretary of the LAI, Chatto believed it was immoral and indefensible for nationalists of one oppressed nation to betray the freedom of other oppressed nations by allying themselves with one imperialism against another in accordance with the maxim 'the enemy of our enemy is our friend'. This is because the nationalists 'do not fight against imperialism as such, they betray their own national revolutionary movement by hindering the militant alliance between it and the revolutionary proletariat of all nations.'[34]

It is unfortunate that one who could formulate the duties of anti-imperialist freedom fighters in such a way in the international context, abandoned around 1930 his own long-held view on a 'united front' against imperialist domination in the national context. It is an irony of fate that just at the time Chatto renounced his 'united front'—shown in his arguments against M.N. Roy's thesis of 1920-1—Roy, his long-standing political rival, made a complete turnaround and embraced Chatto's earlier position and arguments and won a great name for himself in the process. A further irony is that all this happened in Berlin itself—the scene of Chatto's incessant political activity for more than a quarter of a century. In fact, without a word of repentance for his past dogmatic assertions, Roy, in an open statement released in Berlin in early June 1930[135], declared that his expulsion from the Comintern was due to: a) his scant advocacy of a united front with the petty bourgeois revolutionary nationalists in the struggle against imperialism; b) his view that the programme, strategy, and tactics of the struggle in India should be determined not according to an abstract scheme, but in the light of actual conditions; c) his opinion that oppressed middle classes were a revolutionary factor in India and an alliance with them should be sought by the working classes for the common fight against imperialist domination; and d) his criticism of the attitude taken by Indian communists towards the Left wing of the INC, led by Nehru, Iyenger, and Bose. Roy even went on to denounce the Indian communists for toeing the Comintern line as 'political weather cocks', 'job hunters', and 'infantile super revolutionaries'—epithets used for him and his ilk in earlier days.

Because of his ideological transformation, Chatto was obliged to keep aloof from two important Indian events that took place in Berlin in the summer of 1930. He did not sign the open letter to the executive committee of the Labour and Socialist International that was in session in Berlin on 12 May 1930, protesting against the arrest of Gandhi and other repressive measures by the British government in India. M.N. Roy put his signature to the letter along with 25 others, including J. Naidu, R.M. Lohia, and Sundar Kabadi.[136] Chatto also refrained from the initiative by Berlin Indians to establish a branch of the INC. This attitude of Chatto, the most outstanding representative of the Indian community in Berlin, was considered by organizers as 'surprising and regrettable'.[137]

Notes

1. Interviews with A.C.N. Nambiar, Lucie Hecht, and Fritz Grobba.
2. Some of these articles are: 'Die Frau in Indien', *Neue Zuericher Zeitung*, 12 August 1925; 'Indiens nationale Fuehrerin', *Deutsche Allgemeine Zeitung*, 31 December 1925; 'Indiens Fuehrerin', *Frau im Staat*, 8 (4), 1926, pp. 2–5; 'Indiens Dichterin', *Berliner Tageblatt*, 4 September 1926. Most of Smedley's articles of the time were translated from English by Lucie Hecht. Author's interview with Miss Lucie Hecht. It must be noted, however, that Smedley herself did not mention Chatto's relationship with Mrs Naidu in her articles.
3. *Dresdner Neueste Nachrichten*, 14 July 1926.
4. Smedley to Lennon, 19 January [1924], Florence Lennon Papers (FLP).
5. Margarete Buber-Neumann, *Von Potsdam nach Moskau: Stationen eines Irrwegs* (Stuttgart, 1957), p. 107.
6. Babette Gross, *Willi Muenzenberg: Eine Politische Biographie* (Stuttgart, 1967), p. 196. Gross quotes here from the German *Inprekorr*, 6 (68), p. 1065 and no. 52, p. 725.
7. Nehru did not fail to notice this during his visit to Germany in 1926. See Jawaharlal Nehru, *Autobiography* (London, 1936), p. 161.
8. Gross, op.cit., pp. 196–8.
9. On 5 November [1926] Smedley in her letter to Lennon mentioned her unexpected conversation with the British ambassador in Berlin regarding the pan-Asiatic movement in Berlin. FLP.
10. Gross, op.cit., p. 198, quoting W. Muenzenberg, *Fuenf Jahre Internationale Arbeiterhilfe* (Berlin 1926), p. 116.
11. Beatrix Geisel, 'Willi Muenzenberg: Gegen Oeffentlichkeit', a four-part series in *Publizistik & Kunst* (a journal of the Trade Union of Media, Germany),

June–September 1990. See especially part 3, August 1990, pp. 56–9. Among Muenzenberg's co-workers were writers Gustav Regler and Arthur Koestler.
12. Gross, *op.cit.*, p. 201.
13. Interview with A.C.N. Nambiar. Nehru had friendly relations with many members of Chatto's family in India.
14. Circular letters to Hasrat Mohani and Maulana Shaukat Ali in India by Gibarty, Berlin, 9 March 1926. AA Indien Politik 19, *Sozialismus, Bolschewismus, Kommunismus usw.*
15. *Ibid.*
16. *Inprekorr*, 3 August 1926, p. 301f., quoted in Gross, *op.cit.*, p. 199.
17. *Ibid.*
18. Gross, *op.cit.*, p. 200.
19. *Ibid.*
20. *The Indian Quarterly Register* (IQR), vol. II, July–December 1926, Calcutta, p. 322. In an interview, Nambiar told the author how later, in the autumn of 1927, Chatto persuaded the reluctant Motilal Nehru to accept an invitation from the Soviet Union to visit Russia with his son on the occasion of the 10th anniversary of the October Revolution.
21. *Ibid.*
22. For a comprehensive account of the Congress with photographs, speeches, resolutions, and the list of representatives see *Das Flammenzeichen vom Palais Egmont*, published by the LAI in German (Berlin, 1927). See also 'The Anti-Colonial Congress' in IQR, vol. I, nos. 1–2, January–June 1927, pp. 204–11.
23. *Ibid.*, p. 204; *Invitation to the International Congress against Colonial Oppression and Imperialism* by the members of the Provisional Committee, Berlin, 15 December 1926.
24. *Ibid.*, pp. 204–5. See also Dorothy Norman (ed.), *Nehru: The First Sixty Years*, I (London, 1965), pp. 121–2.
25. J. Nehru, 'The British Imperialism in India, Persia and Mesopotamia', a speech delivered at the opening session of the Brussels Congress. See also Dorothy Norman (ed.), *op.cit.*, pp. 122–5; IQR, January–June 1927, pp. 209–11. For the full text in German, see pp. 209–11 and also *Das Flammenzeichen*, pp. 55–60.
26. *Ibid.*, p. 207. See also *Das Flammenzeichen*, p. 62.
27. There were 25 delegates from China, 15 from Great Britain and 7 from India.
28. IQR, January–June 1927, p. 208.
29. *Ibid.*
30. *Ibid.*
31. *Ibid.*, p. 206.
32. *Das Flammenzeichen*, *op.cit.*, p. 220.
33. Buber-Neumann, *op. cit.*
34. S. Gopal, *Jawaharlal Nehru: A Biography*, I (New Delhi, 1975), p. 101.

35. See Nirode K. Barooah, 'Germany and Indian Nationalism after World War I: Nehru-Subhas' Moves for Indo-German Cooperation 1927–38', *Mainstream*, XXXVIII (12), 11 March 2000, p. 17.
36. Ibid.
37. *Cf.* Chatto to Nehru, 20 March 1929, NMML, Jawaharlal Nehru Papers (JNP).
38. In one of his letters to Nehru, Chatto wrote: 'My health has been causing me some anxiety...There are also a number of private difficulties of long standing which I have to contend with, and the fact that my position in Berlin was desperate...[and then about his having to earn money by translation work etc. instead of working for the Indian movement]. It is also for our friends at home to judge whether I should do such work instead of being directly useful to the movement...I am now living under my own name, but find that this causes me innumerable difficulties with Governments. The French have now refused to give me visa, though only 8 weeks ago they gave me without hesitation under my other names.' Chatto to Nehru, Brussels, 23 January 1929, NMML, JNP.
39. Krishna Hutheesing, *With No Regrets* (Bombay, 1952), 2nd edn., pp. 40–1.
40. Gross, *op. cit.*, p. 205. Komsomol = Communist League of Youth.
41. Nehru's report to the Congress Working Committee, quoted in S. Gopal, *op. cit.*, p. 100.
42. Nehru's report to the All-India Congress Committee on the Brussels Congress against imperialism, 10–15 February 1927. IQR 1927, vol. II, July–December, p. 154. Also the typed script of Nehru's report to the AICC in February 1927, found among Chatto's papers at the Dimitroff Museum.
43. Of these three meetings of the executive committee the first one was held in Amsterdam on 28 and 29 March, the second in Cologne (19–20 August) and the third in Brussels on 8 December. Motilal Nehru attended the Brussels session of the general council of the LAI in December 1927. In November 1927, Nehru with his father accepted an invitation to visit the Soviet Union, after which he left for India, arriving at the time of the Madras Session of the INC in December.
44. R. Baldwin to Nehru, Geneva, 4 December 1927, NMML, JNP.
45. Ibid.
46. R. Baldwin to Nehru, Paris, 12 December 1927, NMML, JNP.
47. Chatto to Nehru, 2 April 1928. Intercepted letter. Meerut Conspiracy Trial (MCT), vol. VII, quoted by Horst Krueger in 'Zum Einfluss internationaler Faktoren auf die Herausbildung und Entwicklung der antiimperialistischen Haltung Jawaharlal Nehrus', in E.N. Komarov and others (eds.), *Politik und Ideologie im gegenwaertigen Indien* (Berlin, 1976), p. 333.
48. 'Report on the Development of League Against Imperialism' in *The Anti-Imperialist Review*, 1 (1), Berlin, July 1928, p. 83, edited and published by the LAI (responsible editor V. Chattopadhyaya).
49. Chatto to Nehru, Brussels, 23 January 1929, NMML, JNP.

50. *The Anti-Imperialist Review*, 1 (1), July 1928, pp. 83–4.
51. *Ibid.*, p. 92.
52. *Ibid.*
53. *Young India*, 3 January, 1928, quoted in S. Gopal, *op. cit.*, p. 112.
54. Press release of the LAI secretariat, Berlin, n.d., quoted in H. Krueger, 'Zum Einfluss…', *op. cit.*, p. 322.
55. LAI press release, Berlin, 5 September 1928. *Ibid.*
56. Chatto to Nehru, 3 October 1928, NMML, JNP.
57. Chatto to Nehru, 24 October 1928, MCT, vol. VII, p. 1649, quoted in H. Krueger, 'Zum Einfluss…' *op. cit.*, p. 323.
58. *Ibid.* Krueger, p. 324.
59. Nehru to Chatto, 25 October 1928, NMML, JNP.
60. Chatto to Nehru, 14 November 1928, MCT, vol. VII, p. 1645, quoted in H. Krueger, 'Zum Einfluss…', *op. cit.*, p. 324–5.
61. Chatto to Nehru, 5 December 1928, NMML, JNP.
62. *Ibid.*
63. Nehru to Chatto, 23 January 1929, NMML, JNP.
64. *Cf.* Gopal, *op. cit.*, pp. 122–3.
65. Plassen to AA, Calcutta, 25 August 1928, reporting on the 'Social struggle in India' and quoting also the *Englishman* on M.N. Roy's letter. AA Pol. 19, *Sozialismus, Bolschewismus, Kommunismus usw.*
66. In April 1929 Nehru wrote to Chatto: '…our letters have been spirited away by an ever watchful Government. It is equally probable that my letters do not reach you.' Nehru to Chatto, 25 April 1929, NMML, JNP.
67. Home secretary Haig to all local governments, 21 February 1929, quoted in S. Gopal, *op. cit.*, p. 123.
68. Altogether 33 people were prosecuted, out of whom three were acquitted and one, D.R. Thengdi, died in prison. The others received punishments ranging from transportation for life to three years imprisonment. See R. Page Arnot, 'The Meerut Sentences' in *The Labour Monthly*, 15(2), February 1933, pp. 96–7.
69. 'The Speech of the Prosecutor in the Meerut Case', *The Labour Monthly*, 12 (1), January 1930, p. 25.
70. Nehru to Chatto, 20 June 1929, NMML, JNP.
71. The central defence committee consisted of Dr Ansari as chairman and Girdhari Lal as secretary. The other members were Motilal Nehru, Raghubir Narain Singh, Jyoti Prasad, N.C. Kelkar, K.F. Nariman, V.H. Joshi, and Jawaharlal Nehru. There were local committees as well. Nehru to Chatto, 20 June 1929, NMML, Ibid.
72. Nehru to the secretary of the LAI, 26 June 1929, NMML, AICC Papers, quoted by H. Krueger, 'Zum Einfluss…', p. 326.
73. Otto V. Kuusinen, 'The Revolutionary Movement in the Colonies', *Inprecor*, VIII (68), 1928.
74. League Against Imperialism and for National Independence, *Second Anti-*

Imperialist World Congress (20 July to 31 July, 1929) Frankfurt-on-Main, Germany, Manifesto, p. 4.
75. Emile Burns, 'The World Congress of the League Against Imperialism', *The Labour Monthly*, 11 (9), September 1929, pp. 559–61. Giving examples of ILP leaders who retracted, the author pointed out that Lansbury became chairman of the Labour Party and subsequently a minister of the Labour government; Brockway, Wilkinson, Beckett and Postgate followed the same lead in less exalted positions.
76. Nehru to Chatto, 23 September 1929 and Chatto to Nehru, 30 October and 6 November 1929, NMML, JNP.
77. Nehru to Chatto, 23 September 1929, NMML, *Ibid*.
78. Nehru to Chatto, 25 November 1929, NMML, *Ibid*.
79. Nehru to Chatto, 20 June 1929, NMML, *Ibid*.
80. Chatto to Nehru, 30 October 1929, NMML, *Ibid*.
81. *Ibid*. Maxton, however, remained a member of the LAI's executive committee.
82. *Ibid*.
83. *Ibid*.
84. When speaker after speaker asked where Maxton, the chairman of the ILP, stood *vis-à-vis* the misdeeds of the MacDonald government Maxton, after keeping silent for six days said on the evening before the closing session, 'These facts impose upon me, as a Socialist, the duty of pointing out and opposing strongly the imperialist policy of the Labour Government put into office by the Labour Party. I pledge myself and those associated with me to the League to carry out this duty—openly and fearlessly—recognising that the pursuance of an imperialist policy by the Labour Government constitutes the most deadly menace to the interests of the oppressed masses of the colonies.' See Burns, *op. cit*.
85. Chatto to Nehru, 6 November [mistakenly written October] 1929, NMML, JNP.
86. *Ibid*.
87. *Ibid*.
88. Nehru to Chatto, 26 November 1929, NMML, JNP.
89. Chatto to Nehru, 4 December 1929, NMML, *Ibid*.
90. *Ibid*.
91. *Ibid*.
92. Shiva Rao, an Indian delegate to the ILO in Geneva at this time, said publicly in Europe that Amsterdam's and not Moscow's was the right method. Chatto to Nehru, 29 May 1929, NMML, JNP.
93. Chatto to Nehru, 3 April 1929, NMML, *Ibid*.
94. Nehru to Chatto, 30 January 1930, NMML, *Ibid*.
95. Nehru to the secretariat of the LAI, 30 January 1930, NMML, *Ibid*.
96. *Ibid*.
97. Chatto to Nehru, 26 February 1930, NMML, JNP.

98. E.H. Carr, *The Twilight of Comintern 1930–1935*, (London, 1982), p. 385.
99. V.J. Patel to Nehru, Vienna, 22 July 1931, NMML, JNP.
100. Chatto to Nehru, 26 February 1930, NMML, *Ibid*.
101. Emma Goldman, *Living My Life*, p. 905, quoted by MacKinnons, *op. cit.*, p. 74. Chatto's friend, the Left socialist Ture Nerman of Sweden, also found Chatto to be an anti-British Indian nationalist.
102. Interview with A.C.N. Nambiar. For Chatto's plans with his Italian anarchist friend, Luigi Bertoni, see N.K. Barooah, 'Har Dayal and the German Connection', *The Indian Historical Review*, July 1980–January 1981, nos. 1–2, p. 199.
103. Gross, *op. cit.*, p. 210.
104. Buber-Neumann, *op. cit.*, p. 107.
105. Interview with A.C.N. Nambiar.
106. *China Correspondent, op. cit.*, p. 17
107. V. Chattopadhyaya, 'Unemployment in India', *Inprecor*, 6 March 1930.
108. *Ibid*.
109. V. Chattopadhyaya, 'The Indian Railway Strike', *The Pan-Pacific Monthly*, April 1930.
110. *Ibid*.
111. V. Chattopadhyaya, 'India and the Second International', *The Pan-Pacific Monthly* (San Francisco), no. 37, June–July 1930, p. 13.
112. *Ibid.*, pp. 13–14.
113. *Ibid.*, p. 14.
114. V. Chattopadhyaya, 'The Indian Revolution and the Nationalist Leaders', in *The Pan-Pacific Monthly*, no. 37, June–July 1930, p. 15.
115. *Ibid*.
116. *Ibid*.
117. *Ibid.*, p. 16.
118. *Ibid*.
119. *Ibid*.
120. *Ibid*.
121. *Ibid*.
122. V. Chattopadhyaya, 'Faked Indian Statistics as Imperialist Propaganda', *The Labour Monthly*, 12(9), London, September 1930, pp. 539–45 (unfinished).
123. *Ibid.*, p. 541.
124. *Ibid.*, p. 545.
125. V. Chattopadhyaya, 'The Indian National Congress', *The Labour Monthly*, 13 (5), May 1931, pp. 303–7.
126. *Ibid*, p. 307.
127. V. Chattopadhyaya, 'MacDonald's New Year Honours' List of India: A Document of Imperial Corruption', *Inprecor*, 8 January 1931, p. 5.
128. V. Chattopadhyaya, 'Timber Export and Forced Labour in the Andaman Islands', *Inprecor*, 22 October 1931, pp. 985–6.
129. *Ibid*.

130. V. Chattopadhyaya, 'International Imperialism Arms Afghanistan', *Inprecor*, 3 December 1931, pp. 1122–3.
131. *Ibid.*, p. 1123.
132. V. Chattopadhyaya, 'Buddhism in the Service of Japanese and British Imperialism', *The Anti-Imperialist Review*, 1 (3), January–February 1932, pp. 196–205.
133. *Ibid.*, p. 202.
134. *Ibid.*, p. 203.
135. M.N. Roy, *A Statement regarding my difference with the present leadership of the Communist International* (lithographic circular), Berlin, 8 June 1930. AA, Pol. 5, *Innere Politik, Parlaments- und Parteiwesen in Indien*.
136. *Offener Brief an das Exekutiv-Komitee der Sozialistischen Arbeiter-Internationale*. See AA, Pol. 3, *Pol. Bezieh. Zu Indien*, 1.
137. Sundar Kabadi was the honorary secretary of the provisional committee for organizing a branch of the INC. AA, Pol. 3, *Pol. Bezieh, Zwischen Indien u. fremd. Staaten*.

9

The Birth of the Soviet–Indian Social Scientist Virendranat Agornatovich Chatopadaya 1933–7

1. Escape to the Soviet Union

In August 1931, Chatto on the advice of Georgi Dimitrov, who had been head of the West European Bureau of the Comintern in Berlin since March 1929, and with the help of the Soviet ambassador in Berlin, left Germany for the Soviet Union.[1] He had no other option. The headquarters of the international secretariat of the LAI had been moved to Paris from Berlin, and presumably, since Chatto was barred from entering France, he had to be replaced by Clemens Dutt. The Berlin office of the LAI had long been under observation by the Berlin police, and the danger for the communists, particularly foreign communists, loomed even before the complete takeover of the country by the Nazis. In the middle of 1932, the police raided, ransacked, and closed the LAI building.[2]

The Nazis, who had become the second largest party in the Reichstag in September 1930, began to be domineering ever since. They were not only implacably against communists and social democrats, but also in a special sense against the Indian national struggle for freedom. Shortly after Chatto's departure, Hitler, in his capacity as the supreme Nazi leader, went out of his way to declare that India's move for self-determination was an undesirable development, and he held the view that any weakening of British hold on India would be a calamity. When the statement appeared both in the *Times* of London and the Nazi mouthpiece *Voelkischer Beobachter*, Champakaraman Pillai as the representative of the Federation of Indian Chambers of Commerce and Industry protested rather mildly in a letter to Hitler on 10 December 1931. After a few days, Pillai received a curt and laconic reply from Hitler's private secretary, saying that Herr Hitler remained convinced that it was in the interest of the civilized world to keep British rule in India intact.[3] Chatto judged the new political climate in Germany accurately. He knew that as a stout opponent of British imperialism in India and an ally of the Soviet Union, he would no longer be safe in Germany.

Under an arrangement made between Dimitrov and Dmitrii Manuilsky, secretary of the executive committee of the Comintern, Chatto was to be engaged in one of the Comintern's various sections in Moscow.[4] During March and June 1932, he worked as an editor in the Foreign Workers Publishing House and was engaged in revising the two volumes of the English edition of the *Selected Works of V.I. Lenin*.[5] Later, he worked in the Indian Section of the Byuro Kommunisticheskoy Akademii (Bureau of the Communist Academy) until the end of December 1932.[6] However, in the middle of 1932, a snag arose in the continued employment of Chatto in the Comintern. The reason for this is still not clear, but it would appear that British pressure was at work against him. In May 1932, the AA learnt from a report from the press service of Nauen that the British government had informed its embassy in Moscow that communist propaganda had lately intensified in India and that this propaganda had been directed by Moscow in violation of the Henderson Dowgalsky Agreement which had stipulated non-interference in the internal affairs of each other's country.[7] The British government suspected that this propaganda owed its existence to Chatto's presence in the Soviet Union. Chatto himself was unhappy in the Soviet Union during his first year there, and this information, we do not know how, reached the AA. The AA informed its ambassador in Moscow that if this were true and Chatto wished to return to Berlin, he should be given a visa on the condition that he refrain from all political activity.[8]

It is not clear what made Chatto insecure and anxious in Moscow in the summer of 1932. Neither is the sudden surge of sympathy for him in German official circles. Chatto's anxiety might have been caused due to the scrutiny of a charge of 'political dishonesty' against him which had come before the Comintern Control Commission. Lidiya Karunovskaya, however, thought otherwise. In her memoirs, written long after Chatto's death, she speculated that the source of his anxiety was his alleged involvement in the Curzon Wyllie murder of 1909 and the British attempt at about this time to bring to justice those said to have been responsible for the crime.[9] However, Karunovskaya does not give a detailed account of the case under the Comintern's scrutiny, and it seems more likely, because of the use of the phrase 'political dishonesty', that the cause of Chatto's trouble was his alleged involvement in the Reventlow-Lirau plot of 1922.[10] At that time, the Germans had refrained from taking any action against Chatto on the ground that he had acted in the German interest. This also explains the German sympathy for Chatto in 1932 resulting in the offer of conditional asylum.

Even in the midst of such anxieties, Chatto kept himself busy in Moscow with various intellectual pursuits. For example, while working at the Comintern's Oriental secretariat, he received an assignment in October to write an article on the revolutionary movement in India. The offer came from the editorial office of the journal *Borba Klassov* (Class Struggle), and requested him to complete the assignment by 20 November.[11]

2. ACADEMIC APPOINTMENT AT LENINGRAD

Chatto's insecurity in Moscow ended when Sergey Mironovich Kirov (1886–1934), chief of the Russian Communist Party in Leningrad and the second highest-ranking figure in the Russian political hierarchy, came to his rescue. Mindful of Chatto's interest in linguistics and ethnography, Kirov suggested to the central committee of the Comintern that Chatto be sent to Leningrad to join one of the institutes of the Academy of Sciences of the USSR.[12] While Chatto's employment in Leningrad was thus being planned, the renowned Soviet Orientalist S.F. Oldenburg, who had studied the art and culture of India, recommended that Chatto be engaged in scientific work at the Oriental Institute of the Academy. However, thinking in political terms, the party secretary of the Academy of Sciences, V.P. Volgin, decided that since most of the institutes of the Academy including the Oriental Institute were headed by non-party directors, it would be more suitable to send a communist Chatto to the Institute of Anthropology and Ethnography (IAE) which was headed by the communist humanist, Professor Nikolay Mikhailevich Matorin.[13] Thus, on 1 March 1933, Chatto joined the IAE as a research assistant, grade 1, and was also made head of the Indian section of the Institute. Because of 'his educational qualifications and his wide-ranging knowledge of India, it was expected that Chatto would be of great help to shape the Indian Department in accordance with modern needs.'[14]

Ever since his boyhood, Chatto had pursued an interest in languages and philology. As mentioned in the first chapter, while in England and France, he used to contribute occasional short notices to some philological journals. In Germany and Sweden, he was widely known and respected not only for his trustworthiness and intellectual acumen but also for his expertise in many European languages, including the three Scandinavian languages, like a native speaker.[15] So, although Chatto had yet to master Russian and get acquainted with the theoretical literature on ethnography, he already had a great asset in his ability to read the relevant literature in English, German, Swedish, Danish, Norwegian, Dutch, Italian, and Persian, as well as several Indian languages.[16]

When Chatto joined the IAE, the whole structure of scientific work in the Academy of Sciences was being reorganized. The party organization of the Academy, headed by Volgin, was determined to forge a link between the entire scientific activity of the institutions and the consolidation of socialism in Russia. There was also a plan to expand the entire museum in the interest of the Soviet people. It was expected that this restructuring, on the basis of Marxist-Leninist theory, would help the party, the government, and the entire Soviet people to solve the main task of consolidating socialism in Russia faster.[17] Thus Chatto, from the start, faced two challenges at the IAE. He was not only expected to acquire sufficient theoretical knowledge in ethnography and its allied fields but also to interpret that knowledge in the light of Marxist-Leninist theroies and principles.

Chatto proved an exceptionally quick learner, and his intellectual ability and genial, generous nature made him at once a popular and respected figure at the IAE. This is the verdict of an eyewitness,

The Birth of the Soviet–Indian Social Scientist 287

Andrey Nikolayevich Dalskiy who, besides being a colleague, was the party secretary at the IAE at the time. Dalskiy writes in his memoirs that Chatto not only managed the scientific work in the Indian section efficiently but also actively participated in the restructuring of the Institute's museum expositions as a whole on the basis of historical materialism. Moreover, his quick mastery of conversational Russian enabled him to participate actively in the social life of the Institute in no time.[18] Dalskiy particularly emphasized Chatto's warm relations with the young people in party circles both at the IAE and in the city:

> In the party committee, in the regional committee, in the presidium of the Academy of Sciences, and particularly with the Permanent Secretary, Volgin, Chattopadhyaya enjoyed the authority and trust which he well deserved. Great consideration and trust was shown to him not only by the leadership of the Academy but also by the party organisations and Soviet organisations of Leningrad.[19]

As examples of warmth shown to Chatto by the party in Leningrad, Dalskiy mentions how, on Kirov's order, the Leningrad Soviet put at Chatto's disposal a large two-room flat at Nevskiy Prospect (House no. 146) and later, when Chatto expected the arrival of his German wife Charlotte with her children from Berlin, a separate two-room apartment in the same street (House no. 141) was allotted to him.[20] Till the allotment Chatto stayed in a hotel. Kirov also ordered that Chatto be given an *Insnab-booklet* in order to be able to supply his family with all necessities (with the *Insnab-booklet* foreigners were privileged to buy essential things overriding control). Chatto also received an academic pass which admitted him to the special canteen of the IAE.[21]

These generous gestures were reciprocated by Chatto with zeal and enthusiasm for the party's politico-educational programmes. Both Dalskiy and Karunovskaya have given examples of Chatto's services in this sphere. He guided the work of MOPR which arranged wall newspapers in all the institutes of the Academy; imparted political education through his lectures to foreign specialists working in the Academy[22]; did educational work among the Soviet cadres in the Oriental Institute where he also taught Hindustani; and was active in the *Soyuz Voinstvuyushchikh Bezboszhnikov* (Union of Militant Atheists).[23] On the international day of MOPR on 18 March 1934, traditionally observed on the day of the Paris Commune, a great conference was held in the hall of the Academy of Sciences dedicated to revolutionary movements in capitalist, colonial, and dependent countries. At this conference, Chatto gave a speech narrating his long involvement with the Indian freedom movement in Europe. In this connection, he recalled how he had missed a long-awaited interview with the great leader Lenin in 1921, because of the intrigues and machinations of M.N. Roy. He also named Trotsky, Zinoviev, Bukharin, and Radek who were now discredited leaders in the Soviet Union as fellow conspirators against him.[24]

On 1 February 1934, Chatto was promoted to the position of specialist-ethnographer.[25]

3. ESSAYS EXTOLLING ENGELS AND HIS *THE ORIGIN OF THE FAMILY, PRIVATE PROPERTY AND THE STATE*

The new policy of the IAE to consciously follow and popularize Marxism-Leninism in academic research, and the unwritten terms of Chatto's appointment that he should help the Institute in this direction, suited him down to the ground. He threw himself with great zeal and enthusiasm into the study of the basic theoretical literature on ethnography and ethnographic Indology.[25] After only six months at the job, he gave a talk in Russian in September 1933 at an academic seminar of the IAE on 'Engels' *The Origin of the Family, Private Property and the State* (the first German edition 1884) and its importance in correctly understanding the process of historical development of original Communist society'.[27] Chatto opened his talk with a remark that Lenin had delivered a speech on this work of Engels' at Sverdlovsk University, Moscow, on 11 July 1919, and described it as one of the pillars of modern socialism whose every sentence should be read with avidity and confidence. The lecture made a great impression on the members of the Academy, as did the fact that it was delivered in Russian.[28]

Both Dalskiy and Karunovskaya mention in their memoirs some of Chatto's writings on sociological, anthropological, and philological subjects. 'The socio-economic structure of the Munda tribes' and 'The Indian Community' were among his earliest essays. Then came the enthusiastic preparation by the IAE of a special edition of the journal *Sovietskaya Etnografiya* (Soviet Ethnography) in 1934, with scientific essays devoted to the 50th anniversary of the publication of Engels' above-mentioned work. The volume contained a note and two substantial review articles by Chatto in Russian and showed his profound knowledge and firm grasp of the subjects.

The two-page note by Chatto entitled 'Engels and Shternberg'[29] was on an article by Engels called 'A newly discovered case of group marriage'. Lev Yakovlevich Shternberg (1861–1927) was an anthropologist who made classic ethnographic studies of the Gilyak people of Sakhalin Island and the neighbouring parts of the Eastern Siberian mainland. Shternberg was also active in Russian and Jewish social movements (1902–17). After the Revolution of 1917, he organized the teaching of ethnography at the University of Leningrad with anthropologist V.G. Bogoraz. A strict adherent of Marxist theory, he regarded culture as a creation of mankind as a whole and cultural differences as the outcome of geographical and historical accidents.[30]

In his note, Chatto pointed out that in the Russian translations of Engels' article on Shternberg, the omission of a bracketed question mark put by Engels at one place had not only distorted Engels' statement but also led to some confusion. Chatto gave the background of the whole incident:

On 10 (22) October 1892, at a meeting of the anthropological section of the Society of Friends of Natural History in Moscow, N.A. Yanchuk talked about the information given by Shternberg about the social organisation of the Sakhalin Gilyaks. When a report about this meeting was published in *Russkiye Vedomosti* [Russian News] on 14 (26) October 1892, Engels wrote an article, about six weeks later, entitled 'A newly discovered case of group marriage' in *Neue Zeit* [New Age], the theoretical journal of the German Social Democratic Party.[31] In this article Engels, after a few introductory remarks, presented a translation of the entire report from *Russkiye Vedomosti*. However, while reproducing Shternberg, Engels made a tiny alteration by adding a question mark in bracket to one word. Shternberg in one passage wrote: The gens of a Gilyak consists of all brothers of his father, their fathers and mothers, the children of his brothers and his own children.

But Engels put a question mark after the word 'mothers' in the above passage which, however, had been omitted in the Russian reproductions of Engels' article. Chatto, however, had not the slightest misgiving that, by putting a question mark, 'Engels expressed his doubts as to whether it was possible that in the patriarchal gens of a Gilyak the mother of his father and the mother(s) of his father's brothers could belong to the gens.'[32] Chatto then cited another article by Shternberg on the Sakhalin Gilyaks, published in 1893, in

Etnograficheskoye Obozreniye (Ethnographic Revue)[33] where no mention at all was made of 'mother'. Since it was a fact that Engels wrote to Shternberg at the end of 1892 or at the beginning of 1893 (according to Shternberg's widow, Shternberg lost this letter), Chatto concluded that either in Shternberg's first article the word 'mother' was mistakenly inserted by the printer, or that after receiving Engels' correspondence, Shternberg omitted the word 'mother' from his second article. As in the Russian edition of Engels' work, this article was included without the question mark, Chatto considered it 'unpardonable that any publication of Engels', whether in German or in the Russian translation, should appear without paying the necessary attention to the correctly inserted question mark by Engels.' No doubt, Chatto's note was an important warning not only to scientists in the field but also to Russian translators translating from the original German. A Russian colleague of Chatto's at the IAE praised him for the article, adding that Lenin in his work *State and Revolution* had translated Engels' passages from the original German because the Russian translations of the time were either incomplete or unsatisfactory. He said that Chatto's note confirmed the correctness of Lenin's method.[34]

Chatto's second article in the commemoration volume was a review of the first English edition of Engels' *The Origin of the Family...* translated and published in the USA in 1902, which remained, until then, the only English edition of the book.[35]

Writing in Russian[36], Chatto first wondered why Ernest Untermann's translation had remained the only English edition of the work. He found it astonishing that although Marx and Engels lived in England playing an active role in the workers' movement, and although Engels' work itself was written in England, not a single translation of the work had so far been published there. He wrote:

This fact becomes particularly noteworthy when we think of the early history of organised socialist movement in England which is just as many years old as Engels' book. The Social Democratic Federation was founded in 1884, the year when Engels' book appeared. Out of this and other socialist groupings the British Socialist Party arose in 1912, which, to a certain extent, was connected with the mass organisations of the workers, whose left wing later merged into the Communist Party of Britain. In the same year, 1884, the 'Fabian Society' was also founded—a group of liberal intellectuals considering themselves to be 'socialists'.[37]

Chatto told his readers that after the fourth German edition of the book, several other books were published in England on the early history of the family such as the works of MacLennan, Taylor, Lebboc, Spencer, and Westermark, all of whom Chatto called anti-revolutionary sociologists. But he could not imagine the reason for this neglect of Engels. He went on to surmise that either it was because no market existed for such a book or that the publishers were so contaminated by the poison of bourgeois 'sociology' that they could fight no more against it.[38]

Coming to Untermann's translation, Chatto first praised him and his publishers, Charles Kerr & Co., for publishing not only the present work and Marx's *Capital* but also other works of socialist literature with a view to 'giving the common people an understanding of the existing social institutions'. Chatto also emphasized that such a task ought to be undertaken by socialists since even the best and most radical of bourgeois scholars, like Morgan in his significant work *The Ancient Society*, could not appreciate or understand the existing class struggle, still speaking of 'divine provision' and 'highest common sense' as the creator of history.[39]

However, in Chatto's eyes, Untermann failed to do full justice to Engels' work. Chatto found that Untermann even presented Engels in a distorted way in respect of some essential points, besides making numerous mistakes in the translation. The most evident and oft-repeated mistake in Chatto's view was the wrong translation of the German word *geschlecht*, genus in English and *pol* in Russian. Untermann also mixed up 'gens' with 'genus' and seriously distorted the meaning. Similarly, on the subject of group marriage, he misinterpreted the German word *je* and the Latin text cited by Engels, and thus gleaned a completely opposite meaning to that intended by Engels. Quoting Caesar about the Britons, Engels wrote in German: '*Die Briten je zehn oder zwoelf haben ihre Frauen gemeinsam* (Every ten or twelve Britons have their women in common)', which in Untermann's translation became 'The Britons had each ten to twelve women in common'. Thus Engels' whole argument against MacLennan, who cited Caesar as proof of polyandry being widespread among the Britons, was upheld whereas this quotation pointed merely to the existence of group marriage among the Britons.[40] Chatto found that on cannibalism, too, Untermann wrongly concluded that there was no proof that cannibalism was at any time widespread, whereas Engels said, in the first chapter of his book, that cannibalism arose apparently in the middle phase of savagery and lasted for a very long time and then slowly vanished in the middle phase of barbarism. Here Chatto also quoted from Engels' *Anti Duehring*.[41] He also blamed Untermann for his presumption in translating Engels' passage on marsupials while being completely ignorant of the subject, and took him to task for not understanding the difference between the Indians of India and the American Red Indians.[42]

Chatto emphasized in this review that a translator ought to have a thorough knowledge of the translated language as well as the language into which the translation is to be made. Moreover, he ought to have the right understanding of the subject. It is interesting to note that, before this review appeared, Chatto had already been approached by the Foreign Workers Publishing House to prepare a new English edition of this work and it seems he had already drawn up a plan as to how to set about it. The outline of his plan indicates that apart from a careful edited translation of the text, two forewords and an article about group marriage of the Gilyaks, the new edition would include a critical political and ethnographic introduction, numerous notes, and the following supplements: a) excerpts from letters by Engels on questions mentioned in *The Origin of the Family*...; b) political and ethnographic notes on the text; c) a list of tribes and peoples mentioned by Engels with short notes on them; d) geographical index; e) bibliography; f) biographical notes; g) dictionary of ethnographic terms; h) subject index; and i) an explanatory map.[43]

Chatto's third piece in the Engels commemoration volume of *Sovietskaya Etnografiya* was an elaborate review in Russian of the German edition of the same book by Engels, published by the Foreign Workers Publishing House, Moscow, in June 1934 under the editorship of Ladislaus Rudas.[44] Chatto first pointed out the long-felt need for a new, fully-annotated German edition of the work, since after the publication of the fourth edition with a long foreword by Engels himself in 1891–2, all later appearances of the work were mere reprints without any subject index and other necessary annotations. Emphasizing the book's value to the political education of the working class, Chatto said that a new annotated edition had long been a desideratum for workers in Germany and the German-speaking workers of Europe. With his profound knowledge of history, ethnography, linguistics, and the history of the growth of socialist thought, Chatto then tried to assess the material added by the editor in the light of its usefulness to the political struggle of the workers and peasants in the German-speaking world.

Chatto was extremely disappointed to find that the new German edition was based entirely on the Russian translation which had been published a year ago by the Marx-Engels-Lenin Institute under the editorship of the same Ladislaus Rudas. The introduction as well as biographical and other notes, and the subject index of the Russian edition, were retranslated into German and incorporated into the German edition with numerous errors and inaccuracies. Thus, while praising the Marx-Engels-Lenin Institute for their efforts in bringing out Marxist classics in many European and other languages at a time when the demand of such literature was increasing along with the growth of the influence of the communist party among the working masses, Chatto questioned the validity of making all foreign language editions merely conventional translations of Russian editions. Explaining why a different approach was necessary he said:

The Russian workers enjoying a colossal Marxist mass literature in all fields of knowledge and having gathered such a rich experience in the process of the successful building of socialism have completely other demands than, for example, the English proletariat or the colonial masses fighting for their freedom. There is no doubt that the exactitude of the material of every edition must be checked and affirmed by the Marx-Engels-Lenin Institute, but it seems to us that it is also necessary to take into account the special demands of the foreign workers.[45]

Having thus established the need for a different approach while introducing a Marxist classic to a particular people at a particular point of time, Chatto critically examined Rudas' introduction. Since between January 1933 and July 1934 events unfolded that were of huge importance for the working classes of Germany and Austria, Chatto praised 'comrade Rudas' for dedicating two-thirds of his introduction and all of his notes to the polemics concerning the social-fascist or leftist-opportunist theories of state. But he criticized Rudas for ignoring the national fascism:

The fascist dictatorship by means of its decrees, 'laws', open and secret circular letters, school programmes, text books, and its rule over the press and publishing sector, very actively interferes also with all questions that were dealt with in Engels' work such as the questions of the family, group marriage, monogamy, the situation of women, private property and the state. In view of the fact that a section of the German workers is still partly under fascist influence and that for years they have been infused with a bourgeois anti-Marxist approach to these questions by the Social fascists, it would have been extremely important to enable the German workers to critically unmask the fascist propaganda.[46]

The fact that national fascism and social fascism did not restrict themselves to Germany, Chatto missed in Rudas' introduction a commentary on the characteristics of the bourgeois ethnography since the beginning of the epoch of imperialism. He himself cited these characteristics as being the most important in serving the cause of imperialism. He gave some examples from various Western countries starting with Austria where, he claimed, existed the centre of a very active Jesuit school of ethnography and anthropology headed by Fathers Schmidt and Koppers with their organ *Anthropos*. According to Chatto, Schmidt conducted the Museum of Missiology and Ethnology which had been founded by the Pope himself in the Vatican. The ethnography of this school, he said, 'served not only the struggle against Marxism but was considered as a weapon and scientific auxiliary branch of the Christian missiology which was nothing else but an imperialist euphemism disguising the policy of submission and exploitation of the colonial peoples.' He further added:

What Schmidt and company do for the benefit of the Italian, French and German imperialism is the same as what the Catholic society in Washington, which came into being recently, tries to do for the American imperialism. The Catholic University in Washington has as its aim to teach 'ethnology' to its missionaries—for the better understanding of the primitive peoples.[47]

As for the Anglo-Dutch-American missions, Chatto did not find the situation much different: they worked hand in hand with state civil servants engaged in ethnographic surveys while grim attacks on Morgan and Engels continued in the metropolis. In his view, the 'Californian troika' of Lowie, Kroeber, and Grifford was active in this way, and, in England, a campaign was afoot not only against Morgan and Engels but also against Rivers and other bourgeois ethnologists whose researches confirmed the views of Morgan and Engels. Some of the most active representatives of the so-called 'functionalist school', Chatto said, were Malinovsky and Radcliff-Brown, and, in the Netherlands, Rudolf Steinmetz. In Chatto's opinion, this school was active also in the USA, where the lectures of Lowie enjoyed great popularity and hundreds of petit-bourgeois intellectuals sympathizing with the workers' movement were educated in the anti-Engels spirit which constituted a great danger to the workers' movement in America.[48]

Chatto also pointed to the attacks by English 'functionalists', that is, those who wanted to analyse existing primitive organizations in their current form, without entering into hypotheses for the sake of a 'reconstruction of the past' (Malinovsky, *Man*, 30, 17), who claimed that Morgan, Rivers, and others artificially constructed a 'mixture of relationships' which brought unimaginable confusion into the study of primitive peoples. They maintained that primitive links among relatives were purely individual and only later became 'communalistic' for the sake of legality; the individual family had always existed; neither promiscuity nor group marriage existed in previous times as social form.[49] Chatto then concluded that bourgeois 'schools' had to be exposed in order to arm the workers better in their struggle against theories which, by fair means or foul, were advanced by the agents of the bourgeoisie.[50]

Chatto was critical of Rudas too for not giving sufficient importance to group marriage by way of notes and explanations although Engels himself had enlarged the concerned chapter to 30 pages in his fourth edition. In doing so, Engels unmasked all the social-democratic and bourgeois tendentious mixture from Kautsky to Westermark, and wished to underline the significance of this question and its role not only in the theory of primitive communism but also in the class struggle of the proletariat against the clerical feudal and bourgeois-philistine propaganda of monogamy.[51]

Chatto pointed out many errors of omission and commission in Rudas' notes and commentaries. While referring to the 10 very extensive notes covering 17 pages in small print, relating to six pages of the book itself, and comparing important excerpts from the writings of Marx, Engels, Lenin, and Stalin, Chatto wondered why the editor failed to provide even a single note for the remaining 172 pages. In particular, the editor omitted any mention of Engels' letter to Bebel on 18 (28) March 1875, which Lenin analysed in his booklet *Marxism about the State*. According to Chatto, there were many questions which demanded commentaries. For example, he pointed out, the word 'tum' on page 73 was left without any explanation. The word, properly articulated 'tam', meant 'kin' (in Russian *rod*) among the north-Indian Magars to whom Engels referred in his foreword to the fourth edition. To Chatto's mind the editor could have also said something about the social organization of the Magars whose 'barbarian bravery', he informed, was acknowledged backhandedly by British imperialism in recruiting them for the Indian army. Similarly, terms like 'the Punya tribe', 'the Birmanese', 'the African Barsa' should have been explained.[52]

Since, in Chatto's opinion, Engels' book was 'not a text-book of ethnography but a polemical work', he expected that the colonial peoples mentioned by him 'would have been put into a lively connection with the current revolutionary struggle of the workers and peasants' in those areas. In this connection, he referred to 'Kaffers-Zulus' to whose bravery Engels dedicated an entire paragraph (p. 85). Rudas' edition had only a short footnote on African Zulus, saying that they were crushed by the British in 1879. 'But,' Chatto added, 'the history of the Zulus did not end there. They did not forget this defeat, and every year, on 16 December, "Dingaans Dag" [Dingaan was their leader who was smashed by the Boers on 16 December 1838] is observed with strikes and demonstrations which never end without some bloody conflicts with the imperialist police. Most of the leaders became British agents, but the masses continue the struggle against imperialism.' Chatto said the same was true about the Indian Ho and Santhal tribes. These tribes, expropriated by the British and Indian capital, revolted several times against their enemies until they finally became landless proletariats. Thousands of Hos went to work as industrial workers in the iron-ore mines in Jamshedpur, and thousands of Santhals were taken to Assam to serve as coolies for the planters. The proletarians of both tribes, Chatto said, stood in the first ranks of fighters against feudalism, capitalism, and imperialism.[53]

Chatto also referred to some gross errors made by Rudas in his explanatory notes as a result of sheer carelessness. In one example, Chatto cited a sentence by Engels which ran thus: 'This system...exists almost without changes with the ancient inhabitants of India, among the Dravidian tribes in the Deccan and the Gaura tribes in Hindustan.' The note that Rudas added reads as follows: 'The Deccan is in the south of India. Its southern part is inhabited by tribes who speak Dravidian.' Safeguarding Engels from being misunderstood, Chatto wrote:

> On this, one has to observe: a) Deccan here does not mean Deccan plateau, but the whole of southern India (the Sanskrit word 'dakshina' meaning 'south'). Therefore, one cannot say: 'Deccan is situated in the south of India'; b) the expression 'to speak Dravidian' is just as senseless as 'to speak European'.

Chatto suggested that a footnote on the word 'Hindustan' would have solved the problem. He wrote:

'But while reading Engels' phrase it becomes clear that here we have three geographical meanings: a) India, b) Deccan, c) Hindustan, i.e. the whole of India and her two parts—Deccan and Hindustan. The point is that at the time of Marx and Engels, the word 'Hindustan' was usually applied by the Indians only for the northern part of India (from the Gangetic valley to the north of the river Narbada), whereas 'Deccan' (more correctly 'Daccan') meant the south of India. The present use of the word which equates Hindustan with the whole of India, is the outcome of the capital development and the national movement.

In this connection Chatto found the following quotation from Morgan's *Ancient Society* (1934, p. 218, fn. 1) interesting because of the clear distinction made here between southern and northern India for which Engels used 'Deccan' and 'Hindustan': 'The Turan system prevails until now in Southern India among the Hindus speaking dialects of the Dravidian language, but also in a somewhat different form in Northern India among the Hindus speaking dialects of the Gaura language.'[54] Chatto, however, pointed out that Morgan was mistaken when he spoke of a Dravidian and a Gaura language. Engels corrected this by mentioning the Dravidian and Gaura tribes that included the Pancha Gauras of Kanyakubja, Sarasvat, Gaur, Metila, and Utkal and the Pancha Dravida of Maharashtra, Talinga, Dravida, Karnata and Gujar.[55]

After pointing out some other lapses in the work, from wrong spellings of names to insufficient and confusing explanations in the subject index, Chatto concluded with one more suggestion for the future edition: the value of the work would be substantially enhanced if it included select passages from various correspondences of Engels concerning the subjects dealt with in *The Origin of the Family*... In this way, Chatto thought, it would be possible to obtain valuable material highlighting very diversified questions, such as the significance of Morgan's work, Germanic tribes, Indian and Russian village communities, group marriage, and so on.[56]

4. IN DEFENCE OF MARX AND ENGELS AGAINST THE INFLUENCE OF BOURGEOIS SCHOLARSHIP

Chatto's three pieces in the commemoration volume established him as a scholar in the Soviet Union. He also seems to have received Russian citizenship, for which he had earlier applied, shortly after the publication of these pieces, as his later writings bear his name in the Russian style, as Virendranat Agornatovich Chatopadaya, in accordance with the common practice in Russia to use the father's name after one's own, with the addition of the suffix 'ovich' for males and 'ovna' for females. Encouraged by his enthusiastic recognition as a Marxist scholar, combined perhaps with a feeling of security that the granting of Russian citizenship[57] brought, Chatto now continued with redoubled zeal what he had already begun: to propagate harmonization between scholarship and the party interest.

In 1935, *Sovietskaya Etnografiya* published another substantial review by Chatto, more than 10,000 words long, which brought him further recognition as a serious Marxist scholar.[58] This was a review of a compilation *Iz Arkhiva Lyuisa Genri Morgana* (From the Archive of Lewis Henry Morgan[59]) by one of his colleagues at the IAE, I.N. Vinnikov, head of the Australian Department, and published by the Academy of Sciences.[60] As Chatto mentioned in the introductory part of this investigative review, the book contained a great deal of highly interesting material. First, there were 34 letters to Morgan by some outstanding scientists of his time like Charles Darwin, Herbert Spencer, Henry Maine, Jacob Bachoven, Bandelier, and many others, in which a series of important questions were dealt with: origin and essence of the Roman kin; the question of *gentis enuptio*; kinship structure of the Germanians; the material of Fayson and Howett on marriage, classes, totem divisions, and the like, of Australian tribes; the blood-related family; group marriage; the relations between the uncle from the mother's side and the nephew, and so on. Second, it also contained a table prepared by Morgan himself in 1875, and published for the first time in the book under review, giving the original outline of Morgan's periodization of pre-class society. Third, it contained some superb facsimiles of tables and pages of the original letters. Fourth, it included corrections that Morgan himself had made in his own copy of *Ancient Society*. Fifth, of the 98 published articles as many as 55 had remained unpublished until then. Sixth, it embodied a short description given by D.G. Gilchrist of the newly discovered manuscripts of Morgan. Finally, all the listed documents were presented both in the English original and in Russian translation with the exception of the two English reviews on *Ancient Society* which, for unspecified reasons, appeared only in Russian translation.[61]

After mentioning these facts, Chatto went on to make a sharp criticism of almost everything Vinnikov had done by way of introducing and annotating Morgan's material. He was highly critical of Vinnikov's assertion in the introduction that Engels made Morgan's *Ancient Society* the basis for his *The Origin of the Family...* and thereby 'fulfilled what Marx was not fated to do'. Quoting from the first edition of Engels' work in the German original, Chatto pointed out that Vinnikov's assertion was far-fetched since Engels wrote his work 'in connection with' but not 'on the basis of' Morgan's discoveries. He added that 'to mention only Engels' *The Origin of the Family...* without taking into account all phases of development of the theory of the pre-class society of Marx and Engels embodied in *German Ideology* (1845), *On the Critique of Political Economy* (1859), *Capital* (1867), *Dialectics of Nature* (1873–1882), and *Anti-Duehring* (1878) and culminating in *The Origin of the Family...* was to distort Marx's and Engels' theory on the pre-class society.'[62] Chatto explained that in the 1870s, when Marx and Engels had been occupied with research on pre-class society, the origin of the state, and so on, Morgan's book appeared in 1877, presenting rich factual material particularly regarding the history of the family and kinship, confirming the materialistic understanding of history initiated by Marx 40 years previously and, therefore, 30 years before Morgan's book.

Chatto added several other points to butress his argument. Before Morgan's book became known to Engels, Engels and Marx had already read a huge amount of biological, geological, archaeological, ethnographical, and historical literature by Darwin, Lubbock, Spencer, Dokine, Bachofen, Bancroft, Mauer, Maine, Soom, Kovalevsky, Jaksthausen, Fier, and many others. Chatto quoted a letter that Engels wrote to Kautsky on 26 April 1884, in connection with his review of Morgan's book: 'It would be absurd to only objectively expound Morgan and not to interpret him critically, using the newly achieved results, and in accordance with our views and the conclusions that we have already arrived at.' Again, Engels in Chapter IX of his *Barbarism and Civilisation*, stated clearly that, for the understanding of the economic conditions which broke down clan society, Marx's *Capital* was indispensable. Chatto reinforced his argument with a further quote from Engels: 'The economic considerations which were sufficient for the task which Morgan had put to himself, were completely insufficient for mine, everything was revised by me anew.'[63] Chatto then referred to the fact that Marx devoted special attention to the forms of the family in his thesis in 1859, saying that 'the original form of family is the kin family itself, out of which the private family developed only through its historic disintegration.'[64]

According to Chatto, Vinnikov, while exaggerating Morgan's role in the development of the theory of Marx and Engels on pre-class society, ignored one fundamental point: Engels' *The Origin of the Family*..., as Lenin characterized it, was 'one of the basic works of modern socialism', whereas Morgan's book could be described only as the highest achievement of bourgeois ethnography. Chatto argued that only through the acknowledgement of its importance by the founders of Marxism and leaders of the workers' movement was Morgan's work saved from the 'conspiracy of silence' in the West. He pooh-poohed Vinnikov's remark about 'the greatness of Morgan who managed to rise so high above his surroundings and leave his epoch far behind', and added that although one might talk about greatness with reference to Morgan's scientific achievements as bourgeois evolutionist-materialist, it would be wrong to claim that he had left his epoch far behind. Citing Engels' words in his letter to Starkenburg on 25 January 1894, in which he had described the coincidental appearance of 'so-called great people' at a certain time in a given country, Chatto showed that Engels believed that although Marx had explained the theory of the materialistic interpretation of history, many historians before 1850 had also been progressing towards that conception. In Chatto's view, the same conditions applied to Morgan's case, for he was the expositor of an idea whose time had come.[65]

Chatto showed how both Morgan's friends and enemies alike tried to divest him of any hint of classical socialism while Vinnikov endeavoured to make him the forerunner of Marx and Engels. He first gave the views of 'the bourgeois anti-Morganist' Robert Louis, who wrote in his *Primitive Religion*:

Morgan would of course not have subscribed to many doctrines of classical socialism, but the then leaders of the German workers' movement were attracted to some of Morgan's theses. They translated his books into German and introduced them into the arsenal of socialist philosophy. In this way, specific theories, which by themselves had no relation whatsoever to socialist propaganda, became holy in the eyes of faithful socialists due to indirect circumstances, and the entire book henceforward became a symbol of that complex of feelings which constitute, mainly, socialist psychology.[66]

After this Chatto mentions some other comments from Morgan's friends who proclaimed 'his respectability and suitability for the bourgeois society'. He quoted from McIlvaine's funeral oration:

Our friend had not the least sympathy for materialism to which the hypothesis of revolution may lead and often has led...Even in the far-reaching conclusions which our friend reached in his researches, there is nothing to be found which would contradict the Christian religion and our faith in the Holy Scripture.

Chatto commented that 'although this is an absurd statement, it is nevertheless really true that Morgan was not an atheist.' He pointed out that in *Ancient Society* Morgan even talked about 'God's providence', and his political views were not much different from the general level of bourgeois liberalism in America. Chatto went on to say that

his social environment itself hindered him to see and understand the basic fact of the existence of class struggle, and he himself was so much politically linked with the American bourgeoisie that he could write: 'privileged classes had existed for several thousands of years everywhere with the exception of the United States'.[67]

It is this plethora of background information that Chatto invariably provides which makes his writing specially interesting. Chatto's second line of attack against Vinnikov was the latter's apolitical and insipid annotations. He opened this attack with a caustic remark: 'I.N. Vinnikov obviously believes that a book published by the Academy of Sciences should be 'academic', 'objective', and politically pale and colourless.'[68] The first item he took up was the note Vinnikov added to the name of Wendell Phillips Garrison. Vinnkov wrote:

Garrison, Wendell Phillips (1840–1907), American man of letters. From 1865 to 1906 he was literary editor of the New York journal 'The Nation', where Morgan in 1876 and 1878 published three articles on the Red Indian question. Garrison is the author of the following works: 'What Mr. Darwin saw on his Voyage around the World' (1879); 'William Lloyd Garrison' (4 vols., 1885–1889), a biography of his father, which he wrote together with his brother F.J. Garrison; 'Parables for School and Home' (1879); 'The New Gulliver' (1898); 'Memoirs of Henry Villard' (1904). After his death, the book 'Letters and Memorials of W.P. Garrison' (Cambridge, Mass., 1908) were published.

Reproducing this note, Chatto asked:

What sense does such a note make for the readers of the Soviet Union? What have we learnt from it about the social and political physiognomy of Garrison? Was it just by accident that Morgan's articles or Bandelier's review of *Ancient Society* were published by Garrison in *The Nation*?[69]

Chatto then provided information about Garrison which he considered 'more relevant and useful':

> Garrison was a bourgeois liberal with a certain political tradition. His father Wm. Lloyd Garrison played an outstanding role in the struggle for the abolition of slavery of the Negroes in America. In those days, when the ideas of Etienne Cabe and Charles Fourier created ferment among the masses and the progressive intelligentsia of the United States, Garrison founded 'The Free Press' in 1820, gathered around him the boldest of the young writers and poets—Whittier, Wendell Holmes, Longfellow, Emerson—, and won all of them over to the campaign against the slavery of Negroes. On 1 January 1831, he founded *The Liberator* which became the leading organ of the abolitionists, and devoted himself on the whole to the struggle for the liberation movement. His son, Wendell Phillips, who was born into this tradition, continued the struggle for the rights of the Negroes, and was against lynching. He also took up the Red-Indian question and was in general a progressive liberal.

After this note, Chatto stated: 'Facts like these, it seems to us, are more important for the understanding of Morgan and his epoch than the dry bibliographical enumerations compiled by I.N. Vinnikov.'[70]

Vinnikov had added a similar note to Richard Grant White (1821–85). Vinnikov introduced him as 'an American linguist and known expert on Shakespeare', listing names of some books on Shakespeare written by him. Chatto found this note equally unhelpful and complained, 'Here we do not find a single word which proves that White was a linguistic representative par excellence of the 'brahmins' of New England in Boston who presented arrogant "English" racial and class pretentions of the American Society.' Chatto introduced another interesting episode about White:

> All this racial and linguistic arrogance of White was completely shattered by Fitzedward Hall, professor of the English language at the College in Banaras in India, and later professor of Indian languages at Kings College in London, whose book 'Modern English' in its essence was a crushing rebuke of White. This was the same Fitzedward Hall from whom Morgan in 1861 had received the scheme of Sanskrit terms of kinship with a fairly extensive commentary, which was published in Systems of Consanguinity.[71]

Vinnikov was also criticized for his note on J.W. Powell, founder of the Bureau of American Ethnology. Vinnikov's biographical note on Powell explained that 'when the civil war began, Powell joined the army as a volunteer and during one of the fights lost his right arm.' Chatto pointedly asked: 'But, which army? The army of the slave-owners of the South or the army of the progressive capitalists of the North? They were clearly not the same thing. Even American books find it necessary to mention that Powell joined the Federal Army of the Northerners.' Chatto suspected that Vinnikov abstained from giving such information in order to show 'academic objectivity' which he derided because of his open and unabashed belief in polemical or propagandist writing, whose purpose should be to promote the communist cause and serve the communist state. He, therefore, criticized Vinnikov for his political indifference and lamented that terms like 'socialism', 'socialist', 'class struggle', 'workers' movement' were nowhere to be found in the book. He insisted that: 'We are right in demanding a clear understanding of the fact that science cannot be separated from the political struggle.'[72]

Chatto further charged Vinnikov of not being able to free himself from the influence of the bourgeois scholars. A case in point was his six-page note on the letter to Morgan by Benjamin Alvord. Alvord, Chatto wrote, was an officer of the American Federal Army in the Civil War, posted in Oregon. According to Vinnikov, Alvord's mission was to defend the settlers against the attacks of the Red Indians as also to protect the peaceful Red Indians from the aggression of the whites. Chatto considered this to be the language of the American bourgeoisie and said that, in Soviet language, it should have been written thus: 'Alvord was instructed by the Government on the one hand, to defend the colonizers—the invaders of the Indian territories—from counteractions of the justifiably outraged Red Indians, who defended their independence, and, on the other hand, to win over the Red Indian tribes which had already been subdued by means of cruel military force, for their peaceful exploitation and to use them against the tribes which had not yet been subdued.'[73] Morgan wanted to find out from Alvord the possibilities of settling the Red Indian tribes to a pastoral life, and Vinnikov said the answer given by Alvord was interesting in two ways: On the one hand, it depicted a clear picture of arbitrariness, chaos, and irresponsibility prevailing in the administration of Red Indian affairs, and on the other, it gave the impression that

Morgan had a genuine interest in resolving the Red Indian question in a humane and socially acceptable manner. Chatto rejected this explanation as a bourgeois-liberal outline of facts and asked: 'What was the real situation like when Morgan worked out his plan and wrote to President Hayes?'

Chatto explained the situation from W.T. Hornaday's book *The Extermination of the American Bison* (1889) which gives a clear picture of how the so-called 'pioneers' ('white robbers' in Chatto's terminology) in the 1870s penetrated the western states and annihilated the bison herds of the Red Indians because they needed the hide and fat of the animals for industry which was developing rapidly and which brought them big profits. On the other hand, in the plains cattle and sheep breeding was started and developed rapidly. The feeding grass, which formerly had fed tens of thousands of bison, now served as fodder for sheep and cattle. Huge portions of land were fenced, and the herds of the Red Indians became smaller and smaller as they had no free land for pastures. The result was the complete expropriation of the Red Indians, who responded with armed resistance. Consequently, the army was moved against them. Chatto blamed Vinnikov for not mentioning the decimation of the Red Indian tribes by the whites. He also added that Morgan's plan of introducing pastoral life among the Red Indians was fully in line with the interests and demands of the industrial bourgeoisie and not the philanthropic, humane conception of a scholar. He quoted Morgan's own words in his letter to President Hayes, 'From the economic point of view, we are ourselves directly interested in this...If in the vast central prairies countless herds of domestic animals are bred they will become the source of meat supplies for the entire country east of the Mississipi.' In conclusion, Vinnikov said that 'as was to be expected, all efforts of Morgan and the enormous success he sometimes managed to achieve could not stop the attacks of the young American capital, which on its way swept off with bloody hands everything which hindered its rapid growth.' Did Morgan fight against the young American capital? 'No,' Chatto asserted emphatically, 'Morgan [only] expressed the interests of the liberal bourgeoisie of the industrial capital against the reactionary, agrarian capital based on expropriation and seizure of land.'[74]

Chatto also did not accept Vinnikov's view on the origin of exogamy and totemism, calling it a nominalist point of view. Morgan in *Ancient Society* suggested that the institutions of mankind had sprung up in a progressive connected series, each link the result of an 'unconscious reformatory movement' to extricate society from existing evils, and considered the origin of exogamy the result of such a movement. Vinnikov, however, spoke even of the possibility of a conscious movement and maintained that the entire social institution of exogamy developed from the awareness of the harm of promiscuity and not the other way round.[75]

5. Other Scientific Researches, Academic Rewards, and Dedication in Teaching

Chatto's ethnographic enquiries were primarily concerned with the origin and development of family, systems of relationship, group marriage, and exogamy. In 1936 his bibliographical article, 'Literature of Indian Ethnography', was published in *Sovietskaya Etnografiya*.[76] The same year, in a volume containing papers of the IAE, his article 'Indiyskiye terminy oboznachayushchiye rod' (Indian Terms to mark the Gender) was published.[77] Among the papers left by Chatto, there were also two handwritten drafts in English on the 'Indo-Afghans' and 'Tibet'. 'Indo-Afghans' was written for the *Great Soviet Encyclopaedia*, requested in April 1935.[78] During 1935–6, Chatto was preoccupied with the study of relationship terms, and corresponded with other scientists in the field. In November 1936, he wrote to an Indian anthropologist mentioning a detailed article he had written on the Maler kinship system.[79] A.M. Reshetov, in his biographical sketch— 'V.A. Chatopadaya, Indian Revolutionary and Soviet Ethnographer'—in the volume of biographical sketches of Soviet scientists published by the Academy of Sciences in 1998, cites along with Chatto's contribution to the first edition of the *Great Soviet Encyclopaedia* this significant work on the Maler system of kinship. Chatto also completed an article 'Sistema rodstva u Vedda' (The System of Relationship in the Veda) and prepared a review of another book by Vinnikov entitled *Programma dlya sbora materialov po sistema rodstva i svoystva* (Programme for Collecting Material about the Systems of Relationship and Relationship through Marriage'). According to Reshetov, Chatto had announced: 'I shall soon publish some works which constitute a new way of dealing with these questions.'[80] In April 1935, Chatto helped the Scientific Publication Institute of the USSR in their preparation of *The Great Soviet Atlas of the World*, editing and correcting the notes and checking the correctness of the drawings as far as India and Burma were concerned.[81]

Chatto continued his longstanding interest in linguistic and philological enquiries. In addition to his work at the IAE, he taught Urdu at the Institute of Oriental Studies in Leningrad and later also at the Leningrad Institute of Linguistic Studies. As we shall soon see, he supervised an American Indian doctoral student in the study of his tribal language. These events further whetted his appetite for linguistic enquiry. Among his papers, we find a nine-page handwritten draft in German, with his signature on it, called 'Ueber die Bedeutung der Silbe "pu" im Wort "Punalua"' (On the significance of the syllable 'pu' in the word 'Punalua').[82] A document listing Chatto's writings, formerly preserved in the Dimitrov Museum in Leipzig, mentions a two-page printed review of A.P. Baranikov's book *Hindustani* in 1937.[83]

In December 1934, Chatto applied for professorship at the Institute of Oriental Studies in Leningrad. The chances of his appointment became brighter when, in June 1935, the presidium of the Academy of Sciences conferred upon him the degree of Candidate of Sciences (equivalent to Doctor of Philosophy) in linguistics without his having to defend it. On 15 January 1937, Chatto's appointment as specialist-ethnographer was confirmed.[84] In 1937, Chatto prepared for publication another article 'Sistema rodstva dorodstvovo obshchestva' (System of kinship in a pre-tribal society).[85]

At the IAE, there were two doctoral students under Chatto's supervision, V.E. Krasnodembskiy and I.M. Lekomtsev, and at the Institute of Linguistic Studies, the American Indian Archie Phinney. The memoirs of Karunovskaya and Dalskiy, and Reshetov's biographical sketch on Chatto, tell us about the exceptional help Chatto rendered them on methodology and material collection. Dalskiy and Karunovskaya also write how Chatto was greatly loved and admired by the younger generation of scholars and other co-workers at the Academy. The Chattopadhyaya section of the defunct Dimitrov Museum in Leipzig preserved copies of various scientific papers of Russian scholars in the field of anthropology and ethnography which were presented to Chatto with appreciative and flattering remarks.

One instance of Chatto's fatherly care for his students was long remembered by his colleagues, his contribution to the intellectual development of Phinney, a Numipu (Nez Percé) Indian from Idaho, who came to the Soviet Union for higher education in ethnography.

Phinney originally planned to do ethnographical research on the Indian tribes north of the USA. However, Chatto persuaded him to move to linguistics, and work on his own language, Numipu. He also interceded with the director of the Institute of Linguistics, Ivan Ivanovich Meshchaninov, to move for an extension of Phinney's stay at the IAE. Meshchaninov not only granted this extension but also agreed to give Phinney a special course in linguistics. During the lessons, Chatto volunteered to act as a translator from Russian to English for Phinney. This helped Phinney successfully complete his dissertation on 'The Grammar of the Numipu Language', and also pass other exams on philosophical subjects. With Chatto's help and guidance, Phinney gave a lecture on 'the language of gestures' of his Numipu tribe which was filmed in 1935 by the Lenin State University, and published as a 25-page booklet on the folklore of the Numipu tribe. The booklet included the original version of the folklore, word for word, as collected by Phinney and his mother, as well as a translation into Russian. Both these works were considered of immense importance to linguists, ethnographers, and folklorists.[87]

Phinney was already an accomplished researcher in ethnography and linguistics in the USA before he came to the Soviet Union. He had been a student of Franz Boas, professor of Anthropology at Columbia University, New York. During 1929–30, he collected from his mother 41 tales. These were published in 1934 in a book called *Nez Percé Texts*[88], and formed a volume in the series, 'Columbia University Contribution to Anthropology', under the editorship of Boas. Besides reproducing the tales in the original tongue with word for word English translation, Phinney provided free translations of every tale in English. Since his mother could not speak English at all, Phinney believed that the world of thought and imagination that lay deep inside the Indian soul were truly portrayed in these tales in all their pristine beauty and archaic word formation and free from any corruption from the influence of other Indian tales in circulation.

Phinney's background as a writer and researcher established him as a prestigious figure, and both the IAE and the Institute of Linguistics strove to convert him to Marxism and influence him to view the national question of the American Indians from the Marxist-Leninist angle. At least Chatto took it as a challenge to change Phinney's mind ideologically. In addition to being Phinney's overall academic supervisor, Chatto was asked by the Academy to be Phinney's consultant on 'historical materialism' in 1933, and consultant on the 'national issue' during the semester 1935–6. Under his supervision, Phinney read (however, to Chatto's regret, only the English editions, not the German or Russian ones) such Marxist-Leninist works as *Poverty of Philosophy, The Situation of the Working Class in England, Anti-Duehring, Origin of the Family, Stalin's Marxism and the National and Colonial Question, Questions of Leninism, Lenin and the Historical Materialism*, and so on, besides a host of special brochures on Soviet life and activity and, in particular, on the national question.[89]

On 26 April 1937, when Phinney had to defend his dissertation for the degree of Candidate of Sciences before the examination board, Chatto, as one of the examiners, gave a critical speech approving Phinney's candidature. He pointed out what Phinney had been before and what he was now. According to him, before arriving in the Soviet Union, Phinney had been educated to see society and political history and even his own Indian issue from the point of view of the educated liberal American bourgeoisie. He had held anti-Morgan views, strongly propagated by the schools of Lowie, Kroeber, and Goldenweiser, and his ethnography had been the ethnography of this school. He had known practically nothing of the works of the founders of Marxism-Leninism. He had been sent to the Soviet Union as an exchange student by the well-known American professor, Boas, who had hoped Phinney would undertake a special investigation of the national policy of the Soviet Union. However, this did not happen.[90]

Coming to Phinney's handling of the social organization of the Numipu tribe, Chatto went into great detail and pointed out some methodological shortcomings. However, he highlighted the intrinsic merits of Phinney's work as it was an attempt to view his tribe not as some excavated article to be installed in a museum, but to use its ethnography, folklore, linguistics, and past history as material in practical work for the solution of the national question of the American Indians. He concluded that Phinney was a deserving candidate for the degree and hoped that after returning to his people, Phinney would actively practise the principle of Marxism-Leninism which he had studied in the Soviet Union, and would contribute to making the Indian tribes more progressive as a revolutionary national minority under the red flag of the Communist International and the unconquerable banner of Marx, Engels, and Lenin.[91]

The Birth of the Soviet–Indian Social Scientist 309

A little more than two months after this speech Chatto was arrested and subsequently executed. In the commemoration volume on Soviet scientists, published 60 years later in 1998, the biography of Chatto ends with the following tribute:

> The name and scientific activity of V.A. Chatopadaya deserve the respect and acknowledgement of his colleagues. Although he worked only for a short period [four years] in the field of Soviet ethnography, he had a certain influence on the formation of the new subject which, in particular, was connected with the study of the system of relationship and the development of Soviet ethnographic Indology.[92]

Notes

1. One Russian source gives Chatto's date of departure for the Soviet Union as 23 August 1931. See A.M. Reshetov, 'V.A. Chatopadaya—indiyskiy revolyutsioner i sovietskiy etnograf' (V.A. Chatopadaya—Indian revolutionary and Soviet ethnograph') in N.V. Kyuner (ed.), *Museum of Anthropology and Ethnography* (Russian Academy of Sciences, St Petersburg, 1998), pp. 148–51.
2. Bundesarchiv Koblenz (BAK) R. 134. *Reichskommission fuer Ueberwachung der oeffentlichen Ordnung und Nachrichtensammelstelle im Reichsministerium des Inneren*.
3. Pillai to Hitler, Berlin 10 December 1931; and Hitler's Private Secretary to Pillai, Munich, 24 December 1931. BAK, R. 43 I/45, pp. 270–4; see also A.C.N. Nambiar, 'The Story of My Arrest in Berlin: India and Germany Today', *The Free Press Journal*, Bombay, 6 May 1933.
4. Andrey Nikolayevich Dalskiy, *Vospominaniya* (Memoirs), mss., Leningrad, 29 March 1962, p. 3. These are primarily reminiscences of his friend and colleague, Chattopadhyaya, preserved in the Archive of Orientalists of the Russian Academy of Sciences in Leningrad. F. 138, Op. 1, No. 47.
5. A.M. Reshetov, *op. cit.*, p. 149.
6. *Ibid.*
7. AA to German Embassy, Moscow, 31 May 1932. AA, Pol. 19, *Sozialismus, Bolschewismus, Kommunismus usw*.
8. *Ibid.*
9. Lidiya Eduardovna Karunovskaya, *Vospominaniya o Chattopadhyaya, Virendranath Agornatovich* (Reminiscences of Chattopadhyaya, Virendranath Agornatovich), typed mss. in Russian, Leningrad, May 1970, preserved in the Archive of Orientalists of the Russian Academy of Sciences. F. 138, Op. 1, No. 48, p. 23.
10. See Ch. V, sec. 2.
11. N. Odintsova, the head of the editorial office of Borba Klassov, to Chatto, Moscow, 19 October 1932. A copy of this letter was formerly preserved at the erstwhile DML.

12. Dalskiy, *op. cit.*, p. 4. At that time the seat of the Academy of Sciences was in Leningrad.
13. *Ibid.*, pp. 3–4. Dalskiy himself was the party secretary of the IAE and, as he writes in his memoirs, Chatto was introduced to him on the very first day of Chatto's arrival at the IAE (1 March, 1933) by Director Matorin. Reshetov, *op. cit.*, p. 149.
14. Academy of Sciences of the USSR. Archive Information, '12' October 1945, no. 314–783 / 34 signed by T.I. Lysenko (Academy secretary) and V.P. Kostygova (scientific assistant). A copy of this document was once preserved in the DML; Reshetov, *op. cit.*, p. 149.
15. H. von Glasenapp, *Meine Lebensreise* (Wiesbaden, 1964), p. 76. Interview with Stroemgren who met many of Chatto's contemporaries in Stockholm. Lucie Hecht also told the author: 'He [Chatto] explained to us once the relation between the Indian word *swaraja* meaning self-rule, and the Swedish word *sveridge* meaning "ruling by self". He liked such comparisons of languages and enjoyed discovering similarities.'
16. Reshetov, *op. cit.*, p. 149.
17. Dalskiy, *op. cit.*, p. 3.
18. *Ibid.*, p. 4.
19. *Ibid.*
20. Not much is known about this German wife of Chatto's and her two children. It is clear from Karunovskaya's memoirs that in 1933 this lady and her children were to arrive in Leningrad. But whether they actually did arrive or not is not mentioned either by Karunovskaya or Dalskiy or anyone else.
21. *Ibid.*, pp. 4–5. See also Karunovskaya, *op. cit.*, p. 14.
22. Dalskiy, *op. cit.*, p. 5. Karunovskaya, *op. cit.*, p. 9.
23. Karunovskaya, *op. cit.*, p. 9.
24. Karunovskaya, *op. cit.*, pp. 9–12. Dalskiy, *op. cit.*, p. 5.
25. Academy of Sciences of the USSR. Archive Information '12' October 1956, no. 314–783 / 34. A copy of this document was once preserved in the DML.
26. Reshetov, *op. cit.*, p. 149.
27. Dalskiy, *op. cit.*, p. 8.
28. *Ibid.* Dalskiy names several academic personalities (ethnologist, Professor E.G. Kargarov; historian, Professor B.L. Bogayevskiy; and a member of the Academy of Sciences, D.K. Zelenin) who personally conveyed to him their opinions about Chatto's talk.
29. *Sovietskaya Etnografiya*, 6 (1), 1934, pp. 178–9.
30. *Ibid.*, p. 178.
31. *Neue Zeit*, XI (1), pp. 373–5.
32. Chatto in *Sovietskaya Etnografiya*, 6 (1), 1934, p. 179.
33. 1893, no.2, p. 7.
34. Dalskiy, *op. cit.*, p. 8.
35. Frederick Engels, *The Origin of the Family, Private Property and the State*, translated by Ernest Untermann, Chicago (Charles H. Kerr & Company), 1902.

36. *Sovietskaya Etnografiya*, 6 (1), 1934, pp. 189–92.
37. *Ibid.*, p. 189. This and other quoted passages, including those from Chatto, are my translations from the Russian original.
38. *Ibid.*
39. *Ibid.*, p. 190.
40. *Ibid.*
41. *Ibid.*, p. 191.
42. *Ibid.*
43. *Ibid.*, p. 192.
44. Chatto's review article on Friedrich Engels, *Der Ursprung der Familie, des Privateigentums und des Staats*, edited by Ladislaus Rudas, Moscow-Leningrad (Foreign Workers Publishing House), 1934, in *Sovietskaya Etnografiya*, 6 (1), 1934, pp. 192–9.
45. *Ibid.*, p. 193. My literal translation from Chatto's Russian. Subsequent quotes are also translations from Russian.
46. *Ibid.*, p. 194.
47. *Ibid.*
48. *Ibid.*
49. *Ibid.*, p. 195.
50. *Ibid.*
51. *Ibid.*, p. 193.
52. *Ibid.*, pp. 195–6.
53. *Ibid.*, p. 196.
54. *Ibid.*, p. 197.
55. *Ibid.*, p. 197.
56. *Ibid.*, p. 198.
57. According to Dalskiy, Chatto applied for Russian citizenship in 1923, and Dalskiy supported his application with surety as secretary of the party organization. Dalskiy here does not say whether Chatto was granted citizenship (Dalskiy, *op. cit.*, p. 21). However, Dalskiy quotes Chatto in the course of an academic speech in April 1937: 'No one can live and work in our country [Soviet Russia] for five years without undergoing a profound rebirth.' (Dalskiy, *op. cit.*, p. 12)
58. See *Sovietskaya Etnografiya*, no. 6, 1935, pp. 173–88. The author of the article is named here as V.A. Chatopadaya. For an appreciation of this review article, see Dalskiy, *op. cit.*, p. 9.
59. Lewis Henry Morgan (1818–81): An ethnologist and principal founder of scientific anthropology, Morgan is known especially for establishing the study of kinship and for his comprehensive theory of social revolution. In the early 1840s, he developed a deep interest in American Indians and over his lifetime championed the Indian struggle against white oppression.
60. I.N. Vinnikov, *Iz Arkhiva Lyuisa Genri Morgana*, Works of the Institute of Anthropology and Ethnography of the Academy of Sciences (vol. II), published by the Academy of Sciences of the USSR, M–L, 1935, pp. VII–262.

61. *Sovietskaya Etnografiya*, no. 6, 1935, p. 173.
62. *Ibid.*, p. 174. This and subsequent quotes from this review article are my translations from the original Russian.
63. *Ibid.*
64. *Ibid.*, p. 175.
65. *Ibid.*
66. *Ibid.* Chatto quotes here Louis' book (1925, p. 327). I have retranslated here from Chatto's Russian.
67. *Ibid.*, pp. 175-6.
68. *Ibid.*, p. 176.
69. *Ibid.*, pp. 176-7.
70. *Ibid.*, p. 177.
71. *Ibid.*
72. *Ibid.*
73. *Ibid.*, p. 178.
74. *Ibid.*
75. *Ibid.*, p. 179.
76. 'Literatura pro indiyskoy etnografii', *Sovietskaya Etnografiya*, vol. 3, 1936, pp. 116-21.
77. The volume called *Voprosy istorii doklassovovo obshchestva* (Questions about the History of the Pre-Class Society), Publishing House of the Academy of Sciences of the USSR, 1936; see also Dalskiy, *op. cit.*, p. 9.
78. The letter from the editorial office of the *Great Soviet Encyclopaedia*, 21 April, 1935, signed by Turovskaya. Copies of this document and the draft of the original articles were once preserved at the DML.
79. We have a copy of the letter that Chatto wrote to Susanka Sarkar of the Anthropological Laboratory, Indian Museum, Calcutta, dated 25 November 1936, discussing Maler relationship terms.
80. Reshetov, *op. cit.*, p. 150.
81. Central executive committee of the Scientific Publication Institute (signed by Yestigneyeva) to Chatto, Moscow, 27 April 1935. A copy of this document was at the DML.
82. A copy of this draft was preserved at the erstwhile DML.
83. Handwritten list in Russian of Chatto's academic writings in Russian, DML.
84. Reshetov, *op. cit.*, p. 75; Academy of Sciences of the USSR, document dated '12' October 1956, no. 314-783/34, DML.
85. Handwritten list of Chatto's work in Russian, DML.
86. These papers were published in Russian and international research journals including *American Anthropologist* during 1934-7. Some of the scholars are: V.V. Ginzburg, Y.P. Alkor, Y.P. Averkiyeva, Yuriy Burnakov, V.V. Struve, D.N. Lev, A.N. Dalskiy, and Alexander M. Zolotarev.
87. Dalskiy, *op. cit.*, p. 13.
88. Archie Phinney, *Nez Percé Texts*, pp. XII-498 (New York, Columbia University Press, 1934). See also *Anthropos*, vol. 31, 1936, pp. 295-6 for a

review of Phinney's book.
89. *Ibid*. Dalskiy quoting from Chatto's report on Phinney verbatim.
90. *Ibid*., pp. 14–17.
91. *Ibid*., p. 19.
92. Reshetov, *op. cit.*, p. 151.

10

A Brief Interlude of Happiness and Sudden Death

Chatto lived barely six years in the Soviet Union from the end of August 1931 to his death on 2 September 1937. The first phase of his stay, until he joined the IAE, was full of odd jobs and intense anxieties, as already noted in the first section of the previous chapter. The second phase, that is, the time spent at the IAE from 1 March 1933 till his death, was probably the most creative and fulfilling period of his life. As we shall soon see, this period too was not free from anxiety, as he suspected that the Comintern would come up with new charges against him. Yet his stay at the IAE was a time of great satisfaction and solace largely because of his friendship with a colleague, Lidiya Eduardovna Karunovskaya. It is this friendship and intimacy we will now turn to.

1. CHATTO AND LIDIYA: CONJUGAL HARMONY AND BLISS

When Chatto joined the IAE, Karunovskaya, a Russian about 10 years younger to him, was head of the Indonesian section at the Institute. As Chatto's Indian section was close by, Chatto often sought clarifications of Russian words or passages from her. This contact developed within a very short period into an intimate friendship.[1]

Gregarious and used to the company of people, Chatto hated his lonely hotel room and, later, his apartment. Often he accompanied Karunovskaya to her apartment after work, and would remain there for the whole evening reading and writing. Sometimes he even stayed the night. Karunovskaya lived with her husband, Andrey Danilin, also an ethnographer, and an elderly female relative in a three-room apartment on Serpukhov Street, Leningrad. Chatto was not unwelcome to any of the inmates, and he once observed: 'All here consider me an integral part of the family.'

Danilin, of course, noticed that an emotional attachment was developing between Karunovskaya and Chatto, but he took this in his stride. In August 1933, when Karunovskaya was away at a sanatorium in Khilovo, she received a letter from Chatto describing Danilin's placid demeanour towards him and his philosophical attitude to Chatto's relationship with her:

> When Andrey saw in the morning that I was washing clothes and then cleaning up the room, he said to me: 'Lidiya considers you, not me, as an example, a model.' I replied to him that you are a wonderful woman, and that I love you very much and that he should do everything to make things easier for you. Andrey thought about it. I then asked him whether I should do some washing for him. He replied: 'Yes, but this would be difficult for you.' 'No, no,' I said. He then replied: 'My brain needs to be washed.' I know that he is somewhat confused...[2]

Karunovskaya sensed Chatto's 'desire to bring some order into a disorganised character'. In the same letter, Chatto also confessed his innermost feelings for Lidiya:

> Lidusha, you simply don't know *what* you mean in my life. Wait until we are together. I'll pour out my soul to you, but only do write to me in absolutely clear terms as far as Andrey is concerned. I would like to have absolute clarity on this point so that I don't inflict any pain upon him.[3]

A month later, Chatto wrote to her from Moscow how he always felt at home at her place:

> I must say that it is a great pleasure for me that I have a home at your place. Never did I feel so much at home as I do at your place. I am not tormented by the idea that I am a disturbance to you, and particularly to Andrey. When I talk with you, Andrey gets bored because he cannot take part in our talk. Therefore I have to learn Russian thoroughly, and he has to learn German.[4]

Far from considering Chatto a nuisance or a pest, Karunovskaya herself was drawn to him and saw this an opportunity to escape from her drab and unhappy marriage with Danilin. In her memoirs she described her life with Danilin thus:

> Our life together was poorly organised. We got married when we were students, in the twenties—the years of famine. We ate at the students' canteen; the basic comfort of life was missing, and life somehow developed in such a way that also in the future I had to bear solely the everyday household worries. Chatto could not overlook this. He spoke to Andrey pointing out to him the abnormal situation and advised him to be more attentive to his responsibilities in the household tasks.[5]

In contrast to Danilin's indifference and laid-back nature, Lidiya saw in Chatto a profoundly social, caring, generous, and hardworking person, whose extraordinary capacity for work under any circumstances surprised all his colleagues. Karunovskaya writes:

> He could write and work sitting sometimes on the edge of a table or writing simply on his knees, reacting at the same time to the happenings around him… During the first two years of Chatto's stay in Leningrad, it was particularly rainy, cold and windy making it very difficult for him to get used to the new climatic conditions. He often suffered from a cold, had temperature, complicated by unbearable neuralgic pain in the eyes, kidneys and the back. And yet, as soon as the pain subsided, he would continue his work. Despite his extremely busy routine and his illnesses, Chatto always had time for everyone who needed his advice or a word of comfort or often material help.[6]

Karunovskaya extols Chatto's kind-heartedness to less fortunate co-workers and their children in her memoirs:

> Those were still very difficult years after the War and the destruction caused by the War. Many things, even the most essential ones, were not available for sale. On his [Chatto's] desk in the Institute, he would find notes such as: 'My little son badly needs warm shoes'; 'My mother has fallen ill, she needs butter badly'; 'Do you have ten roubles to spare?' etc. And Chatto, who not desiring to be different from the less fortunate co-workers refused to use the *insnab* coupons [with which foreigners could buy essential items overriding control] would take such coupons from his friends to buy the things asked for in the slips. These things were not always just butter but sometimes also a coat, stockings and other things. For small children of co-workers he would hide in the writing desk of their mothers some dainty titbits. As a result of this, he was often left without money to buy the most essential things for himself.[7]

Chatto's readiness to help the needy and the hardship he suffered in doing so is illustrated in an episode that occurred in the early months of Chatto and Karunovskaya's friendship. In August 1933, during

Karunovskaya's sanatorium stay, Chatto spent his evenings, and sometimes nights, in her apartment. One day he met a 17-year-old Mexican girl, whose passport, money, and other articles had been stolen by someone who was acting as an interpreter for her in Minsk. She came to Leningrad to address her problem to the Italian Consulate which represented the Mexican government, Mexico having no diplomatic representation in the Soviet Union at the time. Chatto arranged accommodation for the girl for the first night at a hotel. But her problem was not solved immediately. So Chatto lodged her in Karunovskaya's flat until the matter was resolved. Although he himself was on sick leave, suffering from a painful influenza, he gave his only woollen sweater to the girl who had arrived in Leningrad in a summer dress. About his decision to put the girl up at Karunovskaya's apartment, Chatto wrote to her:

I cannot talk with you personally, but I think you would agree to this girl staying one night here together with your old lady. I cannot keep her in a hotel, that is certain. But I don't have such a heart to throw her out into the street. I know that most people would be afraid, in particular, the party people. But I feel strong enough to follow my instincts. I only do hope that you would agree. This is the most important thing for me.[8]

When after a few days, the Mexican girl's problem was finally solved, costing Chatto 40 roubles, he wrote to Karunovskaya:

The others have talked much but did not spend a single penny...In any case, I am satisfied that I am not a coward like most of the brave comrades who don't want to shoulder any responsibility.[9]

This episode was a pleasant surprise to Karunovskaya, who wondered how Chatto was able to find time, in spite of being overworked, to rescue the helpless girl, and struck a sympathetic chord in her heart.[10] Surprisingly, even the old lady in Karunovskaya's apartment praised Chatto's character and role in this matter in glowing terms. She wrote to Karunovskaya in Khilovo:

I cannot imagine how he [Chatto] can understand her. He chooses his words patiently so that she might be able to understand him. He is very nice to her. What a human being!...He has sent a telegram to her father in Vera Cruz on his own, spending 30 roubles...What goodness of heart, what noble-mindedness! One can only bow to him and be delighted.[11]

Similarity of thought and feeling brought Chatto and Karunovskaya increasingly close, and before the year was out they married. The date of marriage is not mentioned in Karunovskaya's memoirs. It has been deduced from Chatto memorabilia that she once lent to the Chattopadhyaya Section of the DML. Among the memorabilia, there was a small tile relief, a gift to Chatto and Karunovskaya at their wedding from a Russian restorer of artefacts, Amalia Vasilevna Werner, given 'at the end of 1933'.[12] As if to free Chatto completely from the ghosts of the past, Smedley happened to be in the Soviet Union when Chatto's relationship with Karunovskaya was reaching its culmination. Smedley stayed in the Soviet Union from June 1933 to April 1934. Interestingly enough, she also met Phinney in Moscow, besides meeting Chatto in Leningrad. The reunion with Chatto was friendly and platonic. Chatto told her about his relationship with Karunovskaya, and, happily for him, they parted amicably, finally closing the chapter of a curious relationship full of intense passion, endless depression, and infinite unhappiness.[13]

Apart from Chatto's arrest in 1937, the only other incident that brought some anxiety to the otherwise quiet and peaceful life of Chatto and Karunovskaya happened in 1935. On August 22, when Karunovskaya was away from Leningrad, Chatto wrote to her saying that his 'situation' had become 'more difficult' and that it would require him to go to Moscow to clarify matters.[14] Circumstantial evidence indicates the problem was of a political nature—the old charge of 1932, mentioned in the previous chapter, seems to have appeared again in a different guise. Chatto went to Moscow on 30 August 1935 to discuss the matter with Comintern leaders. Dimitrov[15], his old colleague from Berlin, had just become secretary general of the Comintern and Wilhelm Pieck a secretary. Chatto had had good relations with Dimitrov in Berlin. As one eyewitness described, both understood each other well, and had four characteristics in common: fearlessness, clear foresight, analytical scepticism, and a Homeric laughter.[16] Chatto, therefore, hoped that with Dimitrov's help the problem would soon be over. But he could not talk to any of the central committee members as they were all engaged in long sessions. He, however, met many other comrades who received him warmly, and this pleased him.[17] Chatto came to know that Philip Dengel[18], another friend, had become a member of the Comintern executive Committee and thought of meeting him too. Luckily, Muenzenberg also happened to be in

Moscow then, and he too received Chatto warmly. Commenting on Chatto's problem, Muenzenberg considered 'the whole situation a shame'. Encouraged by Muenzenberg and Dimitrov's presence in Moscow, Chatto wrote to Karunovskaya with hope, 'But now our own people are at the top.' However, he was unable to meet Dimitrov, who was bedridden at the time. He met Muenzenberg again for a long talk, and Clemens Dutt also joined them. Clemens' brother, R.P. Dutt, was a candidate member to the Comintern executive just then. So it was hoped the matter would be easily resolved. Muenzenberg and Dutt decided to meet again the next day to discuss the matter with R. P. Dutt.

Neither hopeless nor hopeful, Chatto wrote to Karunovskaya on 30 August: 'I could not do anything yet since Pieck is so busy and it will be possible for me to talk to him only on 1 September.' On this day, Chatto also met Abani Mukherji, who insisted Chatto should come to his *dacha*.[19] To Chatto's great relief, the dark clouds of foreboding disappeared the very next day. The charge of political dishonesty against him seems to have been dropped again. Chatto wrote to Karunovskaya:

My dear Lidusha, I had so much talk and have so much to tell that I simply don't know where to begin...Above all, I have cleared the matter concerning my cleanliness. This took the whole day.[20]

This Moscow visit was not entirely full of worries for Chatto. He was also able to see the fruits of his earlier academic labour. As we have already seen, he was engaged by the Marx-Engels Institute to revise various language editions of Engels' book *The Origin of the Family...* Also, Rudas, the editor of the German edition, whom Chatto had sharply criticized in his review, approached him at a Moscow café with a request: 'I have read your review. Correct my mistakes in the new edition.'[21] Chatto reckoned that the job would bring him about 2000 roubles. As Lidiya was thinking of studying Bahasa Indonesian in Moscow at the time, Chatto enquired about who would be the most suitable teacher for her, and decided to engage an old Indonesian comrade, Semaoen.[22] Chatto had known him from the LAI days in Berlin. He wrote to Karunovskaya about the importance of her learning the Indonesian language:

I attach great importance to your linguistic and political education, so no sacrifice would be too great. As long as you have me, we must achieve everything. Semaoen comes to Moscow tomorrow, and I will sort out with him the conditions which we can then confirm in writing and carry out the plan.

Chatto advised her to look for an apartment in Moscow on her next official trip and added, 'Maybe I, too, have to settle in Moscow very soon.'[23] On 4 September, Chatto wrote to her again on the same subject:

I will pay Semaoen in advance so that he can secure a room for himself. I shall do everything so that you learn the language perfectly within a year. Then I may 'die' in peace.[24]

Chatto also found many possibilities of writing and publishing during his Moscow visit. For example, he met the Czechoslovakian author and editor, Weiskopf, who wanted to accept Chatto's articles on the Aga Khan and Nepal on a payment basis.[25] After returning to Leningrad, besides writing articles for money, Chatto became busy with teaching and research. On 15 January 1937, he was confirmed as senior research assistant with a salary of 750 roubles per month.[26]

2. Arrest and Execution

While thus engaged in teaching, research as well as propaganda for the party, both inside and outside the IAE, Chatto and Karunovskaya's apartment was raided by the Secret Police on the night between 16 and 17 July 1937. Following a short interrogation and cross-examination, the police whisked Chatto away. Chatto said goodbye to Karunovskaya, embraced her and whispered in her ears that she should inform a Comintern comrade about this occurrence. Unfortunately, she failed to understand the name of this comrade, and sent a telegram to the Comintern the following morning about Chatto's arrest.[27]

This was the time of Stalin's infamous purges, and Karunovskaya must have had a presentiment she was never going to see her husband again. She tried through numerous means to discover Chatto's whereabouts, but it was all in vain. Two months after Chatto's arrest, she was herself summarily dismissed from the Institute. She protested against this dismissal, sending a complaint to Andrey Aleksandrovich Zhdanov, one of the secretaries of the Party's central committee, and, in

March 1939, she was reinstated by a decision of the Police Court. But she had no success in obtaining any clear or accurate information about her husband.[28] In fact, the authorities gave her blatant disinformation. After the 20th Party Congress in 1956, at which the terrible consequences of Stalin's personality cult were criticized, Karunovskaya sent a petition to the chief party leader, N.S. Khrushchev, to check her husband's case. In this petition, she included a 'secret' document recording a decision of the International Control Commission of the Comintern of 10 November 1932, exculpating Chatto from any charge of political dishonesty.[29] As a result, on 15 September 1956, she was given a certificate saying that 'the accusation of Chatopadaya Virendranat Agornatovich was checked by the Military Collegium of the Supreme Court of the USSR on 28 April 1956', and that 'the verdict of 2 September 1937 on him was lifted. In the light of the newly discovered circumstances, the case against him was withdrawn because of the lack of evidence of a crime'. And on 22 March 1958, Karunovskaya was handed a death certificate stating Chatto had died on 6 April 1943. Neither the cause nor the place of death were mentioned.[30]

Even this long-delayed official information was completely wrong. After the dawn of liberalism in Russia in the early 1990s, the Russian historian and India expert Leonid Mitrokhin was one of the first to gain information from KGB archives about the fate of some Indian revolutionaries in the Soviet Union during the notorious purges. He learned that Chatto was sentenced to death by the Military Collegium of the Supreme Court of the USSR on 2 September 1937, and that the sentence was carried out on the same day by a firing squad.[31] In accordance with the egregious practices of the totalitarian state under Stalin, Chatto was formally discharged from his duties on 16 September 1937—14 days after his death.[32]

Following the Secret Police raid, while in prison, Chatto tried to contact Karunovskaya, and to this end arranged for a book parcel to be sent to her which, however, reached only during the war in 1941. Karunovskaya had to pay 6.50 roubles to receive this packet which contained a book, from a Teachers' Institute in Alma-Ata, for learning the Indonesian language. She concluded that Chatto, by means of this ploy, wished her to know he was still alive.[33]

Years after Chatto's death, she recorded this tribute to him:

During the years of his wanderings in foreign countries, Chatto took from the West all the positive things which the West could give him, but he did not forfeit the stamp of special culture of his beautiful motherland. In every one of his gestures, in every word, one could see his innate nobility, his disarming simplicity and the subtleness of his nature. His intelligence, the warmth of his heart and his capacity to understand everybody were expressed in a charming smile which attracted people towards him. I had the great good fortune to be the friend and wife of this astonishingly charming, beautiful man, to break his prolonged loneliness, to be together with him and to be useful to him.[34]

In her memoirs, Karunovskaya gives examples of the high regard and admiration in which Chatto's students held him. One of his students, Berner, wrote:

I am proud that I was his student and that he was not only my teacher but also my friend and elder brother. His beautiful image constantly flashes upon my inward eye, looking just the way I used to see him. The loss, the death of dear Chatto, is a great grief for all who knew him and the greatest crime in the history of our time. Unfortunately, it is irreversible and the perpetrators cannot be punished.

It seems that Soviet authorities pressured some of Chatto's students into denouncing him. But according to Karunovskaya, one of them, Igor Lekomtsev, categorically refused to say anything negative about him.[35]

3. KIROV'S PROTÉGÉ

Chatto and his two Indian compatriots, Abani Mukherji and Gulam Ambia Khan Luhani,[36] were among the many thousands of non-Russian communists who were exterminated by Stalin's Secret Police during 1936–9. The numbers involved in the purges are staggering: they far exceed the total number of their counterparts murdered by Hitler, Mussolini, and all other dictators put together between the two World Wars.[37] The cruel irony is that, while this rampage of murder and mayhem was in full swing, Stalin was simultaneously promulgating 'the most democratic constitution in the world', which explicitly guaranteed the right of asylum to foreign communists and political activists.[38]

Reputable scholars in the field of Comintern history generally agree that these mass murders cannot be imputed to political reasons alone; psychological or psychopathological factors are no less important.[39] However, if we confine ourselves to the consideration of purely political factors, we can perceive the plausible reasons that could have been used to brand Chatto as an enemy of the Soviet state and justify his execution.

Apart from the rank and file, the Comintern members of foreign origin who were massacred by Stalin fall into two categories:

1. Those who had followed Lenin or had cooperated with him before October 1917, or had followed him during the foundation of the Comintern in 1919. All Polish leaders, with two or three exceptions, belong to this category.
2. Leaders of parties that had been outlawed in their own countries and who had sought refuge in the Soviet Union, e.g., leaders from Yugoslavia, Germany, Hungary, Rumania, Finland and the Baltic countries. It is important to note that leaders belonging to legal parties in the European parliamentary democracies, e.g., Britain, France, Sweden, Norway, Denmark and Czechoslovakia, survived the massacre.[40]

Chatto was not a Comintern official, but as a political criminal in the eyes of the British and a member of the German Communist Party, he fell neatly into the second category. Immediately before the dreadful purges began, Chatto was deeply involved in the study of the fundamental writings of Marx, Engels, and Lenin, and had openly praised Lenin.[41] Although publicly devoted to Marx and Lenin for political reasons, Stalin was working clandestinely to establish his personal dictatorship, which brooked no one who showed any signs of an independent mind.[39] There was, however, enough in Chatto's political past to provoke the suspicions of Stalin's minions. Apart from Stalin's xenophobic dislike of foreign communists, Chatto had, in his European days, freely associated with communists, conservatives, anarchists, and socialists in his constant effort to further the cause of the Indian national struggle. As if this were not bad enough for Chatto's safety in the Soviet Union and to give anyone looking for ammunitions to frame him, he was patently a protégé of Sergey Mironovich Kirov (1886–1934), the second most important man in Russia after Stalin. It was he who brought Chatto to Leningrad, and set him on the academic path at the IAE. Kirov was an active, energetic, and popular leader from Leningrad. Since 1932, his popularity was rapidly growing while Stalin's was steadily falling in the wake of the Russian collectivization debacle and famine. There was a growing sense that Russia needed a change, and there were demands for softening the dictatorship and making the system more humane. Kirov sympathized with these demands, and it was he who had most strongly opposed the shooting of old opponents, pleaded for the better treatment of the peasantry and argued for the infusion of new blood in the Party. As Stalin's popularity declined, the search for an alternative leader was widely canvassed, and Kirov seemed to be the clear choice of the people.[43] Then, on 1 December 1934, Kirov was assassinated in Leningrad by a young party member, Leonid Nikolayev. The assassin and suspected accomplices were accused of being Zinovievite terrorists and were speedily shot. Although Stalin showed great grief in public, kissing the body of his assassinated 'friend', no one doubted that Stalin himself was behind the assassination. In fact, many consider the murder of Kirov as the beginning of Stalin's abominable purges.

According to Karunovskaya, 'Chatto considered Sergey Mironovich Kirov his best friend who cared for him.'[44] It seems that Chatto sensed the danger to himself when he heard the news of the murder, for he is reported to have exclaimed prophetically, 'Well, now reprisals against foreigners will begin.'[45] Another two and a half years were to elapse before Chatto's turn came for liquidation, but during this time he seems to have been full of fear and foreboding. This is illustrated by what he said at one of his meetings with Buber-Neumann—an old friend from Berlin and wife of the famous German communist leader, Heinz Neumann[46]—in Moscow in 1937. When hearing from her that her husband had been arrested in Moscow, Chatto said he too was expecting his arrest any night, and added, like the tender and compassionate man that he was, that his greatest anxiety was not so much for his own fate but for the misery in which the murdered men would leave their wives and children.[47]

Before I conclude this chapter, let me note the dubious consolation for Indians that, unlike thousands of foreign communists who were liquidated by Stalin, the Indian victims—Chatto, Mukherji, and Luhani—were at least rehabilitated posthumously.

However, this rehabilitation seems to be part of the cynical game of political courtship that Soviet leaders were playing during the Cold War to cultivate the goodwill of neutral India under Nehru. Equally, at the other end of the spectrum, there was no lack of cynicism in Indian politics either, for neither Nehru nor the post-Nehru leadership in India did anything to rescue Chatto from obscurity, although he was the pivotal figure in waging a relentless propaganda war against British imperialism for almost a quarter of a century. One would have expected the Indian government to recognize his selfless sacrifice and service. Instead, even the centenary of his birth was disgracefully ignored at the official level, and Chatto remains to this day one of the forgotten and unsung heroes in the pantheon of the Indian freedom movement.

NOTES

1. An Indian scholar and Communist, Chinmohan Sehanavis met Karunovskaya in Leningrad in the early 1960s and talked with her about Chatto's period in the Soviet Union. See C. Sehanavis, *Rush Biplab O Prabashi Bharatiya Biplabi* [The Russian Revolution and Indian Revolutionaries Abroad], Calcutta, 1973, pp. 241–3.
2. Karunovskaya, *op. cit.*, p. 19, quoting from Chatto's letter to her on 12 August 1933. This is a translation from the Russian original. The subsequent quote are also translated by me.
3. *Ibid.*
4. *Ibid.*, p. 15 (quoting a letter from Chatto, Moscow, 9 September 1933).
5. *Ibid.*
6. *Ibid.*, pp. 12a–13.
7. *Ibid.*, p. 13. Karunovskaya also adds, 'Chatto loved children very much. He always made jokes with small children, paid attention to them and, in return, they were drawn to him.'
8. *Ibid.*, p. 18.
9. *Ibid.*, p. 20.
10. *Ibid.*, pp. 26–7.
11. *Ibid.*, p. 20.
12. List of memorabilia received by the DML from Karunovskaya, dated 11 June 1969, DML.
13. Janice R. and Stephen R. MacKinnon, *Agnes Smedley: The Life and Times of an American Radical* (Berkeley, 1988), pp. 159–60. Smedley went to the Soviet Union to meet her publishers and give finishing touches to one of her books. At first she had to spend some time in a sanatorium in the Caucasus Mountains for a heart ailment. In Moscow she visited operas and theatres with Phinney.
14. Karunovskaya, *op. cit.*, p. 21.
15. Georgi Dimitrov (1882–1949): Bulgarian communist leader who gained worldwide fame for his defence against Nazi accusations during the German Reichstag Fire on 27 February 1933. The Fire was an excuse for Hitler, the newly-appointed German Chancellor, to issue a decree outlawing his communist opponents. Dimitrov defended himself well and won his acquittal. He later settled in Moscow, and became secretary general of the Comintern executive committee from 1935 to 1943, and encouraged the popular movements against the growing Nazi menace. In 1945, he returned to Bulgaria and became prime minister of the communist-dominated Fatherland

Front government.
16. Interview with Lucie Hecht. Hecht also worked for Dimitrov occasionally while working for Chatto in the LAI.
17. Karunovskaya, op. cit., p. 22.
18. German communist in the Ulbricht and Pieck group.
19. Karunovskaya, op. cit., pp. 22–3.
20. Ibid., pp. 23–4.
21. Ibid., p. 24. Chatto's letter to Karunovskaya, Moscow, 4 September 1935.
22. Semaoen was a member of the Indonesian Communist Party, and had been present at the Brussels Congress of the LAI in February 1927. Later he was elected to the ECCI. See Xenia J. Eudin and Robert C. North, op. cit., pp. 265, 271, 279.
23. Ibid.
24. Ibid., p. 26. 'Inverted commas' in the Russian original.
25. Ibid., p. 23.
26. Academy of Sciences of the USSR. Archive Information, 12 October 1956. A copy of this document was preserved at the DML.
27. Ibid., p. 28.
28. Ibid., p. 29.
29. Ibid., p. 28.
30. Ibid., pp. 28 - 29.
31. Leonid Mitrokhin, 'A Triple Trap: Story of Three Indian Comintern Activists in the years of Stalinist Terror', *Soviet Land*, no. 4, April 1991, p. 30.
32. USSR Academy of Sciences, document of 12 October 1956, No. 314–783/38. A copy was formerly preserved at the DML.
33. Karunovskaya, op. cit., p. 28.
34. Ibid., pp. 27–8.
35. Ibid., pp. 14–5.
36. During the WWI, Abani Mukherji (1891–1937) was associated with the activities of Chatto's Berlin India Committee. Later, he became an Indian member of the Russian Communist (Bolshevik) Party. He had been living in the Soviet Union since 1920, and later became a professor at the University of Moscow. He was executed on 28 October 1937, and rehabilitated posthumously on 26 May 1957. Gulam Ambia Khan Luhani (1892–1938) worked with Chatto in Berlin during and after WWI, and was also a member of Chatto's mission to the Comintern in 1921. He became a member of the Russian Communist Party (Bolshevik) in 1928, and was sentenced to death by firing squad on 17 September 1938. He was rehabilitated on 9 July 1957. For a short account on Mukherji and Luhani see the second part of Leonid Mitrokhin's article in *Soviet Land*, no. 5, May 1991, pp. 22–3.
37. Branko Lazitch, 'Stalin's Massacre of the Foreign Communist Leaders' in Milorad M. Drachkovitch and Branko Lazitch (eds.), *The Comintern, Historical Highlights: Essays, Recollections, Documents* (New York, 1966), p. 170.

38. *Ibid.*, pp. 139–40. Article 129 of the Stalinist Constitution of 1936 read: 'The USSR grants the right of asylum to those foreign citizens who are being persecuted for defending the workers' interests or because of their scientific activity or their struggle for national liberation.'
39. *Ibid.*, p. 172. See also the comment of Herbert Wehner, p. 170.
40. *Ibid.*, pp. 141–2.
41. See the previous chapter and also the draft lecture of Chatto in German that was to be delivered at the MOPR meeting; copy preserved at DML.
42. An overwhelming part of the old Comintern apparatus had disappeared through liquidation, while Dimitrov's secretariat was functioning with a much reduced and predominantly Russian staff. The reduction of the Comintern to a state of suspended animation was actually the expression of Stalin's will. See Branko Lazitch, 'Two Instruments of Control by the Comintern: Emissaries of the E.C.C.I. and the Party Representatives', in Drachkovitch and Lazitch, *op. cit.*, p. 63.
43. See E.H. Carr, *The Twilight of Comintern 1930–1935* (London, 1982), pp. 120–1; also George F. Kennen, *Russia and the West under Lenin and Stalin* (Boston, 1961), pp. 255, 296, 301–3.
44. Karunovskaya, *op. cit.*, p. 28.
45. *Ibid.*
46. Heinz Neumann was a member of the Politburo and, with Remmele and Thaelmann, one of the three leaders of the German Communist Party during the first phase of Stalinization. He served as a Comintern emissary in countries ranging from China to Spain. He was forced to take refuge in the USSR and was arrested in 1937. He disappeared in Soviet jails.
47. Buber-Neumann, *op. cit.*, pp. 107–8, 110. Buber-Neumann herself was arrested in the Soviet Union and, in 1940, delivered to the Nazis.

Bibliography

I. PRIMARY UNPUBLISHED SOURCES

A. Politisches Archiv, Auswaertiges Amt, Bonn, Germany
 1. Englische Besitzungen in Asien 2, Britisch Indien, vols. 1–58 (October 1884–March 1920)
 2. Englische Besitzungen in Asien 2, Britisch Indien, Militaria, vols. 1–18 (November 1885–June 1919)
 3. Englische Besitzungen in Asien 2, Britisch Indien, Fuersten, vol. 1 (May 1887–April 1914)
 4. Preussen 1. Nr. 1g Nr. 2. Reise Sr. K. u. K. Hoheit des Kronprinzen nach Indien, vols. 1–10 (6 October 1910–4 November 1911)
 5. Preussen 1. Nr. 1g Nr. 2 (1911)
 6. Weltkrieg Nr. 11e.
 Entwuerfe von Rundschreiben an den Emir von Afghanistan und indische Fuersten, vol. 1 (March 1915–May 1918)
 7. Weltkrieg Nr. 11f.
 Unternehmungen und Aufwiegelungen gegen unsere Feinde in Indien, vols. 1–48 (August 1914–April 1920)
 8. Weltkrieg Nr. 21. 'Acta Retanta' (May 1915–November 1918)
 9. Akten des AA im Grossen Hauptquartier, vols. 1–2 (March 1915–May 1918)

10. Akten von der Deutschen Botschaft London
    a) Politische Akten-Paket 178–82. Indien (February 1888–December 1909)
    b) Britische Besitzungen, 360. Indien, vols. 1–2. (January 1910–January 1912)
    c) Bekaempfung des Bolschewismus und Kommunismus, vols. 1–2. (October 1920–March 1930)
11. Akten der Deutschen Gesandtschaft Stockholm
    a) 212 Sozialisten Konferenz (1918)
    b) 209 I Sozialisten Konferenz, vols. 1–2. (April 1917–May 1918)
    c) 219 Bolschewismus (1918–20)
    d) 169 XVIII Schwedisch-Englische Verhandlungen (October 1916–August 1918)
    e) 181 I Internationales Komitee Chattopadhyaya–Acharya vols. 1–2 (1917–18)
12. Indien Pol. I, Allgemeine auswaertige Politik (July 1921)
13. Indien Pol. 19, Sozialismus, Bolschewismus (March 1921–January 1926)
14. Indien Pol. 2. Pol. Bezieh. zu Deutschland (February 1922–October 1926)
15. Pol. 3. Pol. Bezieh. England und Indien, vols. 1–2 (September 1920–December 1935)
16. Pol. 1. Allgemeine auswaertige Politik Indiens (September 1920–November 1930)
17. Pol. 2. Pol. Bezieh. Indiens zu Deutschland, vols. 1–5 (May 1920–April 1936)
18. Pol. 2. Indisches Informationsbuero (April 1926–April 1931)
19. Pol. 3. Polit. Beziehg. zwischen Indien u. fremden Staaten, Russland (April 1925–April 1929)
20. Pol. 5. Innere Politik, Parlaments- und Parteiwesen in Indien, vols. 1–9 (May 1920–April 1936)
21. Pol. 5. Innere Politik, Parlaments- und Parteiwesen in Indien (Zeitungsausschnitte) (January 1930–February 1931)
22. Pol. 6. Nationalitaetenfrage, Fremdvoelker, Indien (February 1922–August 1935)
23. Pol. 8. Dipl. und konsular. Vertretungen Indiens im nichtdeutschen Ausland und umgekehrt (April 1920–February 1936)
24. Pol. 10. Deutsche dipl. u. konsular. Vertretungen in Indien, vols.

330   Chatto

        1–2 (April 1920–December 1935)
25. Pol. 11. Nr. 5. Journalisten, Pressevertreter (December 1921–August 1934)
26. Indischer Dichter Tagore (May 1920–December 1921)
27. Pol. 12. Pressewesen (Indien) (February 1922–April 1935)
28. Pol. 12. Sonderheft. Pressewesen (Indien-Presse) (1933–34)
29. Pol. 18. Pazifismus (June 1925–October 1930)
30. Pol. 19. Sozialismus, Bolschewismus, Kommunismus usw. (May 1922–December 1934)
31. Pol. 25. Deutschtum im Ausland (March 1922–January 1935)
32. Pol. 26. Polit. und kulturelle Propaganda, vols. 1–2 (December 1921–January 1936)
33. Pol. 29. Faschismus, Nationalsozialismus und aehnl. Bestrebungen in Indien (July–August 1935)
34. Allgemeines 3. Indien. Allgemeines (February 1929–January 1936)
35. Handel 13. Handelsvertragsverhaeltnis zu Deutschland (January 1925–March 1933)
36. Handel 37. Boykott (June 1922–March 1931)
37. Industrie 3. Industrielle Bezieh. Indiens zu Deutschland (November 1926–November 1934)
38. Wirtschaft 6. Wirtschaftliche Beziehungen zu Deutschland (March 1924–August 1933)
39. Pol. 2. Indien. Polit. Bezieh. Indiens zu Deutschland (May 1936–September 1939)
40. Pol. 5. Innere Politik, Parlaments- und Parteiwesen (August 1936–December 1938)

B. Bundesarchiv Koblenz, Germany

Reichskanzlei, Pol. Auswaertige Angelegenheiten (Asien 1922–32)

1. R 43 I/55   1925–32
2. R 7 VI/7–10   1925–40
3. R 85/70 39   Die Aussichten für die Wirtschafts-beziehungen des Reichs mit Indien nach dem I. Weltkrieg, von Consul Heyer. 13 February 1918
4. Geissler / 55   Niedermayers Bericht über Afghan Expedition
5. R 134   Reichskommission fuer Ueber-wachung der oeffentlichen Ordnung und Nachrichtenstelle im

Reichsministerium des Innern. Lageberichte (1920 –9) und Meldungen (1929–33)

C. Deutsches Zentralarchiv, Potsdam, German*

1. Reichskommissar fuer die Ueberwachung der oeffentlichen Ordnung No. 128. Indische Vereinigungen in Deutschland
2. Handelspolitische Abteilung No. 5432. Jahreshandelsbericht des Konsulats in Calcutta. January 1907–April 1916
3. Indien, Handel Handelsbeziehungen zu Deutschland. 4 vols. (Nos. 45168–71) February 1921–March 1936
4. Reichswirtschaftsministerium No. 968. England, Brit.-Indien, Handelssachen. 17 vols. 1914–19

D. Erstwhile Dimitroff Museum, Leipzig

Some of the surviving papers (copies) from the old Chattopadhyaya Section of the Museum made available to the author by the City Council, Leipzig. The papers had originally come to the Museum as a loan from Chattopadhyaya's widow, Dr Lidiya Karunovskaya.

1. A typed copy of the confidential report submitted by Jawaharlal Nehru to the All India Congress Committee on the International Congress against Imperialism held at Brussels in February 1937.
2. Interview with Nehru by someone in London on 19 February 1936 about the political situation in India (typed ms).
3. Report of a meeting arranged at 9 Guilford Place, London WC 1, on 31 January 1936, at 11 a.m. People present were Nehru, Tufuhin Moore, S.R. Wood, H. Rathbone, Lester Hutchinson, B.P. Bradley, J.R. Cambell, R. Bridgeman, Dr Bhat, Dr Vakil, Ronald Kidd, and Y.S. Ho.
4. A list of publications by Chattopadhyaya in English, Swedish, and Russian (in Chatto's own hand in Russian).
5. Various correspondence of scholars acknowledging the help and assistance they received from Chattopadhyaya.
6. Letter from D. Dombrowskaja-Liau to Chattopadhyaya, Moscow, 27 January 1936, in German.
7. A rough first draft of an article entitled 'Tactical problems of the Indian Revolution', in microfilm strip, 4 pages, dated 1 August

*At the time of consultation of these documents, in 1976, the archive was in the erstwhile German Democratic Republic

1930.
8. 'Some unpublished facts on the Egyptian National Movement', a photocopy of an article in Chattopadhyaya's own hand, written in the period 1931–7, in microfilm strip, 7 pages.
9. A handwritten draft of an article about Tibet by Chattopadhyaya in microfilm strip, 5 pages.
10. Copy of a 9-page draft of a research article in Chattopadhyaya's own hand and with his signature, in German, called 'Ueber die Bedeutung der Silbe "pu" im Wort "Punaluae"' (during the Soviet period).
11. A handwritten copy of a letter by Chattopadhyaya from Leningrad on 25 November 1936, to Susanka Sarkar of the Anthropological Laboratory, Indian Museum, Calcutta, about 'the Maler relationship terms'. 3 pages.
12. Rough draft of an article (handwritten) on 'Indo Afghans', n.d. but of the Soviet period.

E. Public Records Office, London

1. The British Foreign Office (FO) series 371 concerning world-wide activities connected with the German-Indian conspiracies from 1913 to 1922.
   FO 371. Files 2013; 2152; 2332; 2388; 2493–7; 2590; 2693; 2756; 2784; 2787; 2788; 3064; 3067; 3339; 4244; 4358; 6844; 6954; 7300; 8170.
2. FO 395 / 56
       395 / 190
       395 / 246
3. FO 628 Bangkok
       Box 31 (343)
       Box 32 (351)

F. India Office Library & Records, London

1. L/PS/10: German War
       460 Afghan neutrality
       473 Emissaries to Afghanistan/Germans in Persia
       520 German agents in China
       542 Sedition in the Far East, Siam

		544	Sedition in the Far East/Germans in China
		553	Import of arms into Siam and the Far East
2.	L/PJ/6	1338 (1524/15)	Report of the *Komagata* Maru Committee of Enquiry (Calcutta, 1914)
3.	L/PJ/6	(1458/16)	Mandalay Conspiracy Case
4.	L/PJ/6	1405 (4095/15)	The Lahore Conspiracy Case I
		(2181/16)	The Supplementary Lahore Conspiracy Case
5.	Mss. Eur. c. 138		Trial of the Ghadr Conspiracy 1917–18 USA vs. Franz Bopp et al.

G. Riksarkivet (The Archive of the Royal Ministries for Foreign Affairs, Internal Affairs, and Legal Affairs), Stockholm

Parliamentary interpellations in the Swedish Parliament: Questions put to the prime minister in the Swedish Parliament by Stockholm Mayor Carl Lindhagen on the expulsion of Chattopadhyaya from Sweden on 31 May 1921 and the prime minister's reply to them on 14 June 1921 (24 printed pages).

H. Royal Library, Stockholm

Misc. Sven Stroemgren Collection of Chattopadhyaya's books and papers in Stockholm.

Here the letter that Stroemgren wrote to the Indian envoy Padman dated 2 April 1955, from Stockholm, gives some useful information about Chattopadhyaya's political propaganda and social life in Sweden between 1917–21.

I. Stadsarkivet, Stockholm

Lindhagen Papers: Letters.

Here letters to Lindhagen from Taraknath Das, M. Acharya, Har Dayal, and V. Chattopadhyaya of the League Against Imperialism between 1916–29.

J. Det Kongelige Bibliotek, Copenhagen

Karin Michaelis Papers
Letters from Agnes Smedley to Karin Michaelis (1923–33).

K. University of Colorado at Boulder

Florence Becker Lennon Collections:
Letters from Agnes Smedley to Florence Becker Lennon between 1921–7.

L. Arkhiv Vostokovedov, St Petersburg

1. Thesis on India and the World Revolution presented to the Executive Committee of the Communist International and the Congress Commission on the Oriental Question by V. Chattopadyaya, G.A.K. Luhani, and P. Khankhoje, Moscow, July–August 1921.
2. *Zapiska Indusa Chattopadiya (iz Bengali)* (Notes from the Indian Chattopadiya) (from Bengal), Stockholm, 8 January 1920.
3. *Vospominaniya Chattopadhyaya, Virendranat Agornatovich* (Reminiscences of Virendranath Agornatovich Chattopadhyaya) by Karunovskaya, Lidiya Eduardovna. F: 138, Op. 1, No. 48.
4. *Vospominaniya* (Reminiscences) by Dalskiy, Andrey Nikolayevich. F: 138, Op. 1, No. 47.

M. Nehru Memorial Museum and Library, New Delhi: Jawaharlal Nehru Papers

1. Jawaharlal Nehru and V. Chattopadhyaya Correspondence (1928–37)
2. Jawaharlal Nehru and A.C.N. Nambiar Correspondence (1935–8)
3. Jawaharlal Nehru and Roger Baldwin Correspondence (1927–31)

II. PRIMARY PUBLISHED SOURCES

A. Government of India Publications, Calcutta

1. *Political Trouble in India (1909–1917)* by J.C. Ker of the Indian Criminal Intelligence Department, summarizing the information at the disposal of this Department on political and revolutionary agitations of the time (Calcutta, 1917).
2. *Sedition Committee (1918) Report* (Calcutta, 1918).

Bibliography   335

B. Material Preserved at the International Institute of Social History, Amsterdam

1. Published material concerning the League Against Imperialism.
   a) Invitation to the International Congress Against Colonial Oppression and Imperialism
   b) United Front in the Struggle for Emancipation of the Oppressed Nations
   c) Memorandum on Forced Labour by Willi Muenzenberg, V. Chattopadhyaya, and Emile Burns
   d) Resolution on India, Brussels Conference, 9, 10, 11 December 1927
   e) *Das Flammenzeichen vom Palais Egmont* (the official report of the Brussels Congress 10–15 February 1927)
   f) Second Anti-Imperialist World Congress 20–31 July 1928, Frankfurt-on-Main
2. Selected issues of International press correspondence (Inprecor).

C. Biographical Sketches of V. Chattopadhyaya in Russian Encyclopaedias and Other Works from Russia

1. Ja. V. Vasilyev (i.e.), *Bio-bibliograficheskiy slovar uchenykh-zhertv repressiy 1917–1991* (Bio-bibliographical dictionary of scientists, victims of the repression 1917–91).
2. A.M. Reshetov, V.A. *Chatopadaya—Indiyskiy revolyutsioner i sovietskiy etnograf* (V.A. Chatopadaya—Indian revolutionary and Soviet ethnograph), in *Kyunerovskiye chteniya, Rossiyskaya Akademiya Nauk* (Russian Academy of Sciences) (1998), pp. 148–51.
3. Leonid Mitrokhin, *A Triple Trap: Story of Three Indian Comintern Activists in the Years of Stalinist Terror, Soviet Land*, nos. 4–5 April and May 1991, pp. 30–1 and 22–3, respectively.

D. Documentary Works

1. Adhikari, G. (ed.), *Documents of the History of the Communist Party of India*, vol. 1, 1917–1922 (New Delhi, 1971).
2. Degras, Jane (ed.), *Soviet Documents on Foreign Policy*, vol. 1 (London, 1951).
3. Degras, Jane (ed.), *The Communist International 1919–1943: Documents*, vols. 1–3 (The Hague, 1956, 1960, 1965).

4. *Deutsche Dokumente zum Kriegsausbruch* (Berlin, 1927)
5. Drachkovitch, Milorad and Lazitch, Branko (eds.), *The Comintern: Historical Highlights: Essays, Recollections, Documents* (London, 1966).
6. Eudin, Xenia Joukoff and North, Robert C., *Soviet Russia and the East: 1920–1927, A Documentary Survey* (Stanford, 1957).
7. Meijer, Jan M. (ed.), *The Trotsky Papers 1917–1922* (London, 1964).
8. Norman, Dorothy (ed.), *Nehru: The First Sixty Years*, vol. 1 (London, 1965).

III. SELECTED WRITINGS OF VIRENDRANATH CHATTOPADHYAYA

1. 'Indian Anarchism in England' (letter), *The Times* (London), 1 March 1909.
2. 'Indian Anarchism' (a letter), *The Times* (London), 19 March 1909.
3. 'The Extremist Attitude' (letter), *The Times* (London), 12 July 1909.
4. 'Die Revolution in Indien', *Asien*, vol. XIV: 1916, October 1916.
5. 'Zur Lage in Indien', *Asien*, March 1917.
6. 'De sorgliga foerhallandena i Indien: Hur engelsmaennen misskoete landet i socialt och sanitaert haenseende' (The tragic relations in India: British social and sanitary mismanagement), *Nya Dagligt Allehanda*, Stockholm, 30 August 1917.
7. 'Det undertryckta Indien' (The oppressed India), *Folkets Dagblad Politiken*, 13 November 1917.
8. *En bok om England och dess Undertryckta Folk* (A book about England and her oppressed people) (ed.) (Stockholm, 1918).
9. 'Den indiska nationalkongressen' (The Indian National Congress), *Nya Dagligt Allehanda*, 2 January 1918.
10. Sjaelvstaendig regering foer Indien' (Self-supported government for India), *Nya Dagligt Allehanda*, 18 January 1918.
11. 'Indiska fragan beroerd i Brest Litowsk' (Indian question discussed in Brest Litovsk), *Stockholm Dagblad*, 24 January 1918
12. 'Englands vaelde i Indien. Indiska nationalkommitten vaedjar till Labour Partys Konferens' (British rule in India. Indian National Committee's appeal to the Labour Party Conference), *Aftonbladet*, 26 January 1918.

Bibliography 337

13. 'Allmaen skolplikt i Indien?' (General school compulsion in India), *Folkets Dagblad Politiken*, 5 February 1918.
14. 'Vad Indien kraever' (What India demands), *Klockan*, 8 February 1918.
15. 'Tagore befarar en tragisk brytning mellan oest och vaest' (Tagore fears a tragic East-West division), *Klockan*, 16 February 1918.
16. 'Nobelpristagaren Tagore om England och Indien' (Nobel Prize winner Tagore about England and India), *Stockholm Dagblad*, 17 February 1918
17. (An article against Yusuf Ali's propaganda in Sweden), *Stockholm Tidningen*, 2 May 1918.
18. 'Den indiska fragan' (The Indian question), under the pseudonym, Mohamed Ali, *Aftontidningen*, 12 May 1918.
19. (A reply to Yusuf Ali's answer to the India Committee), *Afton Tidningen*, 29 May 1918.
20. 'Konstitutionella reformplaner foer Indien. Engelska foerhoppningar om Montagus indiska resa' (Constitutional reform plans for India: British hopes in connection with Montagu's Indian trip), *Stockholm Dagblad*, 7 June 1918.
21. 'Englands stoersta kulturbragd' (England's greatest cultural deed) (a protest letter against an article in *Socialdemokraten* of 12 June 1918), *Aftonbladet*, 22 June 1918.
22. 'England och Indien: Den indiska nationalkommitténs svar' (England and India: the Indian National Committee's answer to the article 'England's greatest cultural deed'), *Svenska Morgonbladet*, 26 June 1918.
23. 'Indiska homerule roerelsen' (The Indian homerule movement) *Stockholm Dagblad*, 3 August 1918.
24. 'Det engelsk-indiska problemet' (The English-Indian problem), *Nya Dagligt Allehanda*, 3 August 1918.
25. 'Det undertryckta Indien' (The oppressed India) (protest of the Indian National Committee against the assertions of the Swedish prime minister), *Folkets Dagblad Politiken*, 13–14 October 1921.
26. 'Die erwachte Inderin' (The awakening Indian woman), *Deutsche Allgemeine Zeitung*, 29 January (?).
27. 'Die Akali Bewegung' (The Akali Movement), *Deutsche Rundschau*, July 1924.
28. 'Indiens Selbstaendigkeit: Ergebnisse des National-Kongresses' (India's self rule: Results of the Indian National Congress) (under

the pseudonym Reva Prasad Misra), *Deutsche Allgemeine Zeitung*, 7 February 1924.
29. 'Betrayers of the White Man's Cause', *Industrial and Trade Review for India*, August (first half) 1925.
30. 'The German Consul-General Again', *Industrial and Trade Review for India*, September (first half) 1925.
31. 'Das soziale Programm Mahatma Gandhis', *Aus dem Archiv fuer Politik und Geschichte* (Berlin), Sonderdruck (under pseudonym Reva Prasad Misra) (date ?).
32. *Anti-Imperialist Review* (ed.) (Berlin, July 1928).
33. 'Tactical Problem of Indian Revolution', mss. rough draft, 1 August 1930.
34. 'Unemployment in India', *Inprecor*, 6 March 1930.
35. 'The Indian Railway Strike', *The Pan-Pacific Monthly*, no. 35, April 1930.
36. 'India and the Second International', *The Pan-Pacific Monthly*, no. 37, June–July 1930.
37. 'Faked Indian Statistics as Imperialist Propaganda', *The Labour Monthly*, 12(9), September 1930.
38. 'Mac Donald's New Year "Honours" List of India: A Document of Imperialist Corruption', *Inprecor*, 8 January 1931.
39. 'The Indian National Congress', *Labour Monthly*, XIII (5), May 1931.
40. 'Timber Export and Forced Labour in the Andaman Islands', *Inprecor*, 22 October 1931.
41. 'Some unpublished facts on the Egyptian National Movement', mss. (Soviet period).
42. 'International Imperialism Arms Afghanistan', *Inprecor*, 3 December 1931.
43. 'Release the Meerut Prisoners: The Need of an International Campaign', *Inprecor*, vol. XI, 1931.
44. 'Buddhism in the Service of Japanese and British Imperialism', *The Anti-Imperialist Review*, 1 (3), January–February 1932.
45. *Marx: Poverty of Philosophy*, ed. with C.P. Dutt with notes.
46. 'Engels i Shternberg; Primechaniye k statye Engelsa "Vnov otkrytiy sluchay gruppovovo braka"' (Engels and Sternberg; a newly discovered case of group marriage) (in Russian), *Sovietskaya Etnografiya* (Soviet Ethnography), vol. 6, 1934, pp. 178–9.

Bibliography

47. Review in Russian of the book Frederick Engels, *The Origin of the Family, Private Property and the State*. Translated by Ernest Untermann, Chicago (1902). *Sovietskaya Etnografiya*, vol. 6, 1934, pp. 189–92.
48. A review article on Friedrich Engels' book *Der Ursprung der Familie, des Privateigentums und des Staates* as edited by Ladislaus Rudas in Russian, *Sovietskaya Etnografiya*, vol. 6, 1934, pp. 192–9.
49. A review article on *I.N. Vinnikov: Iz Arkhiva Lyuisa Genri Morgana* (1935) (in Russian), *Sovietskaya Etnografiya*, vol. 6, 1934, pp. 173–88.
50. 'Literatura po indiyskoy etnografii' (Literature on Indian Ethnography), *Sovietskaya Etnografiya*, vol. 3, 1936, pp. 116–21.

IV. Interviews* and Correspondence°

*1.	Dr Fritz Grobba	at his Bonn-Bad Godesberg house, July 1972
*2.	Dr W.O. von Hentig	at his house in Seiberbach, near Koblenz, July 1972
*3.	A.C.N. Nambiar	at his house in Zurich, September 1972 and March 1973
*4.	Lucie Hecht	at her house in Muehlheim (Ruhr), November 1972 and January 1973
*5.	Wilhelm von Pochhammer	at his house in Bremen, October 1973
*6.	Sven Stroemgren	at his house in Stockholm, October 1973
*7.	Dr. Thomas Hammer	at his house in Stockholm, October 1973
°8.	Rajani Palme Dutt	March 1973, London
°9.	Arthur Koestler	April 1973, London
*10.	Franz Wesendonk (son of Otto Guenther von Wesendonk)	at his house in Munich, December 1980

*interviews and correspondence
°only correspondence

*11. Aladar Wesendonk (another son of von Wesendonk from his second wife) — at his house in Munich, December 1980
*12. Graefin Margarete von Montgelas (von Wesendonk's second wife) — at her house in Munich, December 1980
°13. Allan Degerman — Uppsala, Sweden, May 1973, mostly about his contact with Har Dayal in Sweden
°14. Dr Bernhard Hegards — Svanesund, Sweden, May 1973, mostly about his contact with Har Dayal in Sweden
°15. Elmo Stiller (son of Gustav Bernhard Stiller) — Stockholm, November 1973 and January 1980, mostly about his father's relationship with Har Dayal and the Berlin India Committee
°16. K. S. Hirleker — Bombay, August 1973

V. CONTEMPORARY NEWSPAPERS AND MAGAZINES (SELECTED)

Aftonbladet (Stockholm)
Afton Tidningen (Stockholm)
The Anti-Imperialist Review (Berlin)
Asien (Berlin)
Berliner Lokal-Anzeiger
Berliner Neueste Nachrichten
Berliner Tageblatt
The Bombay Chronicle
Civil and Military Gazette (Lahore)
The Daily Telegraph (London)
Dagens Nyheter (Stockholm)
Deutsche Allgemeine Zeitung
Deutsche Rundschau
Dresdner Neueste Nachrichten
The Englishman (Calcutta)
Folkets Dagblad Politiken (Stockholm)
Free Hindustan (New York)
The Free Press Journal (Bombay)

Geopolitik (Munich)
Hamburgischer Correspondent
The Indian Annual Register (Delhi ?)
Indo-German Commercial Review (Berlin)
Industrial and Trade Review for India (Berlin)
International Press Correspondence (Moscow)
The Labour Monthly (London)
Leipziger Neueste Nachrichten
Liberty (Calcutta)
Manchester Guardian
Modern Review (Calcutta)
Der Neue Orient (Berlin)
Pan-Pacific Monthly (Australia)
The People (Lahore)
Proceedings of the Central Asian Society (London)
Pro-India (Zurich)
The Statesman (Calcutta)
Stockholm Tidningen
Svenska Morgonbladet (Stockholm)
The Times (London)
The Times of India (Bombay)

VI. SECONDARY REFERENCES: SELECT PUBLISHED WORKS

Baig, Tara Ali	*Sarojini Naidu* (New Delhi, 1974)
Balfour, M.	*The Kaiser and His Times* (London, 1964)
Banaji, J.	'Comintern and Indian Nationalism', in K.N. Panikkar (ed.), *National and Left Movements in India* (New Delhi, 1980)
Barooah, N.K.	*India and the Official Germany 1886–1914* (Frankfurt/Berne, 1977)
–	'Berlin Indians, the Bolshevik Revolution and Indian Politics 1917–1930', *My World* (April 1978)
–	'When the Kaiser's Heart Bled for the Indians', *My World* (November 1978)
–	'German Attitudes Towards India Before 1914', *My World* (Germany, August 1979)
–	'When Afghanistan Was Independent and

	India Under Foreign Rule', *My World* (April 1980)
–	'Why "Max Mueller Bhawans" In India Ought Not To Be Called So', *My World* (December 1980)
–	'Har Dayal And The German Connection', *Indian Historical Review*, VII (1–2), January 1981
–	'Virendranath Chattopadhyaya in Stockholm 1917–1921', *Mainstream* (New Delhi), 1, 8, and 15 March 1986
–	'Germany and Indian Nationalism after World War I: Nehru–Subhas' Moves for Indo-German Cooperation (1927–38), *Mainstream*, 38 (12), 11 March 2000
Von Bernhardi, Friedrich	*Germany and the Next War* (London, 1911)
Boersner, D.	*The Bolsheviks and the National and Colonial Question (1917–1928)* (Paris, 1957)
Bose, A.C.	*Indian Revolutionaries Abroad 1905–1922* (Patna, 1971)
Brown, E.C.	*Har Dayal: Hindu Revolutionary and Rationalist* (New Delhi, 1975)
Brown, G.T.	'The Hindu Conspiracy 1914–17', *Pacific Historical Review*, vol. XVII, no. 3, August 1948
Buber-Neumann, Margarete	*Von Potsdam nach Moskau: Stationen eines Irrweges* (Stuttgart, 1958)
Carr, E.H.	*German-Soviet Relations between the two World Wars 1919–1939* (Baltimore, 1951)
–	*The Bolshevik Revolution 1917–1923*, vols. I, II, and III (London, 1950, 1952, 1953)
–	*A History of Soviet Russia: The Interregnum 1923–1924* (London, 1954)
–	*A History of Soviet Russia: Socialism in one country 1924–1926* (London, 1958)
–	*The Twilight of Comintern, 1930–1935* (London, 1982)
Chirol, V.	'Pan-Islamism', in *Proceedings of the Central*

Bibliography

	Asian Society (London, 1906)
Churchill, R.P.	*The Anglo-Russian Convention of 1907* (Iowa, 1939)
Dahrendorf, R.	*Society and Democracy in Germany* (New York, 1967)
Datta Gupta, S.	*Comintern, India and the Colonial Question 1920–37* (Calcutta, 1980)
Dayal, Har	*Forty-Four Months in Germany and Turkey* (London, 1920)
Deutscher, I.	*The Prophet armed Trotsky: 1879–1921* (London, 1954)
Dignan, Don.	*The Indian Revolutionary Problem in British Diplomacy 1914–1919* (New Delhi, 1983)
Drachkovitch, M.M. (ed.)	*The Revolutionary Internationals, 1864–1943* (Stanford, 1966)
Druhe, D.N.	*Soviet Russia and Indian Communism* (New York, 1959)
Dutta, B.N.	*Aprakashita Rajnaitik Itihas* (unpublished Political History), vol. II, (2nd edition, Calcutta, n. d.)
Engels, F.	*Der Ursprung der Familie, des Privateigenthums und des Staats* (Berlin, 1946)
European Central Committee of the Indian Nationalists	*Roger Casement und Indien* (Stockholm, 1917)
Finsod, Merle	*International Socialism and the World War* (2nd edition, New York, 1966)
Fischer, Fritz	*Germany's Aims in the First World War* (New York, 1967)
Fraser, T.G.	'Germany and the Indian Revolution 1914–18', in *Journal of Contemporary History*, 12(2), April 1977
–	'The Sikh problem in Canada and its political consequences, 1905–1921', in *The Journal of Imperial and Commonwealth History*, vol. VII, October, 1978
–	'India in Anglo-Japanese Relations During the First World War', in *History*, 63 (209),

Gandhi, Sonia (ed.) October 1978
Freedom's Daughter: Letters between Indira Gandhi and Jawaharlal Nehru 1922–39 (London, 1989)

Gankin, Olga Hess and Fischer, H.H. *The Bolsheviks and the World War: The Origins of the Third International* (California, 1960)

Gehrke, U. *Persien in der deutschen Orientpolitik waehrend des I. Weltkrieges* (Stuttgart, 1960)

Geisel, Beatrix 'Willi Muenzenberg: Gegen Oeffentlichkeit', in *Publizistik & Kunst*, nos. 6, 7, 8, and 9, 1990

Gilbert, M. *Britain and Germany between the Wars* (London, 1966)

Von Glasenapp, H. *Meine Lebensreise* (Wiesbaden, 1964)

Gopal, S. *Jawaharlal Nehru: A Biography*, vol. 1 (Delhi, 1975)

Gross, Babette L. *Willi Muenzenberg: Eine Politische Biographie* (Stuttgart, 1967)

Hagenbeck, John *Unter der Sonne Indiens* (Leipzig, 1926)

Haithcox, J.P. *Communism and Nationalism In India: M.N. Roy and Comintern Policy 1920–1939* (Princeton, 1971)

Hammar, Thomas *Sverige at svenskarna: Invandringspolitik utlanningskontroll och asylrat 1900–1932* (Stockholm)

Hitler, Adolf *Mein Kampf* (8th Jaico impression, New Delhi, 1998)

Indian Nationalist Committee (ed.) *Some American Opinions on British Rule in India* (Stockholm, 1917)

– *The International Socialist Congress: Speeches and Resolutions on India* (Berlin, 1917)

Indian Nationalist Party (ed.) *British Rule in India: Condemned by the British Themselves* (London, 1915)

International Publishers (ed.) *The Woman Question: Selections from the Writings of Karl Marx, Frederick Engels, V.I. Lenin, Joseph Stalin* (New York, 1951)

	Internationaler Sozialisten-Kongress Stuttgart 1907 vom 18. bis 24. August (Berlin, 1907)
Jensen, J.M.	'The "Hindu Conspiracy": A Reassessment', *Pacific Historical Review*, XLVIII (1), February 1979
Johnston, Hugh	*The Voyage of the Komagata Maru: The Sikh Challenge to Canada's Colour Bar* (Delhi, 1979)
Keer, D.	*Veer Savarkar* (Bombay, 1966)
Kennen, G.F.	*Russia and the West under Lenin and Stalin* (Boston, 1961)
Kohn, Hans	*The Mind of Germany* (New York, 1960)
Kozma, Ferdinand	'Indische Agitation gegen England' in *Neues Pester Journal* (Budapest, 31 May 1917)
Krueger, H.	'Har Dayal in Deutschland', in *Mitteilungen des Instituts fuer Orientforschung*, vol. X (Berlin, 1964)
–	'Zum Einfluss internationaler Faktoren auf die Herausbildung und Entwicklung der anti-imperialistischen Haltung Jawaharlal Nehrus', in E.N. Komarov et al. (eds.), *Politik und Ideologie im gegenwaertigen Indien*, Akademie der Wissenschaften der DDR, Band 36 (Berlin, 1976)
Landauer, C.	*European Socialism* (California, 1959)
Lazitch, B. and Drachkovitch, M.M.	*Lenin and the Comintern* (vol. I) (Stanford, 1972)
Lenin, V.I.	*On the National and Colonial Questions: Three Articles* (Peking, 1970)
–	*The Awakening of Asia* (Moscow, 1973)
–	*The National Liberation Movement in the East* (Moscow, 1974)
–	*On Imperialism and Imperialists* (Moscow, 1973)
MacKinnon, Janice R. and Stephen R. McInnes, N.	*Agnes Smedley: The Life and Times of an American Radical* (Berkeley, 1988) 'The Labour Movement' in A.J. Toynbee, (ed.), *The Impact of the Russian Revolution 1917–1967* (London, 1967)

Majumdar, R.C.	*History of the Freedom Movement in India* (vol. II) (Calcutta, 1963)
Mayer, A.J.	*Political Origins of the New Diplomacy 1917–18* (New Haven, 1959)
Mikusch, D.V.	*Wassmuss, der deutsche Lawrence* (Leipzig, 1937)
Nambiar, A.C.N.	'The Story of My Arrest in Berlin: India and Germany Today', *The Free Press Journal* (Bombay, 6 May 1933)
Nehru, Jawaharlal	*An Autobiography* (London, 1949)
Persits, M.A.	*Revolyutsionery Indii v Strane Sovietov 1918 - 1921* (Revolutionaries of India in the country of the Soviets 1918–1921) (Moscow, 1973)
Pratap, M. (Raja)	*My Life Story of Fifty-five Years* (Delhi, 1947)
–	'My German Mission to High Asia: How I joined the Kaiser to enlist Afghanistan against Great Britain', in *Asia*, 15(5), May 1925
Rai, Lajpat	*Young India* (New York, 1917)
–	*Autobiographical Writings* (ed. by V.C. Joshi) (Delhi, 1965)
zu Reventlow, Graf E.	*Indien–Seine Bedeutung fuer Grossbritannien, Deutschland und die Zukunft der Welt* (Berlin, 1917)
Ryss, P.	'Stockholm Indians' in *Rech*, reproduced in *Der Neue Orient*, vol. II (Berlin, 1918)
Roy, M.N.	*M.N. Roy's Memoirs* (Bombay, 1964)
Sehanavis, Chinmohan	*Rush Biplab O Prabashi Bharatiya Biplabi* (The Russian Revolution and Indian Revolutionaries Abroad) (Bengali) (Calcutta, 1973)
Sengupta, P.	*Sarojini Naidu: A Biography* (New Delhi, 1974)
Smedley, Agnes	'Indische Frau von gestern und heute', in *Frau: Monatsschrift fuer das gesamte Frauenleben unserer Zeit*, 32 (1924), pp. 239– 44, 279 83

–	'India's Role in World Politics', *Modern Review*, 37 (5) (May 1925), pp. 530–41
–	'Die Frau in Indien', in *Neue Zuericher Zeitung*, 12 August 1925
–	'Indien als entscheidender Faktor der Weltpolitik', in *Zeitschrift fuer Geopolitik*, 2(6) (June 1925), pp. 385–403
–	'Germany's Artist of Social Misery', *Modern Review*, 38 (2) (August 1925), pp. 148–55
–	'Indiens nationale Fuehrerin', *Deutsche Allgemeine Zeitung*, 31 December 1925
–	'Indiens Fuehrerin', *Frau im Staat: Eine Monatsschrift*, 8 (4), 1926, pp. 2–5
–	'Indiens Dichterin', *Berliner Tageblatt*, 4 September 1926
–	'Indians in European Zoological Gardens', *The People*, 3 (10), 5 September 1926, pp. 202–4
–	'Denmark's Creative Women', *Modern Review*, 40 (1) July 1926, pp. 61–6; no. 2, August 1926, pp. 149–53; 3 September 1926, pp. 265–68; 4 October 1926, pp. 366–71
–	'Dr Helena Lange', *Modern Review*, 41 (5), May 1927, pp. 566–72
–	*Daughter of Earth* (Feminist Press edition) (New York, 1973)
–	*China Correspondent* (Pandora edition) (London, 1984)
Sykes, Ch.	*Wassmuss, The German Lawrence* (London, 1936)
Tagore, Rabindranath	'Choto O Boro' in *Rabindra Rachanavali*, vol. 24
Taylor, A.J.P.	*The First World War: An Illustrated History* (London, 1963)
Trumpener, Ulrich	*Germany and the Ottoman Empire 1914–1918* (Princeton University Press, 1968)
Tschiedel, Johannes	'Englands indische Sorge', *Berliner Tageblatt*, 6 March 1914

348 Chatto

Tuchman, Barbara — *The Zimmermann Telegram* (New York, 1958)
Vira, D. — *Lala Har Dayal and Revolutionary Movement of his Times* (New Delhi, 1970)
Yajnik, I. — *Shymamaji Krishnavarma: Life and Times of an Indian Revolutionary* (Bombay, 1950)
Jeman, Z.A.B. — *Germany and the Revolution in Russia 1915–1918* (London, 1958)

Index

Abhinav Bharat, 12–14, 29
Acharya, M. P. T., a member of Savarkar's group in London, 13; his life before coming to London, 14; goes to Berlin from the U. S., 52; member Suez Canal Mission, 66; in Constantinople, 73–4; accompanies Chatto to Stockholm, 101, 116, 126; in Soviet Union, 158
Addison, J., 193
Ahmed, M., one of the earliest members of Oppenheim's India Committee, 43; meets Wesendonk with Chatto and Kersasp, 50; becomes leader of the Baghdad Mission, 70–3
Aiyar, V. V. S., 13–14, 23, 28
Ali, Dawood (P. N. Dutta), 46
Ali, Mohamed, 271–2
Ali, Rajab, 66, 70
Ali Baker, M., 241
Alvord, B., 303
Amin, Govind, 29
Anjuman-e-Akhwan-us-Safa, 9
Annie Larsen, the, 77
Ansari, Dr., 271
Anti-Duehring, 292, 299
Archer, W., 127
Arne, Ture, 113
Avanti, the, 267

Bachoven, J., 298
Baghdad Mission, the, 65–74

Baig, Tara Ali, 9
Bakhale, R. R., 270
Balabanoff (Balabanova), Angelica, 106, 114, 161, 168
Baldwin, R., 253, 256, 262
Balmokand, S., 25
Banerjee, Surendranath, 3, 20, 21
Barakatullah, M., biog. 92 n. 1; his paper *Islamic Fraternity*, 39; proposes Muslims' common cause with Germany, 39–40; in Pratap-Hentig Mission to Kabul, 63; and the idea of provisional government of India, 64; in Soviet Union 158
Baranikov, A. P., 306
Barbusse, H., 253
Bashhamba, Ali Bey, 39, 72, 74
Beard, C., 228
Becker, Dr., 63
Beckett, W. R. D., 77
Bell, J., 162
Bennett, Sir Courtenay, 78
Berkman, A., 231
Bernhardi, General F. von, his *Germany and the Next War*, 37
Bernstorff, Count J. von, 75, 83
Bertoni, L., 135
Bey, Faud, 74
Bey, Kazim, 63
Bhattacharya, Abinash, biog. 40 and n. 30; tries with Chatto for German-Indian revolutionary collaboration, 40–1; in Oppenheim's India Committee, 43

Bleek, Wilhelm, 200
Bloor, E. R., 231
Boas, Franz, his *The Mind of Primitive Man*, 225–6; Phinney's American teacher, 307
Boehm, G. P., 78
Bogoraz, V. G., 289
Borghi, A., 267
Borodin, M., 161, 162
Bose, P. B., 227
Bose, R. B. (Thakur), 82
Bose, Subhas C., 64, 273, 274–5
Bowder, Earl, 231
Branting, K. H., 101, 126 133
Brest Litovsk, 108, 109, 111, 113
Briess, E. E., 73
Bridgeman, R., 253
Brockway, F., 251, 270
Brooks, A., 118
Bryan, W. J., 118, 120
Buber-Neumann, Margarete, 253, 267, 324
Bukharin, N., 288

Cama, Madame B., associates with Krishnavarma and 'India House', 11; publishes *The Talvar*, 22; early background of, 24–5; publishes *Bande Mataram* from Paris, 24, 39; interned in Paris, 42; attends Stuttgart Congress of 2d International, 101
Capital, 299
Carnegie, A., 118
Casement, R., 118
Chakravarty, C. K., 82–6; on Chatto, 90
Chamanlal, 270
Chamberlain, A., 127
Chandra, Harish, 88, 91–2
Chatterton, Mr & Mrs., 11
Chattopadhyaya, Aghorenath, 7–10, 26
Chattopadhyaya, Harindranath, 8

Chattopadhyaya, Mrinalini, 7–8
Chattopadhyaya, Ranendranath, 8
Chattopadhyaya, Suhasini, 8, 190
Chattopadhyaya, Sunalini, 8,
Chattopadhyaya, Virendranath (Chatto) 1, 2, 5; childhood and education in India, 7; father's legacy in, 9–10; studies law in London, 10–11; contributes to journals on linguistics, 11; collaborates with B. C. Pal in England, 15; debates with Krishnavarma in *The Times*, 16–20; friendship with Savarkar, 20; expulsion from Middle Temple for seditious views, 21–2; extols revolutionary nationalism as editor of Madame Cama's *Talvar*, 22; accepts Krishnavarma's scholarship, 23; arrives in Paris, 24; tries to smuggle arms to India from Paris, 25–6; and *L'affaire Savarkar*, 26; remains close to *L'Humanité* circle in Paris, 27; helps Egyptian nationalists in Paris, 27, 28; arrives in Germany, 29; involves in German plans concerning India, 40–1; helps Oppenheim in Indian revolutionary cause, 43–4; meets Har Dayal in Geneva, 49–50; submits memorandum to Wesendonk for direct link with A.A., 50–2; brings 'Oppenheim India Committee' under Indian control, 52–4; persuades Har Dayal and Mahendra Pratap to come to Berlin, 53–4; visits Constantinople to supervise India Committee's work, 71–3; takes measures reg. British spy E. E. Briess, 73; is impressed with Kraft's plan, 79; supports Chandra Chakravarty in U. S., 82–7; assessment of his leadership in

revolutionising attempts, 87–92; Zimmermann writes to, 91; arrives in Stockholm, 101; tries for Indian representation at proposed Socialist Peace Conference, 102 ff; in Stockholm associates with the Finns, the Poles, the Hungarians etc., 103; establishes contact with *Dagens Nyheter*, 103; establishes 'European Central Committee of Indian Nationalists' in Stockholm, 105; greets 'United Muslim Congress' of All Russian Muslim Council at Petrograd, 105; keeps close contact with Zimmerwaldians, 106; negotiates with Troyanovsky for Indo-Russian collaboration, 107–13; complains about non-existence of German official announcement on Indian self-rule, 111; feels diffident about Indo-Russian collaboration from Russia, 113; starts vigorous anti-British propaganda from Stockholm, 116–25; faces British reaction, 125–42; attacks British Indian agent Yusuf Ali in Swedish press, 127–32; jeers at Branting, 133–4; is debarred from political propaganda in Sweden, 134–5; the British fail to get him out of Sweden, 126–7; escapes British plot to kill him in Switzerland, 136–7; Sommerset Maugham spies on and makes him a character of his story, 137; is refused visa to return to Sweden, 138; Lindhagen defends him in Swedish parliament, 138–41; visits Moscow with his Berlin colleagues and submits his 'Thesis on India and the World Revolution' to Comintern, 160–2; fails to get Comintern support, 167–70; and Roy, 170–2; founds 'The Indian News Service and Information Bureau' in Berlin, 178; suffers British and German harassments and poisoning plot, 188; edits anti-British *Indo-German Commercial Review* and *Industrial and Trade Review for India*, 189; escapes Anglo-German plot to transport him to India, 191–5; attacks German racial trade policy, 195–207; criticizes Hagenbeck's 'Indian Show', 207–10; Lucie Hecht's appraisal of, 214; his life with Smedley, 229–42; in League Against Imperialism as one of its two Joint Secretaries, 246–50; his relations with J. Nehru, 253–66; Krishna Hatheesing on, 254–5; Emma Goldman on his anarchism, 267; writes polemical articles on Comintern line, 268–76; criticizes Gandhi's conception of Indian independence, 270; makes uncharitable remarks on S. Naidu, 271; criticizes V. J. Patel, 271; calls Subhas Bose fascist, 274; leaves for Soviet Union and feels insecure, 283–4; Kirov takes him to Leningrad with academic posting, 285–6; guides MOPR work in Leningrad 287; becomes specialist ethnographer in Leningrad, popularises Marxism-Leninism in academic research, 288–97; receives Russian citizenship, 297–8; on British Fabian Society and anti-revolutionary sociologists, 290–1; on national fascism in Germany, 293–4; on Anglo-Dutch-American missions, 294–5; on English functionalists, 295; on Magars, Zulus, Ho and Santhals, 295–6; establishes that Engels' *The Origin of the Family* is not based on

Morgan's Ancient Society, 299; on progressive liberalism of W. P. Garrison, 301–2; on racial linguistic arrogance of R. G. White, 302; extols J. N. Powell, 303; on Benjamin Alvord's attitude to Red Indians, 303; on origin of exogamy and totemism, 304–5; publishes bibliographical article 'Literature of Indian Ethnography', 305; writes on Indian terms to mark the gender, 305; writes on 'Indo-Afghan' and Tibet, 305; writes on Maler kinship system, 305; writes on system of relationship in the Veda, 305; prepares another review of Vinnikov's work on relationship through marriage, 305; applies for professorship at Leningrad Institute of Oriental Studies, 306; receives degree of 'Candidate of Sciences' (Doctor of Philosophy) from Academy of Sciences, USSR, 306; supervises studies of the American Red Indian Archie Phinney 306–8; his biography in commemoration volume on Soviet scientists in 1998, 309; marries L. Karunovskaya, 318; discusses with Muenzenberg and Clemens Dutt in Moscow about his problems, 318–19; gets assignments to edit various language editions of Engels' *The Origin of the Family*, 319; police raids apartment of, 320; gets death sentence and is executed, 321; his relationship with Kirov, 322–4; is posthumously rehabilitated by Soviet Union, 324; ignored by Nehru dynasty and India, 324–5

Chedli, Mustaph, 253

Chiang-Kai-Shek, 248
Chicherin, G., 158, 168
Chirol, V., 135
Cleveland, C. R., 4
Cotton, Sir Henry, defends Indian nationalism, 21; expresses critical views on British in India, 119
Congress, International Anti-Colonial, in Brussels, 248–50; India and China in, 250–3; and J. Nehru, 248–50
Crerar, J., 194

D'Abernon, Lord, 179, 186, 192
Dagens Nyheter, the, Chatto's earliest contact with, 103; Taraknath Das-Gilbert Murray controversy in, 125–6
Dalskiy, A. N., on Kirov's generosity towards Chatto, 287; on Chatto's academic and party work at IAE, 287–8; on Chatto's writings, 288; on Chatto's popularity among students, 306 ff
Darwin, C., 298
Das, H. C., 14, 24
Das, Taraknath, arrives in Berlin, 52; member, Berlin Committee's Suez Canal Mission, 66; clashes with Gilbert Murray in *Dagens Nyheter*, 125; and Agnes Smedley, 227; attacked by Chatto for his opinion about Japan, 274–5
Dasgupta, B. N., 66, 73, 161
Daughter of Earth, 240
Davis, S. O., 250
Dayal Har, reputation as a revolutionary, 1; connection with Savarkar and 'India House', 13; his academic brilliance, 13; edits Cama's *Bande Mataram*, 24; and Egyptian nationalists in Paris, 27; on Krishnavarma, 28; his contact with the official Germans in

Geneva, 42–3; arrives at Constantinople for Afghanistan expedition, 43; and Wassmuss, 46–7; Wangenheim's opinion of, 47–8; goes to Berlin to join the India Committee, 53; is assigned to supervise India Committee's activities in Ottoman Empire from Constantinople, 67; loses interest in India Committee's work, 67–8; antagonises both his colleagues and Indian Muslims in Constantinople, 68–70; in Briess' letter to Pillai, 73; goes to Stockholm only to part with India Committee, 110
de Haas, W., 205
Delbrueck, C., 40
Delbrueck, H., 40
Delhi Manifesto, 264
Demoule, F. T., 126
Dengel, P., 318
Dering, H., 81
Dhingra, M., 3, 13, 14, 15
Dialectics of Nature, 299
Digby, W., 119
Diehn, 80
Dimitrov, G., 283, 284, 318 and n. 15 biog
Djember, the, 78
Dominion Status, Chatto castigates Nehru on, 264–6
Duchésne, Mme, 253
Dufour, Ambassador, 194–5
Durieux, Tilla, 240
Dutch-Scandinavian Socialist Committee, 101–2
Dutt, Clemens, 319
Dutt, R. P., 319
Dutta, B. N., arrives in Berlin from U. S., 52; accompanies Chatto to Constantinople, 73; writes to poet Tagore, 89; joins Chatto to Moscow, 160–1; Pruefer's sympathy for, 186

Ecks, 81
Einstein, A., 206, 253, 262
Elliot, C., 21
Engels, F., his *The Origin of the Family, Private Property and the State*, 288 ff; his article on Shternberg, 289; on North Indian Magars, 295–6; his use of the terms 'India', 'Deccan' and 'Hindustan', 296–7
Etnograficheskoye Obozreniye, 290

Fimmen, E., 253, 262
Fitzmaurice, 135
Folkets Dagblad Politiken, the, 123; publishes Chatto's full-page article 'Bloody, violent policy of Great Britain in India' on 1857 celebration day, 137–8; publishes Chatto's accuses against Sydow, 141–2
'Friends of Freedom for India', 229
Fuller, B., 21

Gadar Party, Gadarites, 74–82
Gandhi, Indira, 2
Gandhi, Mahatma, 1, 7, 257, 258, 276
Garrison, W. P., 301–2
Gehrmann, Dr., 80
Geissler, Consul General, 42, 46, 50
German Ideology, the, 299
Ghose, S., 227–8
Gosh, Aurobindo, 9, 17
Gibarty, L. (Wladislaw Dobos), 247
Gilchrist, D. G., 298
Glasenapp, H. von, 134, 208
Goldman, Emma, 231, 240; on Chatto, 267
Goltz, General von der, 38, 72
Gomez, M., 255
Gorky, M., 106

Grifford, 294
Grobba, F., 212
Gross, Babette, 247, 250, 267
Gullick, D., 136
Gumerus, H., 113, 127
Gupta, H. L., goes to Berlin from U. S., 52; early life, 76; goes back to US as Berlin Committee's representative, 76; meets Jacobsen and Wehde, 77–8; in Japan, 82; is replaced by C. K. Chakravarty as Berlin Committee's representative, 82; Bernstorff's opinion of, 83; arrested in U. S., 86
Gupta, Nalini, 161

Habibullah, Amir, 63–4
Haensing, W., 81
Hafis, Abdul, 70, 136
Hagenbeck, J., 208, 211, 212
Han-sin, Liau, 253
Hardie, J. Keir, 118
Harris, W. T., 118
Hatheesing, Krishna (Nehru), 254–5
Hatta, Mohamed, 253
Hearst, W. R., 118
Hecht, Lucie, 214; on Chatto, 214
Hedin, S., 39
Heinemann, F., 41
Henderson Dowgalsky Agreement, 284
Henry S, the, 78
Hentig, W. O. von, 63, 64
'Hind National Agency', 20
'Hindustan Association' (Berlin), 213
Hitler, A., his remarks on Indians, 213; against weakening British hold on India, 284
Hirtzel, Sir Arthur, 194
Hoglund, Z., 113
Hohenlohe, Ambassador, 67
Hornaday, W. T., his *The Extermination of the American Bison*, 304
Howard, Sir Esmy, 104

Howsin, Hilda M., 68, 136
Huysmans, C., 101, 102
Hydari, Sir Akbar, 10
Hyndman, H. M., 118, 120

Igel, W. von, 83
'Indian News Service and Information Bureau', the formation of, 178; in Lucie Hecht's reminiscences, 214
'India House' (London), 11–15
Indian Sociologist, the, 11
Indo-German Commercial Review, 189, 191
Industrie- und Handelszeitung, 200–6
Industrial and Trade Review for India, the, 189, 201, 205
Innes, Sir Charles, 199

Jacobsen, 78
Jaeckh, E., 43
Jaehnigen, 81
James, Langford, 260
Jaurès, Jean, 26
Jehan-i-Islam, the, 39
Jessen, 80
Johnstone, W. J., 257
Joshi, N. M., 270, 272
Joshi, S. C., 272

Kaiser, Wilhelm II, 34, 35, 63
Kabadi, S., 276
Karunovskaya, L., on Chatto's early anxieties in Soviet Union, 285; on Chatto's academic writings, 288–9; on Chatto's popularity with students, 306, 322; her relationship with Chatto, 314–22; on Chatto's simple living and hard work, 316; on Chatto's kindheartedness, 316–7; marries Chatto, 318; on Chatto's later anxieties, 318; loses her job after Chatto's execution and reinstated, 320–1; approaches N. Khrushchev

about Chatto, 321; gets false official information about Chatto, 321; records her tribute to Chatto, 321–2
Katayama, S., 251, 255
Kaul, M. N., 43
Kennard, Sir Coleridge, 135
Kersasp, H., 43, 49, 65
Khankhoje, P., 65, 161
Kheiri, A. J., and his *Hind-Ikhwat-ul-Islam Anjumani*, 69–70; attends suppressed Muslims' Conference in Stockholm, 124
Kheiri, A. S., 69–70, 124
Khrushchev, N. S., 321
Kienthal Conference, 100
Kingsford, D. H., 14
Kirov, S. M., 285, 322–4
Knipping, Consul General, 77, 80; comments on the Indian revolutionaries, 81–2
Kol, van, 101, 120
Kollwitz, Kaethe, 236, 240, 241
Komagata Maru, the, 51 and n. 99, 88
Kopp, V., 158
Kraft, G. V., 79–80
Krasnodembsky, V. E., 306
Kreuz-Zeitung, the, 35
Krishnavarma, Shyamaji, 3; his Indian Home Rule Society and its mouthpiece *Indian Sociologist*, 11; his India House hostel and its prominent guests, 11; his scholarships to politicians and patriotic Indian students, 11; his kind of nationalism and INC, 12; inmates of his India House during Savarkar's time, 13–14; his controversy with Chatto in *The Times*, 15–20; patches up with Chatto and offers him scholarship, 23; Har Dayal's opinion of, 28; Chatto dissuades Oppenheim to invite him to Berlin, 88

Krober, 294
Kun, Bela, 168

La Follette, R. M., 118
Lahiri, J. N., 52
Lal, Sohan, 81
Lansbury, G., 251
Lassow, von, 72
Latta, R. K., 52, 65
Ledeburg, G., 252
Lekomtsev, I. M., 306
Lenin, V. I., 101, 108, 109, 168, 284, 288, 290, 295
Lennon, Florence, 228, 230, 233, 235, 236
Liberty, the, 274
Liebknecht, K., 228
Lindhagen, C., 106, 123, 124, 125, 138–40
Litvinov, M. M., 158
Lohia, R. M., 276
Longuet, M. J., his legal intervention in Savarkar's case, 26, 27
Louis, R., 300
Lowie, 294
Luhani, G. A. K., 161, 163, 322 and n. 36
Lunacharsky, A., 109
Luxburg, Count Karl Ludwig von, 37
Luxemburg, R., 228

MacDonald, R., 118, 119, 252, 264
Maine, H., 298
Maltzan, Baron von, 191, 193, 194
Maniktala Conspiracy Case, 14
Manuilsky, D., 261–2, 284
Marathey, N. S., 75
Marteaux, A., 253
Martha, the, 138
Martin, Montgomery, 119
Matorin, N. M., 286
Maugham, S., 137; his story on Chatto 137
Maverick, the, 77

Maxton, J., 253, 263, 267
Meerut Conspiracy Cases, 260–1
Mensheviks, the, 106
Mertens, W., 43
Meshchaninov, I. I., 307
Metternich, Ambassador, 72
Michaelis, Karin, 237–9
Mitter, K. K., 25
Mitrokhin, L., 321
Mohammed, Ata, 70
Moller, G., 101, 103. 140
Moltke, General H. von, Chief of the General Staff, 38
Monroe, Thomas, 119
MOPR, 158
Morgan, L. H., 291, 294, 296, 297, 298 and n. 59, 300–1
Mueller, H., 43, 44
Muenzenberg, W., 246–50, 253, 318, 319
Mukherji, Abani, 161, 319, 322 and n. 36
Mukherji, J., 77
Murray, G., 125
Muzaffarpore bomb blast, 14

Nabokov, M. M., 115
Nachrichtenstelle fuer den Orient (Information Service for the Orient) 44, 53 and n. 107, 69
Nadolny, 79
Naidu, J., 248, 276
Naidu, S., 7–10, 271
Nambiar, A. C. N., 190, 206, 209–10
Nambiar, Suhasini, 190
Naoroji, Dadabhai, 119
Nasik Conspiracy Case, 14
Nassarullah, brother of Amir of Afghanistan, 64
Nath, K., 52, 65
Nayik, K., 65, 73, 74
Nehru, J.,X; procures grant from INC for Berlin's Indian Information Bureau, 214; attends the Brussels Congress, 248–53; in executive of League Against Imperialism, 253; his relations with Chatto, 253–266; cedes his and INC's connection with Chatto and LAI, 266; ignores to rescue Chatto from obscurity, 324–5
Nehru, Krishna (see Hatheesing)
Nehru, M., 257, 260
Nerman, Ture, 106, 113, 123
Neumann, H., 253, 324
Niedermayer, Capt., 63
Nikolayev, L., 324
Nimipu, tribe and language, 308

Oldenburg, S. F., 285
Ollen, J. M., 131–2
On the Critique of Political Economy, 299
Oppenheim, Baron M. von, biog. 38 and n. 15; propounds revolutionising India for German war purpose, 38–9; helps Indians from U. S. and other places come to Berlin for preparing revolution in India 43–4; shows paternalistic attitude to Indians, 43–4; opens an office for his 'India Committee', 44–5; is against Indians' 'direct contact' with German Foreign Office, 54; dissuades Indians from propaganda in holy places in Arabia, 67
'Oren', 77
Origin of the Family Private Property and the State, the, 288–97, 299
Otto, R., 48

Pal, B. C., 1, 2, 9, 12, 15, 18, 19, 20, 23
Papen, Capt. F. von, 75, 77, 78
Pasha, Envar, 39, 41, 63, 67
Patel, V. J., 260, 266
Pavlovich, M., 27

Peters, L., 247
Petrie, D., 81
Phinney, A., 306–8, 318
Pieck, W., 318
Pillai, Champakraman, 43, 73, 284
Pochhammer, W. von, against Indian nationalism, 199–200; scepticism about Indians, 203, 205–6
Politt, H., 251, 255
Powell, J. W., 303
Prabhakar, M., 43
Pratap, M., 53, 63, 64, 158
Pruefer, C., 186–7
publications of Berlin Committee, 118

Qayyum, Abdul, 9
Quadt, Baron A. von, 41
Quelch, T., 161

Rab, Abdur, 158
Radcliff-Brown, 294
Radek, K., 106, 161, 168, 169
Radowitz, Chargé d'Affaires, Constantinople, 73
Rai, Lala L., 1, 11, 12, 13, 42, 88, 92, 122, 211
Rakosi, M., 162
Ram Chandra, 68
Rana, S. R., 11, 24, 28, 29, 42
Rao, Shiva, 270
Rappoport, C., 27
Rech, the, 106
Regendanz, H. K., 43
Remy, E., 80, 89
Reshetov, A. M., on Chatto, 305–6
Reventlow, Count, 191
Reynolds, Miss, 28
Richthofen, Baron H. von, 186, 193, 194
Ridout, Major-General D., 80
Riezler, K., 109
Rifaat, M., 28, 42, 73
Rivera, D., 253
Roehr, W., 63

Romberg, Baron von, 136
Rosenberg, M., 250
Roy, M. N. (Martin), 2, 77, 80, 161, 162, 186–87, 227, 276, 288; Roy and Chatto, 170–2
Roy, Tarachand, 213
Rudas, L., 293–6
Ruedt, Baron von Collenberg-Boedingheim, career before Indian posting, 179; relation with British officials in India, 179–80; assessment of Indian movement 180–3; on Indo-German trade, 183–5; against Indian nationalism, 185–6; clashes with Chatto, 199–207; attitude to Berlin Indian Show, 210–12
Rutgers, J., 161

Sachsen, the, 78
Sanger, M., 228, 240
Saklatvala, S., 253
Sarkar, D., 51, 75
Savarkar, V. D., 11, 12, 13, 15, 20, 26, 27
Schiemann, Prof., 35
Schubert, C. T. von, 186, 191, 193, 194
Sekuna, E., 83
Semaoen, 319 and n. 22
Sharma, A. C., 65
Shternberg, L. Y., 289–90
Siddiqui, A., 43
Singh, Ajit, 13
Singh, Basant, 65
Singh, Bhagwan, 82
Singh, Chet, 65
Singh, Jodh, 81
Singh, Lila, 234
Sloan, Jack, 68
Smedley, A., her life before 1920, 225–9; arrives in Berlin, 229; first impression of Chatto, 230–1; accompanies Chatto to Moscow,

160–1; presents statement to Comintern, 162; on German Government's total submission to British, 187–8; describes police torture to her and Chatto, 188; sends articles to Indian journals, 206; writes on Berlin's Indian Show, and complicacies, 211–13; her incident with Heramba Lal Gupta, 231–2; depression and illnesses, 232–3; disharmony with Chatto, 234–42; correspondences with Karin Michaelis, 237–9; finishes her autobiographical novel *Daughter of Earth*, 240; friendship with Tilla Durieux, 240; friendship with Kaethe Kollwitz, 240, 241; relations with Mirza Ali Baker, 241; leaves for China, 241; on Chatto turning communist, 267–8; meets Chatto in Soviet Union 1933, 318
Socialist Peace Conference in Stockholm, 100
Solf, W., 112
Solomon, Prof., 43, 53
Sovietskaya Etnografiya, 288, 292, 298, 305
Spencer, H., 298
Stalin, J., 2, 108, 295, 308, 322, 323
Sterneck, 78
Stiller, 68
Stoedten, Baron L. von, 104
Stroemgren, S.: on Chatto's love of women, 230 and n. 12
Suevia, the, 78
Sunderland, Rev. J. T., 118
Sun Yat-sen, Mme, 253
Sydow, O. von, 139, 140, 141

Tagore, R., 86, 122, 213, 214
Tashkilat-i-Maksusa, 39, 70
Tauscher, H., 75
Teggart, Sir Charles, 10

Thalheimer, A., 162
Tilak, B. G., 1, 9, 12
Troelstra, P. J., 101
Trotsky, L., 108, 109, 115, 121, 288
Troyanovsky, K. M., meets Chatto in Stockholm and invites him to Petrograd, 107–16; and fate of proposed Russian-Indian Society, 111–12; his publications about revolutionary potentialities in the East, 114–16; becomes member of Comintern Commission on Berlin Indians, 162
Tsereteli, I. G., 103
Twain, M., 118

Untermann, E., 291

Vandervelde, E., 249, 252
Varada Sundari Devi, 7, 9
Varma, L. P., 66, 70
Vinnikov, I. N., 298–305
Volgin, V. P., 286
Voretzsch, E., 80, 89
Vorovsky, 109

Wahid, A., 70
Wangenheim, Baron H. von, 38, 39, 41, 47–8
Wardani, El, 27
Wehde, A., 78
Weiskopf, 320
Wesendonk, O. G. von, 50 and n. 94, biog.; his first meeting with Chatto and his colleagues, 50–2; Baltic Baron Uexkuel's opinion of, 52; Zimmermann permits him to deal directly with Indians, 52–3; advises Zimmermann to grant further money to Harish Chandra, 91; against Chatto's coming closer to Bolsheviks, 111–12; generously supports Chatto in his anti-British press propaganda in Scandinavia,

116–17; his tacit approval of Chatto's Balkan (anarchist) plan, 135 ff; writes to Curt Pruefer defending Chatto, 191
White, R. G., 302
Windels, 79, 80, 81, 89
Wyllie, Sir Curzon, 3, 15, 19, 21, 24, 285

Yamato Shimbun, the, 82
Yusuf Ali, A., 127, 128, 129, 130, 131

Zhdanov, A. A., 320
Zimmermann, A., 52, 87; letter to Chatto, 91
Zimmerwald Conference/Movement, 101, 106
Zinoviev, G. E., 168, 169, 288